AN INTRODUCTION TO LOGIC

PROVING THE EXISTENCE OF FISH

...But somewhere, beyond Space and Time,
Is wetter water, slimier slime!
And there (they trust) there swimmeth One
Who swam ere rivers were begun,
Immense, of fishy form and mind,
Squamous, omnipotent, and kind;
And under that Almighty Fin,
The littlest fish may enter in....

(Rupert Brooke, "Heaven," *1914 & Other Poems*, London:
Sidgwick & Jackson, 1915)

AN INTRODUCTION TO LOGIC

Using Natural Deduction, Real Arguments, a Little History, and Some Humour

RICHARD T.W. ARTHUR

SECOND EDITION

broadview press

BROADVIEW PRESS – www.broadviewpress.com
Peterborough, Ontario, Canada

Founded in 1985, Broadview Press remains a wholly independent publishing house. Broadview's focus is on academic publishing; our titles are accessible to university and college students as well as scholars and general readers. With over 600 titles in print, Broadview has become a leading international publisher in the humanities, with world-wide distribution. Broadview is committed to environmentally responsible publishing and fair business practices.

Library and Archives Canada Cataloguing in Publication

Arthur, Richard T. W. (Richard Thomas William), 1950-
[Natural deduction]
    An introduction to logic : using natural deduction, real arguments, a litle history, and some humour / Richard T.W. Arthur. —Second edition.

Revision of: Natural deduction : an introduction to logic with real arguments, a little history, and some humour / Richard T.W. Arthur. —Peterborough, Ont. : Broadview Press, ©2011.

Includes bibliographical references and index.
ISBN 978-1-55481-332-2 (paperback)

    1. Logic—Textbooks. I. Title. II. Title: Natural deduction.

BC177.A78 2016   160   C2016-906853-6

Broadview Press handles its own distribution in North America
PO Box 1243, Peterborough, Ontario K9J 7H5, Canada
555 Riverwalk Parkway, Tonawanda, NY 14150, USA
Tel: (705) 743-8990; Fax: (705) 743-8353
email: customerservice@broadviewpress.com

Distribution is handled by Eurospan Group in the UK, Europe, Central Asia, Middle East, Africa, India, Southeast Asia, Central America, South America, and the Caribbean. Distribution is handled by Footprint Books in Australia and New Zealand.

Broadview Press acknowledges the financial support of the Government of Canada through the Canada Book Fund for our publishing activities.

Canada

Edited by Robert M. Martin

Book design by Chris Rowat Design

PRINTED IN CANADA

This book is made of paper from well-managed FSC® - certified forests, recycled materials, and other controlled sources.

To Gabriella,
without whom this book would only have been logically possible.

Contents

PART II: STATEMENT LOGIC

Preface for Students

This book is intended to do several things for you. Most importantly it is intended to enhance your ability to reason correctly, and to evaluate the reasoning of others. To this end we will learn various forms of argument and rules for making valid inferences, learning also how to symbolize them and construct proofs of validity. As far as possible we will be looking at real arguments that people have made, some of which have made vital contributions to the history of thought. But even those that haven't are generally more interesting than logicians' made-up examples. We will also learn methods for tackling natural arguments directly, i.e., for treating arguments as they actually appear in their original wording. In this way we will steer a judicious middle course between two approaches: a purely formal treatment, and the "informal logic" approach to treating arguments directly that has gained in popularity in recent years. On its own the first approach can be quite difficult and off-putting if you have had little training in formal methods, and may leave you at a loss when faced with the complexities of arguments given in their context; whereas the informal logic approach may do you a disservice in leaving you ignorant of the whole history of logic from Zeno of Elea and the early Buddhists to Bertrand Russell and the Intuitionists, and by ducking any acquaintance with the simple formal rules that have underlain some of the most exciting arguments in science and philosophy. So here I have tried to combine the best of both these approaches, natural deduction techniques and methods for grappling with natural arguments, while at the same time including enough material to help you get a sense of logic's fascinating history.

This text is born out of the conviction that logic can be exhilarating. It can be frustrating; but it can also be emancipating. I have seen students who have spent long years in a cloud of "math anxiety" experience a kind of revelation when they suddenly see how to symbolize and do proofs. Likewise it can be very liberating when you have learnt to spot errors in the arguments of experts on subjects you know little about. But although it can be hard work, there is no reason logic cannot also be fun. It has a close relation with humour, and I have tried to build on this with liberal use of jokes and sketches. I've enjoyed writing this book, and have tried to make it fun as well as instructive. I hope that comes through as you read and work from it.

Preface for Instructors

The rationale for this textbook is entirely pedagogical, based on my experience teaching logic in Canada, Nigeria, and the United States during the past thirty-something years. I have found myself dissatisfied with the dichotomy of approaches to teaching introductory logic. Most approaches to modern deductive logic present logic from the beginning as a formal system, focussing on precise definitions and the proving of derived rules as theorems from a set of primitive rules of inference, using only made-up examples to exemplify the system. It is acknowledged that such an approach makes only tenuous contact with reasoning in natural contexts, but one perseveres in the hope that exposure to such rigour will lead to improved reasoning skills. In my experience, many bright students without much exposure to formal methods, among them philosophy majors who take logic as a requirement, find such a full-blown formal treatment dry, intimidating and remote from their logical intuitions. The alternative approach has been to abandon formal logic for informal logic and critical thinking, and to develop a battery of techniques appropriate to arguments occurring in their natural contexts, such as diagrams of the inference structure of such arguments, and informal means for assessing their worth. Both approaches have their merits, but it seems to me that they both cede too much: the first in abandoning the pretence that introductory logic is designed to help students reason logically; the second in throwing aside the consilience of its new techniques with the traditional analysis of valid inferences; and both for eschewing the whole history of logic, and its role in shaping science and philosophy.

By contrast, my approach in this textbook is to introduce rules of inference in the context of natural arguments, i.e., ones that have actually been offered by historical agents in real-life argumentative contexts, and to apply the formal techniques we learn to such arguments. In this way I try to take maximal advantage of both formal and informal approaches to logic, and at the same time to include more material relating to the history of logic. The aim is for students to complete the course armed with a full understanding of standard logic, propositional, predicate, and relational, as well as with a feel for its historical development, and a better-than-usual ability to apply it to the arguments they are likely to meet outside this course. I have also tried to make my prose lively and readable, with a fair dose of humour to lighten the mood.

To this end, I take a natural deduction approach, bucking the recent trend of relying solely on the method of truth trees (semantic tableaux) for determining validity. The advantage of truth tree methods is readily seen: one can determine whether or not a given argument is valid by a systematic procedure, and, at least in statement logic and unary predicate logic, this is a decision procedure; whereas the natural deduction method does not determine invalidity, for which one has to appeal to supplementary methods such as truth tables, argument diagrams, or the method of counterexamples. But it seems to me that if the fundamental goal of an elementary logic course is to try to hone students' reasoning skills, the natural deduction method has the advantage that it is based on "rules of inference" that correspond fairly closely with the ways we intuitively reason, or at least to rules that are implicit in our reasoning. So although I include chapters on truth trees in the text, I delay their introduction until after students have got a good handle on the rules of inference of natural deduction.

Much attention has been paid here to the order and pace of the introduction of the material. Instead of hitting students with a large batch of rules of inference that are too much to be taken in at once, it introduces them gradually, encouraging rather than de-emphasizing correspondence with their own logical intuitions and competences. In this way it builds students' confidence in logic, and moves on only when a good intuitive understanding is secured, introducing rigour gradually and as the need for definitions and structure makes itself felt. In this spirit, the distinction between primitive and derived rules and the treatment of logic as a formal system is postponed until the students are already in command of an adequate system of rules, as can be done with no disadvantage to their understanding the distinction. Wffs make their first appearance in chapter 12, where formal definitions of argument, argument form or schema, statement and statement form are also given. I treat logic as dealing with the statements that occur in natural argumentative contexts: that is, with *interpreted statements* and the logical forms of arguments. This is why I do not adopt the model-theoretic distinction between two types of validity, a "syntactic" validity based on rules of derivation in an uninterpreted formal system, and a "semantic" validity defined in terms of truth preservation. Instead, as each rule of inference is introduced, its validity is demonstrated by appeal to the overarching definition of formal validity. If an argument has such a form, then it is formally valid; an argument possessing an invalid form, of course, is not necessarily invalid, just because the same argument can be an instance of several different forms.

In this connection, a distinctive feature of the approach taken here is the appeal to a Chrysippean notion of validity, according to which an argument is valid if and only if denying its conclusion is incompatible with accepting all its premises, and otherwise invalid. This definition is the appropriate one for natural arguments, and is distinguished from formal validity, according to which an argument is formally valid if it has a valid argument form. An argument form, on the other hand, is valid if and only if there is no argument of that form which has all true premises and a false conclusion. Thus formal validity is the usual Philonian notion employed in introductory logic. This Philonian notion is therefore what is appealed to in rules of inference (which are valid argument forms), each of which is justified by appeal to the definition of formal validity. Truth tables and truth trees also only establish formal validity or invalidity. The play between these definitions allows for an original resolution of the paradoxes of material implication. It is argued that the Chrysippean definition of validity, together with an application of Grice's notion of *conversational implicature*, allows one to characterize certain forms of argument as formally valid, even though specific arguments instantiating them may be invalid when meaning relations between statements in them are taken into account. How this resolves the Paradoxes of Material Implication is shown in Appendix 1.

In Predicate Logic, a similar appeal to context allows a neater solution to problems of existential import than usually given in introductory texts. Existential import is *implicit* in certain contexts, but not in others. So universal statements do not logically imply existential import, but in certain contexts they can be taken to presuppose it. This leads to a very natural treatment of penevalid arguments, ones whose validity depends upon one of the universal premises being taken to have existential import. Thus we symbolize **A**- and **E**-statements in such a way that no existential import is involved; but if the validity of an argument depends upon an existential import that is implicit in the context, we treat this as an implicit existential premise that must be made explicit. In such a case, the argument will be valid only on that assumption.

There are several other pedagogical innovations, all of them minor, but with a cumulative effect that is significant. Among them are:

a) The method of presenting conditionals and indirect (or reductio) proofs, i.e., proofs which depend on an unasserted or dischargeable assumption (here termed a supposition), is adapted from those of Hurley and Hofstadter, with an indentation for each supposition, and for each subsequent line depending on this supposition until it is discharged. With this method, I have found students make far fewer mistakes than with Lemmon's and Pospesel's method of keeping track of the assumption dependence of each line. The minor innovation is to have suppositions bound to the type of proof: thus the rule introducing suppositions is Supp/CP for a conditional proof, and Supp/RA for a reductio proof, in each case demanding application of the corresponding rule (CP or RA) to discharge the supposition, undent the line, and complete the proof. This is preferable to the liberal assumption rule found in many texts (make any assumption you wish, only discharge it later), which tends to lead students into a strategic mess.

b) The text exploits the structural similarity between these conditional and indirect proofs in formal logic and natural arguments based on suppositions. The method of diagramming natural reductio arguments is indebted to Alec Fisher's *The Logic of Real Arguments*, but the systematic treatment of the correspondence between conditional and indirect proofs in formal logic and natural suppositional arguments is original with this text.

c) New logic diagrams, inspired by those of Charles Dodgson (Lewis Carroll), with debts to John Venn and George Boole for their interpretation. These diagrams generalize very smoothly from arguments involving 2 predicates to those involving 4 or more, and much more naturally than the traditional Venn diagrams. Although these are presented as modifications of Carroll's diagrams, the modifications are significant, and make them easier to use than Carroll's or Venn's, as my students have attested. A comparison of Venn's, Carroll's, and my diagrams is given in Appendix 3.

d) The rules for generalizing from an instance of a universal quantification (UG) and for instantiating an existential quantification (EI) are simplified by the introduction of the notion of *arbitrary individual names*: **i**, **j**, and **k** are arbitrary names used only for EI, and **u**, **v**, and **w** are different arbitrary names used in UG: they are introduced in anticipation of UG, and universal generalizations may only validly be made from instances involving **u**, **v**, or **w**. That these names are arbitrary means that they cannot have occurred either in the symbolization of the argument or on any previous line of the proof, making the statement of any provisos for EI unnecessary. As a result, they cannot occur in the conclusion, and so do not need to be discharged by a separate line of the proof as in Lemmon's rule for Existential Elimination. As for the UG rule, instead of the usual (difficult to remember) 4 provisos, there are now only 2 (needed only in asyllogistic logic): "providing (i) Fu neither is nor depends upon an undischarged supposition involving u, and (ii) Fu was not obtained by an EI step in the proof."

e) The supposition of arbitrary names for the UG and EI proofs corresponds to the supposition of specific examples or cases for the sake of specificity in natural arguments. The distinction of *suppositions for the sake of specificity* from *suppositions for the sake of argument* is original with this text.

There is more material in the textbook than can be comfortably managed in a 12 week semester. This allows considerable scope for adjustment to the different tastes and approaches of instructors by taking different tracks through the material. One track could emphasize the application of logic to natural argument and forego truth trees and logic with identity, finishing with relational logic. Or one could set aside treatment of the complexities of natural argument, omit truth tables in favour of truth trees, and also leave out the theory of the syllogism and argument diagrams. Another option would be simply to remain content with a thorough introduction to logic that stopped short of relational logic, but possibly got as far as logic with identity. These options are outlined in the following table, though clearly many other choices are possible depending on the instructor's own preferences.

Option 1:	Emphasis on natural reasoning	chs. 1-13, 15-19, 20.1, 22, 24.
Option 2:	Natural deduction with trees	chs. 1-12 (but not 2.3, 5.3, 7.3, 9.2, 10.2), 14, 16-17, 19-24.
Option 3:	Statement and predicate logic with identity	chs. 1-19, 21.1-2, 24.

Acknowledgements

All the students I have taught introductory logic, from 1975 to the present, have contributed to making this book what it is. I am indebted most of all to Broadview's copy editor, Bob Martin, to an anonymous referee, to my McMaster colleagues David Hitchcock and Mark Vorobej for their detailed and helpful feedback, and to my former colleagues Phil Gasper and Victor Nuovo for their encouragement and help in the early days at Middlebury. I am also much indebted to all my TAs, Jenn Potton, Sarah Halsted, Adam Harmer, Jayar La Fontaine, Patrick Riesterer, Jim Monier-Williams, Sheldon Hanlon, Paul Sweeney, Haixia Zhong, Qilin Li, Jeremy Proulx, Pat Bondy, Brynna Loppe, Charlene Elsby, Qiang Hao, Zuzanna Chociej, Andrew Pineau, Adam Sopuck, Mark Garron, and above all, Yussif Yakubu, for their suggestions and support; and to the following students for picking up errors: Garon Jones, Chloë Mcintosh, Alfred Cheng, Dave Marsden, Andy Jones, Shival Pawria, Peter Donald, Eric Lebel, Justin Christmas, Sandra Bouranova, Tonya Bonarenko, Massoud Abbasi, Shanda Simpson, Suzanna Curcija, Mohammed Hassan-Ali—my apologies to anyone I have forgotten!

Also, I have a great debt to other textbooks. As any author of a logic text like this will attest, one of the hardest things is to find serviceable real-life examples. So I have made liberal use of examples discovered by other authors, especially Copi and Cohen's *Introduction to Logic* (for ch. 1: 7a, b, e, 9a, c, 10a-d, 11a, c, 13-15, 18; ch. 2: 6b, 11, 13; ch. 3: 13c-h; ch. 5: 16, 18; ch. 13: 11-13; ch. 15: 10, 11, 12; ch. 16: 1-12, 16-18), Pospesel's *Propositional Logic* and *Predicate Logic* texts (for ch. 3: 5i; ch. 6: 15; ch. 8: 1d, i, j, 2a, b, 4a-c, i, f; ch. 19: 1p, 10, 12, 13), and Pospesel and Marans's *Arguments: Deductive Logic Exercises* (for an example in ch. 6 and for ch. 19: 1a, e, k, m, n, v; ch. 16: 15).

I should also like to thank the editors and the whole production team at Broadview for their thorough job in bringing this book to fruition.

For their help in the composition of the second edition I would like to thank Nicolas Fillion and Brad Zurcher of Simon Fraser University, BC, for their positive book review in *Dialogue*, J.M. Kearns of Cape May, NJ for his incisive criticisms of how I previously construed the relation between validity and formal validity, Garry Todd and Tom Adajian for their queries and comments, to David Wright for his witty input, and Broadview's very conscientious anonymous reviewer of the first edition. But my main debt of gratitude is to Nic Fillion of Simon Fraser University, BC, for all his constructive remarks and many detailed suggestions for this new edition.

And, finally, thanks are also due to my colleague Elisabeth Gedge for noticing that the conclusion of my proof on the front cover seems to have been anticipated by the poet Rupert Brooke in his poem "Heaven"!

PART I
ARGUMENTS

Chapter One

Arguments

1.1 INTRODUCTION

One of the difficulties that arise in studying logic is that we are all convinced that we are logical: not necessarily *merely* logical, as Mr. Spock and Data are supposed to be on the TV series *Star Trek*; but we do suppose that we all can be logical when we need to be. (But doesn't there seem to be something a little strange, even paradoxical, about this idea that we can "turn on" our logical mode?) The great French philosopher René Descartes summed it up well when he said:

René Descartes image by
Frans Hals, c. 1580-1666

> Good sense is the best distributed thing in the world: for everyone thinks himself so well endowed with it that even those who are hardest to please in everything else do not usually desire more of it than they possess.—Descartes, *Discourse on Method*, 1637

And it's unlikely that we are all mistaken in thinking that we do have the ability to reason well, as Descartes went on to point out. Our native logical ability does not vary greatly about the mean (although we can of course improve it by concentrating on it, as we shall in this book!), and we all tend to make the same kinds of errors in similar psychological circumstances. All of this we owe perhaps to our biological and social evolution. After all, as Chrysippus observed in ancient Athens, even a dog is capable of reasoning logically to some extent. For suppose it is following the scent of some animal down a path and it comes to a fork in the path. Then if it finds no scent along one of the paths, it will immediately retrace its steps to the fork and try the other (thus implicitly applying the rule of inference called Disjunctive Syllogism!).

But as we all know from experience, having the ability to reason well in a relatively simple situation like the fork is one thing; but to follow a long chain of deductive reasoning, or to follow the logic of a technical argument with many unfamiliar terms, requires a less intuitive and more analytical skill. Consider the following two examples:

> There is no box of mine here that I dare open. My writing desk is made of rosewood. All my boxes are painted, except those that are here. There is no box of mine I dare not open, unless it is full of live scorpions. All my rosewood boxes are unpainted. Therefore my desk is full of live scorpions.
> —Charles Dodgson (aka Lewis Carroll), *Symbolic Logic*

> If the money supply were to increase at less than 5%, the rate of inflation would come down. Since the money supply is increasing at about 10%, inflation will not come down.
> —Alec Fisher, *The Logic of Real Argument*

The first of these arguments, Lewis Carroll's wacky example, is a valid piece of reasoning (provided his writing desk counts as a box—perhaps he couldn't afford a proper desk?). You will prove it to be so later in the book. The second example, as Fisher points out in giving it, is often advanced by monetarist politicians, but should never have been accepted by anyone. It might appear that we would have to know some economics to criticize it—what factors contribute towards inflation? what might bring it down?—but this is not so. We can criticize the argument on logical grounds alone. The conclusion does not necessarily follow from the premises of the argument *as stated*: something else might bring inflation down. If it had been stated that the rate of increase of the money supply were the *only* factor affecting inflation, then the argument would be valid; but this is clearly a much stronger claim. One of the virtues of logic that I will be aiming to promote in this book is that it helps to break through the "cult of the expert" in exactly this way: no matter how expert someone is in a particular subject, if she is to convince her audience, then she must adduce reasons that sufficiently support the point she wants to make. And deciding whether she has done so is precisely a task for logic.

Here I have been happily speaking of "arguments," "conclusions," "premises," "validity," etc. as if you all understand exactly what I mean. But it's time to define our terms. What exactly is an argument in the logicians' sense? The key notions are as follows. First there is an overall *conclusion*: this is the statement the argument is intended to establish. In support of this statement, some other statements are given: these are the *premises* (variant spelling: *premiss, premisses*). The act of drawing a conclusion from some given premises is called the making of an *inference*. We may define an inference as follows:

An *inference* is the drawing of a conclusion from one or more other statements given as premises.

Here

A *conclusion* is a statement inferred from one or more other statements. These statements are the *premises* of the inference.

An argument may now be defined as a chain of inferences from premises to an overall conclusion:

An *argument* is a chain of (one or more) inferences from some initial premises to an overall conclusion.[1]

Thus in a typical argument there may well be several intermediate conclusions which themselves serve as premises for the main conclusion, or perhaps as premises for other intermediate conclusions. One virtue of the above definition is that it is applicable even to these extended arguments that occur in natural contexts, as well as to the simpler, well-formulated examples favoured by logicians. (It is also applicable to the case of the suppositional arguments we'll encounter in later chapters, where an inference may be made on the basis of a previous inference, rather than on the given premises alone.)

These definitions depend crucially on the notion of a *statement*, which we will define as follows:

A *statement* is a sentence (or part of a sentence) that expresses something true or false.

The "something" that it expresses has traditionally been called a *proposition*:

A *proposition* is what a statement expresses as true or false.

Our definition of statement suffices to distinguish it from other types of sentence—for instance, a question, a command, or an exhortation—none of which expresses something that can be true or false. Also, it takes into account that propositions are often expressed

---

[1] Cf. the definition of argument provided in "The Argument Sketch" of *Monty Python's Flying Circus*, the British comedy troupe. There the supposedly naive student defines an argument as "a connected series of statements intended to establish a proposition," a definition that is flatly contradicted by the logic teacher without argument!

by (and statements constituted by) *parts* of sentences, or sentence-fragments.[2] Thus of the following seven sentences from St. Augustine's *City of God*,

(1) Courage, my mind, and press on mightily.
(2) God is our helper, he made us and not we ourselves.
(3) Press on where truth begins to dawn.
(4) Suppose, now, the voice of a body begins to sound.
(5) What, then, is time?
(6) If no one asks me, I know.
(7) But if someone asks me, I cannot give an answer.

only (2), (6), and (7) are statements by our definition. Numbers (1) and (3) are *exhortations* or *commands* that Augustine is making to himself in order to summon up the courage necessary to tackle the difficult question of what time is, and (5) *is* that question. In (4) "the voice of a body begins to sound" is a statement, but the introductory word "Suppose…" signals that it has a special status: Augustine is *supposing* it for the sake of example, rather than *asserting* it. Such a statement is a *supposition*. We will deal with suppositions in chapter 7.

Notice that parts of the other sentences are statements, too: "truth begins to dawn" is a statement, even though sentence (3) as a whole is not. Sentence (2), on the other hand, is not only a statement itself, but also contains the statements "God is our helper" and "he made us and not we ourselves"; and the latter could be analyzed as containing "he made us" and "[it was] not we ourselves [who made us]," each of which could be true or false individually. The sentence as a whole is a compound of these three statements, each of which is not further reducible in this way. But the whole question of how statements are made up out of other statements needs to be treated with some care, and we shall return to it in chapter 3.

SUMMARY

- An **inference** is the drawing of a **conclusion** from one or more other statements given as **premises**.
- An **argument** is a chain of (one or more) inferences from some initial premises to an overall conclusion.
- A **statement** is a sentence (or part of a sentence) that expresses something true or false.
- A **proposition** is what a statement expresses as true or false.
- Thus if a sentence or sentence-fragment does not express something true or false, then it is not a statement. In particular, questions, exhortations, commands, and suppositions are not themselves statements (although they may contain statements).

---

[2] These are, I believe, good grounds for rejecting the customary textbook definition of a statement as "a sentence that is either true or false."

EXERCISES 1.1

1. Based on your understanding of this chapter, *state whether each of the following statements about logic is true or false, and why*:
    (a) We study logic in order to learn how to reason.
    (b) Animals seem to be able to use logic, at least implicitly.
    (c) Logic helps you decide whether something is true even if you know nothing about the subject.
    (d) An argument is the automatic gainsaying of any statement the other person makes.
    (e) Animals don't argue, so they don't use logic.
    (f) The point of an argument is to contradict your opponent.
    Example:
    (f) Wrong: the point of an argument is to persuade someone of something. It is not necessary to take up a contrary position, unless perhaps you are engaged in debate.

2. *Identify which of the following sentences is a statement*, with a brief explanation for your answer:
    (a) My hovercraft is full of eels. (Monty Python's "Hungarian Phrasebook")
    (b) Let the flow of time from some first instant A be represented by the line AB...(Galileo Galilei, *Discorsi*)
    (c) Get thee to a nunnery. (Shakespeare, *Hamlet*)
    (d) Why woulds't thou be a breeder of sinners? (Shakespeare, *Hamlet*)
    (e) O heavenly powers, restore him! (Shakespeare, *Hamlet*)
    (f) Nature never makes leaps. (Gottfried Leibniz)
    (g) 'Scuse me, while I kiss the sky! (Jimi Hendrix, "Purple Haze")
    (h) When the body arrives at B, suppose that a centripetal force acts with great impulse...(Isaac Newton, *Principia*)
    (i) If Gorbachev made a mistake, well, who hasn't? (Russian V-P Alexander Rushkoi, 1991)
    Example:
    (c) Not a statement, since it doesn't express something that can be true or false; it's a command or exhortation.

3. *Identify whether each* of the following sentences or sentence-fragments from the ancient Greek philosopher Heraclitus *is a statement*:
    (a) It is not possible to step twice into the same river.
    (b) The road up and the road down are one and the same.
    (c) Nature loves to hide.
    (d) Knowing neither how to hear nor how to speak.
    (e) Listening not to me but to the logos, it is wise to agree that all things are one.

(f) Let us not make aimless conjectures about the most important things.

(g) If all things were smoke, nostrils would distinguish them.

(h) How could one fail to be seen by that which does not set?

(i) Dogs bark at everyone they do not know.

(j) Turnings of fire: first sea; of sea, half is earth and half lightning-flash.

Example:

(e) This is a statement, since it asserts something that could be true or false.

4. *Determine which of the following sentences* from Albert Einstein *is a statement*:

(a) Science has been charged with undermining morality, but the charge is unjust.

(b) Compare the spirit which animated the youth in our universities a hundred years ago with that prevailing today.

(c) Let every man judge by himself, by what he has himself read, not by what others tell him.

(d) How can cosmic religious feeling be communicated from one person to another, if it can give rise to no definite notion of a God and no theology?

(e) Only the absolute repudiation of all war can be of any use here.

(f) Suppose, for example, that the American, English, German, and French governments insisted that the Japanese government put an immediate stop to their warlike operations in China, under pain of a complete economic boycott.

(g) Mere agreements to limit armaments furnish no sort of security.

(h) May I begin with an article of political faith?

(i) I regard it as the chief duty of the state to protect the individual and give him the opportunity to develop into a creative personality.

Example:

(b) This is not a statement, but a command or exhortation.

5. *For each of the following sentences* from Neal Stephenson's novel *Quicksilver, list any and all statements it contains*:

(a) Enoch rounds the corner just as the executioner raises the noose above the woman's head.

(b) Her knees pimple the front of her apron and her skirts telescope into the platform as she makes to collapse.

(c) The crowd scratches and shuffles.

(d) He's not come to watch witch-hangings, but now that Enoch has blundered into one it would be bad form to leave.

(e) There is a drum-roll, and then a sudden awkward silence.

(f) As they are cutting the limp witch down, a gust tumbles over the common from the north.

(g) If Herr Fahrenheit were here with one of his new quicksilver-filled, sealed-tube thermometers, he would probably observe something in the fifties.

Example:
(a) This sentence is itself a statement, and contains the two other statements: "Enoch rounds the corner," and "the executioner raises the noose above the woman's head."

6. *For each of the following sentences* from Heraclitus, *list any and all statements it contains*:
   (a) This logos holds always, but humans always prove unable to understand it.
   (b) If they are gods, why do you grieve?
   (c) If you grieve, no longer think them gods.
   (d) If it were not for Dionysus that they hold processions and sing hymns to the phallus, it would be a most shameless act.
   (e) Eternity is a child playing a game of checkers, and the king is in the hands of a child.
   Example:
   (a) This sentence is itself a statement, and contains the two other statements: "This logos holds always," and "humans always prove unable to understand it."

1.2 IDENTIFYING ARGUMENTS

1.2.1 INFERENCE INDICATORS

An argument occurs wherever someone is trying to convince someone of something by giving reasons for it. These *reasons* or *grounds* (contained in the *premises*) are given in *support* of some claim (the *conclusion*); that is, an argument is being given whenever one statement is supposed to be *inferred* from others, either by the person giving the argument or by a person hearing or reading it. Of course, arguments are usually given to persuade somebody of something. To do this, people will generally mix in a whole load of rhetoric too; but this is generally what you *shouldn't* be persuaded by. Arguments are the basic units of reasoning, and we use them to express our reasoning even when we have no specific readership in mind.

In natural contexts it is not always easy to tell when an argument is being given, but certain words habitually crop up whenever we are making an inference. Thus when the great natural scientist Sir Isaac Newton began the second "Rule of Reasoning in Philosophy" in his *Principia* with the word 'Therefore,' he was indicating that we should infer it from the first:

(Rule 1) No more causes of natural things should be admitted than are both true and sufficient to explain their phenomena.... (Rule 2) Therefore, the causes assigned to natural effects of the same kind must be, so far as possible, the same.[3]

---

[3] Isaac Newton, *The Principia: Mathematical Principles of Natural Philosophy*, trans. I. Bernard Cohen and Anne Whitman (U of California P, 1999), pp. 794-95.

Similarly Roger Cotes, elaborating on the implications of these rules in the following passage from his preface to the second edition of Newton's masterwork, uses the word 'since' to introduce the reason why we should conclude that gravity is universal:

> Now, since all terrestrial and celestial bodies on which we can make any experiments or observations are heavy, it must be acknowledged without exception that gravity belongs to all bodies universally. (*ibid*, 391)

Words used to indicate the conclusion of an inference, like *So...*, *Thus...*, and *Therefore...*, are called *conclusion indicators*; similarly, words that are often used to indicate the giving of reasons or grounds for the conclusion, like *since...*, *for...*, etc., are called *premise indicators*. Collectively, all such words are known as *inference indicators*, i.e., words indicating that an inference is being made, that an argument is being given. Here are lists of other such inference indicators; neither list is intended to be exhaustive. [Can you think of any other premise or conclusion indicators?]

Conclusion Indicators		
therefore...	consequently...	it follows that...
so...	whence...	proves that...
thus...	in conclusion...	implies that...
hence...	I/we conclude...	demonstrates that...
Premise Indicators		
since...	as...	the reason being that...
because...	for...	follows from the fact that...
given that...	on the grounds that...	for the following reasons...
may be inferred from the fact that...		

CAUTION: you can't be uncritical in using these indicator words to establish whether an argument is being given. Natural language is very flexible, and the same words are pressed to many different uses. Consider: "We haven't made love *since* George fell off his horse," "*Thus* are dreams unmasked," "I was never *given that* chance," "*For* want of a better idea...," "*...as* I have already mentioned," and *so* on!

1.2.2 EXPLANATIONS

Another minor complication arises with explanations. For present purposes we may define an explanation as follows:

> An *explanation* is an account intended to show how it came to be that a fact or event is the way it is.

Now, explanations involve the giving of reasons, just as arguments do, and these are introduced by premise indicators like "for" and "because." But many philosophers hold that not all explanations are arguments. Consider the statement:

He caught AIDS because he got a transfusion of blood infected with the HIV virus.

This passage involves the inference indicator "because...," and we can see that "he got a transfusion of blood infected with the HIV virus" is being given as the cause of his having AIDS. But are we being asked to make an inference? Is it being given as a reason to persuade us that he caught AIDS? Many would say that the statement is being given as a reason *why* he caught AIDS, but it does not seem to be "intended to establish the conclusion" *that* he caught AIDS—this seems to be a fact regarded as given. According to these philosophers, reasons are not always given in support of a conclusion; they are also given to *explain a fact*.

Others disagree, and hold that in explaining a fact you are always giving an argument. Even though the conclusion may be understood, there are many causal hypotheses or accounts you can give of why it has come to pass. In each of these accounts, the (agreed upon) conclusion will be inferred from some putative premises, which may or may not constitute a good argument for the state of affairs in the conclusion having come to pass for those reasons.

This is not an issue we need to resolve here, however. We are interested in explanations only insofar as they can be interpreted as arguments. And we can determine this solely by reference to the above definition of an argument. To see how this works, let's look at another example.

Christopher Columbus wrote of some of the inhabitants of the "New World":

They bear no arms, nor know thereof. For I showed them swords and they grasped them by the blade and cut themselves through ignorance.

That they bear no arms is not being argued for or explained. But what about the natives' knowledge of arms? The premise indicator "For" introduces Columbus' reasons for thinking that the natives did not even know of weapons, which invites us to make the same inference. Thus the statement is best interpreted as constituting an argument. It is at the same time the best explanation of the aboriginals' behaviour. This kind of argument is called *inference to the best explanation*.

1.2.3 IMPLICIT ARGUMENTS

Usually at least one of the above inference indicators will occur when an argument is being offered. But this will not always be so. Sometimes one can only determine the presence of an argument from an examination of its content, or from the surrounding context. Take the following sentence from Jean-Jacques Rousseau's *Emile*:

> Where everything is good, nothing can be unjust, justice being inseparable from goodness.[4]

In this one sentence Rousseau is giving an argument. He is trying to convince us that "Where everything is good, nothing can be unjust." In fact the sentence can be rephrased as two linked statements,

> Where everything is good, nothing can be unjust, [since] justice [is] inseparable from goodness.

with the now explicit indicator 'since' showing that "justice [is] inseparable from goodness" is the premise for the first statement.

Here is a longer passage advancing an argument, where we have to concentrate on trying to understand the argument itself in order to work out what the premises and conclusions are:

> We are perpetually told that without a God there would be no moral obligation; that the people and even the sovereigns require a legislator powerful enough to constrain them. Moral constraint supposes a law; but this law arises from eternal and necessary relations of things with one another; relations which have nothing in common with the existence of a God. The rules of man's conduct are derived from his own nature, which he is capable of knowing, and not from divine nature, of which he has no idea.—Baron d'Holbach (eighteenth-century French atheist)

D'Holbach grants that moral constraint presupposes a law, but denies that this must be a divine law, asserting instead that the law "arises from eternal and necessary relations of things with one another," and from man's own nature. Thus he can be understood as arguing against the claim that "without a God there would be no moral obligation."

Sometimes, too, arguments are proposed using rhetorical questions instead of statements. This is a rhetorical device that should be familiar to anyone from everyday conversation. Here is an example from the philosopher Gottfried Leibniz's famous correspondence with the English cleric Samuel Clarke in the early eighteenth century:

> If space is a property or attribute, it must be the property of some substance. But what substance will that bounded empty space be an affection or property of, which the persons I am arguing with suppose to be between two bodies?—Leibniz, Fourth Letter to Clarke, §8

On the face of it, all we are presented with here is a conditional statement (if...then...) and a rhetorical question. Yet the context (which you do not have here) makes clear that this is intended as an argument against Clarke's prior claim that space is a property.

---

[4] Jean-Jacques Rousseau, "Profession of Faith of a Savoyard Vicar," *Emile*, 1762.

Leibniz wants us to infer that since there is nothing in empty space (more accurately, no bounded substance in a bounded empty space), there is nothing that such a space could be a property of. Thus he is presenting an argument. The conclusion is "space is not a property (or affection or attribute)," and the rhetorical question should be construed as equivalent to the statement "there is no substance that a bounded space between two bodies can be a property of."

In all such cases where there are no explicit inference indicators, you need to ask yourself: Is the author giving or suggesting reasons for accepting a certain proposition? If so, that proposition is the conclusion, and the reasons are the premises. In effect we need to use judgement. If we can construe the passage as an argument without "forcing" this interpretation, then this is what we should do. Also, we should try to make any such argument we impute to the author the strongest possible argument given the evidence at hand, i.e., that argument we believe the author most likely to find acceptable. This advice is usually summed up in the *Principle of Charity*:[5]

> **PRINCIPLE OF CHARITY:** If you can construe a given passage as containing an argument, make it the strongest argument compatible with the available evidence, i.e., that argument you believe the author would be most likely to accept as capturing his or her intentions.

This principle needs to be applied with restraint, however. With enough ingenuity, almost any statements can be *imagined* to be part of an argument. Take the following passage from a newspaper article:

> Seizing what may be his best chance to transform and energize his candidacy, Gore reminded a nationwide television audience that he and Clinton have overseen a booming economy. But Gore said that is not enough.—Michael Kranish, *Boston Globe*

These two statements may suggest all sorts of thoughts to you, depending upon your politics. But no inference is being invited.

1.2.4 ENTHYMEMES

Another difficulty in identifying arguments lies in the fact that they are very commonly presented with one of their premises or their conclusion left unstated. Such arguments

---

[5] "In its most generic sense, 'charity' means giving someone the benefit of the doubt. So, where competing interpretations of a passage are well supported by the evidence to a roughly comparable degree, charity instructs us to attribute to the author of the passage that interpretation which is the *strongest*, or most defensible, interpretation" (Mark Vorobej, *A Theory of Argument*, p. 29).

are called *enthymemes*. Here's an example, taken again from Jean-Jacques Rousseau's *Emile*:

> No material being can be self-active, and I perceive that I am so [i.e., self-active].

Here Rousseau is inviting us to infer from these two statements a conclusion that he regards as too obvious to need stating. You should be able to work out what it is. Any such statement that the Principle of Charity would dictate as being understood in the context to be the unstated conclusion of an inference or argument is called an *implicit conclusion* of that reasoning. Similarly, people often leave out premises that again would be understood to be assumed in the context, *implicit premises*. Natural reasoning often involves both. Consider, for instance, this passage from Monty Python's "Argument Sketch":

> Mr. B: Well, you didn't pay.
> Cust: Aha! If I didn't pay, why are you arguing? I've got you!
> Mr. B: No, you haven't.
> Cust: Yes, I have. If you're arguing, I must have paid!

Here our long-suffering customer seems to be arguing that he must have paid. He does not state this conclusion explicitly, since this is precisely what they are arguing about: it is understood, or *implicit*. Instead he adduces one premise only: "If you are arguing, I must have paid." But it seems that something else is needed in order for the argument to have force (can you see what?).

This will be clearer if we lay out the argument with the convention that premises are stated on separate lines, and the conclusion below a solid line, preceded by the three-dot symbol ∴ for therefore:

If you're arguing, I must have paid.

∴ I must have paid. [implicit]

What is missing is the premise "You are arguing." But it is clear from the context that, even by his own devious criteria, Mr. Barnard admits that he is arguing, and that this is understood by both parties as too obvious to need explicit mention. So we may impute this to the customer:

If you're arguing, then I must have paid.
You are arguing. [implicit]

∴ I must have paid. [implicit]

Again, as always, we shall have to exercise some judgement in determining whether an argument is being offered in cases like these.

SUMMARY

- An argument occurs wherever someone is trying to convince someone of something (the **conclusion**) by giving grounds or reasons for it. The statements giving these purported grounds or reasons are called the **premises**.
- Whenever a conclusion is drawn from some premises, we say that an **inference** has occurred.
- Certain key words often indicate that an inference has been made or is being invited: words such as *since*, *because*, and *for* are **premise indicators**; words such as *therefore*, *hence*, *so*, and *consequently* indicate that a **conclusion** is about to appear. All such words indicating an inference is being made are called **inference indicators**.
- An **explanation** is an account intended to show how it came to be that a fact or event is the way it is. Many philosophers claim that not all explanations are arguments. But here we are concerned with explanations only insofar as they can be construed as arguments.
- **Principle of Charity**: If you can construe a given passage as containing an argument, make it the strongest argument compatible with the available evidence, i.e., that argument you believe the author would be most likely to accept as capturing his or her intentions.
- An **enthymeme** is an argument in which one or more premises or the conclusion (or both) is left unstated. These are called **implicit** premises or conclusions.

EXERCISES 1.2

7. Each of the following passages contains an argument. In each case, *identify any inference indicators*, as well as the *main conclusion* of the argument, restating it as a statement if necessary:
   (a) Logic is a matter of profound human importance precisely because it is empirically founded and experimentally applied.—John Dewey, *Reconstruction in Philosophy*
   (b) Time heals all wounds. Time is money. Therefore money heals all wounds.— "Ask Marilyn," *Parade*, April 12, 1987
   (c) These gentlemen maintain . . . that space is a real absolute being. But this involves them in some difficulties; for such a being must be eternal and infinite. Hence some have believed it to be God himself, or one of his attributes, his immensity. But since space consists of parts, it is not a thing which can belong to God.— Gottfried Leibniz, *Third Letter to Clarke*, §3

(d) Infinite space is immensity; but immensity is not God; and therefore infinite space is not God.—Samuel Clarke, Third Reply to Leibniz, §3

(e) Neither a borrower nor a lender be;
For loan oft loses both itself and friend,
And borrowing dulls the edge of husbandry.—Shakespeare, *Hamlet*, Act 1, Scene 3

8. *Identify which of the following passages contains an argument.* For those that do, *identify the conclusion.*

(a) Tapestries are made by many artisans working together. The contributions of separate workers cannot be discerned in the completed work, and the loose and false threads have been covered over. So it is in our picture of particle physics.— Sheldon Glashow, 1979 Nobel Lecture "Towards a Unified Theory"

(b) For once it was not raining and the sun that came was bright and mildly warm. The air was humid. There were plenty of puddles and mud all along the untarred bits of the road. Since it was the season of heavy rainfall, the tarred roads had developed gaping holes in many places.—Buchi Emecheta, *Double Yoke*, p. 43

(c) It's a beautiful thing, the destruction of words. Of course the great wastage is in the verbs and adjectives, but there are hundreds of nouns that can be got rid of as well. It isn't only the synonyms, there are also the antonyms. After all, what justification is there for a word which is simply the opposite of some other word? A word contains its opposite in itself. Take 'good,' for instance. If you have a word like 'good,' what need is there for a word like 'bad'? 'Ungood' will do just as well...—George Orwell, *1984*, p. 52

(d) If there were any community which rejected the doctrines of modern physics, physicists employed by a hostile government would have no difficulty in exterminating it. The modern physicist, therefore, enjoys powers far exceeding those of the Inquisition in its palmiest days, and it certainly behooves us to treat his pronouncements with due awe.—Bertrand Russell, *My Philosophical Development*, p. 13

(e) There is no portion of matter that is not actually divided into further parts, so that there is no body so small that there is not a world of infinitary creatures in it.— Gottfried Leibniz, *Pacidius to Philalethes*, 1676

(f) Since time is number, the now and before and so on are in time in the same way that a unit and odd and even are in number: the latter are aspects of number, while the former are aspects of time.—Aristotle, *Physics*, 221a13

(g) The prohibition [of suicide] is ridiculous; for what penalty can frighten a person who is not afraid of death itself?—Arthur Schopenhauer, "On Suicide," 1851

(h) According to the dogmatic decrees of the Council of Trent, at the consecration in the Mass the substance of the bread and wine are changed into the Body and Blood of Christ, while the accidents of the bread and wine remain. But if, as Descartes held, extension is identical with corporeal substance, and if qualities are subjective, it seems to follow that there are no real accidents which remain after the conversion of the substance.—Frederick Copleston, S.J., *A History of Philosophy*, vol. IV, p. 126

(i) "This has occurred once, and will occur again," said Euphorbus. "It is not one pyre you are lighting, it is a labyrinth of fire. If all the fires on which I have been burned were brought together here, the earth would be too small for them, and the angels would be blinded."—Jorge Luis Borges, "The Theologians," *The Aleph*, p. 203

Example:

(i) Euphorbus declares all these things to be so, but he gives no reasons. There is no *argument* for his having been burnt at the stake many times.

9. The following passages contain arguments in which the conclusion is left unstated. *Identify the missing conclusion*:

   (a) ...the law does not expressly permit suicide, and what it does not expressly permit, it forbids.—Aristotle, *Nichomachean Ethics*

   (b) Venantius... said that Aristotle had dedicated the second book of the *Poetics* to laughter, and that if a philosopher of such greatness had devoted a whole book to laughter, then laughter must be important.—Umberto Eco, *The Name of the Rose*, p. 126

   (c) Who controls the past controls the future. Who controls the present controls the past.—George Orwell, *1984*

   (d) If there were no empty space, everything would be one solid mass.—Lucretius, *On the Nature of Things*

   (e) If—as I believe I have shown—quantitative data are as subject to cultural constraint as any other aspect of science, then they have no special claim upon final truth.—Stephen Jay Gould, *Mismeasure of Man*, p. 59

10. The following passages contain arguments in which one or more of the premises is left unstated. *Identify the missing premises*:

    (a) Man tends to increase at a greater rate than his means of subsistence; consequently he is occasionally subject to a severe struggle for existence.—Charles Darwin, *The Descent of Man*

    (b) I am an idealist, since I believe that all that exists is spiritual.—J. McT. E. McTaggart, *Philosophical Studies*

    (c) No enthymemes are complete, so this argument is incomplete.—Copi and Cohen, *Introduction to Logic*

    (d) Epicurus maintained that no man had ever seen reason but in a human figure; therefore, the gods must have a human figure.—David Hume, *Dialogues Concerning Natural Religion*

11. The following arguments are *enthymemes*. In each case, *identify the premise or conclusion that has been left unstated*:

(a) When Blair can say, as he did the moment the Chilcot report was published, that it should "lay to rest allegations ... of bad faith, lies and deceit" ..., then you can be sure that his successors will have no hesitation in swindling the public again and again.—Robert Fisk, *The Independent,* July 6, 2016

(b) Now I know, as the doctor says, that love can harm the lover when it is excessive. And mine was excessive.—Umberto Eco, *The Name of the Rose*, p. 336

(c) It is probably true that the least destructive nuclear weapons are the most dangerous, because they make it easier for a nuclear war to begin.—Freeman Dyson, "Weapons and Hope," *The New Yorker*, February 1984

(d) If humanism were right in declaring that man is born to be happy, he would not be born to die. Since his body is doomed to die, his task on earth must evidently be of a more spiritual nature.—Alexander Solzhenitsyn, *Calgary Herald*, July 6, 1978

(e) Dictionaries cannot settle all questions about how words are to be used, nor are they intended to. If they were, then such heated debates as the current one about abortion could be settled by looking up definitions for 'human being' or 'person.'—Joan Hoaglund, *Critical Thinking*

(f) A child who has received no religious instruction and has never heard about God is not an atheist—for he is not denying any theistic claims.—Ernest Nagel, "A Defence of Atheism"

1.3 NATURAL ARGUMENTS

1.3.1 ARGUMENT AND INFERENCE

We have defined an *argument* as a chain of (one or more) *inferences* from some initial premises to an overall conclusion. In the examples so far we have been mainly looking at arguments involving a single inference, with clearly defined premises and conclusion. It is these single-inference arguments whose validity we investigate in our natural deduction systems for Statement and Predicate Logic. As we shall see, proofs of the validity of arguments can be analyzed as depending on a chain of inferences, so that the proofs themselves resemble closely the reasoning we undertake in arguments containing multiple inferences.

Still, it is not so easy to apply the techniques we shall be developing in formal logic unless the arguments are given tidily and explicitly, in the form "premise, premise, premise ∴ conclusion." The actual arguments we are presented with in real life—the arguments we find in conversations, newspaper editorials, cartoons, and so forth—are usually anything but tidy. We've already seen something of this in having to supply them with implicit premises, and sometimes conclusions. But even when we've done this, it is very often the case that the reasoning in them is quite complex, and involves more than one inference. It is about such extended arguments involving multiple inferences that I want to say a little here.

What usually happens when two people argue is that person A makes an assertion, and offers some reasons in support, leaving what she judges to be too obvious (either premises or conclusion of the reasoning) unstated or implicit. Person B then asks for reasons why he should accept certain premises—this requires A to give further arguments for them; or she questions the logical reasoning itself—perhaps giving counterexamples. (An example of this would be the passage from Monty Python's "Argument Sketch" considered in section 2 above, when we were considering enthymemes.) All of us are familiar with this kind of dialectical reasoning. Consequently when we argue, we try to anticipate such objections. We give reasons in support of some of the premises of the main argument, i.e., we give arguments within arguments.

Thus naturally occurring arguments tend to have a good deal of inferential structure. They contain not just one inference from the premises to the conclusion, but inferences from premises to intermediate conclusions, which then themselves serve as premises for the inference to the main point being argued for. With such arguments it is extremely helpful to lay out this structure explicitly using a diagram. Techniques for diagramming arguments are among the most valuable contributions of the "Informal Logic" movement, and to these we now turn.

1.3.2 TECHNIQUES OF DIAGRAMMING

The first thing to do in examining any argument is to see *what is intended to follow from what*. In each case that we can identify this, we have an *inference* from the premise statements to the conclusion. Each such inference will be represented by a downwards arrow, so: $\downarrow$. The following argument is an example (yes, it's a real argument, formulated by a second-century CE philosopher!):

Male lions do not desire other male lions, because lions are not philosophers.

First we shall number the statements, circle or bracket the inference indicator 'because,' and underline the conclusion:

(i) "(1) <u>Male lions do not desire other male lions</u>, (because) (2) lions are not philosophers."

The structure of this simple argument is:

(2)

$\downarrow$

(1)

Although (1) occurs before (2), (1) is asserted to follow logically from (2), as indicated by the premise indicator 'because.' Another way of expressing this assertion of logical dependence is to say that (2) *entails* (1). Not many people would accept the validity of this inference, of course; but we shall return to that issue in the next chapter. For now we are just looking at inferential structure. A slightly more complex example is this:

(ii) "(1) Drug use is wrong because (2) it is immoral, and it is immoral because (3) it enslaves the mind and destroys the soul."—James Q. Wilson, *Newsweek*, January 9, 1989

This argument is diagrammed:

$$(3)$$
$$\downarrow$$
$$(2)$$
$$\downarrow$$
$$(1)$$

Here statement (2) is given as a reason for statement (1), so that it is a premise. But (2) in turn is inferred from statement (3), so that it also functions as a conclusion. Any such statement occurring in an argument that is inferred from one or more other statements in the argument but is not the overall conclusion, is called an *intermediate conclusion*. As the diagram makes clear, the validity of the overall argument will depend on the validity of both inferences, from (3) to (2), and from (2) to (1).

Usually, of course, arguments are more complex than the ones above. In particular, many inferences involve several premises, rather than just one. Here there are two cases to be distinguished: the premises may entail the conclusion *conjointly*; or each of them may entail it *independently*. Here is an example of each kind:

(iii) (1) Universities must expect further cuts because (2) they have suffered less than other sectors of education. But even if that were not so, (1) they should expect further cuts because (3) they are not sufficiently vocationally oriented.

This is diagrammed:

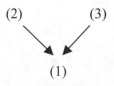

(iv) Since (1) morals have an influence on the actions and affections, it follows that (2) they cannot be derived from reason;... because (3) reason alone, as we have already proved, can never have such an influence.

This is diagrammed:

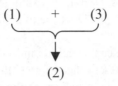

Here now is a more complex argument, one typical of the way arguments occur in natural contexts. It was originally given in note form by Charles Darwin in one of his early notebooks:

(v) The general delusion about free will [is] obvious. Because (1) man has power of action, and (2) he can seldom analyze his motives—[since (3) they are] mostly instinctive, and therefore (4) now great effort of reason [is required] to discover them—(5) he thinks they have none.[6]

First let's ignore the subsidiary argument for premise (2). Premises (1) and (2) jointly support the overall conclusion (5). This gives:

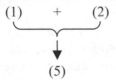

Turning to the subsidiary argument, we see that (3) is given as a reason for (2) by way of (4): it is because motives are instinctive that great effort of reason is required to discover them, and this having to apply a great effort of reason makes it difficult to analyze them. So (3) is given as a reason for (4), and (4) as a reason for (2). This gives:

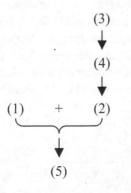

6 Charles Darwin, "Old and Useless Notes," in *Metaphysics, Materialism and the Evolution of Mind*, transcribed and annotated by Paul Barrett (U of Chicago P, 1974), p. 129.

There are other possibilities. A piece of argumentative reasoning may, for example, serve to justify two distinct conclusions. Here is an example from a 1932 essay by the Italian fascist leader, Benito Mussolini, "The Doctrine of Fascism":

(vi) (1) Outside the State there can be neither individuals nor groups (political parties, associations, syndicates or classes). Therefore (2) Fascism is opposed to that Socialism which views the movement of history as the process of class struggle, and (3) analogously it is opposed to class syndicalism.

Here (1) is given to support both (2) and (3):

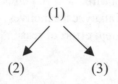

Finally, let's consider the following argument given by the philosopher Spinoza on behalf of Descartes, whose *Principles of Philosophy* he was expounding axiomatically:

(vii) *Proposition 13:* (1) *God by his power conserves the same quantity of motion and rest which he once gave to matter. Demonstration:* Since (2) God is the cause of motion and rest (by (3) Proposition 12), (4) he conserves these by the same power by which he also created them (by (5) Axiom 10 of Part I), and (6) indeed with the same quantity of power (by (7) Corollary to Prop. 20, Part I). QED.

Here "Proposition 12," which I have numbered (3), is that "*God is the principal cause of motion,*" and Axiom 10 of Part I, which I have numbered (5), is "*No lesser cause is required for the conservation of a thing than for its initial creation,*" and the Corollary to Prop. 20 of Part I, which I have numbered (7), is "*God is unchangeable in all his works.*"

Now Spinoza gives (3) as the reason for (2), which, together with (5), is given as a reason for (4). But (4), together with the corollary, (7), is then given as a reason for (6). The "QED" (Latin for "what was to be demonstrated") indicates that Spinoza takes (4) and (6) together to establish the proposition (1). This gives the following inferential structure:

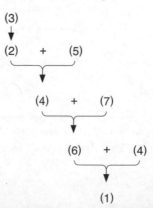

SUMMARY

- Many **natural arguments**—those naturally occurring in speech, in writing, etc.—are **extended arguments** involving more than one inference.
- **Each inference in an extended argument has its own premise(s) and conclusion**.
- The overall point being argued for in an extended argument is the **main conclusion**; in some (rare) cases, there may be more than one.
- The conclusions of the other inferences in the argument are **intermediate conclusions**. An **intermediate conclusion will function as a premise for other inferences** in the argument.
- In an **argument diagram**, **each inference** is represented by a downward pointing **arrow, ↓**.
- Premises may entail a conclusion **conjointly**, in which case they are joined with a +, and the arrow goes from them together to the conclusion; or each may entail it **independently**, in which case there will be an arrow from each premise to the same conclusion.
- The point of an argument diagram is to make explicit what is supposed to follow from what. Only when the inferences have been identified, can we judge how good they are.

EXERCISES 1.3

Analyze each of the following extended arguments as follows: (i) *(bracket) or* box *the inference indicators, set the premises in <triangular brackets>, underline the <u>conclusions</u>, and double-underline the <u>main conclusion</u>, and* (ii) *construct the argument diagram.*

12. (1) Reality is one. It must be single because (2) plurality, taken as real, contradicts itself.—F.H. Bradley, *Appearance and Reality*, 2nd ed., p. 519

13. Because (1) the greatest mitochondrial variations occurred in African people, scientists concluded that (2) they had the longest evolutionary history, indicating (3) a probable African origin for modern humans.—*Science*, May 26, 1995

14. As (1) force is always on the side of the governed, (2) the governors have nothing to support them but opinion. (3) It is therefore on opinion only that government is founded.—David Hume, *Essays, Moral, Political, and Literary*, I, iv, 1777

15. (1) Contrary to what many people think, a positive test for HIV is not necessarily a death sentence. For one thing, (2) the time from the development of antibodies to clinical symptoms averages nearly ten years. For another, (3) many reports are now

suggesting that a significant number of people who test positive may never develop clinical AIDS.—R.S. Root-Bernstein, "Misleading Reliability," *The Sciences*, March 1990

16. (1) Nor is what exists empty in any respect. For (2) what is empty is nothing; and so, (3) being nothing, it would not exist.—Melissus, Fragment B7

17. (1) One should avenge injustices to the best of one's ability and not pass them by; for (2) to do so is just and good, and (3) not to do so is unjust and bad.—Democritus, Fragment B261

18. (1) The promise you make with a gun to your head is devoid of moral or legal force. (2) Nobody is obligated in any way to keep a pledge extracted under duress.—William Saffire, "Made Under Duress," *The New York Times*, June 22, 1995

19. Since (1) there is no single objective world-wide 'now' in special relativity, and since (2) there cannot be multiple rivers of time each of which determines the advance of reality, (3) it follows that there simply is no such thing as the universal, worldwide flux of 'now' or lapse of time consistent with relativity.—Palle Yourgrau, *The Forgotten Legacy of Gödel and Einstein* (Cambridge, MA: Basic Books, 2005), p. 132

20. (1) The central problem evolutionary biology must explain is the existence of complex adaptation. So, (2) natural selection has a special status within evolutionary biology, for (3) complex adaptation can only be explained by natural selection.—Kim Sterelny, *Dawkins vs. Gould* (Cambridge: Icon Books, 2001), p. 168

Example:

16. (1) <u>Nor is what exists empty in any respect</u>. (For) (2) what is empty is nothing; (and so), (3) being nothing, it would not exist.—Melissus, Fragment B7

The 'For' indicates that what precedes it is being argued for. Here, despite the "and so" introducing (3), it seems that (3) must be taken together with (2) to support (1). For we may rewrite (3) as "What is nothing does not exist," which together with (2) entails that "what is empty does not exist," and this is equivalent to "what exists is not empty."

This is diagrammed:

Chapter Two

Validity

2.1 VALIDITY

2.1.1 DEFINING VALIDITY

What constitutes a valid argument? Obviously, if we are to be persuaded by an argument—if we are to accept its conclusion—we must believe the premises to be true. But this will not be enough by itself. Consider for example this single-inference argument:

No NDP leader has been elected as Canadian Prime Minister.
Jack Layton was not elected as Canadian Prime Minister.
Therefore Jack Layton was an NDP leader.

At the time of writing, both these premises are true, but they give us no reason to accept the conclusion, even though that too is true. And even if the premises were not true, we could certainly *imagine* them to be so without feeling at all obliged to accept the conclusion. Thus whether or not the conclusion is true, we have not been given good grounds for accepting it. In such a case we say that *the argument is invalid*, or that *the inference* from the premises to the conclusion *is invalid*.

The root notion of validity is that accepting the premises ought to lead one to accept the conclusion. That is, it cannot be good reasoning if we can accept all the premises (even if we accept them only for the sake of argument) and still deny the truth of the conclusion. This motivates the following definitions:

An argument or inference is *valid* if and only if denying its conclusion is incompatible with accepting all its premises.
An *invalid* argument or inference is one that is not valid.

Here is an example to help clarify the definition.

A body's mass increases without bound as it approaches the speed of light, c.
But mass is directly proportional to energy, according to Einstein's formula.

Therefore it would take an infinite amount of energy to accelerate a body to the speed of light.

Here if we understand and accept both the premises, this is incompatible with denying the conclusion, since the energy we use to accelerate the body must also increase without bound as the body's velocity approaches the speed of light. But that is just what the conclusion asserts. So denying the conclusion is incompatible with accepting all the premises. The argument is therefore judged valid.

This definition of validity harks all the way back to the ancient Greek Stoic logician, Chrysippus. It has very wide applicability, because we will judge differently in different contexts whether statements are *incompatible*. In the above example, for instance, the context is that of modern physics. Given an understanding of mass, energy, acceleration, etc. the denial of the conclusion is incompatible with an acceptance of the premises, even if it is not *logically inconsistent* with them. Two statements are logically inconsistent if there is a logical contradiction between them, that is, if they are a statement and its negation, or if together they entail both a statement and its negation. For example, the statement "This figure is a circle" is logically inconsistent with the statement "This figure is not a circle," since these two statements contradict one another. "This figure is a circle" is also incompatible with the statement "This figure is a square," since if you know the meanings of 'circle' and 'square,' its being a circle precludes its being a square. But judging them incompatible depends on a knowledge of circles and squares, whereas the inconsistency of the first two statements does not depend on meaning or context. In purely formal contexts such as formal logic and mathematics, logical inconsistency is the appropriate standard of incompatibility. When we interpret incompatibility as logical inconsistency, we obtain a narrower kind of validity, *formal validity*, as we shall discuss in the next section. But if we adopt this criterion of validity universally, a very large class of arguments whose reasoning appears perfectly valid will come out as formally invalid. This is because they implicitly appeal to other standards of evidence appropriate to their contexts, and not to purely formal criteria. Our Chrysippean definition will be particularly useful for evaluating the validity of such natural arguments.

We will also apply the over-arching Chrysippean definition to establish the validity of rules of inference in formal contexts, where we will interpret incompatibility as logical inconsistency. As a consequence, validity in such formal contexts will simply be identical with formal validity. This has an important consequence for arguments with logically inconsistent premises. For since one cannot accept a contradiction, it is not possible for one to accept the premises of such an argument and also deny the conclusion, thus making the argument valid—whatever the conclusion might be. As we shall see, this agrees with the rules of formal validity, according to which anything at all follows from a contradiction.

Our definition of validity differs very subtly from one often found elsewhere, where a valid argument is defined as one "such that it is impossible that its premises are all true and its conclusion false." One objection to this rival definition is that it is not easy to see how to apply it if the premises are not actually all true. A particular argument is only given once, with its premises variously having the values of true or false that they do; we cannot change their values to make them all true and then see whether the conclusion is false. We can, however, imagine an argument of the same *form* to have all true premises and a false conclusion, in which case the definition in terms of truth and falsity could then be applied to arguments of this form. We will take this approach in the next section, where we will see that arguments that are instances of a valid form are formally valid.[1]

2.1.2 SOUNDNESS

Now suppose we agree that a given argument is valid. Should we then accept its conclusion? Let's look at an example from the Zen Masters of Logic, *Monty Python*. In their movie *Monty Python and the Holy Grail* (1975), Sir Bedevere manages to elicit the following argument from a group of willing bystanders:

If she's made of wood, she's a witch.
If she weighs the same as a duck, she's made of wood.
Therefore, if she weighs the same as a duck, she's a witch.

Although I haven't given here the reasoning by which he establishes each premise, it is, of course, awful, full of the most flagrant fallacies. Only someone as utterly stupid as the peasants in Sir Bedevere's audience would accept the conclusion. But that's only because the premises are totally ridiculous. If, however, we put that to one side and, for the sake of argument, accept the above two premises, then we have to accept the conclusion. That is, denying the conclusion would be incompatible with accepting the premises, so the argument stated above is valid! (We'll prove it so in chapter 7.)

What this example shows is that in order to be convinced by an argument, we need to be persuaded of more than just the validity of the reasoning. If we are going to accept the argument's conclusion, we also need to be convinced of the truth of the argument's premises. Now it is often said that all that is necessary for a good argument, in addition to the validity of its reasoning, is that *its premises be true*. Such an argument is defined as *sound*:

---

[1] In rewriting this subsection for the second edition, I am much indebted to J.M. Kearns of Cape May, NJ, for his incisive criticisms, and also to Bradley Zurcher and especially to Nicolas Fillion of Simon Fraser University, Burnaby, BC, for their helpful comments and constructive suggestions.

An *argument* is *sound* if and only if it is *valid* and all its premises are *true*. Otherwise it is *unsound*.

A few notorious examples, however, suffice to show that the mere truth of the premises is not enough, in addition to the argument's validity, to make an argument a good one. There is, for instance, a whole range of arguments in which the statement being argued for as the conclusion is already presupposed as one of the premises. Here is a (made-up) example:

(1) A religion is a system of beliefs based on some commitment to the supernatural. Since (2) Scientology is a religion, (3) we know that its credo centres on such a commitment.Therefore, having such a commitment, (4) it must be classified as a religion.

Here the conclusion (4) is derived from the definition (1) and the statement (3). But (2) is given as a premise for (3) (as shown by the premise indicator "since"). This means that (4) is derived from (2) as a premise, but the two statements say the same thing! In case the controversial nature of that subject throws you off, here is another example of the same form:

(1) An irrational number cannot be expressed as the ratio of two integers. Since (2) π is an irrational, (3) we know that it cannot be expressed as the ratio of two integers. Therefore, not being so expressible, (4) it must be an irrational number.

Such arguments are called *circular arguments*. By our definition of validity, they are necessarily valid, because denying the conclusion is incompatible with accepting all the premises.[2] Even if all the premises are true, including the statement in question, clearly this type of argument should not persuade anyone, and therefore should not be regarded as a good argument, even though it is *sound* by the above definition.

Another objection to soundness as a criterion for a good argument is that a valid argument may perhaps have true premises, but if they are not *known to be true*, it will still not be persuasive. Indeed, outside of purely formal contexts, we often do not know for certain whether many of the statements we use as premises are infallibly true. But this will not prevent us from judging whether, given appropriate standards of evidence, we should accept the conclusion on the basis of the premises. But this is just validity.

Thus the concept of soundness does not appear to be an adequate notion for evaluating the strength of arguments. In any case we will make no further use of it in this book after the exercises of this section.

---

[2] Although it does not add to the persuasive force of an argument, there may still be good reason to reiterate a statement made earlier. In chapter 11 we will introduce a rule, Reiteration, that allows us to do just that in the course of a proof of validity.

Finally, notice that in logic, as opposed to uncritical speech, we NEVER speak of an *argument* or the *reasoning* in it as being *true* or *false*; in logic the only thing that can be true or false is a *statement* or *proposition*. Likewise we NEVER speak of a *statement* being *valid* or *invalid*, reserving those terms strictly for *arguments*, *inferences*, or forms of reasoning.

SUMMARY

- An argument or inference is **valid** if and only if denying its conclusion is incompatible with accepting all its premises. Otherwise it is **invalid**.
- This definition is preferred to ones defining a valid argument as one for which it is impossible that its premises are all true and its conclusion false, (1) because it can be successfully applied to a much wider class of arguments than can that definition, and (2) because (unlike that definition) it can be applied whether or not the premises of a given argument are actually all true.
- An argument is **sound** if and only if it is **valid** and all its premises are **true**. Otherwise it is **unsound**.
- However, soundness so defined is inadequate to define a good argument, since (1) circular arguments can be sound but should persuade no one, and (2) whether all an argument's premises are true is something we often do not know for certain, yet we still make judgements about whether it should persuade us of its conclusion.

EXERCISES 2.1

1. Based on your understanding of this section, *say whether each of the following statements is true or false*:
   (a) An argument is valid if the conclusion follows from the premises.
   (b) An argument is valid if all its premises are true.
   (c) If an inference has only one premise but this is incompatible with its conclusion, then it is valid.
   (d) An argument is valid if it is sound.
   (e) An argument is valid if and only if the denial of the conclusion is incompatible with the acceptance of all its premises.
   (f) All circular arguments are valid.

2. *Make a true statement by filling in the gaps below with words taken from among the following set*: {conclusion, deduce, infer, premises, follow from, valid, sound}:
   In a good argument the _____ should _____ the _____. If you are given the premises, you should be able to _____ the conclusion, provided the argument is _____.

3. *Is the following argument valid?*

> Every sound argument is a valid argument.
> Every sound argument has true premises.
> ∴ Every valid argument has true premises.

4. A famous example of a circular argument is that of the "Cartesian Circle." Although scholarly opinion differs on whether Descartes was actually guilty of it, he is alleged to have argued that the fact that clear and distinct ideas have true contents (C) is guaranteed by the fact that an omnibenevolent God exists (G); but we know that an omnibenevolent God exists because this is the content of one of our clear and distinct ideas. Thus we have C because G; but G, because C. *Show that this argument is valid according to the definition of validity given in the text.*

5. Consider the statement "A square has four sides." *Determine whether it is (i) logically inconsistent with, (ii) incompatible with (given the meanings of 'square' and 'triangle'), or (iii) neither incompatible nor logically inconsistent with, each of the following statements:*

    (a) A square has three sides.   (b) A square does not have four sides.

    (c) A triangle has three sides.   (d) No four-sided figure is square.

2.2 ARGUMENT FORMS AND FORMAL VALIDITY

But how are we to tell whether a given argument is valid? Must we determine this on a case-by-case basis, or are there some general forms of reasoning that are good or bad? One way to tell whether a piece of reasoning is valid is to examine another argument *of the same form*. Thus an argument of the same form as the "Jack Layton" argument at the beginning of the section is this:

> None of the Founding Fathers of the US is still alive today.
> Groucho Marx is not still alive today.
> Therefore Groucho Marx is one of the Founding Fathers of the US.

A form of reasoning *cannot* be good if it leads, as does this one, from true premises to a false conclusion. This leads to an alternative definition of the validity of an argument cast in terms of the idea of an *argument form*:

> An argument is *formally valid* if it has a valid argument form; and an argument form is valid if and only if there is no argument of that form which has all true premises and a false conclusion.

This is a more subtle definition than it might at first appear, and there are many traps for the unwary. The first point to notice is that a particular argument is *not* formally valid simply because it happens to have true premises and does not have a false conclusion. What is required is that *no argument of the same form have true premises and a false conclusion*. For example, the following argument has all true premises and a true conclusion:

Every valid argument has a valid argument form.
Every sound argument has a valid argument form.
∴ Every sound argument is a valid argument.

That all sounds good, but the argument is invalid! The problem is with the reasoning, with the *form* of the argument. It *is* possible to think of an argument having the same form as this one which has true premises and a false conclusion. For example:

Every dog has a head.
Every cat has a head.
∴ Every cat is a dog.

From this we can conclude that the following argument form is *invalid*:

Every A has a B.
Every C has a B.
∴ Every C is an A.

This is to be contrasted with Sir Bedevere's argument above. Although it was thoroughly unsound (because the premises were patently false), it had the *valid* form:

If O, then I.
If U, then O.
∴ If U, then I.

We say that the "Sir Bedevere" argument is an *instance* of this form, and that any argument that is an instance of this form is formally valid. From this you may see that we cannot in general tell whether a given argument is *valid* by looking at the truth or falsity of its premises and conclusion. Instead we must concentrate on its form: if it has a valid form, then it is a formally valid argument. If it is formally invalid, then it must be possible to find another argument of the same form that has true premises and a false conclusion.

This definition of formal invalidity relates to the overall definition of validity as follows. In the previous section we defined a valid argument as one for which the denial of its conclusion is incompatible with the truth of all its premises. In applying this to argument forms we interpret this incompatibility purely in terms of the truth and falsity of premises and conclusion: that is, a form is valid if and only if there is no instance of this form with all its premises true and the conclusion false.

But what exactly is an argument form? So far we have proceeded intuitively, identifying arguments as having the same form when they appear to us to have the same elements repeated in the same order. In the Sir Bedevere example, the repeated elements are *statements*: O := "She is made of wood," I := "She is a witch," and U := "She weighs the same as a duck." (In this book I use the notation := to indicate the assignment of a symbol.) In the "Every A has a B" argument form, by contrast, the A and B stand for categories of things, whereas in arguments of the "Jack Layton" and "Groucho Marx" form, they stand for classes of people. Both these latter types can be construed as concerning individuals of which certain *predicates* may or may not hold—"is a Founding Father," "is leader of the NDP," etc. One of the things we shall be doing in this book is learning how to identify various valid forms, as well as developing techniques for proving these forms valid. Arguments of the first kind above, whose form depends on the way constituent statements are joined together, are the subject of **Statement Logic**, and will occupy us in the first part of this book; whereas ones whose forms depend on the way predicates are joined together, are the subject of **Predicate Logic**, which we'll get to in the second part.

So we shall develop a much clearer idea of argument form as we proceed. Nevertheless, before we leave the subject, there is a subtle point concerning argument forms that is important to remember. This is that *an argument may be considered to have a different form depending on how we analyze it*. This can be seen through the above examples. "Every dog has a head" is a statement, and so are "Every cat has a head" and "Every cat is a dog." So if we labelled these statements A, B, and C respectively, the form of that argument *construed as an argument in statement logic* would be:

A
B
―――
∴ C

The same applies to the Sir Bedevere example, where we could have had A, B, and C standing for "If she's made of wood, she's a witch," "If she weighs the same as a duck, she's made of wood," and "If she weighs the same as a duck, she's a witch," respectively. This argument would then have the same form as the one just given, and it is not a valid one. [Why not? Can you think of an interpretation of A, B, and C that proves the form invalid?] What this shows is that *a given argument may be an instance of more than one form*. Consequently, *if we want to prove a given argument invalid, it is not enough to show that the argument has an invalid form*. For it may also be an instance of a valid form, like the Sir Bedevere example, and according to our definition any argument with a valid form is valid. In other words, if we have an argument that is an instance of an invalid form, we are only entitled to say that it is invalid if it is not also an instance of a valid form. So having a valid form proves validity; having an invalid form does not automatically prove invalidity. (Don't worry if this seems confusing at this point; we shall be returning to the issue in chapter 10, by which time you should be a good deal more familiar with argument forms and validity.)

For now it is much more important to *remember the following*: there can be invalid arguments with premises true and conclusion false, with premises true and conclusions true, with premises false and conclusion true, or with premises false and conclusion false. Similarly, there can be valid arguments with premises true and conclusions true, with premises false and conclusion true, or with premises false and conclusion false. There is only one combination that is ruled out: it is impossible for a *formally valid* argument to have *true premises and a false conclusion*.

SUMMARY

- An argument is **formally valid** if it has a **valid argument form**.
- An **argument form** is **valid** if and only if there can be no argument of that form which has all true premises and a false conclusion.
- A given argument may be an instance of more than one form. Thus a formally valid argument may also be an instance of a (different) invalid argument form. This shows that **being an instance of an invalid form does not necessarily make an argument formally invalid**.

EXERCISES 2.2

6. *Invent an argument of the same form as each of the following which has true premises and false conclusion. What does this prove about the form in question?*
   (a) If the Big Bang Theory is correct, there will be microwave radiation corresponding to a temperature of about 3°K in whichever direction in space you choose to look. Since there is such radiation, the theory is obviously correct.
   (b) "J.-J.," I replied, "if it was any of your business, I would have invited you. It is not, and so I did not."—Paul Erdman, *The Crash of '79*
   (c) No electrons are quarks. No quarks are composite particles. So no electrons are composite particles.
   (d) If the orbit is an ellipse, the force law is as the inverse square of the distance. Ergo, if the force law is as the inverse square of the distance, the orbit is an ellipse.

(e) If the money supply increases at less than 5%, the rate of inflation will decrease. Thus, since the money supply is not increasing at less than 5%, inflation will not come down.

Example:
(d) This has the form: If *p* then *q*, so if *q* then *p*. If we replace *p* by "All birds can fly," and *q* by "Swallows can fly," the premise becomes the true statement "If all birds can fly then swallows can fly," but the conclusion becomes "If swallows can fly then all birds can fly." This is false: not all birds can fly. So the argument form is invalid.

7. *Identify whether each of the following statements is true or false*:
   (a) An argument is formally valid if it has a valid argument form.
   (b) An argument is formally invalid if it is an instance of an invalid argument form.
   (c) Every argument with a valid argument form has all its premises true.
   (d) If an argument is an instance of a valid argument form, it cannot be an instance of an invalid argument form.
   (e) No valid argument can be an instance of an invalid argument form.

8. *Identify which of the following symbolically expressed argument forms is valid according to our criterion of validity*, where A and B stand for any statements:
   (a) A. Therefore A.
   (b) A and B. Therefore A.
   (c) A. Therefore B.
   (d) It's not the case that A. Therefore B.
   (e) It's not the case that A. Therefore A.

2.3 EVALUATING NATURAL ARGUMENTS

According to our definition of validity above,

An *argument or inference* is *valid* if and only if denying its conclusion is incompatible with accepting all its premises. Otherwise it is *invalid*.

This applies equally to all arguments, including everyday ones, not just the artificial ones cooked up for logic textbooks. In evaluating such natural arguments, however, there are several wrinkles we need to take into account. The first of the wrinkles is that in an extended argument *there is usually more than one inference involved*. In such a case, in order for the argument as a whole to be valid, *the whole chain of inferences involved in getting to the conclusion must be valid*. We may elaborate this by reference to the arguments of the last section of chapter 1. Thus in argument (ii) of that section,

(ii) (1) Drug use is wrong because (2) it is immoral, and it is immoral because (3) it enslaves the mind and destroys the soul.—James Q. Wilson, *Newsweek*, Januery 9, 1989

each 'because' denotes an inference. Thus both inferences need to be valid for the argument to be valid. Argument (iii), on the other hand, involves two independent inferences:

(iii) (1) Universities must expect further cuts because (2) they have suffered less than other sectors of education. But even if that were not so, (1) they should expect further cuts because (3) they are not sufficiently vocationally oriented.

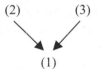

According to our definition of validity, this argument will be valid *either* if (2) validly entails (1), *or* if (3) validly entails (1), or both.

The second wrinkle is that in evaluating the validity of each inference *we will generally need to apply the Principle of Charity to see if any implicit premises need to be supplied*; but this is a matter of some delicacy. It will require us to ask, for each inference: What must the reasoner obviously be supposing if the inference is to be a good one? Might there be some premise that the proposer of the argument is implicitly assuming, which, if accepted, would make the inference valid? For example, in order for the inference in argument (i) of 1.3 to be valid, we would, it seems, have to grant as an implicit premise "Only male philosophers desire other males (of the same species)." This would make the argument valid, but only at the expense of allowing a premise that no one could accept. Either way, the argument would be unsound. So we see that in evaluating natural arguments it may be a matter of judgement whether we regard an inference as invalid or an implicit premise as unacceptable. But in supplying the implicit premise we can offer a more substantial judgement on the argument: instead of just saying that the inference is invalid, we can say that the argument would be persuasive only if the premise "Only male philosophers desire other males" were accepted as true.

Thirdly, in evaluating validity *we will usually need to make a judgement about what standards of evidence are appropriate* to the case. For if we take the criterion that the truth of the premises must be incompatible with the falsity of the conclusion to mean that it must be logically inconsistent with it, very few arguments indeed will come out as valid, even some of the strongest scientific arguments. Take, for instance, Cotes's argument based on Newton's rules of reasoning given above:

> Now, since all terrestrial and celestial bodies on which we can make any experiments or observations are heavy, it must be acknowledged without exception that gravity belongs to all bodies universally.

Here the denial of the conclusion that gravity belongs to all bodies universally is certainly compatible with the premise: there may well be mass-less (and therefore gravity-less) bodies on which physicists of Newton's time simply had not yet made experiments or observations.[3] So Cotes's argument cannot have been valid in the strict sense that the denial of the conclusion was absolutely incompatible with the premises. Yet it seems that to deny that it was a good argument would be to set the standards of evidence appealed to here impossibly high. Where would we be if we rejected all inferences drawn from our experience?

Let's re-express the point as follows. We have called any argument that is valid in the formal sense that the denial of the conclusion is logically inconsistent with the premises *formally valid*. But if we used this standard of logical incompatibility to judge validity in all cases, then virtually none of our knowledge gleaned from facts known through experience could be said to be validly derived. Many philosophers have thought that this shows the need for a separate branch of logic, *inductive logic*, according to which arguments that are not formally valid could be assessed on a scale from weak to strong. Others, including myself, regard the quest for an inductive logic as a hopeless quest. I believe we should bite the bullet and accept that there is a vast array of arguments which are not formally valid, but whose conclusions seem impossible to deny given the premises and *appropriate standards of evidence*. For each such argument we need to ask ourselves:

> *What evidence would convince me of the conclusion?* If the given premises seem insufficient, what else is needed?

Once we ask ourselves these questions, it will usually be possible to identify what further assumption might need to be granted in order for the argument to be valid. If it seems reasonable to assume that all parties would regard it as too obvious to need stating explicitly, it should be added as a further implicit premise.[4]

---

[3] Indeed there are: we now know that photons or particles of light are (in their own rest-frame) massless. But we can't fault Newton or Cotes for not knowing this, since you cannot even make observations on photons in their own rest-frames!

[4] This treatment of the validity of natural arguments is much indebted to Alec Fisher's *The Logic*

Thus, returning to Cotes's argument above, it seems the best assessment would be that the argument is valid, given appropriate standards of evidence.

SUMMARY

- Our definition of argument validity applies equally to **natural arguments**, that is, the usually extended arguments involving several inferences that we encounter in everyday reasoning.
- An argument involving several inferences will be valid **only if all the inferences leading from the premises to the conclusion are valid**. An exception to this is the case of arguments where more than one inference independently leads to the same conclusion: then it is enough if one of the inferences is valid.
- In evaluating the validity of each inference we will generally need to **apply the Principle of Charity** to see if any implicit premises need to be supplied.
- In evaluating validity we will usually need to make a judgement about **what standards of evidence** are appropriate to the case. For **formal validity**, we require that the denial of the conclusion be **logically inconsistent** with the premises. If we used this standard of logical incompatibility to judge validity in all cases, then virtually none of our knowledge gleaned from arguments from experience could be said to be validly derived. Such arguments should be judged according to whether it is impossible to deny their conclusion given the premises and **appropriate standards of evidence**.

EXERCISES 2.3

Evaluate the arguments below as follows. *Identify the main conclusion*, examine the premises, and *ask yourself whether these premises (if you accepted them as true) would be adequate to persuade you of the conclusion. If not, what further premises would be necessary?* (You are not asked to evaluate the truth of the premises.)

9. Matter is divisible, and is therefore destructible, for whatever is divided is destroyed.—Gottfried Leibniz, "Notes on Science and Metaphysics" (1676)

---

of Real Arguments (Cambridge: Cambridge UP, 1988). As we shall see in chapter 5, Fisher claims that judgements about the validity of all natural arguments are amenable to what he calls the Assertibility Question: "What argument or evidence would justify me in asserting the conclusion?" (p. 27). Another approach to the question of what constitutes a good argument is through the notion of *cogency*: see the thorough treatment of argument interpretation and evaluation in terms of this concept in Mark Vorobej, *A Theory of Natural Argument* (Cambridge: Cambridge UP, 2006).

10. Eternity is simultaneously whole. But time has a before and an after. Therefore time and eternity are not the same thing.—Thomas Aquinas, *Summa Theologica*

11. As force is always on the side of the governed, the governors have nothing to support them but opinion. It is therefore on opinion only that government is founded.—David Hume, *First Principles of Government*

12. Each element, such as hydrogen and iron, has a set of gaps—wavelengths that it absorbs rather than radiates. So if those wavelengths are missing from the spectrum, you know that that element is present in the star you are observing.—Rick Gore, "Eyes of Science"

13. Nothing is demonstrable unless the contrary implies a contradiction. Nothing that is distinctly conceivable implies a contradiction. Whatever we conceive as existent, we can also conceive as non-existent. There is no being, therefore, whose non-existence implies a contradiction. Consequently there is no being whose existence is demonstrable.—David Hume, *Dialogues Concerning Natural Religion* (1779), Part IX

PART II
STATEMENT LOGIC

Chapter Three

Statements and Conditionals

3.1 STATEMENTS AND COMPOUNDS

3.1.1 STATEMENTS

What is a statement? As mentioned in chapter 1, this apparently innocent question can lead us quickly into deep philosophical waters. A statement cannot be just a sentence, since sentences have a great variety of linguistic functions. We use them not only to make statements, but to ask questions, issue commands, make exclamations, exhortations, and so forth. But these other functions are by and large identifiable by their grammatical moods, interrogative ("Are you going?"), and Imperative ("Go!," "Let's go!"). So why not say a statement is a sentence (in indicative or perhaps subjunctive mood) used to make an assertion, i.e., a *declarative sentence*? This is close. But the same statement is made by the following three different declarative sentences: "It is raining," "Il pleut," and "Es regnet," the second and third being French and German for the first. And if I say "It is raining" twice in a row, have I made two statements or one? Is "Sean Penn was divorced by Madonna" a different statement than "Madonna divorced Sean Penn"?

These difficulties can be resolved as follows. First we need to distinguish a *type* of sentence from a *token* of the same sentence. Thus a declarative sentence such as "It is raining" is one that could be uttered or written on many different occasions by different people. Each such utterance or act of writing is a token of that sentence-type. Second, among types of sentence we may distinguish the declarative *sentence* (which, when written down or spoken, is subject to grammatical rules), from the *proposition* (what is expressed by a declarative sentence, its content or meaning). Thus "It is raining" is one sentence, and tokens of it may be uttered on any number of occasions. "Il pleut" and "Es regnet" are different sentences, but express the same proposition. Likewise "Sean Penn was divorced by Madonna" and "Madonna divorced Sean Penn": statements in the passive mode ("S was divorced by M") express the same proposition as corresponding active mode statements ("M divorced S"), and from here on will always be so reinterpreted.

Now clearly statements in the sense of utterances are no concern of logic; nor are sentences insofar as they are mere grammatical items. Consequently logic has been said to deal with statements in the last of these senses only, types of statements that are propositions: hence the traditional name for the logic of statements, "Propositional Logic." In the twentieth century, however, the notion of propositions came in for trenchant criticism on the grounds that no one has been able to give an adequate account of when two propositions could be regarded as identical. As a result, most logic texts define a statement as "a sentence that is either true or false." But there are difficulties with this definition too, as noted above and discussed further in the GLOSSARY under STATEMENT; see also PROPOSITION.

Fortunately, we need not resolve this philosophical issue in order to proceed. The definitions already given in chapter 1 of statement and proposition are adequate for our purposes:

A *statement* is a sentence (or part of a sentence) that expresses something true or false.

But to say a statement is true or false is just to say what it asserts is true or false. Thus in this sense, i.e., semantically, a statement may be identified with what it expresses, namely the proposition, which we defined as follows:

A *proposition* is what a statement expresses as true or false.[1]

In contrast to this, a question may ask whether something is true or false, but it does not express something that *is* true or false. Similarly, a command such as "Do up your shoe laces!" does not assert anything true or false; nor does an exhortation such as "Let's go, Blue Jays!" Finally a supposition such as "Suppose you are right" does not itself assert the statement "you are right," although the latter statement is contained within the supposition.

3.1.2 COMPOUNDS

As we saw above, one of the things that these definitions take into account is that propositions are often expressed by parts of sentences. We saw that in a statement like Augustine's "If no one asks me, I know [what time is]," two other statements are contained in it:

---

[1] This definition goes all the way back to Chrysippus of ancient Athens: "A proposition is what can be asserted or denied on its own, for example, 'It is day' or 'Dion is walking.' The proposition gets its name [*axioma*] from being accepted [or rejected]; for he who says 'It is day' seems to accept [*axioun*] that it is day" (Brad Inwood and L.P. Gerson, *Hellenistic Philosophy* [Indianapolis: Hackett, 1988], p. 84).

"no one asks me" and "I know what time is." They are called *components* of the original statement. But not all parts of statements that can be said to express something true or false can be regarded as components. Take for example the following statement, from Umberto Eco's medieval thriller *The Name of the Rose*:

(1) Benno admitted that his enthusiasm had carried him away.[2]

"Benno admitted that" and "his enthusiasm had carried him away" are both parts of a sentence, and each could be taken to express a proposition, so they are statements by the above definition. But the first does not appear to be a component of the whole statement in the right sense. For the second, we could substitute any other statement at all, and still get something meaningful: "Benno admitted that nylon tights tear easily," for example. Try doing that with the first! This motivates the following definitions:

One statement is a *component* of another if substituting it within the original by any other statement whatever still yields a meaningful statement.[3]

A *compound statement* is any statement that contains one or more component statements.

A *simple statement* is any statement that has no components.

To see how this works, consider the following statement:

(2) Bacon was right in saying that the conquest of learning is achieved through the knowledge of languages. (*ibid.*, p. 191)

"Bacon was right in saying that the conquest of learning is achieved" is a statement, as are "learning is achieved through the knowledge of languages," "Bacon was right in saying that," and even "Bacon was right." But none of them are components of the original statement.[4] Substituting the third of these, for example, by "Nylon tights tear easily" yields "Nylon tights tear easily the conquest of learning is achieved through the knowledge of

---

[2] Umberto Eco, *The Name of the Rose*, p. 158. All the statements in this section are taken from this book.

[3] This definition of component statement is due to Copi and Cohen, *Introduction to Logic* (11th edition), p. 301.

[4] Substituting the first of these by "Nylon tights tear easily" yields "Nylon tights tear easily through the knowledge of languages"! You may be able to imagine a context in which this is meaningful; but the original statement must be meaningful when any statement is substituted. Try substituting, say, "Nothing tastes better than lychees."

languages," which is pure gibberish. "The conquest of learning is achieved through the knowledge of languages," however, is a component statement. (Try substituting other statements for it.)

3.1.3 STATEMENT OPERATORS

In Statement Logic we are not concerned with compound statements of all kinds, but only a very delimited class of them. The point can be made by looking at some further examples from Eco's *The Name of the Rose*:

(3) "I began to think [that] I had encountered a forgery."
(4) "Ubertino could have become one of the heretics he helped burn, or [he could have become] a cardinal of the holy Roman church."

Both of these are compound statements according to our definition. In the first, any statement at all could have been substituted for "I had encountered a forgery" and the result would still be a meaningful statement. Similarly in the second, any statements could have been substituted for "Ubertino could have become one of the heretics he helped burn" and "he could have become a cardinal of the holy Roman church," with a similar result. A good way of thinking of this is to imagine the words or phrases "I began to think that" and "or" as *operators* that work on statements to produce other statements. Such operators are usually called *statement connectives* (not a very good term, since the ones that operate on single statements do not "connect" them to anything!). We will call them *statement operators*.

A *statement operator* is a word or phrase which operates on a statement or statements to form a compound statement.

Statement operators that form a compound by operating on only *one* statement are called *unary*; those that join together a *pair* of statements are called *binary*.

Thus the phrases "I believe that," "It must be concluded that," "It is not the case that" are all examples of *unary operators*: they turn *single* statements into other single compound statements. On the other hand, "...or...," "...and...," and "from...it follows that...," are *binary operators*: each joins a *pair* of statements into a compound statement.

Now of all the myriad possible statement operators there are a few that hold special interest for us in statement logic. Naturally these include the inference indicators we have already encountered, that is, the premise- and conclusion-indicators: "Consequently...," "Therefore...," "It follows that...," "...since...," and so forth. But in addition there are those that typically join together statements into the compound statements that constitute the premises and conclusion of commonly occurring single-inference arguments.

There are precisely five of these operators that are basic to logical reasoning. They are:

- "It is not the case that __"
- "if __ then __"
- "__ and __"
- "__ or __,"   and
- "__ if and only if __."

These five are distinguished from other phrases used to make compound statements by the fact that the *truth value*—that is, the truth or falsity—of any compound formed by them is a function only of the truth or falsity of their component statements. That is, for each combination of the truth values of the components there will be a unique truth value—true or false—of the compound. Consequently, these five operators are called *truth-functional operators*.

A *truth-functional operator* is one that forms a compound statement whose truth value is a function of the truth values of the component statements.

All other statement operators are (surprise!) *non-truth-functional*.

This distinction is best illustrated through examples. Statement (1) above is a compound statement formed from the phrase "Benno admitted that__" operating on the component statement "his enthusiasm had carried him away." So "Benno admitted that__" is a unary operator. But when we prefix it to some other statement p, the truth value of the resulting compound statement "Benno admitted that p" depends on whether p is one of those statements that Benno admits! Contrast this with the compound formed from prefixing "[Benno's] enthusiasm had carried him away" by the unary operator "It is not the case that__":

(5) "It is not the case that Benno's enthusiasm had carried him away."

Here if the component is true, the compound is clearly false; and if the component is false, the compound is true; and *this is so for any statements that we care to prefix with this operator*. This is what makes "It is not the case that__" a truth-functional operator. Similar (but not so trivial) considerations apply to the four binary truth-functional operators. We shall investigate how their compounds' truth values vary with the components' in a later chapter.

We have already seen how it is convenient to abbreviate statements by capital letters. In the same way it helps to have abbreviations for the five truth-functional operators. So we introduce special symbols for them, writing

¬A	for	not A (it is not the case that A)	
A → B	for	if A then B	
A & B	for	A and B	
A v B	for	A or B	and
A ↔ B	for	A if and only if B	

Here A and B stand for certain individual statements—*any* statements, compound or simple. Thus in A → B, statement A could be a compound statement. For instance, take the following statement by the ancient Greek Antiphon:

(6) If someone were to bury a bed and the rotting wood came to life, it would become not a bed, but a tree.—*A Presocratics Reader*, p. 105

Here if A is "someone buries a bed and the rotting wood comes to life," and we symbolize "it becomes not a bed, but a TREE" by T, this gives A → T.[5] But A is itself a compound of two statements "someone is BURYING a bed" (B) and "the rotting wood came to LIFE" (L). So we may symbolize it as B & L. This would make the whole statement

B & L → T

Looking at this formula, you may be wondering why you suddenly feel hungry. But you should also notice that it is ambiguous. If you plug back in the component statements, you could get the different statement

(7) Someone is burying a bed, and if the rotting wood were to come to life, it would become not a bed, but a tree.

This statement asserts that someone is actually burying a bed, whereas Antiphon was making no such claim. The ambiguity of formulas like B & L → T is easily removed by using parentheses, just as we do in arithmetic and algebra. The formula 3 + 2/5 can be disambiguated by distinguishing (3 + 2)/5 from 3 + (2/5): these yield the different values 1 and 3.4. Similarly Antiphon's statement (6) should be symbolized

(F6) (B & L) → T

---

[5] Here I am tacitly converting the subjunctive and conditional tenses into indicative mood (and also back again). I should warn, however, that there is a large literature on subjunctive and counterfactual conditionals which I am thereby ignoring.

whereas statement (7) is symbolized

(F7)   B & (L → T)

Here I am using the notation (F6), for example, for the formula symbolizing statement (6). I have also introduced the *convention that the capital letter symbolizing each individual statement will be the first letter of the capitalized word* (sometimes part-word) *in that statement*. I will follow this convention from here on in this book. (I will make sure, however, that different statements are symbolized by different letters.) Thus the formula symbolizing statement (5), "It is not the case that Benno's ENTHUSIASM had carried him away," is

(F5)   ¬E

Note that we do not symbolize statement (5) by E, just because it is a negative statement, a denial. This invokes a further convention regarding symbolizing. This is that *all statements A, B, C,...are to be positive assertions*, rather than denials. Again analogously with algebra, the unary operator '¬' does not need parentheses. There is nothing to be gained in clarity by writing 'Not E' as ¬(E), rather than just plain ¬E. Nor would there be any gain in symbolizing "It is not true that something NEW had not occurred" by ¬(¬N), as opposed to plain ¬¬N. On the other hand, parentheses are necessary for the negation of E & F, that is, ¬(E & F), to distinguish it from ¬E & F.

Finally, there is no gain in clarity from writing parentheses around the outside of the whole of a compound statement standing by itself, e.g., by writing (F6) as

(F6*) ((B & L) → T)

Nevertheless, we can understand such parentheses as being there implicitly in (F6) without having to write them in. This means that it is neater to think of the binary operators as *always* introducing parentheses (or equivalent groupers, like [brackets] and {braces}), with the understanding that the outermost ones do not need to be written in explicitly. All of this can be summed up neatly by the following set of rules:

Rules of statement formation
  (i)   (*unary operator*) if A is a statement, then ¬A is also a statement.
  (ii) (*binary operators*) if A and B are both statements, then (A * B) is also a statement, where '*' stands for any of the binary operators '&', 'v', '→', and '↔'. Likewise, so are [A * B] and {A * B}.
  (iii) (*convention regarding outermost groupers*) in any compound formed by the binary operators, the outermost groupers are understood, rather than explicitly written in: e.g., {A * [B * C]} is written A * [B * C].

One final point: you should appreciate that some paraphrase may be necessary when symbolizing. Thus "Emily is here, and so is Fred" would be understood as "EMILY is here, and FRED is here."

Now let's look at some examples, taken from John Horgan's irreverent and rambunctious interviews with scientists and intellectuals in his book *The End of Science*:

(a) If in fact it [physics] were just a social CONSTRUCT, it would have FALLEN apart long before this.—Steven Weinberg (p. 74) $C \rightarrow F$
This is a simple "if...then..." statement. We'll be looking at these in the next section. The binary operator '$\rightarrow$' introduces parentheses, but since these are outermost, we regard them as understood.

(b) If I didn't spend my life CONCENTRATING on string theory, I would simply be MISSING my life's calling.—Edward Witten (p. 68) $\neg C \rightarrow M$
Here the "if-clause" is a negative statement.

(c) If there's going to be such a TOTAL theory of physics, in some sense it couldn't conceivably [have] the CHARACTER of any theory I've seen.—Roger Penrose (p. 179)
Here the "then-clause" is a negative statement. $T \rightarrow \neg C$

(d) My position in linguistics is a MINORITY position, and it ALWAYS has been.—Noam Chomsky (p. 150) $M \& A$
This a simple conjunction of M and A, where A is understood to be the statement "My position in linguistics has ALWAYS been a minority position."

(e) If you've got a BEAR by the tail, there comes a point at which you've got to LET it go, and STAND back.—Thomas Kuhn (p. 46) $B \rightarrow (L \& S)$
Here the "then-clause" is a compound of "there comes a point at which you've got to let it GO" and "[there comes a point at which you've got to] STAND back."

(f) I have opinions that I DEFEND rather vigorously, and then I find out how SILLY they are, and I GIVE them up!—Paul Feyerabend (p. 50) $D \& (S \& G)$

(g) Evolution no doubt OCCURS, and it's been SEEN to occur, and it's occurring NOW.—Lynn Margulis (p. 129) $O \& (S \& N)$

(f) and (g) could have as well been symbolized by (D & S) & G and (O & S) & N, but *not* by D & S & G and O & S & N, or by (D & S & G) or [O & S & N], etc.

(h) Before it was very easy. Either you believe in Jesus CHRIST, or you believe in NEWTON.—Ilya Prigogine $C \lor N$
Here C := "you believe in Jesus CHRIST," N := "you believe in NEWTON."

SUMMARY

- One statement is a **component** of another if substituting it within the original by any other statement whatever still yields a meaningful statement.
- A **compound statement** is any statement that contains one or more component statements.

- A **simple statement** is any statement that has no components.
- A **statement operator** is a word or phrase which operates on a statement or statements to form a compound statement.
- Statement operators that form a compound by operating on only one statement are called **unary**; those that join together a pair of statements are called **binary**.
- A **truth-functional operator** is one that forms a compound statement whose truth value (truth or falsity) is a function of the truth values of the component statements.
- The five truth-functional operators we shall be concerned with are:

not-A   if A then B   A and B   A or B   and   A if and only if B.
$\neg A$ $A \rightarrow B$ A & B   A v B $A \leftrightarrow B$

Symbolizing conventions:
- The capital letter symbolizing each individual statement will be the first letter of the capitalized word (sometimes part-word) in that statement.
- We use the letters A, B, C, ... to symbolize positive assertions, rather than denials.
- A compound formed by one of the binary operators comes with groupers, e.g., parentheses—$(A \rightarrow B)$, $(A \& B)$, $(A \vee B)$, $(A \leftrightarrow B)$—but the outermost groupers of a compound statement are understood, rather than written explicitly, e.g., $C \vee (A \rightarrow B)$.

EXERCISES 3.1

1. *State whether each of the following statements* from Michael Ondaatje's *The English Patient* is *simple or compound. Identify the component statements in each compound statement.*
   (a) She heard a far grumble of thunder. (p. 62)
   (b) If a man leaned back a few inches he would disappear into darkness. (p. 143)
   (c) In Canada pianos needed water. (p. 63)
   (d) We stood up at the end and you walked off the table into his arms. (p. 53)
   (e) He is a writer who used pen and ink. (p. 94)
   Example:
   (e) "He is a writer" is a statement, but is it a component statement? If we substitute for it, say, "Malebranche was born in Paris," we get "Malebranche was born in Paris who used pen and ink," which is not meaningful. So it is not a component statement of (e), which is therefore simple.

2. *Identify any statement operators in the following statements* by various scientists quoted by John Horgan in *The End of Science*. In each case *identify whether it is truth-functional* or *non-truth-functional*, and whether it is *binary* or *unary*.

(a) [Bohm] insisted that reality was unknowable. (p. 90)

(b) We still live in the childhood of mankind.—John Archibald Wheeler (p. 83)

(c) As we have discovered more and more fundamental physical principles, they seem to have less and less to do with us.—Steven Weinberg (p. 73)

(d) If Edward Witten is a philosophically naive scientist, Weinberg is an extremely sophisticated one…(p. 72)

(e) Since I know a little bit about global economic models, I know they don't work! —Philip Anderson (p. 210)

(f) The situation cannot declare itself until you've answered the question.—John Archibald Wheeler (p. 82)

(g) It's a very deep position, but I also think it's very deeply wrong.—Stephen Jay Gould (p. 136)

Example:

(g) 'But' is a *binary* operator, connecting "It's a very deep position" with "I also think it's very deeply wrong." Since the whole statement can't be true if either of the components is false, 'but' is *truth-functional*. "I also think it's very deeply wrong" is also a compound statement, though, formed from the *unary* operator 'I also think [that]' and "it's very deeply wrong." 'I also think [that]' is clearly *non-truth-functional*.

3. Symbolize the following statements from Eco's *The Name of the Rose*:

(a) "If from this conjunction a BABY was born, the infernal RITE was resumed." (p. 63)

(b) "Providence did not WANT futile things glorified." (p. 127)

(c) "If the window had been OPEN, you would immediately have THOUGHT he had thrown himself out of it." (p. 29)

(d) "The DAYS of the Antichrist are finally at hand, and I am AFRAID, William!" (p. 66)

(e) "In the BEGINNING was the Word, and the Word was WITH God, and the Word was GOD." (p. 3)

(f) "I could sit at the TABLE with the monks, or, if I were EMPLOYED in some task for my master, I could stop in the KITCHEN." (p. 105)

(g) "If it was STIRRED properly and promptly, it would remain LIQUID for the next few days, thanks to the cold climate, and then they would make BLOOD puddings from it." (p. 77)

(h) "Adelmo THREW himself of his own will from the parapet of the wall, struck the ROCKS, and SANK into the straw." (p. 103)

(i) "If Adelmo FELL from the east tower, he must have GOT into the library, someone must have first STRUCK him so he would offer no resistance, and then this person must have found a way of CLIMBING up to the window with a lifeless body on his back." (p. 103)

3.2 CONDITIONAL STATEMENTS

Anyone who has watched or listened to a baseball game will be familiar with this kind of post-game analysis:

(1) If he makes the CATCH, they're OUT of the inning.

This is about a crucial play that happened hours before. Translated out of baseball-speak into English it means

(2) If he had made the CATCH, they would have been OUT of the inning.

(But of course, he didn't; the opposing team capitalized on his error and scored seven unearned runs.) Baseball-speak has no sense of the subjunctive whatever. It also lacks tenses, expressing all actions, past, present, or future as taking place in a kind of timeless present. Now this may be a regrettable impoverishment of language, but it does have the merit of making clear what follows from what. And since that's what we're concerned with in logic, we do exactly the same here when we symbolize statements. We make no distinction between the two statements above, symbolizing them both as

(F1) C $\rightarrow$ O

In fact the same formula would symbolize a great variety of English sentences:

(3) *Had* he made the catch, they would have been out of the inning.
(4) His having made the catch *implies* they'd be out of the inning.
(5) *Should* he make the catch, they'll be out of the inning.
(6) They would have been out of the inning, *if* he had made the catch.
(7) *Provided* he makes the catch, they're out of the inning.
(8) They're out of the inning, *provided* he makes the catch.
(9) His making the catch *will result in* their being out of the inning
   (and even, in baseball-speak,
(10) He makes the catch, and they're out of the inning.
   —though this way of expressing a conditional is particularly confusing if
   you've just turned on the radio. Are they saying he made the catch or not?).

(2) through (10) can be re-expressed as statement (1), which is said to be *in standard form*.

Conditional statements are so often involved in logical reasoning that it is convenient to have some terminology for talking about them. The "if-clause"—here "he makes the catch"—is called the *antecedent*, Latin for that which comes before (the arrow). The "then-clause" (in this case the 'then' is tacit) is called the *consequent*—represented here by "they're out of the inning."

The important thing to note here is that the antecedent, despite its name, does not always come first in a natural language statement. It is the statement following the word 'if' (or 'provided that,' or whatever phrase is equivalent to it). It comes first logically, in that it states the *condition* for the other statement's holding. So don't just blindly symbolize "They're OUT of the inning if he makes the CATCH" as O → C: that's wrong. Put the statement in standard form, then symbolize.

The crucial thing we are trying to capture about conditionals in formal logic is the notion of "following from." The one thing we can't have if the consequent follows from the antecedent is for the antecedent to be true and the consequent false. This is what makes the operator '→' truth-functional: it operates on the antecedent and the consequent in such a way that there is no statement of the form "antecedent consequent" with a true antecedent and a false consequent. Such a conditional is called a *truth-functional* or a *material* conditional. The subject of conditionals is complex and philosophically interesting, and whole books have been written on it. In ordinary discourse there is generally a meaning-relationship or some relation of relevance between the antecedent and the consequent. Thus "If you fall down those steps, you will hurt yourself." Such a relationship is not necessary, however, for the truth-functional operator: it simply has to preserve the fact that a true antecedent does not lead to a false consequent.

Of course, not every statement containing the word 'if' is a conditional. (I wondered if you'd noticed. It looks as if you're following all this very well. As if you wouldn't, with your intelligence!) The main culprits seem to be 'ifs' that could be replaced by 'whethers,' and 'ifs' that could be replaced by 'thoughs.' "As if..." and "What if...?" introduce fictional scenarios, and really shouldn't cause you any confusion. The combinations 'even if' and 'only if' require more discussion, though, and I'll come back to these later.

A slightly more insidious bogus conditional is a kind of literary device, which is easier to present by way of example than to explain:

If Einstein had succeeded in transforming time into space, Gödel would perform a trick yet more magical: He would make time disappear. (Palle Yourgrau, *A World Without Time* [Cambridge: Basic Books, 2005], p. 6)

Obviously it is not being asserted that Gödel's performing this trick is somehow conditional on Einstein's accomplishment, which is in fact being taken for granted here. The 'if' here seems to be roughly equivalent to 'whereas.'

Finally, there are complex conditionals, those whose antecedents or consequents are themselves conditional statements. In symbolizing these, it is prudent to proceed on a step-by-step basis:

(i) Symbolize the component statements.
(ii) Put all the conditionals in their standard "If C then O" form.
(iii) Symbolize the conditionals from the innermost ones outwards.

Here's an example:

If *US Shipyard*'s own bid to acquire the property FAILS, the company would be interested in a LEASE so long as the payments are REASONABLE.

(i) If F, then L so long as (i.e., provided that) R.
(ii) If F, then if R, then L.
(iiia) If F, then (R → L)
(iiib) F → (R → L)

SUMMARY

- A **conditional statement** is a statement asserting that one statement (say, B) is conditional on another (say, A): if A then B. The 'if' statement A is called the **antecedent**, the dependent statement B is called the **consequent**.
- A **truth-functional** or **material conditional** is one such that a true antecedent does not lead to a false consequent.
- **Complex conditionals** are those whose antecedents or consequents are themselves conditional statements.

EXERCISES 3.2

4. *Which of the following are conditional statements? Rephrase any such statements that are not in standard form.*
   (a) We will refund in full if the article is defective.
   (b) Were I to say that, I would be wrong.
   (c) You are looking at me as if you know something.
   (d) If I were a carpenter and you were a lady, would you marry me anyway?
   (e) You may enter provided you are a member.
   (f) Since you ask politely, I will explain.

5. *Symbolize the following conditional statements using the first letter of each capitalized word for the components, which must all be positive statements:*
   (a) If you TRAVEL every path you will not FIND the limits of the soul.—Heraclitus
   (b) If I had a HAMMER, there'd be no more FOLK singers.—comedian Billy Connolly
   (c) If Indonesia does not END the violence, it must INVITE the international community to assist in restoring security.—US President Bill Clinton

(d) Nobody is going to want to continue to INVEST there if they're going to ALLOW this sort of travesty to go on.—US President Bill Clinton

(e) If God did not EXIST, it would have been necessary to INVENT him.—Voltaire

(f) If something EXISTS without any effect at all, its existence is NEGLIGIBLE.—early Buddhist doctrine

(g) Were I the MOOR, I would not be IAGO.—Shakespeare's *Othello*

(h) If there were no CHRYSIPPUS, there would be no STOA.—Stoic philosopher Chrysippus

(i) I am extraordinarily PATIENT provided I get my OWN way in the end.—British PM Margaret Thatcher

(j) If an argument is VALID, then, as long as its premises are TRUE, it is also SOUND.—definitions of validity and soundness

(k) Should the Red Sox SWEEP the Yankees in the weekend series, they will get the WILD card, provided the Blue Jays LOSE tomorrow.

(l) If you think you UNDERSTAND it [quantum theory], that only shows you don't KNOW the first thing about it.—Niels Bohr

6. *Render each formula* (a)-(d) *into a readable English Statement* using the dictionary provided:

C := The standings given in the paper are CORRECT.
S := The Red Sox SWEEP the Jays in their weekend series.
W := The Athletics will qualify for the WILD card.
T := The Athletics win TWO more games.

(a) $S \rightarrow \neg W$
(b) $C \rightarrow (T \rightarrow W)$
(c) $S \rightarrow (\neg T \rightarrow \neg W)$
(d) $C \rightarrow \{S \rightarrow (T \rightarrow W)\}$

7. *Symbolize the following conditional statements* from Shakespeare's *Othello*, Act II, Scene 3, using the first letter of each capitalized word for the components:

(a) IAGO: If I can FASTEN but one cup upon him,
With that which he hath drunk tonight already,
He'll be as full of QUARREL and offense
As my young mistress' dog.

(b) OTHELLO: If I once STIR,
Or do but LIFT this arm, the best of you
Shall sink in my REBUKE.

3.3 MODUS PONENS

3.3.1 ARGUMENT FORM AND SUBSTITUTION INSTANCE

The ancient Buddhists denied that there is some unchanging substance or matter underlying all the changing qualities we observe. Their view was that since qualities change from one moment to the next, the correct way to express this is to say that there are different things at each different moment. That is, they were committed to the premise that

If qualities are REAL, they are THINGS.[6]

which we may symbolize $R \rightarrow T$. Interestingly, their main opponents, the Sānkhyas, also agreed with this statement, but had an entirely different view of the world. They denied that qualities were things, and consequently asserted the unreality of the changing qualities that we see, claiming that only eternal matter is real.

In the terminology explained above, then, the Buddhists held the antecedent of the conditional to be true—in logical parlance, they *affirmed the antecedent* of the conditional—and therefore inferred its consequent. That is, they argued:

If qualities are REAL, they are THINGS.	$R \rightarrow T$
But qualities are real.	R
So they are things.	$\therefore T$

It's convenient to have a way of writing the symbolization of a single-inference argument like this all on one line, which we do as follows, separating the premises by commas:

$R \rightarrow T, R \therefore T$

This inference is as basic as you can get in logic. All languages have some counterpart to the conditional, and it simply means that the consequent follows from the antecedent. Thus anyone who affirmed a conditional and its antecedent but refused to allow that the consequent followed, could not be said to have understood what a conditional means. In other words, it is impossible to deny the validity of inferring the consequent from a conditional and its antecedent. We can see this by reverting to our definition of formal validity: *no argument of this form can have all true premises and a false conclusion*, that is, the conditional and its antecedent both true and the conclusion false.

---

[6] For this and following portrayals of Buddhist logic I am indebted to Shcherbatskoi, F.I., Dharmakirti, and Dharmottara, *Buddhist Logic* (New York: Dover Publications, 1962). The conditional appears on p. 97.

The argument form was well summarized by Chrysippus, a Stoic logician teaching in Athens in the third century BCE, who proposed five basic argument schemata, of which this was the first:

If the first, then the second
The first
———————————
Therefore the second

Here "the first" and "the second" are placeholders for any individual statements. We'll use lower-case letters p, q, etc., instead. These are called *statement variables*, by analogy with the variables in algebra. They stand for *any* statements, whereas the capital letters we have used to represent individual statements are analogous to constants. Any individual argument having a given form is said to be an *instance* or *substitution instance* of that form. The premises and conclusions of the argument must be *substitution instances* of the corresponding variables. For example, the Buddhists' argument is an instance of the valid argument form

$$p \rightarrow q, p \therefore q$$

since R is substituted everywhere for p, and T is substituted everywhere for q. Similarly, the abstract argument

$$\neg E \rightarrow (B \vee C), \neg E \therefore B \vee C$$

is also an instance of this form, with $\neg E$ substituted for p and $(B \vee C)$ for q.

> An argument is a **substitution instance** of a given argument form if it is obtainable from the form by systematically substituting each occurrence of a given statement variable in the form by the same individual statement, whether simple (e.g., P), or compound (e.g., Q $\vee$ R).
>
> Thus $\neg E \rightarrow (B \vee C), \neg E \therefore B \vee C$ is a substitution instance of the form $p \rightarrow q, p \therefore q$.

The rule of inference encapsulating the above valid argument form is known by its Latin name, *modus ponens* (the mood that affirms the antecedent).[7]

---

[7] Actually, the full name of this rule is *modus ponendo ponens*, "the mood affirming [the second term] by affirming [the first]." As we shall see, this contrasts with *modus tollendo tollens*, "the mood denying [the first term] by denying [the second]," as well as the two forms of the disjunctive syllogism recognized by the Stoics, which the medieval scholars called *modus tollendo ponens*, and *modus ponendo tollens*.

> **Modus Ponens (MP)**
> From a conditional statement and its antecedent, infer the consequent.
> *In symbols:*
> From $p \rightarrow q$ and p, infer q.

This rule of inference is so fundamental and so obvious that it is virtually never explicitly appealed to in natural reasoning, except possibly when you are really beating an illogical opponent over the head with the illogic of his reasoning. But we can't get very far with more complex arguments unless we include it among the basics. Once we have basic rules of inference like this, though, we can prove the validity of more complex arguments. This is the idea behind *natural deduction*, where we set up formal proofs in the style of geometrical proofs. Let's look at an example.

Imagine a Buddhist arguing with a Sānkhya as follows:

If qualities are OBSERVABLE then they must be REAL. So you should accept that qualities are THINGS, since you accept that if they are real they are things.

This is an enthymeme with a suppressed premise "qualities are observable." We symbolize it as follows:

$$O \rightarrow R, R \rightarrow T, O \therefore T$$

The idea of a formal proof is simple: we aim to derive the conclusion on the last line. First we state the premises on separate lines, then any subsequent line is derived from those above it by applying our rules of inference:

(1) $O \rightarrow R$ Prem
(2) $R \rightarrow T$ Prem
(3) O   Prem
(4) R   1, 3 MP
(5) T   2, 4 MP

Notice that in the right-hand column we give the justification for each line. The premises are labelled 'Prem.' Line 4 is obtained from lines 1 and 3 by an application of Modus Ponens, and line 5 is similarly obtained from lines 2 and 4. Tacitly, we are applying a procedure first identified by the Stoics, called the *dialectical rule*: "if we have premises that yield a conclusion, then we have in effect also the conclusion among the premises, even if it is not explicitly stated." So far as we know, the Stoics did not set up formal proofs, but instead proved the validity of other argument forms schematically by repeatedly applying this rule together with their five basic rules of inference. Clearly, this amounts to the same thing. A proof such as the one above proves the formal validity of every inference from the premises to a succeeding line derived by valid rules of inference, and therefore the formal validity of an argument from the premises to the conclusion of the last line.

3.3.2 AFFIRMING THE CONSEQUENT

In the witch scene from *Monty Python and the Holy Grail*, already encountered in chapter 2, a crucial part of Sir Bedevere's reasoning is this:

> *Bedevere:* Tell me, what do you do with witches?
> *Crowd:* Burn them!
> *Bedevere:* And what do you burn apart from witches?
> *Crowd:* More witches!...[pregnant pause].... Wood?
> *Bedevere:* So why do witches burn?
> *Crowd:* 'Cos they're made of wood?
> *Bedevere:* Good!

Sir Bedevere seems to be encouraging the crowd to reason along these lines:

> If witches are made of wood, they'll burn. Witches burn. Therefore they're made of wood.

Obviously, this is invalid reasoning, as we can see by considering another argument of the same form:

> If airliners were lighter than air, they'd fly above the ground. Airliners fly above the ground. Therefore they're lighter than air.

This argument has the same form as Sir Bedevere's. All its premises are true, yet its conclusion is false. So the form is invalid. Hence, any argument that has this form (but is not also an instance of some other valid form) is invalid. This is the case for Sir Bedevere's argument. We can also see it is invalid by applying the root definition of validity: even if we were to accept all its premises, this would still be compatible with denying the conclusion.

This invalid form of argument is beguilingly similar to modus ponens. In the latter we *affirm the antecedent* of the conditional in order to infer its consequent; here we *affirm the consequent* of the conditional in order to make the faulty inference to its antecedent. Hence the name of the fallacy:

Fallacy of Affirming the Consequent (FAC)
$p \rightarrow q, q \therefore p$ *INVALID!*

The *Python* argument is intended for humorous effect. Yet the mistake is embarrassingly common. Here's a somewhat controversial example. Few scientists have reasoned with the same kind of logical rigour as Sir Isaac Newton. Nevertheless, he appears to have been guilty of something like this fallacy on one occasion. When Edmond Halley (of comet fame) came from London to visit the reclusive professor in his rooms at Cambridge in 1684, he asked him what curve a planet would describe if it was attracted to the Sun by a force reciprocal to the square of its distance. Newton immediately replied that it would be an ellipse, but, on failing to find his calculation among his papers, promised to redo the calculation and send it to Halley. The end result was perhaps the greatest scientific classic of all time: Newton's *Principia*. But as his opponents pointed out to his embarrassment, what Newton proved in the first edition of his *Principia* was that if the curve was an ellipse, the law of force would be the inverse square law—the converse of what Halley had asked for. In effect Newton was arguing

If the curve is an ellipse, the law of force will be the inverse square law. Thus given Halley's assumption that the law of force is the inverse square law, it follows that the curve is an ellipse.

This fallacy also occurs (all too often) in formal proofs done on autopilot—like this:

(1) F → G   Prem
(2) F → H   Prem
(3) H   Prem
(4) F   2, 3 MP   *ERROR! This is the fallacy FAC!*
(5) G   1, 4 MP

SUMMARY

- In stating **argument forms** we use placeholders for any individual statements called **statement variables**, denoted by the lower case letters p, q, etc. By analogy with the variables in algebra, they stand for **any** statements, whereas the capital letters we have used to represent individual statements are analogous to the particular values of the variables in algebra.
- An argument is a **substitution instance** of a given argument form if it is obtainable from the form by systematically substituting each occurrence of a given statement variable in the form by the same individual statement, whether simple (e.g., P), or compound (e.g., Q ∨ R). Thus ¬E → (B ∨ C), ¬E ∴ B ∨ C is a substitution instance of the form $p \rightarrow q, p \therefore q$.
- The rule of inference **modus ponens (MP)** is
  From $p \rightarrow q$ and p, infer q.
  From a conditional statement and its antecedent, infer the consequent.

- The **validity** of this argument form follows from our definition of formal validity: it is impossible for q to be false if $p \rightarrow q$ and p are both true.
- The argument form $p \rightarrow q, q \therefore p$ is INVALID, and is known as the **fallacy of affirming the consequent (FAC)**.

EXERCISES 3.3

8. *Prove the validity of the* "How do you know she's a witch?" *argument* from Monty Python's *Holy Grail*, using the symbolization suggested:

If she's MADE of wood, she's a WITCH. If she weighs the same as a DUCK, she's made of wood. She weighs the same as a duck. Therefore, she's a witch.

Prove the validity of the following abstract arguments:

9. A, A $\rightarrow$ (B $\rightarrow$ C), B $\therefore$ C

10. A, A $\rightarrow$ (A $\rightarrow$ ¬B) $\therefore$ ¬B

11. (P & Q) $\rightarrow$ R, P & Q, R $\rightarrow$ ¬S $\therefore$ ¬S

12. ¬P $\rightarrow$ (Q v R), (Q v R) $\rightarrow$ S, ¬P $\therefore$ S

13. ¬(F & G) $\rightarrow$ (Q v R), ¬P $\rightarrow$ ¬(F & G), ¬P $\therefore$ Q v R

14. F $\rightarrow$ G, (F $\rightarrow$ G) $\rightarrow$ H $\therefore$ H

15. (F $\rightarrow$ G) $\rightarrow$ H, H $\rightarrow$ F, F $\rightarrow$ G $\therefore$ G

16. (F $\rightarrow$ G) $\rightarrow$ (G $\rightarrow$ P), P $\rightarrow$ Q, F $\rightarrow$ G, F $\therefore$ Q

17. President Clinton, breaking a long silence over the atrocities in East Timor, was quoted as saying:

"It would be a PITY if the Indonesian recovery were CRUSHED by this. But one way or the other, it will be crushed by this if they don't FIX it."—*The Boston Globe*, Sept 10, 1999

By symbolizing and constructing a formal proof, show what follows from the President's remarks if one adds the assumption that "they don't fix it."

Chapter Four

Negation

4.1 SYMBOLIZING NEGATIONS

4.1.1 NEGATIONS

The *negation* of a statement is what we get when we precede it by the operator "It is not the case that…" The latter is a truth-functional operator, symbolized by the logical negation symbol, '¬'. There are of course several ways of making a negation in English or any other natural language. Take the following statement from Jimi Hendrix's *1983 (a merman I should turn to be)*:

(1) I can HEAR Atlantis full of cheer.

If we symbolize this by H, then its negation ¬H would symbolize any of the following variants:

(2) I can *not* hear Atlantis full of cheer.
(3) I *can't* hear Atlantis full of cheer.
(4) *It is not the case that* I can hear Atlantis full of cheer.
(5) *It is false that* I can hear Atlantis full of cheer.
(6) *It is untrue that* I can hear Atlantis full of cheer.

(2)-(6) are all examples of negative statements. As stated in the previous chapter, our convention is that upper case letters symbolize positive assertions only, so that we must use '¬' when symbolizing negative statements. As we also saw, no parentheses are used between '¬' and the statement it operates on. Thus if M symbolizes the statement "I MIND," and S "SIX turned out to be nine," the statements below are symbolized as follows:

(7) It is untrue that I don't mind. $\neg\neg M$
(8) If six turned out to be nine, I don't mind. $S \rightarrow \neg M$
(9) If six didn't turn out to be nine, I don't mind. $\neg S \rightarrow \neg M$

On the other hand, parentheses are always understood as occurring whenever the four *binary* operators join statements into compounds, even if they are not explicitly written. Thus the formula $\neg(S \rightarrow \neg M)$ symbolizes

(10) *It is false that* I don't mind if six turned out to be nine. $\neg(S \rightarrow \neg M)$

4.1.2 CONTRADICTORIES

There's one subtlety to beware of in symbolizing negations, concerning statements like the following:

(11) Some people can't get ENOUGH.

The temptation here is to symbolize this as $\neg E$, where E represents

(12) Some people *can* get enough.

But (12) is not the negation of (11). It does not say that (11) is false. In fact, both statements could easily be true. The negation of (11) is

(13) It is not the case that some people can't get enough.

which (as you will see, if you think carefully) is equivalent to

(14) Everyone can get enough.

The negation of (12), on the other hand, is

(15) It is false that some people can get enough.

which is equivalent to

(16) No one can get enough.

From this we can see that in some cases a simple 'not' in a statement does not always have the force of a negation. If a statement is true, its negation must be false; and conversely, if a statement is false, its negation must be true. In other words, a statement and its negation must *contradict* one another. The notion of contradictory statements is captured in the definition:

> Two statements p and q are *contradictories* if the truth of p is incompatible with the truth of q, and the falsity of p is incompatible with the falsity of q.

Thus of the preceding statements, (11) and (13) are contradictories, as are (11) and (14), (12) and (15), and also (12) and (16). But (14) is not the contradictory of (16). For although the truth of "Everyone can get enough" is incompatible with the truth of "No one can get enough," both the statements could be simultaneously false. Contrariwise, (11) and (12) could both be true, even if they could not both be false. So in each of these cases we are dealing with an opposition that is something less than outright contradiction. We will come back to these types of opposition in chapter 18 below.

SUMMARY

- If S symbolizes a given statement, then ¬S symbolizes its **negation**: "it is not the case that S," or an equivalent. In general, $\neg p$ is the negation of p.
- Any two statements p and q are **contradictories** if the truth of p is incompatible with the truth of q, and the falsity of p is incompatible with the falsity of q.

EXERCISES 4.1

1. *Symbolize* the following statements using the first letter of each capitalized word for the components:
   (a) Atheists are not our PREACHERS.—Edmund Burke
   (b) We are not AFRAID to follow truth wherever it may lead, nor to TOLERATE any error so long as reason is left free to combat it.—Thomas Jefferson
   (c) Newton seems not to have entirely NEGLECTED the study of metaphysics.—Jean Le Rond d'Alembert
   (d) It is impossible that men should not at length have REFLECTED on so wretched a situation.—Jean-Jacques Rousseau (R := "Men should have reflected . . ."; interpret "it is impossible that" as "it is not the case that")
   (e) The British are not the CONVERTS of Rousseau, not the DISCIPLES of Voltaire.—Edmund Burke (there's an implicit 'and' here)
   (f) If you TRAVEL every path you will not FIND the limits of the soul.*—Heraclitus
   (g) If I had a HAMMER, there'd be no more FOLK singers.*—Billy Connolly (*remember, F should be a positive statement)

2. *Render* each formula (a)-(e) *into a readable English Statement* using the dictionary provided:
   G := There is a GOD.
   V := We must still VENERATE justice.
   B := We are to BELIEVE Montesquieu.
   Example: G → ¬B: *Answer*: If there is a God, we are not to believe Montesquieu
   - (a) ¬G
   - (b) B → (¬G → V)
   - (c) ¬B → (V → ¬G)
   - (d) G & ¬B
   - (e) (V & G) → ¬B

3. *Which pairs of the following statements are contradictories?*

   (a) He tied the laces on his right shoe.

   (b) He untied the laces on his right shoe.

   (c) He did not tie the laces on his right shoe.

   (d) He tied the laces of both his shoes.

   (e) He didn't untie the laces on his right shoe.

4.2 MODUS TOLLENS

4.2.1 MODUS TOLLENS AND DOUBLE NEGATION

A second rule of inference identified by Chrysippus in ancient Athens corresponds to the valid argument form:

If the first, then the second
Not the second
<hr>
Therefore not the first   i.e., $p \to q, \neg q \therefore \neg p$

Here, given the conditional, one *denies the consequent*, and therefore infers the negation of its antecedent:

> **Modus Tollens (MT)**
> From a conditional statement and the negation of its consequent, infer the negation of its antecedent.
> *In symbols:* From $p \to q$ and $\neg q$, infer $\neg p$.

If we adopt the Principle of Bivalence, according to which either a given statement is true or its negation is, then the validity of this argument form follows from the validity of Modus Ponens. For according to MP, we cannot affirm the truth of $p \rightarrow q$ and p and the falsity of q, i.e., the truth of $\neg q$. But by the Principle of Bivalence, the falsity of $\neg p$ amounts to the same thing as the truth of p.[1] This means that we cannot affirm the truth of $p \rightarrow q$ and $\neg q$ and the falsity of $\neg p$, thus establishing the validity of the argument form MT. This rule of inference was much beloved by the Sãnkhyas, the ancient Indian materialist philosophers mentioned in the previous chapter. There we saw them opposing the Buddhists with the argument:

If qualities are REAL, they are THINGS. But they are not things. Hence they are not real. Symbolized: $R \rightarrow T, \neg T \therefore \neg R$

This is an instance of the argument form modus tollens, with the individual statement R substituted for the statement variable p and T substituted for q. Its proof is correspondingly trivial:

(1) R → T   Prem
(2) ¬T   Prem
(3) ¬R   1, 2 MT

Often, however, we will need to substitute *negations* of statements for one or both of the variables p and q. Modus tollens arguments of this type are called *mixed modus tollens* arguments. The Sãnkhyas, it seems, were particularly fond of them, for they expressed the essence of their whole doctrine as a series of five mixed modus tollens arguments. The first of these was:

If the effect did not PRE-EXIST in its material cause, it could not be CREATED (since nothing can be created out of nothing). However, it is created. Therefore it does pre-exist in its material cause.[2]

This is a 2-inference argument. We'll ignore the subsidiary argument for the conditional premise for now, and concentrate on the inference to the main conclusion from the conditional together with the second statement, which we may symbolize:

¬P → ¬C, C ∴ P

---

[1] The Principle of Bivalence may seem blindingly obvious, but in fact it has been denied by the Intuitionists, as we shall see in chapter 24.

[2] I have modified the argument somewhat. In Shcherbatskoi's rendition, it runs: "If the effect did not pre-exist, it never could be created out of nothing. However, it is created. Therefore it does pre-exist (in its material cause)" (Shcherbatskoi et al., *Buddhist Logic*, p. 294).

Now if we try to prove this, we have to substitute $\neg$P for the statement variable p and $\neg$C for the variable q in the conditional. But then in order to apply *modus tollens* we would need the negation of the consequent, $\neg q$, which would be $\neg\neg$C, whereas we have just C. Of course, if the principle of bivalence holds, we know that $\neg\neg$C is equivalent to C; but in order to do a formal proof, we need an explicit rule of inference to legitimate this inference:

> ### Double Negation (DN)
> From any statement infer the negation of its negation, and vice versa.
> From p infer $\neg\neg p$; from $\neg\neg p$ infer p.

This is really two rules rolled into one. The validity of the first rule—from p infer $\neg\neg p$—is fairly straightforward: you cannot assert the truth of p and at the same time assert $\neg p$ without contradiction. So, given p, $\neg p$ must be false: that is, given p, it is impossible to deny that $\neg\neg p$ is true. The validity of the second version of DN, however—from $\neg\neg p$ infer p—relies on the Principle of Bivalence, which asserts that every statement is either true or false—there is no third option, such as its being undecidable whether it is true or false. It is only if one knows for sure that either p or $\neg p$ is true that one can establish the truth of p from the falsity of $\neg p$.[3] But let's put those doubts aside for now, and assume the Principle of Bivalence. If we know that p or $\neg p$ is true and that $\neg p$ is false, then p cannot also be false. Thus, given p or $\neg p$, from $\neg\neg p$ we may validly infer p. This completes the justification of the validity of both versions of DN.

Now we can utilize both MT and DN to prove the Sãnkhyas' syllogism:

(1) $\neg$P $\rightarrow$ $\neg$C   Prem
(2) C   Prem
(3) $\neg\neg$C   2 DN
(4) $\neg\neg$P   1, 3 MT
(5) P   4 DN

Note that both lines (3) and (5) are necessary. We have a tendency to do DNs in our heads. But in a formal proof every inference must be made explicit. As another example, I'll prove the validity of the abstract argument:

$\neg$C $\rightarrow$ D, C $\rightarrow$ E, $\neg$D $\therefore$ E

(1) $\neg$C $\rightarrow$ D   Prem
(2) C $\rightarrow$ E   Prem
(3) $\neg$D   Prem

---

[3] It may be the case that p is undecidable. In that case one might be able to prove that the assumption that $\neg p$ can be proved leads to a contradiction without this constituting a proof of p. This was the reasoning of Brouwer and the Intuitionists.

(4) ¬¬C   1, 3 MT
(5) C   4 DN
(6) E   2, 5 MP

4.2.2 DENYING THE ANTECEDENT

Symmetry demands a fallacious form of argument standing in the same relation to *modus tollens* as the fallacy of affirming the consequent does to *modus ponens*. I wouldn't dream of disappointing symmetry; here it is:

Fallacy of Denying the Antecedent (FDA)
$p \rightarrow q, \neg p \therefore \neg q$ *INVALID!*

Again, we are all capable of committing this fallacy, even though it is hoped we could recognize our mistake immediately it was pointed out. Alan Turing gives an example of this kind of fallacy in his seminal article on artificial intelligence. In considering some objections, he frames the following argument (while conceding that it is never quite stated in such a glaringly fallacious way):[4]

> If each man had a definite set of rules of conduct by which he regulated his life he would be no better than a machine. But there are no such rules, so men cannot be machines.— Alan Turing, "Computing Machinery and Intelligence," *Mind*, 59, 1950, p. 452.

That is, adopting some obvious symbolization, R → M, ¬R ∴ ¬M.
    Clearly, this is an instance of the INVALID form denying the antecedent, FDA.

SUMMARY

- The rule of inference **modus tollens (MT)** is
  From $p \rightarrow q$ and $\neg q$, infer $\neg p$.
  From a conditional statement and the negation of its consequent, infer the negation of its antecedent.
- The **validity** of this argument form follows from our definition of formal validity: it is impossible for $\neg p$ to be false if $p \rightarrow q$ and $\neg q$ are both true, assuming bivalence.

---

[4] I am indebted to Dr. Thomas Adajian of James Madison University for reminding me that Turing was only reporting this fallacy, not committing it, as I mistakenly wrote in the first edition. For a more charitable interpretation of such arguments, see Burke, Michael B. "Denying the Antecedent: A Common Fallacy?", *Informal Logic*, 16.1, 23-30.

- The rule of inference **double negation (DN)** is
  From p infer $\neg\neg p$; from $\neg\neg p$ infer p.
  From any statement infer the negation of its negation, and vice versa.
- The **validity** of these argument forms follows from our definition of formal validity: it is impossible for $\neg\neg p$ to be false if p is true, and for p to be false if $\neg\neg p$ is true, assuming bivalence.
- The argument form $p \rightarrow q, \neg p \therefore \neg q$ is INVALID, and is known as the **fallacy of denying the antecedent (FDA)**.

EXERCISES 4.2

4. The great Dutch physicist Christiaan Huygens opposed the Cartesian idea that light propagates instantaneously through the ether by an action passed from one spherical ether particle to the next, arguing that instead *it must be transmitted successively*:

> "For if the movement were not transmitted SUCCESSIVELY, the spheres would all move TOGETHER at the same time, which does not happen."—C. Huygens, *Treatise on Light*, p. 13; quoted from Sabra's paraphrase in *Theories of Light from Descartes to Newton* (Cambridge: Cambridge UP, 1981), p. 211

Symbolize and then prove the validity of Huygens's argument.

Prove the validity of the following abstract arguments:

5. $A, A \rightarrow (B \rightarrow C), \neg C \therefore \neg B$

6. $C \rightarrow A, A \rightarrow B, \neg B \therefore \neg C$

7. $C \rightarrow A, A \rightarrow \neg B, B \therefore \neg C$

8. $A \rightarrow (B \rightarrow C), \neg(B \rightarrow C) \therefore \neg A$

9. $\neg H, (F \rightarrow G) \rightarrow H \therefore \neg(F \rightarrow G)$

10. $F \rightarrow \neg(G \rightarrow H), G \rightarrow H, G \rightarrow F \therefore \neg G$

11. $\neg(F \ \& \ G) \rightarrow (Q \lor R), \neg P \rightarrow \neg(F \ \& \ G), \neg(Q \lor R) \therefore P$

12. $(F \rightarrow G) \rightarrow (G \rightarrow P), P \rightarrow Q, F \rightarrow G, \neg Q \therefore \neg F$

13. *Each of the following passages contains or reports an argument that is an instance of either* MP, FAC, MT, *or* FDA. *Identify which it is:*

(a) If Dion is a horse, then Dion is an animal. But Dion is not a horse. Therefore Dion is not an animal.—an old example of the Stoics'

(b) Men have been perplexed in well-nigh every age by a sophism which the ancients called the "Lazy Argument," because it tended towards doing nothing, or at least towards caring for nothing and only following one's inclination for the pleasure of the moment. For, they said, if the future is necessary, that which must happen will happen, whatever I may do. But the future, so it is said, is necessary...— Leibniz, *Theodicy*, 1710 (Huggard trans., p. 54)

(c) If Pluto, according to Halliday's calculations, had a diameter of more than 4,200 miles, then an occultation would have occurred at MacDonald, and the records clearly indicated that it did not. Thus Pluto must be that size or smaller; it cannot be larger.—Thomas Nicholson, "The Enigma of Pluto," *Natural History*, March 1967

(d) A theoryless position is possible only if there are no theories of evidence. But there are theories of evidence. Therefore, a theoryless position is impossible.—Henry Johnstone, Jr., "The Law of Non-Contradiction," *Logique et Analyse*, n.s. vol. 3, 1960

(e) Total pacifism might be a good principle if everyone were to follow it. But not everyone does, so it isn't.—Gilbert Harman, "The Nature of Morality"

(f) And there is nothing good or bad by nature. For if good and bad exist by nature, then it must be either good or bad for everyone, just as snow is something cold for everyone. But there is nothing which is good or bad for everyone in common; therefore, there is nothing good or bad by nature.—Pyrrho, from Diogenes Laertius' *Life of Pyrrho* (Inwood and Gerson, *Hellenistic Philosophy*, p. 181)

(g) I *do* know that this pencil exists; but I could not know this, if Hume's principles were true; *therefore*, Hume's principles, one or both of them, are false.—G.E. Moore, *Some Main Problems of Philosophy*

(h) If number were an idea, then arithmetic would be psychology. But arithmetic is no more psychology than, say, astronomy is. Astronomy is concerned, not with ideas of the planets, but with the planets themselves, and by the same token the objects of arithmetic are not ideas either.—Gottlob Frege, *Foundations of Arithmetic*

(i) (29) Pilate then went unto them, and said, What accusation bring ye against this man? (30) They answered and said unto him, If he were not a malefactor, we would not have delivered him up unto thee.—Holy Bible, John 18: 29-30 [this is an enthymeme]

14. *Prove the validity* of Carneades the Academic's argument against fate:

"If there are ANTECEDENT causes for everything that happens, then everything happens within a closely knit WEB of natural connections. If this is so, then NECESSITY causes everything. And if this is true there is nothing in our power. There is, however, something in our POWER. But if everything happens by FATE, everything happens as a result of antecedent causes. Therefore, it is not the case that whatever happens happens by fate."—Cicero, *On Fate* (quoted from Inwood and Gerson, *Hellenistic Philosophy*, p. 130)

15. The following "proofs" (of invalid abstract arguments) contain *mistakes in the application of rules of inference*; (a) contains one, (b) two. *Identify them*:

    (a) A → D, ¬D, C → ¬A ∴ C
       (1) A → D   Prem
       (2) ¬D   Prem
       (3) C → ¬A   Prem
       (4) ¬A   1, 2 MT
       (5) C   3, 4 MP

    (b) F → G, F → ¬H, H ∴ ¬G
       (1) F → G   Prem
       (2) F → ¬H   Prem
       (3) H   Prem
       (4) ¬F   2, 3 MT
       (5) ¬G   1, 4 MT

16. James R. Brown writes that the central argument of David Bloor's book, *Knowledge and Social Imagery*, is "that it is not evidence, but instead social factors, which cause belief." He then reasons: "If *Knowledge and Social Imagery* is right, then it is destined to have no direct impact on intellectual life. But since it has had an impact, it must be false" (James R. Brown, *The Rational and the Social* [London: Routledge 1989], p. 42). This argument may be reconstructed as follows:

    If Bloor's central argument is RIGHT, then it is not EVIDENCE which causes belief. But in that case Bloor's argument could have no IMPACT on intellectual life. Since it has had such an impact, it must therefore be wrong.

    Symbolize and then prove the validity of Brown's argument.

17. A former logic student of mine wrote to inform me that the course material for prepping for a police entrance exam he was to sit contained the following question:[5]

---

5 Thanks to Eric Lebel for this example.

"If I go to university, then I can become an engineer. I am not going to go to university."

Which of the following should I conclude from this?

A) There are other university courses.

B) I can become an engineer through other avenues.

C) I will not be an engineer.

D) None of the above.

They give C) as the right answer. Is it? If not, why not?

4.3 INFERENCE AND IMPLICATION

Logicians make a sharp distinction between inference and implication. It is regarded as one of the cardinal sins of logic to confuse the two, although in everyday speech we tolerate a fair amount of looseness in the use of the words 'infer' and 'imply.' The basic distinction is that *inferring* is *drawing a conclusion* from a statement or set of statements: it is *something people do*; whereas *implying is a relation between statements*: this relation can hold whether or not anyone makes or accepts the statements concerned. It is true that we can talk about someone's implying something by a certain statement; but this is elliptical for the statement that person makes implying some other statement. Even in everyday usage, it is a gross mistake to talk of one statement's inferring another.

Still, there's a close relation between inferences and implications that is worth looking further into. What is the difference between the following?

If p then q.   or $p \rightarrow q$
p. Therefore q. or $p \therefore q$

I can still remember when I was learning logic (back in the last millennium) this was something that really stumped me. The similarity may seem overwhelming: both assert that one statement, q, follows from another, p. There is a fundamental difference, though, as I was to learn from my tutor: in the first case, it is simply the notion of consequence that is being asserted, i.e., that q follows from p. In the second case, p is being asserted, and q is being asserted to follow from it.

An example may help clarify. Suppose someone were to say

(1) If the mind ACTS on the brain, it must be MATERIAL. $A \rightarrow M$

This is not at all the same as saying

(2) The mind ACTS on the brain. Therefore it must be MATERIAL. $A \therefore M$

The first statement simply asserts a consequence of the idea of the mind's being able to act on the brain. It could just as well be asserted by an opponent of this view as by a materialist. But the second asserts both that the mind does act on the brain, and that as a consequence it must be material.

The context of such statements as (1) is of course all important in deciding how to interpret them. If (1) were said in a context in which A is being taken for granted, then it could be interpreted as an enthymematic argument inviting us to infer M:

A → M, A (implicit) ∴ M (implicit)

The fact that such enthymemes are common perhaps accounts for the confusion we have between (1) and (2). On the other hand, though, if (1) were uttered in a context where everyone agreed that M is absurd, then it could be interpreted as a different enthymeme, one in which we were expected to infer the falsity of the antecedent:

A → M, ¬M (implicit) ∴ ¬A (implicit)

Closely related to the above confusion is the confusion between 'if' and 'since.' Contrast

(3) The mind must be MATERIAL, if it ACTS on the brain.

with

(4) The mind must be MATERIAL, since it ACTS on the brain.

Statement (3) is equivalent to statement (1) and has the same symbolization, A → M. Statement (4) is equivalent to statement (2) and has the same symbolization, A ∴ M. Thus the argument

SNELL and DESCARTES cannot both have been the first to discover the Law of Refraction. Since Snell had discovered it earlier, it follows that Descartes was not the first discoverer of the law.

is NOT symbolized: ¬(S & D) ∴ S → ¬D. The correct symbolization is ¬(S & D), S ∴ ¬D.

SUMMARY

- Inference and implication are both concerned with one statement's following from another. The difference is that **inferring** is *drawing a conclusion* from a statement or set of statements: it is *something people do*; whereas **implying** *is a relation between statements*: this relation can hold whether or not anyone makes or accepts the statements concerned.
- This is related to the difference between an **argument** such as A ∴ M and the corresponding **conditional statement** A → M. In the argument **A is asserted**, and **M is asserted to follow from it**; in the conditional, **neither A nor M is asserted**: all that is asserted is that **M follows from A**, or that A implies M.

EXERCISES 4.3

18. *Symbolize the following three arguments:*

   (a) I THINK, therefore I AM.
   (b) If there are no proofs, then there are proofs, since there are no proofs if and only if there is a proof of that. [P := there are proofs]
   (c) If an infinite aggregate were a TRUE whole, it could not be EQUAL to its proper PART. But it is equal to its proper part. This implies that it is not a true whole.

For the following three arguments, *(i) identify what is wrong with the symbolization given, (ii) give a correct symbolization and (iii) a proof of validity.*

19. Johnson cannot be PRAISED for leading a successful campaign, since he LIED. You can't be praised for being successful if you lie.

   $L → ¬P ∴ ¬P → L$

20. Since the polar ice caps are MELTING, we know there is GLOBAL warming. For if the ice caps are melting, the temperature of the seas must be unusually HIGH. Their temperature would not be high without global warming.

   $M → G, M → H ∴ ¬G → ¬H$

21. (**CHALLENGE**) If Bloor's argument has been INFLUENTIAL, then it is EVIDENCE which causes belief. So, since Bloor's argument has been influential, and if that argument is CORRECT it is not evidence which causes belief, Bloor's argument must be incorrect.

   $I → E, (I \& C) → ¬E ∴ ¬C$

Chapter Five

Conjunction

5.1 SYMBOLIZING CONJUNCTIONS

A *conjunction* is simply two statements joined by the statement operator 'and,' symbolized '&.' The component statements are called *conjuncts* (from the Latin for things joined together). We have already seen some examples in the exercises of chapter 2. For example, in the statement

(1) "The DAYS of the Antichrist are finally at hand, and I am AFRAID, William!"

which we symbolize D & A, the conjuncts are D := "The DAYS of the Antichrist are finally at hand" and A := "I am AFRAID, William!" To assert a conjunction is to assert that both the conjuncts are true; similarly, to deny a conjunction is to deny that both the conjuncts are true, to suppose a conjunction is to suppose that both the conjuncts are true, and so forth.

'And' is not the only word we use in English to express conjunctions. Just as was the case with conditionals, there are many different ways of expressing them. Take, for instance, this statement by Stephen Jay Gould about a position he opposes:

(2) It's a very deep position, but I also think it's very deeply wrong.

When Gould asserts (2) he is asserting both that "It's a very deep position" (P) *and* that (he thinks) "It's very deeply wrong" (W). Similarly, anyone denying (2) would be denying that both statements are true (and thus effectively asserting that one or both of them is false). Note that the denial that both are true would be symbolized ¬(P & W), and not ¬P & ¬W, which would assert that both are false. Gould uses 'but' as opposed to 'and' to draw some contrast between the two. He might have expressed the same thing by

(3) *Although* it's a very deep position, I think it's very deeply wrong.

(4) *Even though* it's a very deep position, I think it's very deeply wrong.

(5) It's a very deep position; *yet* I think it's very deeply wrong.

(6) It's a very deep position; *however*, I think it's very deeply wrong.

(7) *Not only* is it a very deep position, *but* I also think it's very deeply wrong.

All of statements (2) to (7) are expressed in standard form as

(8) It's a very deep position, and I also think it's very deeply wrong.

because this is the extent to which they could do work in an argument (as opposed to rhetoric). They all have the same logical force, if not the same rhetorical force. All are symbolized as P & W.

Here's something I'll be saying more than once: Language use is very plastic. Not every occurrence of 'and' should be symbolized by '&.' Take the following threat issued by a character in one of Dickens's novels:

(9) "Stand on your HEAD again, and I'll CUT one of your feet off."

The logical force of this is clearly the conditional H $\rightarrow$ C: "*If* you stand on your head again, *then* I'll cut one of your feet off." H & C would wrongly assert both that "You are standing on your head again" and that "I will cut one of your feet off," losing the whole point of the threat. You just have to use some common sense in symbolizing. Two more examples of pseudo-conjunctions:

(10) Frankie and Johnny were sweethearts. (traditional folk song)

(11)...it meant having to try and steal that film back somehow. (Michael Ondaatje, *The English Patient*)

(10) is not equivalent to the conjunction of "Frankie was a sweetheart" and "Johnny was a sweetheart"; nor can (11) be read as conjoining "it meant having to try" with "steal that film back somehow." Similar considerations apply to Heraclitus' statement "The road up and the road down are one and the same." In a similar vein, "I love pork and beans" is not the same as "I love pork and I love beans," since what is loved is the combination, not each separately.

But sometimes, when what follows 'and' is not a statement, a conjunction really is what is meant. Thus

(12) "That goes for HARRY, and ME too."

This would be paraphrased "That goes for HARRY, and that goes for ME too": H & M.

Finally, there is a whole slew of statements that begin with 'And' or one of its synonyms, where the 'And' does not join two statements into a conjunction, but simply introduces the whole statement following. The King James version of the Bible abounds with such statements, e.g.,

(13) And the whole congregation of the children of Israel ASSEMBLED together at Shiloh, and SET up the tabernacle of the congregation there.—Joshua 18: 1

You might be tempted to symbolize this as '& A & S,' but that is ill-formed. Here only the second 'and' is our binary statement operator forming a conjunction. The first 'And' serves to connect this statement with those preceding it into a continuous narrative, and this is a function that an initial conjunction will often perform. Similarly, in the context of an argument, a beginning 'And...,' 'But...,' 'Yet...,' 'Moreover,...,' or 'However, ...' might also serve simply to link premises. Either way, it does not get symbolized. The proper symbolization of (13) is simply A & S (with outermost parentheses understood). Remember, *each binary operator binds two statements and puts groupers around the outside*, with the convention that the outermost groupers need not be explicitly written. Thus {A → [B & C]} is written A → [B & C].

SUMMARY

- A **conjunction** is any two statements joined by the binary statement operator 'and.' Symbolically, it is the compound statement *p & q* produced by the operation of the ampersand operator, '&,' on any two component statements, *p*, *q*, which are called **conjuncts**.
- In English a conjunction can be indicated not only by 'and,' but also by 'but,' 'although,' 'even though,' 'yet,' and equivalents.
- In writing the conjunction as *p & q*, the outermost groupers are understood. Remember, *each binary operator binds two statements and puts groupers around the outside*, with the convention that the outermost groupers need not be explicitly written. Consequently, when a conjunction is a component of a compound statement, the groupers must be written in. Thus A → (B & C), A & [¬B & C], ¬(A & B) → (C & D).

EXERCISES 5.1

1. *Which of the following are conjunctions?* For those statements that are, *identify the conjuncts*.
   (a) And this is what I was trying to tell you, but you wouldn't listen.
   (b) He came into the room, put his hat on the peg, and slumped into a chair.
   (c) Yet there was nothing we could do to persuade her.

(d) Your word is a lamp for my feet, and a light for my path.

(e) I hate vain thoughts, but I love your law.

(f) Let my soul live, and it will praise you.

(g) Although her teeth were crooked, she had lovely eyes, and a well-shaped nose.

Example:

(a) Here the 'And' is not a binary operator. But the 'but' is. In standard form: <u>this is what I was trying to tell you</u>, and <u>you wouldn't listen</u>.

2. *Symbolize the following statements using the first letter of each capitalized word for the components, and the statement operators* →, ¬, *and* &.

(a) She WETS her hands and COMBS water into her hair till it is completely wet.

(b) In the kitchen she doesn't PAUSE but GOES through it and CLIMBS the stairs. ([a, b] from Michael Ondaatje, *The English Patient*)

(c) Names are to DISTINGUISH us from other men, and I am the ONLY man who exists or ever has existed.

(d) It ended, not in a NOZZLE as I almost expected, but in a HEAD of sorts.

(e) Fortunately, you might say, he shook me LOOSE, TEARING off the leg at the knee, and he didn't SEE where the rest of me fell.

(f) I TIED up the stump and CRAWLED away, but I'm DONE. ([c-f] from George Gaylord Simpson, *The Dechronization of Sam Magruder*)

(g) Although Mulroney had PROMISED Canadians that his judicial appointments would be non-partisan, it was EVIDENT to Russell and Ziegel that this had been far from the case. (Stevie Cameron, *On the Take*)

(h) If you consider Japan as an EIGHT-hundred pound gorilla, the European community is a TWELVE-hundred pound gorilla, and far BETTER placed to benefit from the new opportunities in the old Soviet Union. (George Carver, Center for Strategic and International Studies)

(i) Of course, if Pluto were the ONLY object beyond Neptune, this explanation of its orbit, though COMPELLING in many of its details, would have remained UNVERIFIABLE.—Renu Malhotra, "Migrating Planets," *Scientific American*

(j) ... if the members of some group have a COMMON interest or objective and if they would all be BETTER off if that objective were acHIEVED, it has been thought to follow logically that the individuals in that group would, if they were RATIONAL and SELF-INTERESTED, ACT to achieve that objective.—Mancur Olson, *The Logic of Collective Action* (F81) (H := that objective is acHIEVED)

3. Render each formula (a)-(d) into a colloquial English Statement using the dictionary provided:

A := Cook is a liar.

B := Cook is a gentleman.

C := Perry is a liar.
D := Perry is a gentleman.
    (a) A & B
    (b) A & ¬C
    (c) A → (¬C & ¬D)
    (d) [(A & B) & (¬C & ¬D)]

5.2 RULES OF INFERENCE FOR CONJUNCTION

At the beginning of the last section we said that to assert a conjunction is to assert that both the conjuncts are true; and similarly, to deny a conjunction is to deny that both the conjuncts are true (i.e., to assert that at least one of them is false). These two considerations motivate the rules of inference for conjunction. The first leads us to formulate two very obvious rules:

> **Simplification (Simp)**
> From a conjunction, infer either one of its conjuncts.
> *In symbols:* From p & q, infer p or infer q.

The inverse of this is

> **Conjunction (Conj)**
> From any two statements stated separately, infer their conjunction.
> *In symbols:* From p and q stated separately, infer p & q.

The formal validity of these rules is trivial. We cannot assert that both p and q are true and then deny that p is true, or deny that q is true, on pain of contradiction. Likewise we cannot deny that p and q are together true having asserted them as premises without contradicting ourselves.

    Here's an example that puts both rules into action, a proof of the validity of the abstract argument:

R → S, T & R ∴ S & T
    (1) R → S   Prem
    (2) T & R   Prem

Here in order to infer anything from the conditional (1), we need to derive its antecedent first:

    (3) R   2 Simp
    (4) S   1, 3 MP

That's half the conclusion. We also need

(5) T   2 Simp

giving

(6) S & T   4, 5 Conj

With these two rules we can prove something intuitively obvious to us, namely that given *p* & *q* we can infer *q* & *p*. (For those with an eye for connections with algebra, this proves the *commutativity* of &.) I'll leave this as an exercise.

The second consideration mentioned above—that to deny a conjunction is to assert that at least one of the conjuncts is false—means that if one of them is known to be true, the other must be false. This is the grounds for the third rule of inference involving conjunction, first formulated by the Stoics as the third of their five basic argument schemata in the Third Century BCE:

Not both the first and the second
The first

Therefore not the second

For instance:

SNELL and DESCARTES cannot both have been the first to discover the Law of Refraction. Since Snell had discovered it earlier, it follows that Descartes was not the first discoverer of the law.
Symbolized: $\neg$(S & D), S $\therefore$ $\neg$D

The formal validity of this argument is established as follows: it is contradictory to deny S & D and also to assert S and D; so it is contradictory to assert $\neg$(S & D) and S and also deny $\neg$D. This entails that the inference from $\neg$(S & D) and S to $\neg$D is formally valid by our definition. The rule of inference encapsulating the validity of this form is

---

Conjunctive Syllogism (CS)
From the denial of a conjunction and the assertion of one of its conjuncts, infer the denial of the other conjunct.
In symbols: From $\neg$(*p* & *q*) and *p*, infer $\neg$*q*. From $\neg$(*p* & *q*) and *q*, infer $\neg$*p*.

Here's an example (abstracted from one of the exercises):

It is not true that God CAN act, yet DOES not. But God certainly can act. Therefore he evidently does.
Symbolized: $\neg$(C & $\neg$D), C $\therefore$ D

A proof would proceed as follows:

(1) ¬(C & ¬ D)   Prem
(2) C   Prem
(3) ¬¬D   1, 2 CS
(4) D   3 DN

Here's a harder example: A, B, C → ¬(A & B) ∴ ¬C & A

(1) A   Prem
(2) B   Prem
(3) C → ¬(A & B) Prem

Nothing follows from these premises directly. But looking at the conclusion you can see that we already have A, so we only need to prove ¬C. Now on examining the premises more closely, you can see that the first two give A B, which is equivalent to the negation of the consequent of (3), which will allow a Modus Tollens to ¬C. Thus

(4) A & B   1, 2 Conj
(5) ¬¬(A & B)   4 DN
(6) ¬C   3, 5 MT
(7) ¬C & A   6, 1 Conj

SUMMARY

- The rule of inference **simplification (Simp)** is
  From *p* & *q*, infer either *p* or *q*.
  From a conjunction, infer either one of its conjuncts.
- The **validity** of this argument form follows from our definition of formal validity:
  it is impossible for *p* to be false if *p* and *q* are both true.
- The rule of inference **conjunction (Conj)** is
  From *p* and *q* stated separately, infer *p* & *q*.
  From any two statements stated separately, infer their conjunction.
- The **validity** of this argument form follows from our definition of formal validity:
  it is impossible for *p* & *q* to be false if *p* and *q* are both true.
- The rule of inference **conjunctive syllogism (CS)** is
  From ¬(*p* & *q*) and *p*, infer ¬*q*.
  From the denial of a conjunction and the assertion of one of its conjuncts, infer the denial of the other conjunct.
- The **validity** of this argument form follows from our definition of formal validity:
  it is impossible for ¬*q* to be false if ¬(*p* & *q*) and *p* are both true.

EXERCISES 5.2

Prove the validity of the following abstract arguments:

4. A, A → B ∴ A & B

5. A, (A & B) → C, B ∴ A & C

6. A & B, B → (¬C & D) ∴ ¬C & A

7. (D & E) → F, D & ¬F ∴ ¬E

8. ¬(D & B), B, ¬D → E ∴ E

9. D, ¬(B & ¬E), B ∴ D & E

In the following *erroneous* proofs, (a) *identify the mistakes made in applying rules of inference*, and (b) *provide a correct proof* of the abstract argument given.

10. A → ¬B, C & B ∴ ¬A & C
    (1) A → ¬B   Prem
    (2) C & B   Prem
    (3) B   2 Simp
    (4) ¬B   3 DN
    (5) ¬A   1, 3 MT
    (6) C   2 Simp
    (7) ¬A & C   5, 6 CS

11. A → ¬(C & E), C & A ∴ ¬E
    (1) A → ¬(C & E)   Prem
    (2) C & A   Prem
    (3) A   2 Simp
    (4) ¬(C & E)   1, 3 MP
    (5) ¬C   4 Simp
    (6) ¬E   4, 5 CS

12. (D & B) → ¬(D & E), D & E ∴ ¬B
    (1) (D & B) → ¬(D & E)   Prem
    (2) D & E   Prem
    (3) ¬(D & B)   1, 2 MT
    (4) ¬B   2 Simp

13. In a cartoon, a man discovers an item in the newspaper:
    Man: Uncle Phil! Didn't you say the name of that doctor is Jackson Barnum Tufts?
    Uncle Phil: Yep, that's the man. Is there somethin' in the paper about him?
    Man: Yes—a small item. He's returning to Boston—from a three months stay in *Switzerland*!
    Uncle Phil: How can that be?
    Man: That doctor couldn't have been in Miami and Switzerland at the same time!
    Uncle Phil: Omigosh!
    What is Uncle Phil inferring? What rule of inference does this involve?

14. In his *Principles of Descartes' Philosophy*, the great Dutch philosopher Baruch Spinoza presented one of Descartes' arguments as follows:
    If ERROR were something positive, God would be its CAUSE, and by Him it would continually be PROCREATED. But this is absurd. Therefore error is nothing positive.
    By claiming that "this is absurd," Spinoza is denying that God could be the cause of error and that error could be continually propagated by him. Use this information to *symbolize and then prove the validity* of this argument.

15. (**CHALLENGE**) In a rather rambling letter to the editor of *Philosophy Now* (no. 23, Spring 1999, p. 43), Don Crew writes:
    "The position taken by my colleague Tristan Jones (*Philosophy Now*, no. 22) speaks of belief in an Omnipotent, Omniscient God and then adopts the Euclidian Cartesian position 'God cannot create a triangle with more than 180 degrees.' This view is not consistent with the Theist position, that 'for God all things are possible.'
    If God cannot act he is not Omnipotent; if God can act and does not, he is not Good. Tristan Jones' position is that of the non-realist; i.e., God is an anthropological phenomenon which provides social and psychological benefits to the believer."
    It's hard to follow Crew's reasoning. But let's try this: Granting Crew the three implicit premises 'God is OMNIPOTENT,' 'God is GOOD,' and 'If God CAN and DOES act, then he REALLY exists,' show that these together with the two statements contained in the first sentence of the second paragraph entail that 'God really exists.'

16. (a) *Symbolize the explicit premise* of the following enthymeme, rendering "if he were not" as "if there were a GOD who is not JUST":
    If there is a GOD, my dear Rhedi, he must necessarily be JUST; for if he were not, he would be the most WICKED and imperfect of all beings.—Baron de Montesquieu, *Persian Letters*
    (b) *Prove that if one grants Montesquieu the implicit premise* that "there is a GOD and he is not the most WICKED and imperfect of all beings," *it follows from this together with his explicit premise (as rendered above)* that "God must necessarily be JUST."

17. (**CHALLENGE**) *Prove the validity of the following argument*, given by Leibniz in the early eighteenth century against Clarke's claim that space is a property of God:

I have still other arguments against this strange imagination that space is a PROPERTY of God. If it be so, space belongs to the ESSENCE of God. But space HAS parts: therefore there WOULD be parts in the essence of God. [But this is not true.]

Here the "therefore" has to be interpreted as "in that case," i.e., "if E and H."

5.3 EVALUATING EXTENDED ARGUMENTS

At this point we turn from our consideration of single-inference arguments, and go back to extended arguments involving more than one inference. In the last section of chapter 1 we looked at a very useful method for analyzing such arguments, where we represent their inference-structure by means of diagrams. In this method, each inference is represented by a downward-pointing arrow, going to each inferred statement from the premise(s) or reason(s) given in support of it. It is important not to confuse these *downward*-pointing arrows '↓,' which represent *inferences*, with the *horizontal* arrows '→,' which represent *implications*. As explained at the end of the previous chapter, I may assert an implication, say "If BLACK holes do not exist, cosmology will need a complete OVERHAUL," ¬B → O, without asserting ¬B and without inferring O. On the other hand, if I assert both the conditional containing the implication and the antecedent, from these one could infer the consequent by modus ponens. Then we would have the single-inference argument

$$¬B → O, ¬B ∴ O$$

Now, in a single-inference argument, the inference-structure is straightforward: it simply goes from the premises, taken jointly, to the conclusion. So the above argument would be diagrammed:

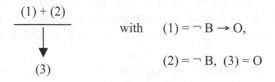

$$\text{with} \quad (1) = ¬\,B → O,$$
$$(2) = ¬\,B, \ (3) = O$$

Here the downward arrow would represent the inference from the premises to the conclusion, which in this case we know is a valid one, since it is an instance of modus ponens. In other cases we will be able to prove inferences valid by symbolizing the numbered statements and using formal proofs.

Now let's proceed to arguments having more complex inferential structures. Once we have identified all the inferences, we can ask whether each of these inferences is valid. We will not generally be able to prove their validity: formal logic covers too little natural reasoning for that. But we will be able to apply the definition of validity in all cases to make an intuitive assessment: *for a valid inference, the denial of the conclusion is incompatible with accepting all the premises.* So for each inference we will be able to ask: given what seem to be appropriate standards of evidence, would it be possible to accept the premises and still deny the conclusion?[1] Asking this question will often help to tease out implicit premises which, when granted, render the inference in question valid. As an example, consider the following argument by Chrysippus against Epicurus' idea that atoms undergo causeless swerves in their motions, as reported by the Roman philosopher Cicero:

(1) If there is a motion without a cause, not every proposition will be true or false. For (2) what will not have effective causes will be neither true nor false. But (3) every proposition is either true or false. Therefore, (4) there is no motion without a cause.— Cicero, *On Fate*[2]

As usual, I have numbered the statements for ease of reference. I have also boxed the *inference indicators* 'For' and 'Therefore.' The 'For' indicates that (2) is given as a reason for (1), whilst the 'Therefore' indicates that (4) is intended as the main conclusion, which it seems on inspection we are to infer from (1) and (3) together. Thus there are two inferences, one from (2) to (1), the other from (1) and (3) together to (4). We represent each such inference by a downwards arrow, so: ↓. Then the inferential structure of the whole argument looks like this:

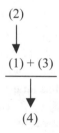

$$(2)$$
$$\downarrow$$
$$(1) + (3)$$
$$\downarrow$$
$$(4)$$

Now let's investigate how good an argument it is. To do this we will work backwards from the conclusion. What is the argument for (4)? We see that it is supposed to follow from (1) and (3). Does it validly follow? Could you deny (4) having accepted (1) and (3)? In fact, you should be able to prove that the inference from (1) + (3) to (4) is formally valid using statement logic. (**Exercise:** do that! Let M := there is a MOTION without a

---

[1]   For this formulation and its use in determining the validity of inferences, I am indebted to Alec Fisher, *The Logic of Real Arguments* (Cambridge: Cambridge UP, 1988). Fisher dubs it the "Assertibility Question": "What argument of evidence would justify me in asserting the conclusion C? (What would I have to know or believe to be justified in accepting C?)" (pp. 22, 27).

[2]   Quoted from the translation of Brad Inwood and Lloyd P. Gerson, *Hellenistic Philosophy*, p. 37.

cause, P := every PROPOSITION will be true or false; then this inference is: M → ¬P, P ∴ ¬M.) This means we should accept the conclusion if we accept both (1) and (3). But there is a subsidiary single-inference argument for (1). Does it validly follow from (2)? Not as it stands; but it would be valid if we allowed an implicit premise, (2a) "if there is a motion without a cause, there is something that does not have an effective cause." This seems true, and reasonable to assume as something too obvious to be worth stating. This would make the argument for premise (1) go as follows:

(1) If there is a motion without a cause, not every proposition will be true or false. (For) (2) what will not have effective causes will be neither true nor false, [and (2a) if there is a motion without a cause, there is something that does not have an effective cause].

Thus we have:

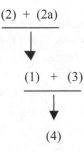

$$(2) \ + \ (2a)$$

$$(1) \ + \ (3)$$

$$(4)$$

You have proved the inference from (1) and (3) to (4) valid. What about the inference to (1)? Rigorously, it is an argument in predicate logic. But we can approximate it in statement logic if we symbolize "there is a motion without a cause" by W, "every proposition is true or false" by P, and "everything has an effective cause" by E. Then the argument is basically ¬E → ¬P, W → ¬E ∴ W → ¬P. This is valid—in fact it is an instance of the rule of inference known as Hypothetical Syllogism, which we shall encounter later.

We can now give an evaluation of the argument. Since both inferences are valid, and (2a) is certainly true, then the only way we can resist the conclusion is for either (2) or (3) to be false, since these are the only other independent premises. Personally, I would need further argument to convince me of the truth of (2). Interestingly, though, according to Cicero's analysis, Epicurus effectively chose to accept (2) and deny (3), that every proposition is true or false: he introduced the idea of a causeless motion, or swerve, precisely to avoid the strict fatalism that Chrysippus embraced.

Now let's try some more complex examples, bringing together the techniques for analysis of real arguments we have learned so far: identifying inference indicators, premises, and conclusions; interpreting which parts of sentences are statements and which are phrases performing other functions, and rephrasing accordingly; construing parts of statements or rhetorical questions as statements; supplying missing premises and conclusions; and evaluating soundness of reasoning into validity of inferences and truth or falsity of premises. We can restate all that as a procedure or method as follows:

(i)   first, mark up the argument: bracket or box the inference indicators, set the premises in <triangular brackets>, underline the conclusions, and double-underline the main conclusion.

(ii) supply any premises or conclusions that you consider to be implicit, i.e., necessary for the validity of an inference, and likely to be regarded as too obvious to be worth stating.

(iii) diagram the inference structure.

(iv) give an assessment of the validity of the argument. You need to evaluate whether each inference is valid, without necessarily being able to prove it by statement logic. Ask yourself, given what seem to be appropriate standards of evidence, would the premises be sufficient to convince me of the conclusion? (When you have been through this step, you may recognize the need for further implicit premises.)

Here's an example:

In the long run, Mr. Lindsay argues, (1) lower inflation could make income distribution more equal. For one thing, (2) some of the measured gain in the incomes of the well-to-do has been caused by sharply higher interest income. But (3) that income is partly compensation for the erosion of financial wealth from inflation and (4) would decline with declining inflation. For another, (5) the fact that housing would become more affordable should make the distribution of wealth more equal by spreading home ownership more widely.

Here there are two independent lines of reasoning for the overall conclusion, introduced by "For one thing" and "For another." This tells us that (1) is the overall conclusion, and (5) is the second reason given for it. But what of (2), (3), and (4)? (2) and (3) together entail (4), that the higher interest income of the wealthy would fall if inflation were lower, which is itself evidence for (1). This gives the following when it is marked up, with redundant material excised, and implicit material inserted:

(1) lower inflation could make income distribution more equal. For one thing, (2) <some of the measured gain in the incomes of the well-to-do has been caused by sharply higher interest income>. But (3) <that income is partly compensation for the erosion of financial wealth from inflation> and (4) <[such sharply higher interest income] would decline with declining inflation>. For another, (5) <the fact that housing would become more affordable should make the distribution of wealth more equal by spreading home ownership more widely>.

Diagram:

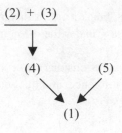

Evaluation:
Assuming (2) and (3) are true, (4) would seem to follow. This would make income distribution more equal, so (1) appears to follow validly from this. Again, if (5) is true, (1) seems to follow. So the argument appears valid.

> (1) Nothing is demonstrable unless the contrary implies a contradiction. (2) Nothing that is distinctly conceivable implies a contradiction. (3) Whatever we conceive as existent, we can also conceive as non-existent. (4) There is no being, therefore, whose non-existence implies a contradiction. (5) Consequently there is no being whose existence is demonstrable.—David Hume, *Dialogues Concerning Natural Religion* (1779)

Here the inference indicators are "therefore" and "consequently" (which we box), and these indicate that the very last statement (5) is the overall conclusion, and that (4) is a premise for it. Does (4) entail (5) by itself? No, but it does entail it if (1) is true. So (5) is inferred from (1) and (4) together. What about (4)? The "therefore" indicates that it follows from what precedes it, and it is readily seen that it follows from (2) and (3) together. This gives:

> (1) <Nothing is demonstrable unless the contrary implies a contradiction.> (2) <Nothing that is distinctly conceivable implies a contradiction.> (3) <Whatever we conceive as existent, we can also conceive as non-existent.> (4) <There is no being, therefore, whose non-existence implies a contradiction>. Consequently (5) there is no being whose existence is demonstrable.

Diagram:

(2) + (3)

↓

(4) + (1)

↓

(5)

Evaluation:
The inferences from (2) and (3) to (4), and from (4) and (1) to (5), seem valid. Can we then agree with the premises? (1) states a valid argument strategy (the *reductio ad absurdum*, which we'll study later), so we know this statement is true. I also cannot find any fault with (2) or (3), so I find myself obliged to accept Hume's conclusion that we cannot demonstrate the existence of any being (including God) from first principles.

EXERCISES 5.3

Instructions for nos. 18-23: (i) *mark up the argument: bracket or box the* inference indicators, *number the statements* (1), (2) *etc.,* set the premises in *<triangular brackets>, underline the* conclusions, *and double-underline the* main conclusion; (ii) *supply any premises or conclusions that you consider to be implicit,* i.e., necessary for the validity of an inference and likely to be regarded as too obvious to be worth stating; (iii) *diagram the inference structure;* (iv) *give an evaluation of the argument.*

Example:
18. Democratic laws generally tend to promote the welfare of the greatest possible number; for they emanate from the majority of the citizens, who are subject to error, but who cannot have an interest opposed to their own advantage. The laws of an aristocracy tend, on the contrary, to concentrate wealth in the hands of the minority; because an aristocracy, by its very nature, constitutes a minority. It may therefore be asserted as a general proposition that democratic laws benefit more citizens than do aristocratic laws. —Alexis de Tocqueville, *Democracy In America*, ch. XIV, 1831
(i) (1) Democratic laws generally tend to promote the welfare of the greatest possible number; for (2) <they emanate from the majority of the citizens>, (3) <who [although they] are subject to error, but who cannot have an interest opposed to their own advantage>. (4) <The laws of an aristocracy tend (on the contrary), to concentrate wealth in the hands of the minority>; because (5) <an aristocracy, by its very nature, constitutes a minority>. It may therefore be asserted, as a general proposition that (6) democratic laws benefit more citizens than do aristocratic laws.
(ii) See (iv).
(iii)

$$(2) + (3) \qquad (5)$$
$$\downarrow \qquad\qquad \downarrow$$
$$(1) \quad + \quad (4)$$
$$\downarrow$$
$$(6)$$

(iv) Although (2) and (3) support (1) validly, it is hard to see why one should believe (3). Why couldn't citizens of a democracy pursue laws that were contrary to their advantage—say refusing to join a larger economic union like the EU even though this might be disastrous for their economy? Also, (4) does not seem to follow from (5) without assuming some other premise, such as (5a) that every group in power enacts laws so as to increase its wealth; this may be historically true, but it still seems overly cynical. If (1) and (4) are granted, something like (6) will validly follow.

19. Wealth is not sought except for the sake of something else, because of itself it brings us no good, but only when we use it, whether for the support of the body or for some similar purpose. Now the highest good is sought for its own, and not for another's sake. Therefore wealth is not a man's highest good.—St. Thomas Aquinas, *Summa Contra Gentiles*, p. 55 in *Basic Writings of St. Thomas Aquinas* (New York: Random House, 1945)

20. It is not the young man who is to be congratulated for his blessedness, but the old man who has lived well. For the young man at the full peak of his powers wanders around senselessly, owing to chance. But the old man has let down his anchor in old age as though in a harbour, since he has secured the goods about which he was previously not confident by means of his secure sense of gratitude.—*Vatican Collection of Epicurean Sayings*, from Inwood and Gerson, *Hellenistic Philosophy*, pp. 29-30

21. [*Fictional detective Sherlock Holmes's explanation to his associate Dr. Watson, of how he knew Watson had come from Afghanistan*]: From long habit the train of thoughts ran so swiftly through my mind that I arrived at the conclusion without being conscious of intermediate steps. There were such steps, however. The train of reasoning ran, "Here is a man of medical type, but with the air of a military man. Clearly an army doctor, then. He has just come from the tropics, for his face is dark, and that is not the natural tint of his skin, for his wrists are fair. He has undergone hardship and sickness, as his haggard face says clearly. His left arm has been injured. He holds it in a stiff and unnatural manner. Where in the tropics could an English army doctor have seen so much hardship and got his arm wounded? Clearly in Afghanistan."—Sir Arthur Conan Doyle, *A Study in Scarlet*, 1887

22. Since some animals are born in earth, others in water, others in air, Aristotle thinks it is absurd to suppose that no animals are born in that part of the cosmos which is most suited for the production of animal life. Now the stars reside in the aether; and since aether is the rarest element and is always alive and moving, an animal born in it must have the keenest perception and the swiftest motion. Thus, since the stars are born in the aether, it is proper that these should have perception and intelligence. From which it follows that the stars should be reckoned among the gods.—Cicero, *On the Nature of the Gods*, from Inwood and Gerson, *Hellenistic Philosophy*, p. 109; modified by reference to Ross's translation

23. (**CHALLENGE**) (a) *Analyze and diagram* the following argument given by Isaac Newton in his First Letter to Bentley (Thayer, pp. 47-48), showing that it is a single inference argument, *and (b)—granting him the two implicit premises* (2a) "If there were a natural cause determining the planets' regular motions, this would also determine the COMETS to move in the same way, and if so, they could not then move all manner of ways, etc.," and (2b) "If the planets' motions do not spring from any natural cause alone, they must be impressed by an intelligent agent"—*construct a formal proof of its validity*:

The motions which the planets have now could not spring from any NATURAL cause alone, but were impressed by an INTELLIGENT agent. For since comets descend into the region of our planets and here move all MANNER of ways,—going sometimes the same way as the planets, sometimes the contrary way, and sometimes in planes inclined to the ecliptic, and at all kinds of angles—it is plain that there is no natural cause which could determine the planets to move the same way and in the same plane, without considerable variation; which must have been [impressed by an intelligent agent].

Chapter Six

Disjunction

This chapter concerns the statement operator 'or,' symbolized by the wedge 'v.' A compound statement formed from two components by this operator is called a *disjunction*. The component statements are called *disjuncts* (from the Latin for "things disjoined"). Here's an example. Suppose a real estate agent is showing someone around a house, but when she turns on the basement light switch, nothing happens. She might say:

(1) Either the BULB has gone, or the FUSE has blown.

We symbolize this as: B v F

The wedge is the third of our binary operators. Like the arrow and the ampersand, it connects two statements and forms from them another statement. And like them, its symbolization involves the introduction of groupers (parentheses, brackets, or braces), with the convention that outermost groupers are left implicit. On the other hand, the formula B v F → ¬L is not well-formed: it is ambiguous between

(F2) (B v F) → ¬L   a conditional whose antecedent is a disjunction, and

(F3) B v (F → ¬L)   a disjunction whose second disjunct is a conditional.

In (F2), which is a conditional, we say that the *governing operator* is the arrow, →. In (F3), which is a disjunction, it is the wedge, v, that is the governing operator. If B and F symbolize the component statements in (1), and L is "the light will come on," (F2) and (F3) say quite different things; respectively,

(2) If the bulb has gone or the fuse has blown, the light won't come on.

(3) Either the bulb has gone, or the light won't come on if the fuse has blown.

Now often when we assert a disjunction we do not intend to rule out that both the disjuncts might be true. Consider statement (1) again, for instance. The bulb's having gone and the fuse's having blown are two alternative explanations of the light's not coming on, but they are not mutually exclusive possibilities. If it turned out that both explanations were correct, the real estate agent wouldn't consider her statement (1) to be untrue. On the other hand, suppose she had said:

(4) Either my car keys are here in my HANDBAG or I must have LOCKED them in my car.

Here the alternatives are exclusive: if she found the keys in her handbag, she would infer that she had not locked them in her car.

This shows us that 'or' is used in at least two different ways in everyday language. The first statement is an example of the *inclusive 'or'*: it includes the possibility that both the bulb is a dud and the fuse is blown. The second is an example of the *exclusive 'or'*: it is understood to exclude the possibility that the keys might be both in the estate agent's handbag and locked in her car. So we are confronted with a choice: Which of these two senses of 'or' should we take as the primary one for our purposes in logic? The Stoic logicians chose the exclusive sense; modern logicians have adopted the inclusive 'or.' Nothing important depends on the choice, since each can be expressed in terms of the other, using negation and conjunction too. Consequently we shall take the inclusive sense as basic, and adopt the following convention when symbolizing:

> *We shall always take disjunctions to be inclusive* and symbolize them
> $p \vee q$, *unless they contain "but not both"* (or an equivalent expression),
> in which case we shall symbolize them as $(p \vee q) \mathrel{\&} \neg (p \mathrel{\&} q)$.

Thus to assert a disjunction is to assert that one or the other or both the disjuncts are true; similarly, to suppose a disjunction is to suppose that one or the other or both the disjuncts are true; to deny a disjunction is to deny that either of the disjuncts is true, i.e., to assert that neither of them is true. This motivates the rules of inference for disjunction that we will encounter in the next section.

We could, of course, have made the other choice, and taken the exclusive sense as basic. In fact the Stoic logicians of Ancient Greece did just this in formulating the first system of statement logic. Thus we could symbolize the exclusive 'or' by $\oplus$, and call any compound formed from A and B formed by the exclusive 'or,' $A \oplus B$,[1] an *alternation* (or *exclusive disjunction*). Having taken the inclusive sense as basic, however, we can still express the exclusive 'or' in terms of it. For the exclusive 'or' is either one or the other, but not both; in symbols:

$$p \oplus q = (p \vee q) \, \& \, \neg(p \, \& \, q).$$

Similarly, had we adopted the exclusive 'or,' we could have expressed the inclusive 'or' in terms of it: see exercise 5.

There is one case, however, where it does not matter whether we use the exclusive or the inclusive (or.) This is when we have statements of the form p or $\neg p$; for example, "Either you AGREE, or you don't agree." This *is* an exclusive 'or'; but the alternative $\neg(A \, \& \, \neg A)$ is already ruled out, since $(p \, \& \, \neg p)$ is automatically false, whatever p is. Consequently $(A \vee \neg A) \, \& \, \neg(A \, \& \, \neg A)$ is equivalent to $(A \vee \neg A)$.

Other uses of the word 'or' occur in ordinary language. One, the *'or' of equivalence*, indicates that the two words it joins are equivalent in meaning, as in

The *middle* or *soft commissure* consists almost entirely of gray matter.[2]

Another is to express alternatives that are not presented as statements, especially in locutions involving "whether...or...."[3] Neither of these 'ors' will occur in an inferential context, however. When reasoning we would simply decide which of two terms marked by the 'or' of equivalence to use; and if the "whether...or..." occurred in the context of an argument, it would be recast as a regular disjunction: "either...or...."

So it is as well to be aware of these different 'ors'; but you need not worry about them: unless you see a "but not both," you may happily use the wedge in symbolizing arguments.

SUMMARY

• A **disjunction** is any two statements joined by the binary statement operator 'or.' Symbolically, it is the compound statement $p \vee q$ produced by the operation of the wedge operator, '$\vee$,' on any two statements, p, q. The components p and q of any disjunction $p \vee q$ are called **disjuncts**.

---

[1] Some logicians use the symbol $\wedge$ for the exclusive 'or.' It should be noted, however, that the conventions for logical signs are not yet uniform, and in many systems $\wedge$ is used instead of & to stand for 'and' and its synonyms.

[2] *Gray's Anatomy* (New York: Bounty Books, 1977), p. 671.

[3] In Latin they had several different words for these different 'ors': AUT was generally exclusive, VEL inclusive, as was -VE on the end of a word, whilst the 'or' of equivalence was denoted by SIVE or SEU. "Whether...or..." was usually AN...AN....

- In English the word 'or' is often ambiguous between inclusive and exclusive senses. An exclusive disjunction (or **alternation**) is so called because it excludes the possibility that *p* and *q* are both true, whereas the inclusive 'or' includes this possibility.
- In symbolizing disjunctions, we always take them to be inclusive and symbolize them *p* ∨ *q*, *unless they contain the phrase "but not both"* (or an equivalent expression), in which case we shall symbolize them as **(*p* ∨ *q*) & ¬(*p* & *q*)**.

EXERCISES 6.1

1. *Symbolize the following statements using the first letter of each capitalized word for the components:*
   (a) The man's a SCOUNDREL, or my name is not AUGUSTA Davenport.—Philip Pullman, *Count Karlstein*
   (b) The earth does not FEEL as if it is spinning, nor does the observational evidence SUGGEST any such thing.—Timothy Ferris, *Coming of Age in the Milky Way*, p. 34
   (c) ...all those things God revealed to the prophets, were revealed to them either in WORDS, or in VISIBLE forms, or in both words and visible forms.—Spinoza, *Theological-Political Treatise* ch. 1 (Curley, *A Spinoza Reader*, p. 12)
   (d) ...he will imagine now SIMON, or now JAMES,...but not both at once.—Spinoza, *Ethics* II, p. 126
   (e) Neither REASON nor MATHEMATICS nor mAPS were any use to me.—Christopher Columbus (quoted from Ferris, *Coming of Age*, p. 55)
   (f) If I speak in the TONGUES of men and of angels, but have not LOVE, I am a noisy GONG or a clanging CYMBAL.—Holy Bible, 1 Corinthians 13
   (g) Anyone WITHOUT a labor book, or filling in his or her labor book INCORRECTLY, or making FALSE statements, will be PROSECUTED with the utmost vigor under the wartime regulations.—Boris Pasternak, *Doctor Zhivago*
   (h) But if she LOST it, /Or made a GIFT of it, my father's eye / Should HOLD her loathed and his spirits should hunt /After new FANCIES.—Shakespeare, *Othello*, Act III, Scene 4
   (i) Either God EXISTS or there is no God.—Frederick Copleston, *A History of Philosophy*, p. 170 [Consider: is anything gained by making the exclusive character of this 'or' explicit?]
   (j) Either we REINVENT our traditions of egalitarianism and liberalism to accommodate the realities of today's global economy or...we will simply...either become another ECHO-IMAGE of the United States or become a region WITHIN it.—Richard Gwyn, *Nationalism Without Walls: The Incredible Lightness of Being Canadian*

2. *Identify the governing operator in each of the following abstract statements:*

(a) ¬A ∨ ¬C

(b) ¬(A ∨ ¬C)

(c) A ∨ (¬B → ¬C)

(d) P → ¬(A & B)

(e) ¬B → (¬A ∨ ¬C)

(f) (B ∨ ¬C) & ¬(B & ¬C)

3. *For each of the following sentences that is or contains a disjunction, identify the disjuncts:*
   (a) Village greens or commons…are beloved features of many Vermont villages today…—Jan Albers, *Hands on the Land*
   (b) Our own creations may soon turn on us and make us their slaves, or worse still, decide we are expendable.—John McCrone, review of *QI: The Quest for Intelligence*, Kevin Warwick
   (c) The more reality or being each thing has, the more attributes belong to it.—Spinoza, *Ethics* II, p. 51
   (d) Now, whether he kill Cassio, / Or Cassio him, or each do kill the other, / Every way makes my gain.—Shakespeare, *Othello* Act V, Scene 1
   (e) It is estimated that between four and six tonnes of heroin is either processed in Turkey or transits through the country each month.—*Guardian Weekly*, September 2000
   (f) The result of a professional hockey game should not be that we are lucky to escape paralysis or are lucky to have our eyesight, after wilful acts of violence.—Dallas Stars Center, Mike Modano

4. *Render each formula (a)-(d) into a colloquial English Statement using the dictionary provided:*
   A := All our actions are determined.
   B := We have free will.
   C := Morality is possible.
   Example: ¬B → ¬C: *Answer*: If we don't have free will, morality is impossible.
   (a) A ∨ B
   (b) (B ∨ ¬C) & ¬(B & ¬C)
   (c) B → (¬A ∨ ¬C)
   (d) A ∨ (¬B → ¬C)

5.(**CHALLENGE**) As explained in the text, the Stoic logicians took as basic the exclusive 'or,' $\oplus$, which may be expressed in terms of the wedge $\lor$ as follows:

$$p \oplus q \equiv (p \lor q) \,\&\, \neg(p \,\&\, q)$$

How would you express the inclusive 'or' in Stoic logic? Give an analogous formula to represent $p \lor q$ in terms of $\oplus$ and $\&$.

6.2 RULES OF INFERENCE FOR DISJUNCTIONS

6.2.1 DISJUNCTIVE SYLLOGISM

In the last section we said that to assert a disjunction is to assert that one or the other or both the disjuncts are true. But this means that if we know in addition that one of the disjuncts is false, then the other one must be true. This is the foundation for the following rule (also true for alternations), noted by Chrysippus the Stoic:

The first or the second.
Not the first.
_____
Therefore the second.

For instance:

> Either wealth is an EVIL or wealth is a GOOD; but wealth is not an evil; therefore wealth is a good.—Sextus Empiricus, *Against the Logicians*
> *Symbolized:* E $\lor$ G, $\neg$E $\therefore$ G

The formal validity of this argument is established as follows: it is contradictory to assert E $\lor$ G and at the same time to deny E and G; therefore it is contradictory to assert E $\lor$ G and $\neg$E and also deny G. The rule of inference encapsulating the validity of this form is

> *Disjunctive Syllogism* (**DS**)
> From the assertion of a disjunction and the denial of one of its disjuncts, infer the other disjunct.
> *In symbols:*
> From $p \lor q$ and $\neg p$, infer q.
> From $p \lor q$ and $\neg q$, infer p.

Here's an example. When Galileo pointed his telescope at the heavens in the early seventeenth century, he was able to observe all the phases of the planet Venus, thus proving that it goes around the sun (and not, as in the Ptolemaic system, around the earth). Physics Professor Verne Booth explains:

This was a triumph of the greatest importance for the Copernicans, for in the Ptolemaic system Venus could never get far enough away from the sun to show a full phase. The fact that Venus displays a full set of phases constitutes the one conclusive proof that it revolves around the sun.

Restating to bring out the underlying logic:

Either the PTOLEMAIC system is correct, or Venus revolves around the SUN. If the Ptolemaic system is correct, Venus could never get far enough away from the sun to show a FULL phase. The fact that Venus displays a full set of phases constitutes the one conclusive proof that it revolves around the sun.

Symbolized: $P \vee S$, $P \rightarrow \neg F$, F $\therefore$ S

A proof would proceed as follows:

(1) $P \vee S$ Prem
(2) $P \rightarrow \neg F$ Prem
(3) F Prem
(4) $\neg\neg F$ 3 DN
(5) $\neg P$ 2, 4 MT
(6) S 1, 5 DS

The sharper among you may have noticed that the alternatives in the first statement are mutually exclusive: if P is true, S is false, and vice versa. You may then have wondered whether anything is lost in representing what is strictly an alternation as a disjunction. Let's see. If we had made the exclusive 'or' explicit, (1) would have been symbolized $(P \vee S) \& \neg(P \& S)$. This would have required us to put in an extra step (numbered (0) here):

(0) $(P \vee S) \& \neg(P \& S)$ Prem
(1) $P \vee S$ 1 Simp
(2)…etc.

Clearly, putting in this extra step doesn't affect the logic of this proof. This is because DS is a valid rule for alternations as well as disjunctions. So in this case no harm comes from having represented the first premise as a disjunction, nor will it if the only rule being applied is DS. In contrast, the following rule identified by the Stoics is valid only for alternations:

The first or the second. $p \oplus q$
The first. p
Therefore not the second. $\therefore \neg q$

This rule is NOT valid for disjunctions, precisely because the disjuncts are not mutually exclusive alternatives. However, note that if we represent an alternation in terms of disjunction, we have to explicitly include the fact that we have "Not both the first and the second," since p ⊕ q is represented by $(p \lor q)$ & $\neg(p$ & $q)$. But then we have

The first or the second.	$p \lor q$
But not both the first and the second.	$\neg(p$ & $q)$
The first.	p
Therefore not the second.	$\therefore \neg q$

the last three lines of which are simply *conjunctive argument*. Therefore this rule is simply subsumed under the CS rule. What all this means in practice is that in symbolizing an argument you can simply assume that you are dealing with disjunctions, unless the argument rides on the exclusivity of the disjuncts. That will be made clear by an expression like "but not both." But as soon as you make this explicit, DS and CS can do the job.

Here's a slightly harder example.[4] The top FBI official investigating the crash of TWA flight 800 off the coast of New York in July, 1996, announced four months later that mechanical failure was the most likely cause of the crash. Like the fictional investigator Sherlock Holmes, he reasoned by eliminating the alternative possibilities:

> The crash was caused either by a MECHANICAL failure, or a BOMB, or a GUIDED missile. But the evidence shows that it wasn't caused by a bomb, nor was it caused by a guided missile. So the cause was mechanical failure.

Symbolized: (M ∨ B) ∨ G, ¬B & ¬G ∴ M

(1) (M ∨ B) ∨ G	Prem
(2) ¬B & ¬G	Prem
(3) ¬G	2 Simp
(4) M ∨ B	1, 3 DS
(5) ¬B	2 Simp
(6) M	4, 5 DS

You may be wondering why I symbolized this as (M ∨ B) ∨G, rather than M ∨ (B ∨ G). Actually, these formulas are equivalent: each entails the other, as we'll soon prove. I chose the one that was more convenient for the proof. [Note that we could have symbolized the second premise as ¬(B ∨ G); in that case it would have been more convenient to symbolize the first as M ∨ (B ∨ G), since then M would follow from these two premises in one line by DS.]

---

[4] This example is due to Howard Pospesel, *Propositional Logic* (3rd ed., Inglewood Cliffs: Prentice Hall, 1998), p. 132.

6.2.2 DISJUNCTION

Disjunctive Syllogism is a rule for eliminating a disjunction. Is there a rule for introducing one? Yes, there is. It's so simple that it appears fishy, so I'll introduce it somewhat obliquely. Consider statement (2) of the previous section, "If either the BULB has gone or the FUSE has blown, the LIGHT won't come on," symbolized $(B \vee F) \rightarrow \neg L$. Assume this is true, and that we discover that the fuse has indeed blown. We should be able to infer that the light will not come on. But when we try a proof we become stuck:

(1) $(B \vee F) \rightarrow \neg L$ Prem
(2) F   Prem

We should be able to get to $\neg L$. But to do so we need to acknowledge that, knowing that the fuse has blown, we of course also know that either the bulb has gone or the fuse has blown. For to assert a disjunction is to assert that one or the other (or both) of the disjuncts is true; so if we know one is true, we know the disjunction of this with another statement—any other statement—is also true. This is the rule

---

Disjunction (**Disj**)
From any statement, infer its disjunction with another statement.
In symbols:
From p (stated alone), infer $p \vee q$.
From q (stated alone), infer $p \vee q$.

The validity of this argument form is established as follows: one cannot assert p to be true and at the same time deny that either p or q is true; similarly, one cannot assert q to be true and at the same time deny that either p or q is true. The argument form is therefore valid by our definition of formal validity.

    With this rule we can complete the above proof:

(1) $(B \vee F) \rightarrow \neg L$ Prem
(2) F   Prem
(3) $B \vee F$ 2 Disj
(4) $\neg L$ 1, 3 MP

The reason this rule appears fishy at first is that, once we are given the first disjunct, the disjunction follows *whatever the second disjunct is*. The second disjunct appears to come out of thin air. I think what confuses us is that to *form* a disjunction, we need to have both of the disjuncts, and the wedge connecting them. But this is about *inferring* the disjunction; we are concerned with rules of inference, not rules of formation. Secondly, the rule is unfamiliar. I think this is because it is weaker to assert $B \vee F$ than it is to assert B, and we are not used to inferring something weaker, and thus losing information. But the above proof shows that we sometimes need to; and the reasoning justifying the rule is completely consistent with what is meant by disjunction.

Now I should mention a PITFALL FOR THE UNWARY. There are many analogies between conjunction and disjunction. For some students, there is an overwhelming temptation to regard the analogy as complete. So they imagine there is a counterpart to *Simplification*:

<u>*NOT A VALID RULE OF INFERENCE!!*</u>
 From a disjunction infer either one of its disjuncts.
In symbols: *YOW!*
 From $p \vee q$ infer p alone; from $p \vee q$ infer q alone.

This is UTTERLY INVALID! From the true statement that I am either a philosopher or a billionaire, you cannot validly infer that I am a billionaire! Here's an example of a proof that contains both it and another error. As an exercise, see if you can spot them before reading on:

A, (A ∨ B) → C ∴ B ∨ C

                                      ERRORS in this proof!

(1) A	Prem	
(2) (A ∨ B) → C	Prem	
(3) A ∨ B	1 Disj	
(4) C	2, 3 MP	
(5) B	3 Simp	*YOW!*
(6) B ∨ C	5, 4 Disj	*YOW!*

The invocation of 'Simp' in line (5) is the utterly invalid move just described; but also in line (6) there a confusion between Disj, which needs only one of the disjuncts, and Conj, which needs both. A valid proof would have the same first four lines, but would end:

    (5) B ∨ C   4 Disj

6.2.3 DE MORGAN'S LAWS

A third rule of inference concerning disjunction was implicit in what I said in section 1 about denying a disjunction: to deny a disjunction is to assert that neither of the disjuncts is true, i.e., that they are both false. Similarly, to deny a conjunction is to deny one or the other or both of its conjuncts. Thus we have the pair of rules known as De Morgan's Laws:

De Morgan's Laws (DM)
(1) From the denial of a disjunction, infer the conjunction of the denials of each of its disjuncts, and vice versa.
(2) From the denial of a conjunction, infer the disjunction of the denials of each of its conjuncts, and vice versa.
In symbols:
From $\neg(p \lor q)$, infer $\neg p \ \& \ \neg q$, and vice versa.
From $\neg(p \ \& \ q)$, infer $\neg p \lor \neg q$, and vice versa.

Notice how this differs from the action of negation in algebra, where $-(a + b) = -a + -b$. There we say that the negation "distributes" across addition. One way to remember De Morgan's Laws is as follows. When distributing $\neg$ across a conjunction $p \ \& \ q$, the $\&$ turns into a $\lor$; and when distributing $\neg$ across a disjunction $p \lor q$, the $\lor$ turns into an $\&$. But I find it easiest to remember them by the following formulas:

'Not either' is equivalent to **'neither.'**
'Not both' is equivalent to **'either not one or not the other.'**

NOT VALID RULES OF INFERENCE!!
Above all, remember that it is INVALID to infer $\neg p \ \& \ \neg q$ from $\neg(p \ \& \ q)$ and vice versa, and to infer $\neg p \lor \neg q$ from $\neg(p \lor q)$, and vice versa.

We will prove the validity of De Morgan's Laws later by deriving them using our other valid rules of inference. They are named after the nineteenth-century English logician Augustus De Morgan. Actually they were known in antiquity; they are given his name in recognition of his contributions to the development of modern logic.

Augustus De Morgan (left) was born in Madurai in India, where his father served for the British East India Company. Apart from his contributions to logic, in which he was a founder of the algebra of relations, he is known for introducing the term "mathematical induction," and has a crater on the moon named in his honour.

Here are proofs of two abstract arguments that put De Morgan's Laws into action:

$\neg$(A $\lor$ B), B $\lor$ C $\therefore$ C
(1) $\neg$(A $\lor$ B)	Prem
(2) B $\lor$ C	Prem
(3) $\neg$A $\&$ $\neg$B	1 DM
(4) $\neg$B	3 Simp
(5) C	2, 4 DS

$\neg$T, (R $\&$ S) $\rightarrow$ T $\therefore$ $\neg$R $\lor$ $\neg$S
(1) $\neg$T	Prem
(2) (R $\&$ S) $\rightarrow$ T	Prem
(3) $\neg$(R $\&$ S)	1, 2 MT
(4) $\neg$R $\lor$ $\neg$S	3 DM

As another example, suppose we had symbolized the TWA Flight 800 example above as (M $\lor$ B) $\lor$ G, $\neg$(B $\lor$ G) $\therefore$ M. De Morgan's Laws allow us to prove its validity as follows:

(1) (M $\lor$ B) $\lor$ G	Prem
(2) $\neg$(B $\lor$ G)	Prem
(3) $\neg$B $\&$ $\neg$G	2 DM
(4) $\neg$G	3 Simp
(5) M $\lor$ B	1, 4 DS
(6) $\neg$B	3 Simp
(7) M	5, 6 DS

SUMMARY

- The rule of inference **Disjunction (Disj)** is
  From p (stated alone), infer $p \lor q$; from q (stated alone), infer $p \lor q$:
  From any statement, infer its disjunction with another statement.
- The **validity** of this argument form follows from our definition of formal validity: it is impossible for $p \lor q$ to be false if p (resp. q) is true.
- The rule of inference **Disjunctive Syllogism (DS)** is
  From $p \lor q$ and $\neg p$, infer q; from $p \lor q$ and $\neg q$, infer p:
  From the assertion of a disjunction and the denial of one of its disjuncts, infer the other disjunct.
- The **validity** of this argument form follows from our definition of formal validity: it is impossible for $p \lor q$ to be true, and yet for both p and q to be false.

- **De Morgan's Laws (DM)** are the rules of inference:
  From $\neg(p \vee q)$, infer $\neg p \mathbin{\&} \neg q$, and vice versa:
  From the denial of a disjunction, infer the conjunction of the denials of each of its disjuncts, and vice versa; and
  From $\neg(p \mathbin{\&} q)$, infer $\neg p \vee \neg q$, and vice versa:
  From the denial of a conjunction, infer the disjunction of the denials of each of its conjuncts, and vice versa.
- The **validity** of De Morgan's Laws will be proved later by deriving them from our other valid rules.
- The argument form $p \vee q \therefore p$ or $p \vee q \therefore q$ is *INVALID*!

EXERCISES 6.2

Prove the validity of the following abstract arguments:

6. $\neg(A \mathbin{\&} B)$, $A \vee C$, $\neg C \therefore \neg B$

7. $D \vee \neg E$, $B \rightarrow E$, $\neg D \therefore \neg B$

8. $A \vee C$, $A \rightarrow B$, $C \rightarrow D$, $\neg D \therefore B$

9. $A \rightarrow B$, $(A \vee C) \vee D$, $\neg C \mathbin{\&} \neg D \therefore B$

10. E, $(E \vee F) \rightarrow \neg G$, $H \rightarrow G \therefore E \mathbin{\&} \neg H$

In the following *erroneous proofs*, (a) *identify the mistakes made in applying rules of inference*, and (b) *provide a correct proof* of the abstract argument given.

11. $(D \vee B) \rightarrow C$, D, $\neg C \vee E \therefore E$
(1) $(D \vee B) \rightarrow C$	Prem
(2) D	Prem
(3) $\neg C \vee E$	Prem
(4) C	1, 2 MP
(5) E	3, 4 DS

12. $(M \vee N) \mathbin{\&} P$, $M \rightarrow O$, $\neg(O \mathbin{\&} P) \therefore N$
(1) $(M \vee N) \mathbin{\&} P$	Prem
(2) $M \rightarrow O$	Prem
(3) $\neg(O \mathbin{\&} P)$	Prem

(4) ¬O	3 Simp
(5) ¬M	2, 4 MT
(6) N & P	1, 5 DS
(7) N	6 Simp

13. (A & B) → C, ¬C v D, ¬D & A ∴ ¬B

(1) (A & B) → C	Prem
(2) ¬C v D	Prem
(3) ¬D & A	Prem
(4) ¬C	2 Simp
(5) ¬A & ¬B	1, 4 MT
(6) ¬B	5 Simp

14. H v C, F v G, ¬(G & H), ¬C ∴ F

(1) H v C	Prem
(2) F v G	Prem
(3) ¬(G & H)	Prem
(4) ¬C	Prem
(5) ¬C v H	4 Disj
(6) H	4, 5 DS
(7) ¬G	3, 6 CS
(8) F	2, 7 DS

15. An article in the *Miami News* reports the difficulties of a married couple contending with an unplanned birth:

> About a year ago, their troubles began. Mrs. Mathias was having medical problems, and went to a doctor who told her "she either had a tumor or was pregnant," Mr. Mathias said. "We were scared because she couldn't be pregnant and we thought it had to be a tumor," he said.[5]

Symbolize and prove the validity of the Mathias's reasoning.

16. "If ANYONE knows anything about anything," said Bear to himself, "it's OWL who knows something about something," he said, "or my name's not Winnie-the-POOH," he said. "Which it is," he added. "So there you are."[6]

Symbolize and prove the validity of Pooh's reasoning.

---

[5] Bill Gjebre, "Unplanned Birth Nearly Cost Marriage," *Miami News*, February 2, 1976; quoted from Pospesel, *Propositional Logic* (3rd ed.), p. 126.

[6] Quoted from Benjamin Hoff, *The Tao of Pooh* (Penguin, 1982), p. 23.

17. *Symbolize the following argument and prove its validity.*
    Either Clarkson travelled at her OWN expense or it was paid for by Canadian TAX-PAYERS. If she had gone at her own expense, then she would have flown in a COMMERCIAL jet. But she flew in a GOVERNMENT jet. Clearly if she did that she did not fly in a commercial jet, so we can conclude that Clarkson's travel was paid for by Canadian taxpayers.

Prove the validity of the following abstract arguments:

18. G & H, ¬(¬H ∨ I) ∴ G & ¬I

19. R ∨ S, ¬(S & T), T ∴ R

20. E → ¬(F ∨ G), F ∴ ¬E

21. (A ∨ B) → C, ¬C ∨ D, ¬D ∴ ¬B

22. ¬(M ∨ N), K → M, L → N ∴ ¬(K ∨ L)

23. (D ∨ B) → ¬(C & E), C & D ∴ ¬E

24. ¬D, B → (C ∨ D), C → D ∴ ¬B

25. **(CHALLENGE)** F → (C & E), ¬(C ∨ D) ∴ ¬F

26. **(CHALLENGE)** One of the reasons De Morgan's Laws were not better known in antiquity is that *they are not valid for alternations* (*exclusive disjunctions*). They were therefore not part of Stoic Logic, which adopted the exclusive as opposed to the inclusive 'or.' As we shall see below, De Morgan's Laws are examples of *equivalence rules*: since each of the expressions ¬(p ∨ q) and ¬p & ¬q entails the other, they are *logically equivalent*. This means that one expression can be substituted for the other. Using this notion of equivalence,
    (a) *Show that* ¬(p ⊕ q) *is not equivalent to* ¬p & ¬q by using the definition of p ⊕ q in terms of disjunctions and conjunctions, and applying equivalences such as De Morgan's Law and Double Negation to the resulting expressions to find a formula for ¬(p ⊕ q) that is different from ¬p & ¬q.
    (b) *Show that* ¬p ⊕ ¬q *is not equivalent to* ¬(p & q), again by using the definition of p ⊕ q in terms of disjunctions and conjunctions, and applying equivalences such as De Morgan's Laws and Double Negation to the resulting expressions to find a formula for ¬p ⊕ ¬q that is different from ¬(p & q).

Chapter Seven

Conditional Proof

7.1.1 DISJUNCTIONS IN CONDITIONALS

In 1942 Adolf Hitler made a prediction about the course of the Second World War:

(1) If we do not get the oil from GROZNY or MAIKOP, we will LOSE the war.

Statements such as these can be tricky to symbolize. First, we need to remember that each capital letter symbolizes a (positive) statement, not a single word: so G := We get the oil from Grozny, and M := We get the oil from Maikop. But should we symbolize the whole compound statement by $\neg(G \lor M) \rightarrow L$, or is it $(\neg G \lor \neg M) \rightarrow L$? To decide, we could reason as follows: if Hitler gets the oil from one or the other city, he presumably thinks he can still win. It is only if he doesn't get it from both that he thinks he is in trouble, that is, if $\neg G \& \neg L$. But that is equivalent to $\neg(G \lor M)$, by De Morgan's Laws. So the first symbolization is correct. Again, $(\neg G \lor \neg M)$, by DM, is equivalent to $\neg(G \& M)$, "not both"; but he didn't say "If we do not get oil from *both* GROZNY *and* MAIKOP...," so the second symbolization is wrong.[1]

---

[1] Actually, according to another source, what Hitler said was: "If I do not get the oil of Maikop *and* Grozny, then I must end the war." That would have been symbolized $\neg(M \& G) \rightarrow E$ (with E := I must END the war). For those interested in history as well as logic, the Germans took Maikop but were unable to take Grozny, and lost the war. But Grozny, the Chechen capital, was not so lucky later on: it was levelled by the Russians in 1996 and again in 1999.

7.1.2 'UNLESS'

A related question is how do we symbolize "unless"? How, for instance, should statement (2) be translated?

(2) Unless Thou wert INCOMPREHENSIBLE Thou wouldst not be GOD.—Cardinal Newman

It seems similar to (1): couldn't we rephrase it

(3) If Thou weren't INCOMPREHENSIBLE Thou wouldst not be GOD?

This suggests that "unless" is equivalent to "if not." We can check this by a similar retranslation of (1):

(4) Unless we get the oil from GROZNY or MAIKOP, we will LOSE the war.

This works. But what about (5)?

(5) Either we get the oil from GROZNY or MAIKOP, or we will LOSE the war.

This also appears to be equivalent, thus suggesting that $\neg(G \lor M) \to L$ is equivalent to $(G \lor M) \lor L$. We'll prove this equivalence in the next chapter. What it means for now is that

'**unless** p, q' can be symbolized either by $\neg p \to q$ or by $p \lor q$.

So how should we symbolize (2) above?

7.1.3 'OTHERWISE,' 'ELSE'

Another couple of English operators that seem to be construable either as disjunctions or conditionals are the words 'otherwise' and 'else' (or 'or else'). That these are equivalent is suggested by the following two translations of Heraclitus' fragment 40,[2] an enthymeme:

(6) Much learning does not teach anyone to have intelligence; for else it would have taught Hesiod and Pythagoras, and again, Xenophanes and Hecataeus.

---

[2] The first is quoted from Bruno Snell's *The Discovery of Mind* (Mineola, NY: Dover, 1982), p. 144; the second from *A Presocratics Reader*, ed. Patricia Curd, trans. Richard McKirahan, Jr. (Indianapolis: Hackett, 1996), p. 31.

(7) Much learning does not teach insight. Otherwise it would have taught Hesiod and Pythagoras, and moreover Xenophanes and Hecataeus.

If we symbolize "Much learning teaches insight" by M, and the compound conjunction "it would have taught Hesiod and Pythagoras, and moreover Xenophanes and Hecataeus" by T, we have: Not M. For *else* [or, *otherwise*] T. Implicitly, we also have "But not T." That is,

Not M. For if M then T; but not T.

i.e.,

(F6) $M \rightarrow T, \neg T \therefore \neg M$

This is just an instance of Modus Tollens. Alternatively, just as with *unless*, we could have construed *else* as an 'or,' but this time with the first disjunct implicit, i.e., we could take "Not M. For else T" as "Not M. For either not M or T." Then the argument would be symbolized

(F7) $\neg M \vee T, \neg T \therefore \neg M$

This is just an instance of Disjunctive Argument. Comparing this with the previous symbolization shows the close relationship between DS and Modus Tollens. In sum, the enthymemic argument

'*p*. **Otherwise** *q*' can be symbolized either by $\neg p \rightarrow q, \neg q \therefore p$
or by $p \vee q, \neg q \therefore p$.

EXERCISES 7.1

1. *Symbolize the following statements using the first letter of each capitalized word for the components:*
   (a) The Brooklyn Museum of Art will LOSE its $7.3m subsidy unless it SCRAPS the Sensation exhibition.—New York Mayor Rudy Giuliani
   (b) If they think it is important to throw feces at NATIONAL or RELIGIOUS symbols, they can pay for it THEMSELVES.—New York Mayor Rudy Giuliani [N := they think it is important to throw feces at NATIONAL symbols, R := they think it is important…at RELIGIOUS symbols.]
   (c) The mayor says Ofili's work is OFFENSIVE to Catholics, and that he will also END the museum's lease and take over its BOARD unless it toes his LINE.—"Hillary Backs Britart Show that New York Seeks to Ban," *Manchester Guardian Weekly* 161, #14

(d) Unless I SEE it with my own eyes, and HEAR it with my own ears, I will never BELIEVE it.—Charles Dickens

(e) If the CAREER-ending or LIFE-threatening violence does not stop, [Dallas Stars centre Mike] Modano says he will get OFF the ice for good.—Associated Press report, October 8, 1999 [C := the career-ending violence stops, L := the life-threatening violence stops.]

(f) Nothing can BE or be CONCEIVED without GOD.—Spinoza, *Ethics* II, P15 [construe "without God" as "unless GOD exists"]

(g) If one body PUSHES another, it cannot GIVE the other any motion unless it LOSES as much of its own motion at the same time; nor can it TAKE away any of the other's motion unless its own is INCREASED by as much.—René Descartes, *The World*, second law of nature

2. "*q* unless *p*" can be symbolized either by $\neg p \to q$ or by $p \lor q$. Show that whichever way it is done, (i) taken together with $\neg p$ it entails *q*, and (ii) taken together with $\neg q$ it entails *p*.

3. *Symbolize and prove the validity* of the following argument from the *Science Times*.[3] (It is an enthymeme: you will need to supply the implicit premise.)

"People were presumably FLOATING some kind of boats as early as 50,000 years ago, or how else could humans have first SETTLED Australia."

4. (**CHALLENGE**) (a) *Symbolize* and (b) *prove the validity* of this paraphrase of Descartes' argument for the non-existence of atoms:

It is impossible that there should exist ATOMS, that is, pieces of matter that are by their very nature indivisible. Otherwise, however small we imagined them to be, they would still have to be EXTENDED. But either they are not extended, or we can divide them in our THOUGHT; and anything we can divide in our thought, must, for that very reason be DIVISIBLE. But by hypothesis, they cannot be divisible.

7.2 MORE RULES INVOLVING CONDITIONALS

7.2.1 CONDITIONAL PROOF AND SUPPOSITION

In the previous section we said that "unless *p, q*" can be symbolized either by $\neg p \to q$ or by $p \lor q$. In particular, the statement

(8) Unless you are going to PAY for lunch, I will need my WALLET.

---

[3] "Early Pharaohs' Ghostly Fleet," *New York Times*, Tuesday, October 31, 2000 p. D4.

would be symbolized by either ¬P → W or P ∨ W. This suggests that ¬P → W and P ∨ W are logically equivalent, that we can derive each from the other. Here is a justification of ¬P → W being derivable from P ∨ W:

> Suppose ¬P. Assuming P ∨ W is true, we can then infer W by Disjunctive Syllogism. So if ¬P is true, W is too. But that's exactly what the statement ¬P → W says!

This argument has the form:

> Suppose *p*. But then, given the other premises, *q* follows. Therefore *p* → *q*.

That this is a valid argument form, I hope the above discussion has made intuitively apparent. It is an extremely useful one too, and we shall set it up as a rule of inference. The first thing to notice, though, is that it begins by making a *supposition*: *p* is not actually given as a premise, it is simply assumed for the sake of argument. We see what follows from it, given the other premises. Whatever follows from it—say *q*—is then made *on that supposition*, i.e., follows *provided the supposition is true*. The concluding step of the argument simply states this: *q* is true, provided *p* is, or, if *p*, then *q*. The rule of Conditional Proof can then be described as follows:

Conditional Proof (CP)
To prove a conditional statement, suppose the antecedent as a statement on a separate line, with justification Supp/CP. If from this supposition, together with other premises, you can derive the consequent, then infer the conditional, discharging the supposition.
In symbols:
   From a derivation of *q* from the supposition of *p*, infer *p* → *q*.

This is how we set the above argument out as a proof:

(1) P ∨ W   Prem
 |(2) ¬P   Supp/CP
 |(3) W   1, 2 DS
(4) ¬P → W   2-3 CP

There are some important things to note here.

- We have a new kind of justification in line 2: we are *supposing P to begin a conditional proof*, and we denote this by "Supp/CP."

- All the lines that are derived using that supposition are *indented* or "pushed in," with a vertical bar to the left, to show that they only follow on that supposition.

- Line 4, however, does not depend on the supposition; instead, it summarizes what has gone on in lines 2-3: (given the premise P ∨ W) then, supposing ¬P, W. Otherwise put: (given the premise P ∨ W), if P then W. What was supposed is now the antecedent. Since it no longer depends on the supposition, we "pop out" or *outdent* (if that's the opposite of "indent").

- Note the justification for line 4: since it summarizes the derivation *beginning in line 2* and *ending in line 3*, it is written 2-3 CP (i.e., lines 2 *through* 3) to indicate this.

- It should be noted when we make a supposition, we are still entitled to use the premises of the argument—or anything derived from them. On the other hand,

- once we have discharged the supposition—in the proof above, with the step of conditional proof—we cannot thereafter use any premises that still depend on the supposition. Thus we could NOT continue the above proof by inferring W from lines (4) and (2) as follows:

(1) P ∨ W   Prem
  |(2) ¬P   Supp/CP
  |(3) W   1, 2 DS
(4) ¬P → W   2-3 CP
(5) W   2, 4 MP   *—INVALID!!*

since line (2) is something we have supposed, not something we are given. We can summarize these last two observations in the following rule:

Constraints on Use of the Supposition Rule

A supposition may be made at any point in a proof. After the supposition is made, any premises or statements derived from the premises may be used in applying further rules of inference. But once a supposition has been discharged, neither it nor lines depending on it may be used in the remainder of the proof. Thus

At any line in a proof, rules of inference may be applied to whole statements in any previous lines, provided they have the *same indentation*, or *an indentation to the left*.

At any line in a proof, rules of inference may **not** be applied to whole statements in any previous lines that have an *indentation to the right* of that line.

A proof is not complete until all suppositions have been discharged—that is, the last line of the proof (containing the conclusion) must have *the same indentation*, or *an indentation to the left* of the indentation of the first.

Here's another example of a proof with the conditional proof strategy, Supp followed by CP:

$P \rightarrow (Q \rightarrow R) \therefore (P \& Q) \rightarrow R$

(1) $P \rightarrow (Q \rightarrow R)$	Prem	
(2) $P \& Q$	Supp/CP	*—push in (supposition made)*
(3) P	2 Simp	
(4) $Q \rightarrow R$	1, 3 MP	
(5) Q	2 Simp	
(6) R	4, 5 MP	
(7) $(P \& Q) \rightarrow R$	2-6 CP	*—pop out (supposition discharged)*[4]

The justification of the formal validity of CP can be achieved as follows. Granted we have the supposition p and a valid derivation of q from p and other premises $\{r, s, \dots\}$, then q cannot be false if p is true, given the other premises $\{r, s, \dots\}$. But this is the definition of the truth-functional conditional (see chapter 3): a statement of the form $p \rightarrow q$ is one such that q cannot be false if p is true. It follows that from p and a valid derivation of q from p and other premises $\{r, s, \dots\}$, $p \rightarrow q$ follows, given the other premises $\{r, s, \dots\}$.

Finally a point that can hardly be stressed too much: *a successful proof cannot end with the conclusion on an indented line—a statement on an indented line is not proven, but still depends on a supposition.*

7.2.2 THE HYPOTHETICAL SYLLOGISM

Now here's a proof of the validity of an argument whose form itself embodies a common inference pattern:

$A \rightarrow B, B \rightarrow C \therefore A \rightarrow C$

(1) $A \rightarrow B$	Prem	
(2) $B \rightarrow C$	Prem	
(3) A	Supp/CP	*—push in (supposition made)*
(4) B	1, 3 MP	
(5) C	2, 4 MP	
(6) $A \rightarrow C$	3-5 CP	*—pop out (supposition discharged)*

This argument has the valid form: $p \rightarrow q, q \rightarrow r \therefore p \rightarrow r$. The traditional name for this argument form is the Hypothetical Syllogism (or the Chain Rule). Now that we have derived it, we can use it as a rule of inference in any proofs. It runs as follows:

---

[4] I owe the "push in/pop out" terminology to Douglas Hofstadter, *Gödel, Escher, Bach: The Eternal Golden Braid* (New York: Basic Books, 1999).

> **Hypothetical Syllogism (HS)**
>
> From two conditionals, the first of which has as consequent the same statement the second has as antecedent, derive the conditional whose antecedent is the antecedent of the first, and whose consequent is the consequent of the second.
>
> *In symbols:*
>
> From $p \to q$ and $q \to r$ (stated separately), infer $p \to r$.

As an example of its use, let's prove valid the inference we imputed to Cicero in chapter 5:

> If there is a motion WITHOUT a cause, not every PROPOSITION will be true or false. For what will not have EFFECTIVE causes will be neither true nor false, and if there is a motion without a cause, there is something that does not have an effective cause.
>
> *Symbolized:* $\neg E \to \neg P$, $W \to \neg E$ ∴ $W \to \neg P$
>
> (1) $\neg E \to \neg P$ Prem
> (2) $W \to \neg E$ Prem
> (3) $W \to \neg P$ 1, 2 HS

This is a simple substitution instance of the Hypothetical Syllogism, with W for p, $\neg E$ for q, and $\neg P$ for r.

Here's a more complicated example of a conditional proof, involving two suppositions and making use of CP twice:

$(P \& Q) \to R$ ∴ $P \to (Q \to R)$
(1) $(P \& Q) \to R$ Prem
  | (2) P   Supp/CP   —*push in, aim to prove* $Q \to R$
    | (3) Q   Supp/CP   —*push in, aim to prove* R
    | (4) P & Q   2, 3 Conj
    | (5) R   1, 4 MP
  | (6) $Q \to R$ 3-5 CP   —*pop out*
(7) $P \to (Q \to R)$ 2-6 CP   —*final pop out*

It is worth reminding you here of the restriction on the supposition rule that only the lines above that have *the same indentation* or an *indentation to the left* may be used at any given line. For example, on line (6) lines (3) to (5) cannot now be used. You cannot, for example, derive R from lines (3) and (6), as in this faulty proof of $P \to R$ from the same premises:

(1) $(P \& Q) \to R$ Prem
  | (2) P   Supp/CP   —*push in, aim to prove* $Q \to R$
    | (3) Q   Supp/CP   —*push in, aim to prove* R
    | (4) P & Q   2, 3 Conj
    | (5) R   1, 4 MP

(6) Q → R	3-5 CP	—*pop out*
(7) R	3, 6 MP	*INVALID! WRONG!*
(8) P → R	2-7 CP	—*final pop out*

SUMMARY

- The rule of inference **Conditional Proof (CP)** is
  From a derivation of any statement q from the supposition of p, infer $p \rightarrow q$.
- The line on which the supposition is made is justified Supp/CP, and this line and all lines depending on the supposition are indented; the line on which the conditional is derived is undented, because the application of CP discharges the supposition.
- The **validity** of this argument form follows from our definitions of formal validity and of a truth-functional conditional: it is impossible for $p \rightarrow q$ to be false if q cannot be false when p is true.
- The rule of inference **Hypothetical Syllogism (HS)** is
  From $p \rightarrow q$ and $q \rightarrow r$ (stated separately), infer $p \rightarrow r$:
  From two conditionals such that the consequent of the first is identical to the antecedent of the second, infer the conditional with antecedent of the first and consequent of the second.
- The **validity** of this argument form was proved using CP once and MP twice.

EXERCISES 7.2

5. *Prove the logical equivalence* of $p \rightarrow q$ and $\neg q \rightarrow \neg p$ by constructing *proofs of the validity of the following two abstract arguments:*
   (a) P → Q ∴ ¬Q → ¬P
   (b) ¬Q → ¬P ∴ P → Q

Prove the validity of the following abstract arguments:

6. A → B, A → C ∴ A → (B & C)

7. A → ¬B ∴ B → ¬A

8. Q → (P → R) ∴ P → (Q → R)

9. ¬A → B ∴ ¬B → A

10. C → D ∴ (D → E) → (C → E)

11. A ∴ (A → B) → B

12. C → D, D → ¬E ∴ E → ¬C

13. C → D, D → E ∴ ¬E → ¬(C v D)

14. A → B, (C & D) → A ∴ C → (D → B)

Identify the errors in the following proofs.—Here an error is *a mistake in applying a rule of inference*; although any subsequent lines depending on a line derived by an incorrect application of a rule may also not follow, this does not count as a separate mistake. A correct application of a rule of inference must be a *substitution instance* of the rule; and the justification must also be given properly: 1, 3 MT, etc.

15. (1) (D & O) → ¬P   Prem   [to prove P → ¬O]
        (2) P   Supp/CP
        (3) ¬(D & O)   1, 3 MT
        (4) ¬O   3 Simp
    (5) P → ¬O   2-4 CP

16. (1) P → ¬O   Prem   [to prove D & (O → ¬P)]
    (2) D   Prem
        (3) O   Supp/CP
        (4) ¬P   1, 3 MT
    (5) O → ¬P   3, 4 CP
    (6) D & (O → ¬P)   2, 5 Conj

17. (1) (D & O) → ¬P   Prem   [to prove P → ¬O]
        (2) P   Supp/CP
        (3) ¬¬P   2 DN
        (4) ¬(D & O)   1, 3 MT
        (5) D v ¬O   4 DM
        (6) ¬O   5 Disj
    (7) P → ¬O   2-6 CP

18. (a) *What fallacy is committed* in the following faulty proof?
    (1) P → O   Prem   [to prove ¬P → (D & ¬O)]
    (2) D   Prem
        (3) ¬P   Supp/CP
        (4) ¬O   1, 3 MT
        (5) D & ¬O   2, 4 Conj
    (6) ¬P → (D & ¬O)   3-5 CP

(b) *Is it possible to prove this inference valid?* Give a reason for your answer.

19. A spokesman for the lobster fishermen of Nova Scotia, objecting to the court's decision to uphold the treaty rights of the Mi'kmaq native people, quoted on CBC radio, September 23, 1999: "As long as status INDIANS are out there fishing there are going to be NON-status Indians fishing too; and as long as there are non-status Indians there are going to be WHITES out there fishing. And if all these people are fishing the lobster conservation programme is in JEOPARDY." His implicit conclusion: [Therefore if status Indians are allowed to fish lobster out of season, the entire conservation program is in jeopardy.]
    (a) *Symbolize* and (b) *prove the validity* of this argument.

20. Summarizing Spinoza's opinion, Frederick Copleston writes: "If God were DISTINCT from Nature and if there were substances OTHER than God, God would not be INFINITE. Conversely, if God is infinite, there cannot be other substances."—*A History of Philosophy*, vol. IV, 217
    (a) *Symbolize both statements*, and *prove that the first follows from the second.*
    (b) *Prove that the second follows from the first if one grants the extra premise* that <God is distinct from Nature>.

21. (**CHALLENGE**) *Prove that* Q *follows from the premise* P & ¬P.
    Q, of course, could be anything; and the premise is self-contradictory. So (if you can do it) you will have proved that *from a contradiction, anything follows.*

7.3 SUPPOSITION IN NATURAL ARGUMENT

Suppositional arguments are quite common in natural reasoning. We make suppositions in an argument for a variety of reasons, but they boil down to essentially two:

(1) we suppose something *for the sake of example*, that is, for the sake of giving specific content to some general principle or observation or method.

or

(2) we suppose something *for the sake of argument*, that is, in order to show what follows from this particular premise if one adopted it.

Here is an example of each:

Suppose that a college dormitory has 200 students. Those who watch an hour or more of television on any given day always watch for less than an hour the next day. One fourth of those who watch television for less than an hour one day will watch an hour or more the next day. Half of the students watched television for an hour or more today. Therefore 25 students will watch television for an hour or more tomorrow.[5]

Clearly the conclusion still depends on the supposition: if there were 80 students in the dorm, say, then (retaining all the other premises) we would conclude that 10 students will watch television for an hour or more tomorrow. The supposition gives us a definite number to work with; we are supposing that the dorm has 200 students for the sake of being able to do a specific calculation. Compare this with the following argument:

> Suppose that the wall had been left in place after the final renovation. The obstruction would have made it impossible for the spectator's eye to see through the house and outside. This would cause the axis of the structure to be nearly completely undetectable to those within, which in turn would lead to an oppressive feeling of claustrophobia.[6]

Here the consequence deduced in the conclusion is not a desired feature of architectural design. But, it is being argued, this is what would follow if we had left the wall in place. So this is an argument justifying not having left the wall in place. The supposition is made not to assert that the wall should have been left in place, but in order to assert that it should not. The supposition was made for the sake of argument, in order to be subsequently refuted.

How then should we treat such arguments? The supposition is not being asserted as true; so the argument will not be unsound if it should turn out that the supposition is false. Nevertheless, everything that is concluded from it is concluded *only on that supposition*, or, *under that hypothesis*. So every conclusion that depends upon it is also unasserted. In marking up an argument, we shall denote all such unasserted statements with a superscript prefix 'u' for "unasserted," ^{u}thus. All statements so designated in an argument will be analogous to the indented lines in a Conditional Proof. In addition, we shall treat the word "Suppose...," or equivalent expressions such as "supposing that...," "Let us assume for the sake of argument that...," etc., as *supposition indicators*. Otherwise we shall proceed as normal, numbering the other statements, indicating <premises>, conclusions, etc.

In constructing a diagram of the inference structure, we shall flag the original supposition or suppositions with the prefix (Supp), to show they are not given premises. All subsequent statements depending on the supposition will be designated with a superscript prefix before the line number, thus: $^u(3)$.

The two examples above will then come out as follows:

(Suppose that) $^u(1)$ <a college dormitory has 200 students>. (2) <Those who watch an hour or more of television on any given day always watch for less than an hour the

---

[5] *Elementary Linear Algebra*, Roland E. Larson and Bruce H. Edwards (Boston: Houghton Mifflin, 1999), p. 102.

[6] *Architectural Digest*, May 1989, p. 71.

next day.> (3) <One fourth of those who watch television for less than an hour one day will watch an hour or more the next day.> (4) <Half of the students watched television for an hour or more today.> Therefore ᵘ(5) 25 students will watch television for an hour or more tomorrow.

Diagram:

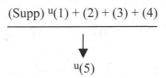

(Supp) ᵘ(1) + (2) + (3) + (4)

↓

ᵘ(5)

(Suppose that) ᵘ(1) <the wall had been left in place after the final renovation>. ᵘ(2) <The obstruction would have made it impossible for the spectator's eye to see through the house and outside.> ᵘ(3) This would cause <the axis of the structure [to be] nearly completely undetectable to those within>, ᵘ(4) which (in turn) would lead to an oppressive feeling of claustrophobia.

Diagram:

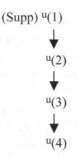

(Supp) ᵘ(1)

↓

ᵘ(2)

↓

ᵘ(3)

↓

ᵘ(4)

Here clearly we could supply extra premises that could be regarded as implicit, such as (1a) <if the wall had been left in place, it would have obstructed the spectator's line of sight to the outside of the house>, (2a) <if the spectator's line of sight to the outside were obstructed, the axis of the structure would be nearly completely undetectable>, and (3a) <if the axis of the structure were undetectable, this would lead to an oppressive feeling of claustrophobia>. These have the effect of making every inference valid, and leaving the spotlight on the truth or falsity of these added premises. For to doubt the inference from (2) to (3) is simply to doubt the truth of (2a), and so with the other inferences. So adding these premises does not alter the soundness of the argument.

A better candidate for an element of the argument left implicit might be a final inference which we are left to make for ourselves, namely to the conditional if (1), then (4) by Conditional Proof: if the wall had been left in place after the final renovation, this would lead to an oppressive feeling of claustrophobia. We diagram this as follows:

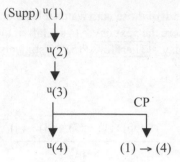

$$(\text{Supp}) \ ^u(1)$$
$$\downarrow$$
$$^u(2)$$
$$\downarrow$$
$$^u(3)$$

$$\text{CP}$$

$$^u(4) \qquad (1) \rightarrow (4)$$

Here the extra "leg" of the diagram represents the inference from the reasoning from the supposition (1) to (4), explicitly summarizing it as a conditional. This is simply a different representation of the same thing we already saw in formal proofs: from the derivation of (4) on the supposition of (1) we infer (1) → (4).

Now let us compare that with the first argument above, about the college dorm. We could interpret this also as a conditional proof: that, given premises (2), (3), and (4), then (1) → (5): "if a college dormitory has 200 students, then 25 students will watch television for an hour or more tomorrow." But it doesn't seem very natural to end there. The number 200 was chosen for the sake of definiteness; any other multiple of 8 would have worked just as well. In fact, we would expect a conclusion generalizing from such specific individual numbers to some *variable*: say that "if a college dormitory has $8n$ students, then n students will watch television for an hour or more tomorrow (where n is a positive integer)." Provided the number 200 was suitably arbitrary with respect to the other premises, a generalization like this will be acceptable. We shall return to such reasoning in looking at Universal Generalization in Predicate Logic below.

Finally, concerning the wall argument, we note that we could have added one final element that is more or less implicit: "Since an oppressive feeling of claustrophobia is undesirable, it is better that the wall not be left in place in the final renovation." This consists in another premise, (4a) <an oppressive feeling of claustrophobia is undesirable>, and a new final conclusion, (4b) <u>it is better that the wall not be left in place in the final renovation.</u> Clearly (4b) follows from (4) together with (4a). But in chapter 10 we will outline a more natural way of dealing with arguments designed to refute their starting supposition: the *reductio ad absurdum*.

EXERCISES 7.3

Instructions for numbers 22-25: (i) *mark up the argument:* bracket the (supposition indicators), box any |inference indicators|, set the premises in <triangular brackets>, underline the <u>conclusions</u>, and double-underline the <u>main conclusion</u>; (ii) *identify unasserted statements with a prefix superscript* u, *and* (iii) *diagram the inference structure, supplying the conditional proof step where it has been left implicit.*

22. Just for the sake of argument, suppose (1) David Duke is elected President of the United States. Then (2) our great country would fall fifty years back in her quest for equality for all her people.—*Boston Herald*, March 14, 1992, p. 34

23. (1) Suppose that only good researchers can be effective college teachers. In that case it follows that (2) a faculty member will be an effective teacher *only if* he or she is a good teacher. (3) From this it follows that if a faculty member is an effective teacher, then he or she must be a good researcher. (4) Therefore every effective college teacher must be a good researcher. (5) So, if only good researchers can be effective college teachers then every effective college teacher must be a good researcher. (6) Therefore we could ensure that the university will excel in research by basing tenure decisions solely on teaching effectiveness.—Stephen Thomas, *Practical Reasoning in Natural Language* (2nd ed.)

24. (1) Suppose the government imposes a tax of $1 per paperback novel. (2) Buyers perceive no change in their willingness to purchase, so (3) they view their demand for paperback books as being stable. However, (4) publishers view demand as having decreased because (5) the after-tax prices they receive are reduced by $1 for each novel sold. Therefore, (6) an increase in taxes causes a decrease in demand.—Ralph T. Byers and Gerald W. Stone, eds., *Macroeconomics* (London: Scott, Foresman and Co., 1989), p. 50

25. Suppose, (1) at full throttle, the escaping CO_2 gas exerts a constant force of 100 N on the wagon. (2) A constant frictional force which opposes the motion is 50 N. The masses relevant to the problem are: (3) the mass of the wagon [is] 30 kg., and (4) the mass of the driver [is] 70 kg. Since (5) the net force is equal to the product of mass times acceleration, and (6) velocity is equal to the product of acceleration and time, (7) the time it takes the wagon to go from rest to a speed of 5 m/s at full throttle is 10 s.—Robert Prigo, Physics class handout, Middlebury College, 1992

26. (**CHALLENGE**) Richard Dawkins describes a model of an evolutionary strategy as follows:

Another kind of war game that Maynard Smith has considered is the 'war of attrition.' This can be thought of as arising in a species that never engages in dangerous combat, perhaps a well-armoured species in which injury is very unlikely. All disputes in this species are settled by conventional posturing. A contest always ends in one rival or the other backing down. To win, all you have to do is stand your ground and glare at the opponent until he finally turns tail. Obviously no animal can afford to expend infinite time threatening; there are important things to be done elsewhere. The resource he is competing for may be valuable, but it is not infinitely valuable. It is only worth so much time and, as at an auction sale, each individual is prepared to spend only so much on it. Time is the currency of the two-bidder auction.

Dawkins then proposes the argument:

Suppose (1) all such individuals worked out in advance exactly how much time they thought a particular kind of resource, say a female, was worth. (2) A mutant individual who was prepared to go on just a little bit longer would always win. (3) So the strategy of maintaining a fixed bidding limit is unstable.[7]

Supplying any premises you take to be implicit, i.e., necessary for the validity of an inference and likely to be regarded as too obvious to be worth stating, *mark up and diagram the argument as above.*

27. (**CHALLENGE**) In 1705 at the age of 30 Samuel Clarke published his *A Demonstration of the Being and Attributes of God,* which included the following argument:

Since the persons I am discoursing to cannot but own that the supposition of the being of God is in itself most desirable and for the benefit of the world that it should be true, they must of necessity grant further that, supposing the being and attributes of God to be things not indeed demonstrable to be true but only possible and such as cannot be demonstrated to be false, as most certainly they cannot; and, much more, supposing them once made to appear probable and but more likely to be true than the contrary opinion; nothing is more evident, even upon these suppositions only, than that men ought in all reason to live piously and virtuously in the world and that vice and immorality are, upon all accounts and under all hypotheses, the most absurd and inexcusable things in nature.[8]

Re-expressed in modern English, with inessential elements pared away:

Since (1) the persons I am discoursing with cannot help admitting that to suppose God exists is most desirable and beneficial for the world, [they must of necessity grant further that], supposing (2) the being and attributes of God are things not indeed demonstrable to be true but only possible and such as cannot be demonstrated to be false; and moreover, supposing (3) that once they are made to appear probable and only more likely to be true than the contrary opinion; then nothing is more evident, even upon these suppositions only, than that (4) men ought in all reason to live piously and virtuously in the world and that vice and immorality are, upon all accounts and under all hypotheses, the most absurd and inexcusable things in nature.

Supplying any premises you take to be implicit, i.e., necessary for the validity of an inference and likely to be regarded as too obvious to be worth stating, *mark up and diagram the argument as above.*

---

[7] Richard Dawkins, *The Selfish Gene* (Oxford: Oxford UP, 1989), pp. 75-76.

[8] Samuel Clarke, *A Demonstration of the Being and Attributes of God,* ed. Ezio Vailati (Cambridge: Cambridge UP, 1998), pp. 6-7.

Chapter Eight

Biconditionals

8.1 NECESSARY AND SUFFICIENT CONDITIONS

8.1.1 'ONLY IF'

Consider the statement:

(1) Your insurance company will PAY up for CDs stolen from your car *only if* you LOCKED the car door.

Which of the following two statements is this equivalent to?

(2) Your insurance company will PAY up for CDs stolen from your car *if* you LOCKED the car door.   *Symbolized:* L → P

(3) *If* your insurance company PAYS up for CDs stolen from your car, you must have LOCKED the car door.   *Symbolized:* P → L

This question is probably causing you some puzzlement. So far we have assumed that the statement following the 'if' is the antecedent, which means that (1) should be symbolized by L → P. But that symbolizes statement (2), which doesn't seem to say the same thing. One could imagine someone having locked the car door, but left the window open, or forgetting to submit a claim; in which case, even if (1) is true, (2) does not follow.

One way to sort this out is to see what else these statements are equivalent to. Intuitively, (1) seems equivalent to:

(4) Your insurance company will not PAY up for CDs stolen from your car if you did not LOCK the car door.   *Symbolized:* ¬L → ¬P

Now suppose you locked the car door. It does not follow that your insurance company will pay up—that would be denying the antecedent! But suppose the company pays up. Assuming (4) is true, we can then infer that you must have locked the car door (by Modus Tollens and a couple of Double Negations). But that's exactly what statement (3) says! So we have (1) is equivalent to (4), and (4) is equivalent to (3). Therefore (1) is equivalent to (3). What we have proved is that "P only if L" is symbolized as P → L. This contrasts with "P if L" which would be the same as "If L then P," and thus would get symbolized L → P. So, in general, whereas

p **if** q	is equivalent to **if** q **then** p and is symbolized as	$q \rightarrow p$
p **only if** q	is equivalent to **if** p **then** q and is symbolized as	$p \rightarrow q$

Putting the all-important little word 'only' in front of an 'if' switches antecedent to consequent, and vice versa.

Here's an example involving the little word 'only.' Recently Spanish researchers claimed to have found evidence for a black hole circulating around another star in the constellation Scorpius. They found an abundance of the elements oxygen, magnesium, silicon, and sulphur in the spectrum of the visible star. "The only way you can produce an abundance of these elements is through several billions of degrees," said Rafael Rebolo, co-author of the study and researcher at the Institute of Astrophysics in the Canary Islands. "The only way to reach these temperatures is when a star goes to a supernova situation." If we use the key

> A := an ABUNDANCE of the elements oxygen, magnesium, silicon, and sulphur has been produced. T:= the TEMPERATURE must have been several billion degrees. S := the invisible star went SUPERNOVA.

we can re-express Rebolo's two statements as A only if T, and T only if S; symbolized A → T and T → S. (The complete argument is given as exercise 3 for this chapter.)

> *One final note of caution: do not confuse "**only if**" with "**if only**."*

The following line from a classic pop song:

> (5) I'll be home for CHRISTMAS, if only in my DREAMS.—Kim Gannon and Walter Kent

would NOT be symbolized C → D. In fact, this is not even a conditional statement.

8.1.2 NECESSARY AND SUFFICIENT CONDITIONS

Another way of expressing statement (1) is in terms of necessary conditions:

(1) Your insurance company will PAY up for CDs stolen from your car *only if* you LOCKED the car door.

could be re-expressed as

(6) That you LOCKED your car door is a *necessary condition* for your insurance company to PAY up for CDs stolen from your car.

That is, "P only if L" is equivalent to "L is a necessary condition for P." This tells us that **necessary conditions are consequents**.

The conditions we have been used to—those expressed in the *if*-clause—are antecedents. We call these *sufficient conditions*, since it is sufficient for the antecedent to be true in order for the consequent to follow. Here's an example:

(7) The fact that our existence has duration is sufficient to demonstrate the existence of God.—Descartes, *Principles of Philosophy*, I, 21

Re-expressed:

(8) If our existence has DURATION, the existence of GOD can be demonstrated.
Symbolized: D → G

Thus **sufficient conditions are antecedents**.

SUMMARY

- *p* if *q* is equivalent to **if *q* then *p*** and is symbolized as *q* → *p*.
  —in this case, *q* is said to be a **sufficient condition** for *p*.
- *p* only if *q* is equivalent to **if *p* then *q*** and is symbolized as *p* → *q*.
  —in this case, *q* is said to be a **necessary condition** for *p*.

EXERCISES 8.1

1. *Symbolize the following statements using the first letter of each capitalized word for the components:*
    (a) A faculty member will be an effective TEACHER only if he or she is a good RESEARCHER.—Stephen Thomas, *Practical Reasoning in Natural Language*

(b) Only if the statesmen have behind them the will to peace of a decisive MAJOR-ITY in their own countries can they ATTAIN their great end.—Albert Einstein, *Ideas and Opinions*

(c) This drug is LEGAL in the United States only when the user is STRADDLING a state line.—Steve Martin, *Pure Drivel*

(d) The SETTLEMENT of the West could only take place if the Indian barrier were REMOVED—Winston Churchill, *A History of The English-Speaking Peoples*, vol. 4, 1958

(e) Having taken INTRODUCTORY logic is a necessary condition for ENROLL-ING in the Intermediate Logic course in Philosophy.

(f) A thing is TRUE only if it can be PROVED.—Umberto Eco, *Foucault's Pendulum*, p. 206

(g) The fact that our existence has DURATION is sufficient to demonstrate the EXIS-TENCE of God.—René Descartes, *Principles of Philosophy* [D := our existence has DURATION, E := we can demonstrate the EXISTENCE of God]

(h) It is only when the intellect decides PREMATURELY . . . that it FALLS prey to error and uncertainty.—Ernst Cassirer, *The Philosophy of the Enlightenment*

(i) Should the Dolphins WIN their division and DEFEAT the Western Champion, the American Conference title game will be held in MIAMI Jan. 2 only if the RUNNER-UP team beats Cleveland.—Sports pages

(j) The only way the BILLS and the CHARGERS can get to the playoffs is if JACK-SONVILLE loses.—TV sportscaster

(k) The mere presence of a SUBSTANCE is not sufficient for PERCEPTION.—Leibniz, 3rd paper to Clarke, 11 [S := A SUBSTANCE is merely present, P := there is PERCEPTION]

(l) Only if we succeed in ABOLISHING military service altogether will it be pos-sible to EDUCATE the youth in a spirit of reconciliation, joy in life, and love toward all living creatures.—Albert Einstein, *Ideas and Opinions*

2. *Which of the following statements is naturally construed as a conditional statement? (no need to symbolize):*

(a) Often a hen who has merely laid an egg cackles as if she had laid an asteroid.—Mark Twain

(b) The sick do not ask if the hand that smoothes their pillow is pure . . .—Oscar Wilde

(c) Should Senator Ervin run again, he would be a formidable opponent.—Newspaper

(d) I never encountered any proposition so doubtful that I could not draw from it some quite certain conclusion, if only the conclusion that it contained nothing certain.—René Descartes, *Philosophical Writings* I, 125

(e) And if Hitler can identify that point in the hollow center of the earth, which is also the exact center of the sky, he will be Master of the World, whose king he is by right of race.—Umberto Eco, *Foucault's Pendulum*, p. 514

3. In 1999 Spanish researchers claimed to have found evidence for a black hole circulating around another star in the constellation Scorpius. They found an abundance of the
elements oxygen, magnesium, silicon, and sulfur in the spectrum of the visible star.
"The only way you can produce an abundance of these elements is through several
billions of degrees," said Rafael Rebolo, co-author of the study and researcher at the
Institute of Astrophysics in the Canary Islands. "The only way to reach these temperatures is when a star goes to a supernova situation." The argument is completed
by noting that the invisible star has a mass of about 40 times the mass of our sun, and
if a star had this mass and went supernova, then (according to current theory) a black
hole would result.—*Boston Globe,* Thursday, September 9, 1999
Using the following key, (a) *symbolize the argument* and (b) *prove its validity:*
   Key: A := an ABUNDANCE of the elements oxygen, magnesium, silicon, and
   sulphur has been produced; T:= the TEMPERATURE was several billion degrees.
   S := the invisible STAR went supernova; M := the invisible star has a MASS of
   about 40 times the mass of our sun; B := the invisible star is a BLACK HOLE.

8.2 BICONDITIONALS

8.2.1 SYMBOLIZING

Although rather rare in colloquial speech, biconditionals are beloved by logicians because
of their use in definitions. They are conditionals which "go both ways": if p then q, and if
q then p. This is more commonly expressed as "p if and only if q." (Remember, "if p then
q" is equivalent to "p only if q"; and "if q then p" is equivalent to "p if q.") Where they
come into their own is in any context where we are trying to be very precise about what
we mean, particularly in giving definitions. Here is an example from "possible world
semantics," a branch of logic where possibility and necessity are construed in terms of
being true in possible worlds:

   (1) *Necessarily A is true in world x if and only if A is true in all worlds.*[1]

Denoting "*Necessarily A is true in world x*" by N and "*A is true in all worlds*" by A, this
could be symbolized as $(N \rightarrow A) \,\&\, (A \rightarrow N)$. But it proves convenient to have a shorthand for "if and only if," and for this we introduce our fifth statement operator, $\leftrightarrow$ by the
following definition:

$p \leftrightarrow q =_{\text{def}} (p \rightarrow q) \,\&\, (q \rightarrow p)$

---

[1] Quoted from Bas van Fraassen, *Laws and Symmetry* (Oxford: Clarendon P, 1989), p. 69.

Here the symbol =**def** stands for "is by definition equivalent to." This is a *stipulative definition*, so-called because we have simply stipulated how the double arrow is to be understood, rather than, say, clarifying the meaning of something previously understood. Thus statement (1) above gets symbolized as N ↔ A.

At this point it will be useful to introduce a new term, the *converse* of a conditional. This is what we get from swapping its antecedent with its consequent:

> The statement formed by exchanging the antecedent and consequent of a conditional is its **converse**. *In symbol*s, the **converse** of $p \to q$ is $q \to p$.

With this terminology, the above definition says that a biconditional is equivalent to the conjunction of a conditional and its converse. There are some synonymous expressions for "*p* if and only if *q*." The philosopher Bas van Fraassen prefers the expression "exactly if," as in

(2) World *y* is *physically POSSIBLE* relative to world *x* exactly if the LAWS of *x* are all true in y.
Symbolized: P ↔ L.

Logicians abbreviate the expression "if and only if" by the made-up word "iff"; this is fine in written form, but confusing aurally, since it sounds the same as plain 'if.' The briefest synonymous expression I know of in English is "just in case," which has only three syllables to the four of "exactly if."

Another equivalent form is implicit in the example below:

(3) CHINA will sign the ban on nuclear weapons testing, but only if the US signs first.

This appears to be a conjunction of C and C only if U. But that would entail U (by Modus Ponens). So that cannot be the meaning. Further reflection shows that it must mean that China will sign if and only if the US does so first: C ↔ U.

8.2.2 CONVERSATIONAL IMPLICATURE (ADVANCED LEVEL MATERIAL)

The above example raises the question: can't "only if" statements always be regarded as disguised biconditionals? If a mother promises her son, for instance, that he will be allowed to watch television only if he finishes his homework, and then refuses to let him watch after he has finished on the grounds that she had said "only if," he would be rightly indignant. This is an example of what has been called, following the pioneering work of H.P. Grice, "conversational implicature." In the context of a conversation, our statements commit us to more than what those statements imply in a narrow logical sense, i.e., if they are literally interpreted. This is illustrated by the following fictional dialogue between Mr. Barnard and a certain Ms. C. who storms into his office with her clothes on fire:

She: Is there a fire extinguisher near here?
He: Yes, there is.
She: Well, could you tell me where it is?
He: Yes, I most certainly could!
She: DO it!!
He: There's a fire extinguisher on the eighth floor, next to the staircase.

Suppose Ms. C. now discovers (i) that the extinguisher on the eighth floor is out of order, (ii) that there is one much closer, near the staircase on the same floor, and (iii) that Mr. B. knew both these facts very well, having participated in a fire drill that very morning. We can safely infer that Ms. C. (if she has not been burnt to a crisp in the meantime) will be more than "rightly indignant" at Mr. B. Yet he has not answered any of her questions untruthfully—just in such a way as to undermine the normal pragmatic assumptions implicit in such an exchange: for instance, that the fire extinguisher she is interested in is the nearest one, that it is in working order, and so forth. Such assumptions are said to be *conversational implicatures* of Mr. B.'s statement (and indeed of Ms. C.'s questions, which Mr. B. has infuriatingly answered without taking them into account).

For our purposes here, we shall certainly have to be alive to conversational implicatures *in evaluating natural arguments*. This means that if they are relevant to the soundness of an inference, we will have to treat them as implicit premises that need to be made explicit. As is the case with all implicit premises, however, we only need to make them explicit if they are relevant to the soundness of an inference. Otherwise, if we are *symbolizing a statement taken out of context*, we will, wherever possible, symbolize the statement literally, without guessing at what the speaker intended to say. For instance, the statement

(4) I can MAKE it to my appointment if I RUSH.

will be interpreted as a simple conditional, $R \rightarrow M$, even though the speaker probably intended it to be understood as a biconditional, $R \leftrightarrow M$. Likewise "only if" statements will be interpreted as simple conditionals unless, as in example (3) above, that proves impossible. Statements like (3), i.e., ones having the form "*p*, but only if *q*," have to be interpreted as biconditionals, $p \leftrightarrow q$.

8.2.3 RULES OF INFERENCE

Now there is a sense in which $\leftrightarrow$ is not really a new operator, $p \leftrightarrow q$ being merely an abbreviation for a conjunction of two conditionals. Still, if a biconditional occurs in an argument, we need to have rules of inference that allow us to derive statements from it, and to derive it from other propositions. The following rule is simply a conversion of the above definition:

> **Biconditional Equivalence** (BE)
> From a biconditional statement, infer the conjunction of the
> corresponding conditional and its converse, and vice versa.
> *In symbols:*
> From $p \leftrightarrow q$ infer $(p \rightarrow q)$ & $(q \rightarrow p)$, and vice versa.

Here's an example of its use in a proof of $A \rightarrow \neg B, \neg B \leftrightarrow C, C \rightarrow A \therefore A \leftrightarrow C$

(1) $A \rightarrow \neg B$	Prem	
(2) $\neg B \leftrightarrow C$	Prem	
(3) $C \rightarrow A$	Prem	
(4) $(\neg B \rightarrow C)$ & $(C \rightarrow \neg B)$	2 BE	
(5) $\neg B \rightarrow C$	4 Simp	
(6) $A \rightarrow C$	1, 5 HS	—*N.B. this use of HS*
(7) $(A \rightarrow C)$ & $(C \rightarrow A)$	6, 3 Conj	
(8) $A \leftrightarrow C$	7 BE	

Here's a more complicated example, making use of CP too:

$F \rightarrow G, (\neg F \& H) \rightarrow \neg G, H \therefore F \leftrightarrow G$

(1) $F \rightarrow G$	Prem	
(2) $(\neg F \& H) \rightarrow \neg G$	Prem	
(3) H	Prem	
(4) G	Supp/CP	—*to prove $G \rightarrow F$, suppose G...*
(5) $\neg\neg G$	4 DN	
(6) $\neg(\neg F \& H)$	2, 5 MT	
(7) $\neg\neg F$	3, 6 CS	
(8) F	7 DN	... *and derive F*
(9) $G \rightarrow F$	4-8 CP	—*pop out*
(10) $(F \rightarrow G)$ & $(G \rightarrow F)$	1, 9 Conj	
(11) $F \leftrightarrow G$	10 BE	

SUMMARY
- The biconditional $p \leftrightarrow q$ is defined as $p \leftrightarrow q =$**def** $(p \rightarrow q)$ & $(q \rightarrow p)$.
- The **converse** of the conditional statement $p \rightarrow q$ is $q \rightarrow p$.
- The rule of inference **biconditional equivalence (BE)** is
  From $p \leftrightarrow q$ infer
  $(p \rightarrow q)$ & $(q \rightarrow p)$, and vice versa:
  From a biconditional statement, infer the conjunction of the corresponding conditional and its converse, and vice versa.

EXERCISES 8.2

4. *Symbolize the following statements using the first letter of each capitalized word for the components:*

(a) We can emphasize these APPLIED areas most effectively if, and only if, we emphasize also the FUNDAMENTAL areas of research.—College memo

(b) North Vietnam will MEET with US negotiator Henry Kissinger Monday but only if the US will AGREE to sign the peace agreement Tuesday on schedule.—Newspaper article

(c) If and only if it [a motion on racial research] is approved by a MAJORITY of the AAA membership will it become an OFFICIAL position of the American Anthropological Association.—Bulletin

(d) [C]ertain premises IMPLY *A* exactly if *A* is TRUE in every possible world in which those premises are true.—Bas van Fraassen, *Laws and Symmetry*, 54

(e) A transferable utility game has a NON-EMPTY core if and only if it is BALANCED.—P. Jean-Jacques Herings and Arkadi Predtetchinski, "A Necessary and Sufficient Condition for Non-emptiness of the Core of a Non-transferable Utility Game"

(f) The assistantship will be offered to McGRAW if and only if she does not get a tuition WAIVER; and it will be offered to SPIEGELMAN if not offered to McGraw.—Department Minutes

(g) A CONJUNCTION is true iff BOTH conjuncts are true.—Logician Howard Pospesel

(h) The Internal Revenue Service is not REQUIRED to make available to the public, except upon WRITTEN request, written determinations that relate solely to approval of any adoption of or change in a taxpayer's method of accounting under IRC §446(e).—Internal revenue manual

(i) A is a necessary condition for B just in case B is a sufficient condition for A.—Online Encyclopedia Nationmaster.com

5. *Render each formula* (a)-(c) *into a statement in colloquial English* using the dictionary provided, translating "if not" as "unless," and adopting the clearest word ordering:

D := We will all DIE eventually; C := A CURE for aging is found; A := An ACCIDENT befalls us.

(a) $\neg C \rightarrow D$

(b) $C \rightarrow (D \leftrightarrow A)$

(c) $D \leftrightarrow \neg C$

Prove the validity of the following abstract arguments:

6. $S \leftrightarrow U, \neg S \therefore N \vee \neg U$

7. $E \leftrightarrow F \therefore F \leftrightarrow E$ ·

8. $\neg J \rightarrow (K \& L), K \rightarrow \neg J \therefore \neg J \leftrightarrow K$

9. $F \rightarrow G, G \rightarrow (F \vee \neg H), H \therefore F \leftrightarrow G$

10. $\neg B \vee A, \neg B \rightarrow \neg A \therefore A \leftrightarrow B$

11. $Q \rightarrow P, \neg(Q \& R) \rightarrow \neg P \therefore P \leftrightarrow Q$

12. **(CHALLENGE)** $\neg(P \leftrightarrow Q) \therefore \neg(Q \leftrightarrow P)$

13. **(CHALLENGE)** $\neg[\neg(R \rightarrow A) \vee \neg(A \rightarrow R)] \therefore R \leftrightarrow A$

14. An editorial in the *Huntington Herald-Dispatch* argued: "Since the First Amendment to the Constitution forbids government from restraining the publication of news, it clearly follows that the government is equally powerless to compel the publication of news or opinion."—*Miami News*, September 1973
Supplying the implicit premise <The First Amendment allows the government to COMPEL the publication of news just in case it allows it to RESTRAIN the publication of news>, *symbolize and prove the validity of this argument.*

15. In chapter 10 we shall be looking at a rule of inference called *reductio ad absurdum*. Logician Howard Pospesel justifies the rule with the following argument:
Argument *x* is VALID if and only if it is…logically IMPOSSIBLE for its premises and the denial of its conclusion all to be true. If a CONTRADICTION can be derived from the premises of *x* and the denial of its conclusion, then it is logically impossible for the premises and the denial of the conclusion all to be true. Therefore, the derivation of a contradiction from the premises of *x* and the denial of its conclusion is a sufficient condition for the validity of *x*.[2]
Symbolize and prove the validity of this argument.

16. In justifying the equivalence of 'P only if L' with 'If P then L' at the beginning of the chapter it was effectively argued that: 'P only if L' is true exactly if 'Not P unless L' is true, and 'Not P unless L' is true if and only if 'If P then L' is true.
Symbolizing 'P only if L' by O, 'Not P unless L' by U, and 'If P then L' by I, *prove that it follows that* 'P only if L' *is true just in case* 'If P then L' *is true.*

---

[2] Howard Pospesel, *Introduction to Logic* (first ed., Prentice Hall, 1984), p. 73; slightly truncated.

Chapter Nine

Dilemmas

9.1 DILEMMAS

Sextus Empiricus was a Skeptic. He doubted all kinds of things that people normally accepted as true, including the reality of change, of becoming, and of perishing. He was also a good logician. Here is an argument he reports against the reality of perishing in which his logical acumen is apparent:

> If Socrates died, he died either when he was living, or when he was dead. But he did not die when he was living, since the same person would be both living and dead. And he did not die when he was dead either, since then he would have died twice. Therefore Socrates did not die.—Sextus Empiricus, *Selections*, trans. S.G. Etheridge

This is an example of what logicians call a ***dilemma***. Ordinarily, we use that word to refer to any kind of unwanted predicament, but logicians use this word in a very precise sense:

> A **dilemma** is an argument involving a disjunction, which shows that each of the two disjuncts leads to a certain conclusion—often an undesired or surprising one.

In debating, especially, this way of arguing can be very effective. You can get your opponent to accept that the disjunction is true, so that he must commit himself to one or other of the disjuncts. If you can then show that each of them leads to an undesirable or impossible consequence, your opponent will be "impaled on the horns of a dilemma."

Sextus' dilemma is an extended argument in which the two 'since's' give subsidiary reasons for the second and third premises, "Socrates died when he was LIVING," which we symbolize L, and "Socrates died when he was DEAD," symbolized D. Ignoring the subsidiary reasons for the moment, and putting S for "SOCRATES died," we may symbolize the main inference as follows:

$S \rightarrow (L \lor D), \neg L, \neg D \therefore \neg S$

We can prove this inference's validity as follows:

(1) $S \rightarrow (L \lor D)$	Prem
(2) $\neg L$	Prem
(3) $\neg D$	Prem
(4) $\neg L \ \& \ \neg D$	2, 3 Conj
(5) $\neg (L \lor D)$	4 DM
(6) $\neg S$	1, 5 MT

Sextus' dilemma involved a disjunction, but the disjunction was the consequent of a conditional. More typically, a dilemma will have a disjunction standing alone as one of its premises, and its proponent will argue that each of the disjuncts leads to a certain conclusion. If the conclusion is itself a disjunction, this is known as a *complex constructive dilemma*; if the conclusion is non-disjunctive, it is called a *simple constructive dilemma*:

> A **simple constructive dilemma** is an argument with a disjunctive premise, each of whose disjuncts implies the conclusion. Its form is: $p \lor q, p \rightarrow r, q \rightarrow r \therefore r$.
>
> A **complex constructive dilemma** is an argument with a disjunctive premise, each of whose disjuncts implies a different consequent, and whose conclusion is the disjunction of these consequents. Its form is: $p \lor q, p \rightarrow r, q \rightarrow s \therefore r \lor s$.

Here is an example of each. The first concerns President Nixon's dilemma in the "Watergate" scandal:

> The decision of the Supreme Court in *US versus Nixon* (1974), handed down the first day of the Judiciary Committee's final debate, was critical. If the President DEFIED the order, he would be IMPEACHED. If he OBEYED the order, it was increasingly apparent, he would be impeached on the evidence.[1]

As is so often the case with dilemmas, the conclusion is left implicit: Nixon would be impeached. As also happens sometimes, the initial disjunction is considered too obvious to be worth stating: either Nixon would defy the order or he would obey it. Making these elements explicit, we have the simple constructive dilemma:

---

[1] Victoria Schuck, "Watergate," *The Key Reporter*, Winter 1975-76; quoted from Irving M. Copi and Carl Cohen, *Introduction to Logic* (11th ed., Upper Saddle River, NJ: Prentice Hall, 2001), p. 294.

[D ∨ O], D → I, O → I ∴ [I]

Our example of a complex dilemma is due to Abraham Lincoln, who was particularly adept at formulating dilemmas:

> But the proclamation, as law, either is valid, or is not valid. If it is not valid, it needs no retraction. If it is valid, it cannot be retracted, any more than the dead can be brought back to life.[2]

Symbolizing "the proclamation, as law, is VALID" by V, "the proclamation NEEDS to be retracted" by N, and "the proclamation CAN be retracted" by C, and supplying the implicit conclusion, we get: V ∨ ¬V, ¬V → ¬N, V → ¬C ∴ [¬N ∨ ¬C]

Here is a proof of the validity of the first argument, and thus of any other of the same form: D ∨ O, D → I, O → I ∴ I

(1) D ∨ O		Prem
(2) D → I		Prem
(3) O → I		Prem
	(4) ¬ I	Supp/CP
	(5) ¬D	2, 4 MT
	(6) ¬O	3, 4 MT
	(7) ¬D & ¬O	5, 6 Conj
	(8) ¬(D ∨ O)	7 DM
(9) ¬I → ¬(D ∨ O)		4-8 CP
(10) ¬¬(D ∨ O)		1 DN
(11) ¬¬I		9, 10 MT
(12) I		11 DN

As you can see, this is not a very easy proof. It involves supposing that the conclusion is false, and showing that on this supposition the premise is false, so that given the truth of the premise, the conclusion follows by Modus Tollens. So for convenience we introduce the form of the simple constructive dilemma as a rule of inference:

Dilemma (**DL**)
From a disjunction and two conditionals whose antecedents are the disjuncts, and which have the same consequent, infer their consequent.
In symbols:
From $p ∨ q, p → r$, and $q → r$, stated separately, infer r.

---

[2] Letter to James C. Conkling, 26 August 1863; also taken from Copi and Cohen, p. 288.

Using this, we may prove the validity of both the dilemmas above. The first is a simple substitution instance, with D for p, O for q, and I for r:

$D \vee O, D \rightarrow I, O \rightarrow I \therefore I$

(1) D ∨ O	Prem
(2) D → I	Prem
(3) O → I	Prem
(4) I	1, 2, 3 DL

Note the justification for DL: it involves citing 3 separate lines: (1) the disjunction, (2) (first disjunct → conclusion), (3) (second disjunct → conclusion).

The second proof is more involved. The basic strategy is DL, but before we can apply that we need to get two conditionals which have the conclusion as consequent and the disjuncts as their antecedents: $V \vee \neg V, \neg V \rightarrow \neg N, V \rightarrow \neg C \therefore \neg N \vee \neg C$

(1) V ∨ ¬V	Prem
(2) ¬V → ¬N	Prem
(3) V → ¬C	Prem
(4) V	Supp/CP
(5) ¬C	3, 4 MP
(6) ¬N ∨ ¬C	5 Disj
(7) V → (¬N ∨ ¬C)	4-6 CP
(8) ¬V	Supp/CP
(9) ¬N	8, 2 MP
(10) ¬N ∨ ¬C	9 Disj
(11) ¬V → (¬N ∨ ¬C)	8-10 CP
(12) ¬N ∨ ¬C	1, 7, 11 DL

Two further dilemma argument forms have traditionally been identified, the destructive dilemmas:

> A **simple destructive dilemma** is an argument of the form:
> $p \rightarrow r, p \rightarrow s, \neg r \vee \neg s \therefore \neg p$.
> A **complex destructive dilemma** is an argument of the form:
> $p \rightarrow r, q \rightarrow s, \neg r \vee \neg s \therefore \neg p \vee \neg q$.

You can probably see that just as each constructive dilemma was a kind of disjunctive form of *modus ponens*, each destructive dilemma is a kind of disjunctive form of *modus tollens*. Proofs of their validity are left as exercises [Exercises 1, 2].

SUMMARY

- A **dilemma** is an argument involving a disjunction, which shows that each of the two disjuncts leads to a certain conclusion, usually unwanted or surprising.
- Of the 4 common valid forms of dilemma—**simple** and **complex constructive dilemmas**, and **simple** and **complex destructive dilemmas**—the simple constructive dilemma is chosen as the rule of inference.
- **Dilemma** (DL): From $p \lor q, p \to r,$ and $q \to r$, stated separately, infer r.
  From a disjunction and two conditionals whose antecedents are the disjuncts, and which have the same consequent, infer their consequent.
- All four forms may be proved valid using the rules of inference we already have.

EXERCISES 9.1

1. The argument form $p \to r, p \to s, \neg r \lor \neg s \therefore \neg p$ is called *simple destructive dilemma.* *Prove its validity.*

2. The argument form $p \to r, q \to s, \neg r \lor \neg s \therefore \neg p \lor \neg q$ is called *complex destructive dilemma. Prove its validity.*

3. Another of Abraham Lincoln's dilemmas:
   Circuit Courts are USEFUL, or they are not useful. If useful, no State should be denied them; if not useful, no State should have them. Let them be provided for all, or abolished as to all.[3]
   Symbolizing "All States should have them" by A, and "No State should have them" by N, and reading "Let them be provided for all, or abolished as to all" as $\therefore$ A $\lor$ N, *prove the formal validity of Lincoln's dilemma.*

Prove the formal validity of each of the following abstract arguments:

4. P $\lor \neg$Q, P $\to$ R, $\neg$Q $\to$ S, $\neg$S $\to \neg$R $\therefore$ S

5. V $\lor \neg$V, $\neg$V $\to$ (P $\lor$ Q), V $\to$ Q $\therefore$ P $\lor$ Q

6. (A & B) $\to$ (C $\lor \neg$A), $\neg$C, A $\therefore \neg$B

7. M, (M $\lor$ E) $\to$ S $\therefore$ S

---

[3] Lincoln, Annual Message to Congress, 3 December 1861; again, from Copi and Cohen, p. 291.

8. E ∨ F, F → G, ¬E ∨ G ∴ G

9. T, N → F, T → (N ∨ F) ∴ F

10. ¬(J & ¬K), ¬J → L, ¬L → ¬K ∴ L

11. ¬U, O → G, ¬(O ∨ G) → U ∴ G

12. **(CHALLENGE)** D ↔ E, E ∨ F, F → G, ¬G ∨ D ∴ D

13. **(CHALLENGE)** A ∨ B, A → (C ∨ B), B → ¬A ∴ C ∨ ¬A

14. Lewis Carroll, the author of *Alice in Wonderland*, was a logician (perhaps confirming your fears about logic causing mild insanity!). Not surprising, then, to find arguments such as the dilemma contained in this passage:

    Soon her eye fell on a little glass box that was lying under the table: she opened it, and found a very small cake, on which the words "EAT ME" were beautifully marked in currants. "Well, I'll eat it," said Alice, "and if it makes me larger, I can reach the key; and if it makes me smaller, I can creep under the door; so either way I'll get into the garden, and I don't care which happens!"

    Symbolizing "It will make me LARGER" by L, and "I can reach the KEY" by K, "It will make me SMALLER" by S, "I can CREEP under the door" by C, and "I'll get into the GARDEN" by G, and supplying two implicit conditionals and an implicit disjunction (assume that it will make her either larger or smaller), *prove that Alice will get into the garden.*

15. According to the Buddhist scholar Fedor Shcherbatskoi, the Buddhists claimed it is useless to give a definition of what a thing really is:

    If the thing is KNOWN, they maintain, its definition is USELESS, and if the thing is not known, it is still more useless, because it is impossible.—N. Kandalï (Shcherbatskoi, *Buddhist Logic*, p. 146)

    This can be read as an enthymeme with implicit conclusion and implicit premise (the disjunction). *Supply these implicit elements, symbolize, and prove its validity.*

16. Tim Parks reports a dilemma remarked on by a British social scientist as follows:

    Bateson remarks among other things on the fact that the schizophrenic's apparent state of subjection does not allow him to comment on his mother's contradictory behaviour. She rejects affection, demands affection, then criticizes him for an inhibition she had herself just induced. Ultimately, Bateson claims, the patient is up against the impossible dilemma: "If I am to KEEP my tie to mother, I must SHOW her that I love her; but if I do show her that I love her, then I will LOSE her."—Tim Parks, "Unlocking the Mind's Manacles," *New York Review of Books*, October 7, 1999

Implicit here for the patient are the premises that <I will LOSE my mother precisely if I do not KEEP my tie to her>, as well as the disjunction that <I must either SHOW her that I love her, or not>. What follows from this? *Set out a formal proof.*

17. The problem of evil can be expressed as a dilemma for theism:

    Evil EXISTS. But if this is so, then either God cannot PREVENT evil, or he does not WANT to prevent evil. If God cannot prevent evil, he is not OMNIPOTENT. And if he doesn't want to prevent evil, he is not BENEVOLENT. Therefore either God is not omnipotent or he is not benevolent.

    Symbolize the argument, and prove its validity.

18. The physicist Lee Smolin has argued as follows:

    If the laws of physics exist eternally and independently of the universe, then the reasons for them are beyond our rational comprehension. But if they are created by natural processes acting in time, it becomes possible that we may come to understand why they, and ultimately our world, are as we find them.

    Thus, no less than for any other regularities we observe in the world, the extent to which we bring the laws of physics inside of time is the extent to which we make them amenable to rational understanding.[4]

    This argument can be expressed as a dilemma as follows:

    If the laws of physics exist ETERNALLY and independently of the universe, then they are not rationally COMPREHENSIBLE. But if they are created by NATURAL processes acting in time, then it becomes possible to BRING the laws of physics inside time. And if the laws are brought inside time they will become rationally comprehensible. But the laws of physics either exist eternally or are created by natural processes acting in time, so it follows that they are rationally comprehensible if and only if they can be brought inside time.

    Symbolize the argument, and prove its validity.

9.2 NATURAL DILEMMAS

In examining reasoning based on the conditional proof in the last chapter, we saw that it depended on the following insight: we may summarize a piece of reasoning from a supposition p to a consequence q as "Supposing p, q"; but this amounts to the same thing as saying "If p, q." As a result of this equivalence, it is often the case that the explicit conditionalization step—the concluding step of a conditional proof—is left implicit in natural reasoning. The reader of a chain of reasoning that establishes q on the hypothesis or supposition p is left to draw the conclusion that $p \rightarrow q$ for him- or herself.

---

[4] Lee Smolin, *The Life of the Cosmos* (Oxford: Oxford UP, 1997), p. 210.

A similar thing occurs in some dilemmas too. Sometimes a consequence will be inferred from a disjunct through some chain of reasoning, and also from the other disjunct, making it the conclusion of a simple constructive dilemma, but with no explicit conditional statements. If the dilemma is complex, a different consequent will be inferred from the second disjunct, and the disjunction of these inferred as the overall conclusion. In such cases, the reasoning is suppositional, sometimes explicitly so, but more often implicitly: the disjunct is supposed, and things are inferred from it. Here's a schematic example of a complex constructive dilemma:

A or B. From A it follows that C, because D. Suppose, on the other hand, that B is true. Then, given that E, it follows that F. Therefore C or F.

Here the first leg establishes that, given D, C follows on the supposition of A. That is, given D, it is inferred that A → C, even though this is not stated. Similarly, in the second leg, it is argued that, given E, F will follow from the supposition of B, i.e., B → F, even though the conditional is not stated explicitly. Then, since one of the two suppositions must be true—A v B—the conclusion C v F follows (it's a complex constructive dilemma, whose validity we proved above). So we could diagram this as follows:

Diagram:

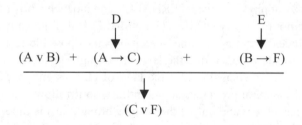

Let's put some flesh on this skeleton, and look at a real-life example. *Protagoras* was perhaps the greatest of the "Sophists," the first people in Ancient Greece to offer to take up as a profession the teaching of various intellectual skills (mainly *rhetoric*, the art of acquitting oneself well in public discourse—essential for lawyers, then as now). The following apocryphal story concerns a certain Euathlus, who had hired Protagoras to teach him rhetoric in preparation for a career as a lawyer. Since he could only afford half the fee, it was agreed that he would pay the second installment after Euathlus had won his first case. But after some time had passed, Euathlus had still not gone into practice, and Protagoras, worried about his reputation and getting low on cash, decided to sue him (how things change, eh?). In court, Protagoras argued to the jury as follows:

Euathlus maintains he should not pay me, but this is absurd. For suppose he wins this case. Since this is his first appearance in court, he should then pay me, because he has won his first case. On the other hand, suppose he loses the case. Then he ought to pay me because this is the judgement of the court. Therefore, since he must either win or lose the case, he must pay me.

Here the first statement can be regarded as a restatement of the main conclusion "Therefore...he must pay me." Let's read it that way. Then on marking up we get:

(1) Euathlus maintains he should not pay me, but this is absurd. For (suppose) ᵘ(2) <he wins this case>. Since (3) <this is his first appearance in court>, ᵘ(4) he should then pay me, because (5) <he has won his first case>. On the other hand, (suppose) ᵘ(6) <he loses the case>. Then ᵘ(7) he ought to pay me because (8) <this is the judgement of the court>. Therefore, since (9) <he must either win or lose the case>, (10) he must pay me.

Here the first leg establishes that, given (3) and (5), then (4) follows on the supposition of (2). That is, given (3) and (5), it is inferred that (2) → (4). Similarly, in the second leg, it is argued that, given (8), then (7) will follow on the supposition of (6), i.e., (6) → (7). But (7) is the same as (4). Thus, since (9) either (2) or (6) must be the case—(2) v (6)—the conclusion (10) = (4) = (7) follows (it's a simple constructive dilemma). So we diagram this as follows:

Diagram:

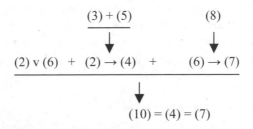

Euathlus had learned well from Protagoras, however. For he replied in kind. His argument is given as an exercise for analysis in Exercise 19 below.

As another example of a natural dilemma, let's look at this one from Voltaire. He reports the view of the Unitarians, who did not believe in the doctrine of Original Sin. Although he claims to "shudder in the reporting" of such a "profound superstition," Voltaire gets his message across by equipping them with a strong argument in the form of what we may call a "trilemma," a dilemma beginning with three disjuncts:

It is to offend God, they say, it is to accuse him of the most absurd barbarity, to dare to say that he made all the generations of men in order to torment them by eternal sufferings on the pretext that their first father ate some fruit in a garden... "How horrible," exclaim the strict Unitarians, "to calumniate the Creator by imputing continual miracles to him in order to damn forever people whom he has given life for so little time! Either he created souls from all eternity, so that on this supposition, since they will be infinitely older than Adam's sin, they will have no connection with him. Or these souls are formed every time a man sleeps with a woman, and in that case God is continually on the watch for every consummation of sex in the universe in order to create the spirits whom he will make eternally unhappy. Or God is himself the soul of all people, and in that case he damns himself. Which of these three suppositions is the most horrible and most senseless?"—Voltaire, *Philosophical Dictionary*[5]

Marking up the trilemma:

Either ᵁ(1) <[God] created souls from all eternity>, (so that on this supposition), since (2) <they will be infinitely older than Adam's sin>, ᵁ(3) they will have no connection with him. Or ᵁ(4) <these souls are formed every time a man sleeps with a woman>, and in that case ᵁ(5) God is continually on the watch for every consumation of sex in the universe in order to create the spirits whom he will make eternally unhappy. Or ᵁ(6) <God is himself the soul of all people>, and in that case ᵁ(7) he damns himself. (8) Which of these three suppositions is the most [are all] horrible and most senseless?

We are offered three alternatives: either (1) he created souls for all eternity, or (4) these souls are formed every time a man sleeps with a woman, or (6) God is himself the soul of all people. Supposing (1), given (2), (3) will follow. Supposing (4), (5) will follow. Supposing (6), (7) will follow. But, (8) implies, since each of the three consequences is horrible and senseless, so must the three alternatives supposed. Since, it is also implied, these are the only way that original sin could happen, that doctrine must be false.

EXERCISES 9.2

19. In the text Protagoras' argument against Euathlus was given and analyzed. *Give a similar analysis of Euathlus' rejoinder, marking it up and diagramming it:*

    Protagoras maintains that I should pay him, but it is this which is absurd. For suppose he wins this case. Since I will not have won my first case, I do not need to pay him, according to our agreement. On the other hand, suppose he loses the case. Then I do not have to pay him, since this is the judgement of the court. Therefore, since he must either win or lose the case, I do not have to pay him.

---

[5] This is my adaptation of Theodore Besterman's translation (London: Penguin, 1972), p. 332.

20. (**CHALLENGE**) In Plato's *Apology*, Socrates gives the following argument in the form of a dilemma to prove that death is something to be desired. *Restate the main inference in your own words, symbolize, and prove its validity:*

> Death is one of two things. It is either annihilation, and the dead have no consciousness of anything, or, as we are told, it is really a change—a migration of the soul from this place to another. Now if there is no consciousness but only a dreamless sleep, death must be a marvellous gain...If death is like this, then, I call it a gain, because the whole of time, if you look at it in this way, can be regarded as no more than one single night. If on the other hand, death is a removal from here to some other place, and if what we are told is true, that all the dead are gone there, what greater blessing could there be than this, gentlemen?...How much would one of you give to meet Orpheus and Musaeus, Hesiod, and Homer?—Plato, *Apology*

21. (**CHALLENGE**) In his second letter to Clarke in their famous controversy, Gottfried Leibniz posed a dilemma for Sir Isaac Newton, who had claimed that God would need to intervene from time to time to keep the same quantity of motion in the universe. *Supply the implicit conclusion of the argument, symbolize, and prove its validity:*

> If God is obliged to mend the course of nature from time to time, it must either be done supernaturally or naturally. If it is done supernaturally, we must have recourse to miracles in order to explain natural things, which [is absurd], for everything may easily be accounted for by miracles. But if it is done naturally, then God will...be comprehended under the nature of things, that is, he will be the soul of the world. [But it is agreed that it is false and heretical to claim that God is the soul of the world.]—Leibniz, *Second Letter to Clarke*, §12

22. (**CHALLENGE**) According to the historians of science Shapin and Schaffer, the chemist Robert Boyle posed a powerful dilemma for the materialist philosopher Hobbes. *Restate the main inference in your own words, symbolize, and prove its validity:*

> In 1675 Boyle spelt out Hobbes's dilemma. If "every body needs an outward movent [sc. something which moves it], it may well be demanded, how there comes to be any thing locally moved in the world?" Hobbes would need to appeal to some external prime mover, such as God. But if God were immaterial, then Hobbes would be compelled to admit that motion was generated by the interaction of matter and something immaterial. On the other hand, if God were material (and "Mr. Hobbes, in some writings of his, is believed to think the very notion of an immaterial substance to be absurd"), then Hobbes would be compelled to attribute inherent motion to this form of matter. Thus, either Hobbes would concede that motion was a product of spirit, or that motion was innate in matter.—*Leviathan and the Air Pump*, p. 204

23. (**CHALLENGE**) The main inference of the trilemma from Voltaire given in the text may be summarized as follows:

> There is ORIGINAL Sin only if one or other of these three alternatives is true: either God created souls for all ETERNITY, or these souls are FORMED every time a man sleeps with a woman, or God is himself the SOUL of all people. But if God created souls for all eternity they would have no CONNECTION with him. On the other hand, if these souls are formed every time a man sleeps with a woman, God would be continually on the WATCH for every consummation of sex in the universe in order to create the spirits whom he will make eternally unhappy. Finally, if God is himself the soul of all people, in that case he DAMNS himself. But since the consequents of these three conditionals are all false, the doctrine of Original Sin must also be false.

Symbolize and prove the validity of this main inference.

Chapter Ten

Reductio Arguments

We come now to what is perhaps the most important rule of inference after *modus ponens*. Certainly it has been at the creative heart of logic through the years, despite its not being part of the formal logic taught in universities until the twentieth century. As we'll see below, Galileo Galilei used the *reductio ad absurdum* argument form to brilliant effect in demolishing the physics of Aristotle, even while pouring scorn on the sterile logic he had learned in the Schools. The *reductio* is a way of refuting a proposition by showing that it leads to an absurdity, by *reducing it to absurdity*—hence the Latin name, which translates as "reduction to an absurdity." Generally, of course, such a reduction cannot be achieved without enlisting the aid of other premises. But this very fact explains the rhetorical force of this style of arguing: you refute your opponent's proposition by getting her agreement on a number of premises, supposing the proposition at issue, and then showing that together with those premises the supposition leads to an absurdity. Given those premises, therefore, the supposed proposition must be false.

In general the absurdity will be some concrete statement that all the arguers agree cannot be upheld: that is, given background assumptions held in common, a statement that is clearly *factually false*. In the context of formal arguments however, we need something stronger for the absurdity: a statement which cannot be true *by virtue of its form*, namely a *logical contradiction*, of the form $p \ \& \ \neg p$.

This kind of reasoning has a long and very distinguished history, going all the way back to the dawn of philosophy and mathematics in Ancient Greece. In fact, one of the most important arguments in the whole history of mathematics made use of it: a proof that the sides of a certain right triangle cannot be put into a ratio of one whole number to another—or, as we would say, that the square root of two is irrational. Some background for this is provided in the box on the next page. The right triangle in question is an isosceles triangle whose shorter sides are each of length 1, so that by Pythagoras' Theorem

147

the square of its hypotenuse h must be $1^2 + 1^2 = 2$. The argument depends only on some simple facts about natural numbers, such as premise (E): if a square is even, its root must be even too. It goes as follows:

> Suppose the ratio of h to one of the other sides is a to b, where any factor common to a and b has been divided out. Thus a and b cannot both be even, since their common factor of 2 would have been divided out. Now $h^2 = a^2/b^2 = 2$, so that $a^2 = 2b^2$. Thus a^2 is even. Therefore by premise (E), a is even, and we can express this as $a = 2c$, where c is another natural number. Combining this with $a^2 = 2b^2$ gives $4c^2 = 2b^2$. Therefore $b^2 = 2c^2$, so that b^2 is even. Therefore, by (E), b is even too. Consequently both a and b are even. But this contradicts our earlier conclusion. Therefore the original supposition is false: h to 1 cannot be expressed as a ratio of a to b: it is irrational.[1]

Pythagoras was a sage and a mystic of the sixth century BCE, who established a religious cult (the "Brotherhood") in a far-flung colony of Greece near Croton in what is now southern Italy. What distinguished him from his twentieth-century counterpart, Jimmy Jones—I mean, apart from the fact that even when they were attacked by the townsfolk he did not force his followers to commit suicide by drinking poisoned Kool-Aid—was his immense learning. He systematized all he had learned of mathematics and music from Babylonian and Egyptian priests, and single-handedly started theoretical science. (The very words 'theory,' 'philosophy,' musical 'harmony,' 'geometry,' and 'theorem' were all coined by him or his followers; we still know the name Pythagoras today in association with the theorem about right-angled triangles he was credited with discovering.) The results he discovered in music, geometry, and number theory, fused together with mystical elements into an all-embracing cosmology, were the mysteries into which the adepts of his cult were initiated. The Pythagoreans believed that "all is number," that everything in the universe has an associated natural number (> 1) ('justice,' for example, has the number 4—perhaps in the sense that we still speak of a "square deal"), and one of the deepest articles of faith of the Brotherhood was the *rationality* of the cosmos. This meant not just that the cosmos is rational in that it makes sense, but that, since everything has its number, any two things must be in a *ratio* of such numbers, such as 3 to 4. In this setting, one can only wonder that it was one of these very Pythagorean adepts who discovered the fateful result that there are two things—sides of a right-angled triangle, no less—which cannot possibly be in the ratio of two whole numbers.

What happened to the ill-fated soul who discovered this awful truth is lost in the mists of legend. But mathematics was never the same again.[2] Nor apparently was philosophy, for

---

[1] It is not known for certain that the irrationality of the square root of 2 was discovered by this argument, but it appears likely, and by the time of Aristotle the argument was well known as a paradigm of this kind of reasoning.

[2] The discovery of the irrationality of the square root of 2 led to a long divorce of arithmetic from geometry in the West, and a reconciliation was only effected by the introduction of Islamic learning: the "Al Jibra" (now spelled 'algebra') of the great Islamic mathematician Al-Khowarizmi (hence "algorithm") led to the formulation of algebraic geometry by Viète, Descartes, and Fermat in the seventeenth century, and eventually to the recognition of irrationals as numbers.

Zeno of Elea (another Italian Ancient Greek), apparently inspired by the Pythagoreans, began to use this style of reasoning to prove the paradoxical philosophy of his mentor, Parmenides. For example, in support of Parmenides' claim that all that exists is One, Zeno proposed the following argument:

> If many things exist, it is necessary for them to be as many as they are, and neither more nor fewer. But if they are as many as they are, they will be finite. If many things exist, the things that exist are infinite. For there are always others between the things that exist, and again others between them. And in this way the things that exist are infinite.[3]

It is readily seen that this argument is a *reductio ad absurdum* where the absurdity is a direct contradiction. From the supposition that many things exist, it is shown that the things that exist are finite, and then that the things that exist are infinite (i.e., not finite), a direct contradiction. (So what is the implicit conclusion of the argument?) Zeno's introduction of this kind of reasoning into philosophy probably marks the starting point of the study of logic. At any rate, Euclides, a disciple of Socrates who studied the philosophy of Parmenides and Zeno of Elea, was the founder of the Megarian school which gave rise to Stoic Logic. And Socrates himself, so far as we can tell, was much taken with a method of proving things by taking a prized belief of one of his interlocutors, and then showing that it leads to absurd or unwelcome consequences. For instance, in the *Meno* Plato has Socrates argue that supposing virtue could be taught, then Athenian worthies would have taught it to their sons. But, as is well known, neither Pericles nor Themistocles nor Aristides succeeded in making their sons virtuous. This kind of reasoning is known as the Socratic 'elenchus.' As William and Martha Kneale have argued, this "differs from the Zenonian in that the consequences drawn from the hypothesis need not be self-contradictory but may on occasions be simply false" (*The Development of Logic*, p. 9). They may also simply be undesirable, as we saw with the "claustrophobia" example in the last section of chapter 7. Historically, all types of argument that suppose something in order to demonstrate its falsity have been called *reductio ad absurdum*, reduction to absurdity, whether the consequence drawn from the supposition is a strict logical contradiction (as in the Zenonian elenchus, sometimes called *reductio ad impossibile*); or something known to be empirically false (as with the virtuous sons); or something that is simply unacceptable (as with the claustrophobic house).

For our rule of inference, though, we will take the Zenonian elenchus that is appropriate to formal arguments: the supposition must lead to a logical contradiction. To this end we define an explicit contradiction as a statement of the form $q \ \& \ \neg q$, where q as always is a variable standing for any individual statement, such as C, or A $\&$ $\neg$B, or (A $\vee$ B) $\rightarrow$ C, etc. Thus (A $\&$ $\neg$B) $\&$ $\neg$(A $\&$ $\neg$B) is an explicit contradiction, and so is $\neg$P $\&$ $\neg\neg$P; on

---

[3] Jonathan Barnes, *Early Greek Philosophy*, p. 154; see pp. 150-58 of the same work for discussion of this and Zeno's other famous paradoxes.

the other hand, D → ¬D is not. It is handy (particularly for long contradictions) to have a symbol for an explicit contradiction:

The symbol ⊥ stands for any *explicit contradiction* of the form q & ¬q.

(This symbol will be a particularly useful shorthand for the long formulas we will encounter in Predicate Logic.) Now we may state the rule of inference:

Reductio ad Absurdum **(RA)**

To prove a statement false, suppose the statement: if an explicit contradiction is derivable from this supposition together with other premises (if needed), then infer the negation of the original statement.

In symbols:

From a derivation of ⊥ (i.e., q & ¬q) from the supposition of p, infer ¬p.

Here is an example of the use of the RA rule in a proof. It concerns the expression "unless p, q." In chapter 7 we concluded that it could be symbolized equally well by ¬p → q and by p ∨ q, but so far we have only proved (in chapter 7) that the second of these entails the first. Now we will prove that ¬p → q entails p ∨ q. In what follows we are using the statement variables p and q to prove the validity of an argument form directly.

(1) ¬p → q	Prem
(2) ¬(p ∨ q)	Supp/RA
(3) ¬p & ¬q	2 DM
(4) ¬p	3 Simp
(5) q	1, 4 MP
(6) ¬q	3 Simp
(7) ⊥	5, 6 Conj
(8) ¬¬(p ∨ q)	2-7 RA
(9) p ∨ q	8 DN

Points to note:
- as with the Conditional Proof rule, we begin with a *supposition*, and this is denoted by "Supp/RA" to indicate that we are *supposing* ¬(p ∨ q) *to begin a reductio ad absurdum proof.*
- we indent the supposition and all the lines that depend upon that supposition.
- on line (7) we derive the contradiction ⊥, which must be stated explicitly.
- line (8), however, does not depend on the supposition; instead, it summarizes what has gone on in lines 2-7: given the premise ¬p → q, then, supposing ¬(p ∨ q), a contradiction follows. Concluding that the supposition must have been wrong *discharges the supposition.*
- note the justification for line (8): since it summarizes the derivation *beginning in line* (2) and *ending in line* (7), it is written 2-7 RA (i.e., lines 2 through 7) to indicate this.

A proof of validity of this rule may be given as follows: Granted we have the supposition p and a valid derivation of $\bot$ from p and other premises $\{r, s, \ldots\}$, then $\bot$ cannot be false if p is true, given the other premises $\{r, s, \ldots\}$. But $\bot$ is a logical contradiction, and is therefore false. So p cannot be true, given the other premises $\{r, s, \ldots\}$. It follows that from p and a valid derivation of $\bot$ from p and other premises $\{r, s, \ldots\}$, $\neg p$ follows, given the other premises $\{r, s, \ldots\}$.

As we'll see, this powerful rule allows us to construct proofs for a huge variety of valid arguments and argument forms. Let's give some examples. First, the form of the *reductio ad impossibile* discovered by the Stoics: $p \rightarrow q, p \rightarrow \neg q \therefore \neg p$

(1) $p \rightarrow q$		Prem
(2) $p \rightarrow \neg q$		Prem
	(3) p	Supp/RA
	(4) q	1, 3 MP
	(5) $\neg q$	2, 3 MP
	(6) $\bot$	4, 5 Conj
(7) $\neg p$		3-6 RA

Next, the Law of Tautology: $p \vee p \therefore p$

(1) $p \vee p$		Prem
	(2) $\neg p$	Supp/RA
	(3) p	1, 2 DS
	(4) $\bot$	2, 3 Conj
(5) $\neg\neg p$		2-4 RA
(6) p		5 DN

Third, the vitally important Law of Excluded Middle: $p \vee \neg p$: this is logically true, and so does not depend on any premises at all. But we may still prove it by supposing its negation and then aiming for a contradiction:

	(1) $\neg(p \vee \neg p)$	Supp/RA
	(2) $\neg p \,\&\, \neg\neg p$	1 DM
(3)	$\neg\neg(p \vee \neg p)$	1-2 RA
(4)	$p \vee \neg p$	3 DN

Such proofs of statements with no given premises are very important in logic. We will return to them in chapter 12.

Some of the rules we have already proved can be proved more simply in terms of the other rules together with RA, for instance, MT. An instance of the latter form of argument is provided by an abbreviated version of an argument we already encountered in chapter 4, ex. 12. J.R. Brown writes that the central argument of David Bloor's book, *Knowledge and Social Imagery*, is "that it is not evidence, but instead social factors, which cause belief." He then reasons: "If *Knowledge and Social Imagery* is right, then it is destined to have no direct impact on intellectual life. But since it has had an impact, it must be false." If we symbolize "*Knowledge and Social Imagery* is right that it is not evidence, but instead SOCIAL factors, which cause belief" by S, and "*Knowledge and Social Imagery* is destined to have a direct IMPACT on intellectual life" by I, we have

$S \rightarrow \neg I, I \therefore \neg S$
(1) $S \rightarrow \neg I$ Prem
(2) I   Prem
  | (3) S   Supp/RA
  | (4) $\neg I$ 1, 3 MP
  | (5) $\bot$ 2, 4 Conj
(6) $\neg S$ 3-5 RA

Finally, let's tackle a more complex proof, this one of the formal validity of the abstract argument: $Z \rightarrow (A \rightarrow \neg B), \neg Z \rightarrow \neg B \therefore \neg(A \& B)$

(1) $Z \rightarrow (A \rightarrow \neg B)$ Prem
(2) $\neg Z \rightarrow \neg B$ Prem
  | (3) A & B   Supp/RA   —we suppose this and aim for a contradiction
  | (4) A   3 Simp
  | (5) B   3 Simp
  | (6) $\neg\neg B$ 5 DN
  | (7) $\neg\neg Z$ 2, 6 MT
  | (8) Z   7 DN
  | (9) $A \rightarrow \neg B$ 8, 1 MP
  | (10) $\neg B$ 4, 9 MP
  | (11) $\bot$ 5, 10 Conj
(12) $\neg(A \& B)$ 3-11 RA

Notice how the RA strategy is dictated by the fact that there is no obvious way to proceed directly. The supposition is simply the negation of what we are trying to prove (granting a double negation). Then we simply try to work in the information contained in both the given premises until we reach a contradiction.

SUMMARY

- The symbol $\bot$ stands for any *explicit contradiction* of the form $q \& \neg q$.
- The rule of inference **Reductio ad Absurdum (RA)** is
  From a derivation of $\bot$ (i.e., $q \& \neg q$) from the supposition of p, infer $\neg p$.
  From a derivation of an explicit contradiction from the supposition of a given statement together with other premises, infer the negation of the supposition.

- The line on which the supposition is made is justified Supp/RA, and this line and all lines depending on the supposition are indented; the line after the contradiction has been derived is undented, because the application of RA discharges the supposition.
- The **validity** of this argument form follows from our definition of formal validity: p cannot be true given the other premises $\{r, s, \ldots\}$ if a false statement is validly derived from them. But $\perp$ is logically false. Therefore $\neg p$ follows, given $\{r, s, \ldots\}$.

EXERCISES 10.1

1. *Prove the validity* of the argument form Modus Tollens: $p \to q, \neg q \therefore \neg p$, using MP and Conj in a *reductio* proof.

2. *Prove* the Commutative Law for Disjunction: $p \lor q \therefore q \lor p$.

3. Use a *reductio* strategy to *prove* the Law of Clavius: $\neg p \to p \therefore p$.

4. As a sister argument form to the *reductio ad impossibile*, the Stoics proved the form: $p \to q, \neg p \to q \therefore q$. Up till now, we have treated arguments of this form as dilemmas with the disjunction $p \lor \neg p$ left implicit. But strictly, this last premise is a tautology that adds no new content to the argument, and the argument form is provably valid without it. The form is exemplified in the following passage from Rudyard Kipling's *Rikki-Tikki-Tavi*, when Nagaina, a King Cobra whose husband had recently been slain, hisses at the son of the man who killed him:

   > Wait a little. Keep very still.... If you MOVE, I STRIKE, and if you do not move, I strike.[4]

   What should the boy infer? *Supply the implicit conclusion and prove the validity of the argument using a reductio strategy.*

5. Prove the validity of the simple constructive dilemma $p \lor q, p \to r, q \to r \therefore r$ (*without* using DL) by using MT, DS, MP (or MT), and Conj in a *reductio* proof.

Prove the validity of the following dilemmas using reductio proofs:

6. $V \to \neg N, V \to C, \neg\neg N \lor \neg C \therefore \neg V$

7. $K \to U, \neg K \to U, K \lor \neg K \therefore U$

8. $U \lor \neg U, U \to A, \neg U \to N \therefore A \lor N$

---

[4] Rudyard Kipling, *The Jungle Book* (Garden City, NY: Doubleday, 1964), p. 146; taken from Pospesel, *Propositional Logic*, 3rd ed., p. 79.

9. $A \rightarrow B, \neg(B \ \& \ D), \neg A \lor D \therefore \neg A$

10. $P \lor Q, Q \rightarrow (R \lor S), \neg R \ \& \ (P \lor \neg S) \therefore P$

11. $\neg S \rightarrow N, P \rightarrow \neg N, \neg\neg M \lor P \therefore M \lor S$

12. In his witty and captivating book *Gödel, Escher, Bach*, Douglas Hofstadter reports the following Zen meditation exercise, or Kôan, called "Gantô's Ax":

> One day Tokusan told his student Gantô, "I have two monks who have been here for many years. Go and examine them." Gantô picked up an ax and went to the hut where the two monks were meditating. He raised the ax, saying, "If you SAY a word I will CUT off your heads; and if you do not say a word, I will also cut off your heads."[5]

Hofstadter asks: "What if the ax were an axiom?" To answer, *symbolize* what Gantô says to the monks, *guess what bloody conclusion it entails, and prove this.*

13. One of the most celebrated paradoxes in the history of logic is the Liar Paradox. It has its origin in a line in a poem by Epimenides the Cretan: "The Cretans, always liars, evil beasts, idle bellies!" Thus a Cretan is saying "All Cretans are liars."[6] But perhaps the most concise formulation is "I am lying." In an episode of *Star Trek*, Spock uses this as a way to escape the grip of an evil computer, which apparently reasons as follows: "He SAYS he is lying. If he says he is lying and he IS lying, then he is not lying. But if he says he is lying and he is not lying, then he is lying." *Symbolize* and *prove* that this entails that *he is lying and he is not lying.*

14. As mentioned earlier, the problem of evil can be posed as a dilemma for theism:

> If God is perfectly LOVING, he must WISH to abolish evil; and if he is all-POWERFUL, he must be ABLE to abolish evil. But evil EXISTS; therefore God cannot be both omnipotent and perfectly loving.[7]

Supply the unstated premise <If God wishes to abolish evil and is able to do so, then evil does not exist>, *and prove the validity of the argument.*

15. You may be familiar with the concept of a "Catch-22." It originates with Joseph Heller's novel of that name:

---

[5] Gyomay M. Kubose, *Zen Koans*, p. 178; quoted from Hofstadter, *Gödel, Escher, Bach*, p. 189.

[6] Medieval discussion stemmed from the comment of the apostle St. Paul: "It was a Cretan himself, one of their own prophets, who spoke the truth when he said 'All Cretans are liars, wicked beasts and lazy gluttons'" (*Letter to Titus*, 1).

[7] John Hick, *Philosophy of Religion* (Englewood Cliffs, NJ: Prentice-Hall, 1989), p. 40; again lifted from Pospesel, *Propositional Logic*, p. 77.

Yossarian tried another approach: "Is Orr crazy?" "He sure is," Dr. Neeker said. "Can you ground him?" "I sure can. But first he has to ask me to. That's part of the rule." "Then why doesn't he ask you to?" "Because he's crazy," Doc Daneeka said. "He has to be crazy to keep flying combat missions after all the close calls he's had. Sure, I can ground Orr. But first he has to ask me to." "That's all he has to do to be grounded?" "That's all. Let him ask me." "And then you can ground him?," Yossarian asked. "No. Then I can't ground him." You mean there's a catch?" "Sure there's a catch," Doc Daneeka replied, "Catch-22. Anyone who wants to get out of combat duty isn't really crazy." There was only one catch and that was Catch-22, which specified that a concern for one's own safety in the face of dangers that were real and immediate was the process of a rational mind. Orr was crazy and could be grounded. All he had to do was ask; and as soon as he did, he would no longer be crazy and would have to fly more missions. Orr would be crazy to fly more missions and sane if he didn't, but if he was sane he had to fly them. If he flew them he was crazy and didn't have to; but if he didn't want to he was sane and had to. Yossarian was moved very deeply by the absolute simplicity of this clause of Catch-22 and let out a respectful whistle.[8]

The heart of this argument is: "If Orr was CRAZY, he could be GROUNDED if he ASKED to be. But he could be grounded only if he asked. And if he asked, he would no longer be crazy and could not be grounded." *Symbolize, and prove that it follows that* Orr could not be grounded. (You will find one premise to be redundant.)

16. (**CHALLENGE**) Prove the Distributive Law for '&' over 'v' *by proving valid*:
    (a) A & (B v C) ∴ (A & B) v (A & C)
    (b) (A & B) v (A & C) ∴ A & (B v C)

17. (**CHALLENGE**) Prove the Distributive Law for 'v' over '&' *by proving valid*:
    (a) A v (B & C) ∴ (A v B) & (A v C)
    (b) (A v B) & (A v C) ∴ A v (B & C)

18. (**CHALLENGE**) In a critique of deconstructionism, E.O. Wilson construes its underlying premise as "Each author's meaning is unique to himself; nothing of his true intention nor anything else connected to objective reality can be reliably assigned to it... That is what Jacques Derrida, the creator of deconstructionism, meant when he stated the formula *Il n'y a pas de hors-texte* (There is nothing outside the text). At least, that is what I think he meant, after reading him, his defenders, and his critics with some care. If the radical postmodernist premise is correct, we can never be sure what he meant. Conversely, if that *is* what he meant, it is not certain that we are obliged to consider his arguments further" (*Consilience*, p. 41).

---

[8] Joseph Heller, *Catch-22* (New York: Dell, 1961), p. 47.

Wilson persuades himself that he has found a paradox loosely analogous to the liar paradox. But has he? Symbolizing the "radical postmodernist premise" <Each author's meaning is UNIQUE to himself; nothing of his true intention nor anything else connected to objective reality can be reliably assigned to it> as U, and <We can be SURE that the formula *Il n'y a pas de hors-texte* means U> as S, the last two statements of the above paragraph may be represented as U → ¬S and S → ¬U. Is this a paradox?

19. (**CHALLENGE**) In his *Physics* (6.6, 237a20-28), Aristotle gave the following argument that nothing could change in an instant:

> Suppose (1) something has changed from state A to state B in an instant. Then (2) it cannot have changed to state B in the same instant at which it is in state A, for (3) in that case it would be in state A and state B at the same time…(4) If however it changed to state B in a different instant, there will be an instant of time in-between, since (5) no two instants can be touching. Since therefore (6) it has changed in an interval of time, and (7) every interval of time is divisible, (8) in half the time it would have completed another change, and again, in half of that time, another, and so on forever. Consequently, (9) it had to be changing previously.

Construing this argument as a dilemma as follows, *symbolize* and *prove its validity*:

> If the thing CHANGED from state A to state B in an instant, this must have been in the SAME instant, or a DIFFERENT instant. It cannot have been in the same instant (for the reasons given). But if it were in a different instant, then it must already have BEEN changing. But if it had already been changing, it would not have changed in an instant. Therefore it is not the case that a thing can change from state A to state B in an instant.

10.2 NATURAL REDUCTIO ARGUMENTS

The *reductio ad absurdum* is the high point of logic. Even some of logic's most hostile critics, such as René Descartes and Galileo Galilei, did not hesitate to employ this rule to prove some of their most powerful results. That should probably be restated: the logic they were hostile to in the seventeenth century was the arid version of Aristotle's logic taught in the universities, by means of which you could check the validity of syllogisms you already knew to be valid, but which you could not use to generate new results. What distinguishes reductio arguments, however, is precisely the creative use to which they can be and have been put, starting as we have already seen with the Pythagoreans and Zeno. In this section we will examine some of these natural *reductio*s, and propose a technique for diagramming them.

Let's begin with the following argument proposed by the seventeenth-century polymath Gottfried Leibniz, taken from an unpublished early dialogue on the problems of the continuum:

> I do not believe a fastest motion is intelligible. Suppose there is such a thing as a fastest motion. Then some wheel may be set spinning so that its rim is moving with the fastest motion. Now if we conceive one of its radii to be extended beyond its rim, then

any point we take on the extended radius outside the wheel will be spinning with a motion faster than the rim, that is, faster than the fastest. Since there is nothing to stop us conceiving the radius so extended, something will be moving faster than the fastest motion. But this is contradictory. Therefore there is no such thing as a fastest motion.[9]

Marked up:

(Suppose) ᵘ(1) <there is such a thing as a fastest motion>. Then ᵘ(2) <u>some wheel may be set spinning so that its rim is moving with the fastest motion</u>. Now (3) <if we conceive one of its radii to be extended beyond its rim, then any point we take on the extended radius outside the wheel will be spinning with a motion faster than the rim>, that is, ᵘ(4) <[the point will be moving] <u>faster than the fastest</u>>. Since (5) <there is nothing to stop us conceiving the radius so extended>, ᵘ(6) <u>something will be moving faster than the fastest motion</u>. But (7) this is a contradiction. Therefore (8) <u>there is no such thing as a fastest motion</u>.

The technique for diagramming this is a natural extension of our techniques for suppositional arguments, taking into account the *reductio* strategy: the supposition and everything that depends on it are unasserted. The argument shows that the supposition leads to something that either (i) contradicts a premise or the supposition itself, or (ii) is absurd or unacceptable according to appropriate standards. This is often made clear by an explicit statement, as here: "this is a contradiction," or "but this is absurd." Then from this reasoning to an absurd consequence, we conclude the contradictory of the original supposition. To show that the conclusion follows from the reasoning, rather than from any one of the premises or intermediate conclusions by themselves, we symbolize the inference to the overall conclusion as branching off to the side, as we did with natural CPs:

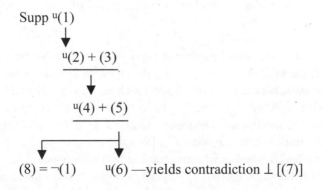

Supp ᵘ(1)

ᵘ(2) + (3)

ᵘ(4) + (5)

(8) = ¬(1)   ᵘ(6) —yields contradiction ⊥ [(7)]

---

[9] This is a quotation, with minimalist alterations to make the logic clearer, from Gottfried Leibniz's dialogue, *Pacidius to Philalethes*, in *G.W. Leibniz: The Labyrinth of the Continuum*, ed. and trans. R.T.W. Arthur (Yale UP, 2001), p. 179.

Galileo Galilei image by Justus (Giusto) Sustermans, 1597-1681.

Galileo Galilei (1564-1642) provided some beautiful reductio arguments against some of the chief tenets of Aristotle's physics, which was the standard physics taught in the universities in his time. Perhaps everyone's favourite is the following, in which Galileo appears to prove that bodies will fall with the same speed whatever their weight. What is amazing about this is that he appears to prove it *a priori*, i.e., without an appeal to experience (even though he had satisfied himself of its truth through testing it experimentally). It occurs in a dialogue where Galileo has one character (Sagredo) claim that he has done an experiment in which a hundred-pound cannonball and a half-ounce musket ball are dropped through a height of two hundred braccia (about 170 feet), and has determined that the cannonball "does not anticipate the musket ball's arrival on the ground by even half a span"—i.e., is no more than about 3 inches ahead of it on landing. The dialogue continues:

SALVIATI: But even without experiment, it is possible to prove clearly that a heavier moving body does not move more rapidly than another less heavy one, provided both bodies are of the same material, and in short such as those mentioned by Aristotle. But tell me, Simplicio, whether you accept that each falling body acquires a definite speed fixed by nature, a speed which cannot be increased or diminished except by the use of force or some impediment that retards it. [Simplicio acquiesces.]

Then if we had two bodies whose natural speeds were unequal, it is evident that on uniting the two, the faster one would be partly slowed down by the slower one, and the slower one would be somewhat speeded up by the faster one. [Again Simplicio agrees.]

But if this is so, and if it is also true that a large stone moves with eight degrees of speed, say, while the slower moves with four, then when they are joined together, their composite will move with a speed less than eight degrees. But the two stones joined together make a larger stone than the one which moved with eight degrees of speed; therefore this greater stone moves less rapidly than the lighter; which is contrary to your supposition. Thus you see how, from the supposition that a heavier body moves more rapidly than a lighter one, I infer that the heavier body moves less rapidly. (Galileo Galilei, *Discorsi*, 1638)

The basic argument is relatively straightforward, and can be rephrased as follows:

Suppose Aristotle is right in claiming that a heavier body falls through the same medium more rapidly than a lighter one made of the same material, in such a way that the natural speeds are proportional to their weights. Then if the two are united, the heavier one will be slowed down by the lighter, and the lighter speeded up by the heavier one. So the combined stones will move more slowly than the heavier one alone. But the two stones joined together make a heavier body than the larger stone. Therefore the heavier body (the combined system) moves more slowly than the lighter (either stone by itself). But this contradicts Aristotle's supposition. Therefore the supposition is false.

Marked up:

(Suppose) ᵘ(1) <Aristotle is right in claiming that a heavier body falls through the same medium more rapidly than a lighter one made of the same material, in such a way that the natural speeds are proportional to their weights>. Then ᵘ(2) <if the two are united, the heavier one will be slowed down by the lighter, and the lighter speeded up by the heavier one>. So ᵘ(3) the combined stones will move more slowly than the heavier one alone. But (4) <the two stones joined together make a heavier body than the larger stone>. Therefore ᵘ(5) the heavier body (the combined system) moves more slowly than the lighter (either stone by itself). But (6) this contradicts Aristotle's supposition. Therefore (7) the supposition is false.

Diagram:

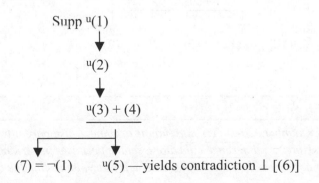

Let's conclude by examining Zeno's argument from the previous section, where he is trying to refute the supposition of his opponents that *there are many things*:

> If many things exist, it is necessary for them to be as many as they are, and neither more nor fewer. But if they are as many as they are, they will be finite. If many things exist, the things that exist are infinite. For there are always others between the things that exist, and again others between them. And in this way the things that exist are infinite.

The first leg of the reductio argues that under the supposition that they are many, they must be finite in number. The second leg argues that on the same supposition they must be infinite. It is left implicit that this is contradictory, and that therefore the supposition is false. Making this reductio structure explicit involves interpreting "if" as "supposing," something that will often be necessary in analyzing reductios:

> I̶f̶ (Supposing) ᵘ(1) many things exist, ([then]) ᵘ(2) <u><it is necessary for them to be as many as they are, and neither more nor fewer></u>. But (3) if they are as many as they are, they will be finite. [(Therefore) (4) <u>they are finite</u>.] I̶f̶ (Supposing) (5) <many things exist>, (6) <u>the things that exist are infinite</u>. (For) (7) <there are always others between the things that exist, and again others between them>. (And in this way) (8) <u><the things that exist are infinite></u>. [(9) But this contradicts (4). (Therefore) (10) <u>it is not the case that many things exist.</u>]

Diagrammed:

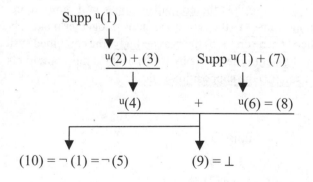

Supp ᵘ(1)

ᵘ(2) + (3)   Supp ᵘ(1) + (7)

ᵘ(4)   +   ᵘ(6) = (8)

(10) = ¬ (1) = ¬ (5)   (9) = ⊥

Instructions for numbers 20-26: (i) *mark up the argument: use parentheses for (supposition indicators), box any* inference indicators*, set the premises in <triangular brackets>, reinterpreting and cancelling material where necessary, underline the* conclusions, *and* *double-underline the* <u>*main conclusion*</u>; (ii) *identify unasserted statements with a prefix superscript* u, *and* (iii) *diagram the inference structure*, supplying the supposition or the inference to its negation if either of these has been left implicit.

20. In the text we represented Jim Brown's argument about Bloor's book *Knowledge and Social Imagery* as an instance of *modus tollens*. The same argument can be construed as a *reductio ad absurdum* as follows:

    Suppose (1) Bloor's central argument is right. Then (2) it is not evidence which causes belief. But in that case (3) Bloor's argument could have no impact on intellectual life. Since (4) it has had such an impact, (5) it must therefore be wrong.

21. Cicero reports Chrysippus to have argued as follows:

    Supposing (1) the gods do not exist, (2) what can there be in nature better than man, seeing that (3) he alone possesses that highest possible mark of distinction, reason? (4) But that there should be a man who believes there to be nothing in the whole world better than himself is crazy arrogance. (5) Therefore there is something better. (6) Therefore god really does exist.[10]

22. In *My Philosophical Development*, Bertrand Russell gives the following argument in support of his view that many entities we believe to exist owe their credibility to inference:

    (1) Your own eyes as visual objects belong to the inferred part of the world...(2) The inference to your own eyes as visual objects is essentially of the same sort as the physicists' inference to electrons, etc.; and, if (3) you are going to deny validity to the physicists' inferences, (4) you ought also to deny that you know you have visible eyes—(5) which is absurd, as Euclid would say.

23. In Chapter 5, ex. 17 we examined the following argument given by Leibniz against Clarke:

    I have still other arguments against this strange imagination that (1) space is a property of God. (2) If it be so, space belongs to the essence of God. But (3) space has parts: therefore (4) there would be parts in the essence of God. (5) *Spectatum admissi.*

    (Here the words *Spectatum admissi* are the beginning of a quote from Horace, which can be translated as "If you saw such a thing, friends, could you restrain your laughter?"—i.e., "But this is absurd!") Interpret this argument as a *reductio* argument against the supposition that <space is a property of God>.

---

[10] Cicero, *On the Nature of the Gods*, 2, 16; quoted from the translation of Long and Sedley, *The Hellenistic Philosophers*, p. 325.

24. Ocellus Lucanus long ago asserted the eternity of the world with the argument: (1) The world must have been eternal, because (2) it is a contradiction for the universe to have had a beginning, since, (3) supposing it had a beginning, (4) it must have been caused by some other thing, but then (5) it would not be the universe.[11]

25. (**CHALLENGE**) The Latin poet Lucretius gave a famous argument for the infinity of space in his *De Rerum Natura* (*On the Nature of Things*), written in the time of Jesus Christ:

Suppose for the moment that (1) the totality of space is finite. Therefore (2) it will have a boundary or limit. Then (3) someone at the very edge could run up to its outermost limit and hurl a flying javelin, with the result that (4) the javelin would either keep going in the direction it was thrown, or would meet an obstruction that would stop it. (5) You must concede and choose one of these alternatives, and either one cuts off your escape and forces you to admit that the universe stretches without end. (6) For if there is something that obstructs it, and stationing itself as a limit, prevents it travelling in the direction it was aimed, then what it started from was not the limit. (7) Likewise, if it keeps going beyond the limit, then what it started from was not the limit. (8) Therefore a limit cannot exist anywhere, so that (9) the totality of space must be infinite.[12]

26. (**CHALLENGE**) In his *Two New Sciences*, Galileo has the character Simplicio say of the proposition that <u>a falling body acquires forces so that its speed increases in proportion to the space traversed</u> that it "ought to be accepted without hesitation or controversy," thus setting up Simplicio himself for a fall. Salviati replies that this is as false and impossible as that motion should be completed instantaneously, and here is a very clear demonstration of it. Supposing (1) the velocities are in proportion to the spaces traversed, ... then (2) these spaces are traversed in equal intervals of time; (3) if, therefore, the velocity with which the falling body traverses a space of eight feet were double that with which it covered the first four, (just as one distance is double the other), then the time intervals required for these traversals would be equal. But (4) for one and the same body to fall eight feet and four feet in the same time is possible only in the case of instantaneous motion; but (5) to suppose all falling bodies fall instantaneously is absurd; therefore (6) it is not true that its velocity increases in proportion to the space.[13]

---

[11] Quoted from Samuel Clarke, *A Demonstration of the Being and Attributes of God*, ed. Ezio Vailati (Cambridge: Cambridge UP, 1998), pp. 24-25.

[12] Titus Lucretius Carus, *De Rerum Natura*, 1, 958-97. Translation of A.A. Long and D.N. Sedley; much adapted.

[13] Galileo Galilei, *Dialogues Concerning Two New Sciences*, trans. Henry Crew and Alfonso de Salvio (New York: Dover, 1954); slightly adapted.

27. (**CHALLENGE**) Consider again Aristotle's argument given in number 19 above, that nothing could change in an instant. This time *take it to be a reductio* in which statement (9) is in contradiction with (1), *mark it up,* and *diagram it.*

28. (**CHALLENGE**) In his fascinating book *The Golden Ratio*, Mario Livio presents the following argument from the famous medieval theologian Maimonides as a good example of the *reductio* style of argument:

> The basic principle [of all monotheistic religions] is that there is a First Being who brought every existing thing into being. For if it be supposed that he did not exist, then nothing else could possibly exist.

Is this a valid reductio? If so, give an analysis using the techniques of this chapter.

29. (**CHALLENGE**) In *The Life of the Cosmos*, Lee Smolin gives the following presentation of Jacob Bekenstein's argument that "the maximum amount of information that any system can contain is proportional to the area of its boundary":

> According to the laws of thermodynamics, (1) no process is allowed that can decrease the entropy of a system. Suppose that (2) inside some boundary, a system exists that contains more entropy than could be contained by any black hole that would fit inside the boundary. It turns out that in this case (3) one can always add energy to the system until it is so dense that it must collapse to a black hole. But then (4) the entropy goes *down* to that of a black hole that could be contained inside the boundary. (5) [According to premise (1)] this is impossible, so there must be something wrong with the assumption of the argument, which was that a system can have more entropy than the largest black hole that fits into the same region. So (6) the entropy of any system contained within a finite region is bounded. But then (7) the information it can contain is also bounded, as (8) entropy is a measure of information.[14]

Sketch a diagram for this reductio.

30. (**CHALLENGE**) In 1615 Peter Fonseca gave the following argument against the idea that space is a "true being":

> Space is not a true being, for if it were, it would either be an uncreated being, which is appropriate only to God; or a created being, which it cannot be, since space could not have begun to exist, for wherever it is now, there necessarily it always was and always will be.[15]

---

[14] Lee Smolin, *The Life of the Cosmos*, p. 274; slightly adapted.

[15] *Commentarium Petri Fonsecae Lusitani* (1615), translated from the Latin given in Edward Grant, *Much Ado about Nothing* (Cambridge: Cambridge UP, 1981), p. 327.

Letting T := space is a TRUE being, U := space is an UNCREATED being, G := only GOD is uncreated, C := space is a CREATED being, B := space BEGAN to exist, A := wherever it is now, there necessarily it ALWAYS was and always will be, (a) *diagram the inference structure*; (b) *give a formal proof of the validity of the main inference*: if T, then U or C. But ¬U; and ¬C. Therefore ¬T.

Chapter Eleven

Review and Consolidation

11.1 RULES OF INFERENCE

11.1.1 RULES OF INFERENCE AND EQUIVALENCE RULES

From among the valid argument forms we have considered, we have selected some of the most useful as Rules of Inference. These we have proved valid using our definition of validity, and then used them to prove the validity of other argument forms. It's time now to systematize what we have established so far. Our rules of inference can be divided into two classes: the Rules of Inference proper, in which the inference goes only one way, and the Equivalence Rules, in which one statement entails the other *and vice versa*. First the one-way rules of inference, in which we derive a statement on one line from one, two, or three separate statements, each on its own line:

Modus Ponens (MP) From $p \rightarrow q$ and p, infer q.	*Modus Tollens (MT)* From $p \rightarrow q$ and $\neg q$, infer $\neg p$.
Simplification (Simp) From $p \& q$, infer p. From $p \& q$, infer q.	*Conjunction (Conj)* From p and q, infer $p \& q$.
Conjunctive Syllogism (CS) From $\neg (p \& q)$ and p, infer $\neg q$. From $\neg (p \& q)$ and q, infer $\neg p$.	*Disjunction (Disj)* From p (stated alone), infer $p \vee q$. From q (stated alone), infer $p \vee q$.
Disjunctive Syllogism (DS) From $p \vee q$ and $\neg p$, infer q. From $p \vee q$ and $\neg q$, infer p.	

Conditional Proof (CP)
From a derivation of q from the supposition of p, infer $p \rightarrow q$.

Hypothetical Syllogism (HS)	*Dilemma (DL)*
From $p \rightarrow q$ and $q \rightarrow r$, infer $p \rightarrow r$.	From $p \lor q$, $p \rightarrow r$ and $q \rightarrow r$, infer r.

Reductio ad Absurdum (RA)
From a derivation of $\bot$ from the supposition of p, infer $\neg p$.

Now the equivalence rules, in which the inference goes from a single statement on one line to a single statement on another:

Equivalence Rules

Double Negation (DN)	*De Morgan's Laws (DM)*
From p infer $\neg\neg p$; from $\neg\neg p$ infer p.	From $\neg(p \lor q)$, infer $\neg p \,\&\, \neg q$, and vice versa. From $\neg(p \,\&\, q)$, infer $\neg p \lor \neg q$, and vice versa.
Biconditional Equivalence (BE) From $p \leftrightarrow q$ infer $(p \rightarrow q) \,\&\, (q \rightarrow p)$, and vice versa.	

To these equivalence rules we will add two new rules, *Material Implication* and *Transposition*. They are defined as follows:

Material Implication (MI)	*Transposition (TR)*
From $p \rightarrow q$ infer $\neg p \lor q$, and vice versa.	From $p \rightarrow q$ infer $\neg q \rightarrow \neg p$, and vice versa.

Material Implication is the traditional name for the equivalence of $p \rightarrow q$ and $\neg p \lor q$, the two alternative ways of translating 'Unless,' proved in the texts of chapters 7 and 10, respectively. The Transposition rule, constituted by the equivalence of $p \rightarrow q$ and $\neg q \rightarrow \neg p$, was proved in chapter 7, exercise 5. Here are some examples of their use:

$\neg A \rightarrow \neg(B \lor C), A \rightarrow D \therefore (B \lor C) \rightarrow D$
(1) $\neg A \rightarrow \neg(B \lor C)$ Prem
(2) $A \rightarrow D$ Prem
(3) $(B \lor C) \rightarrow A$ 1 TR
(4) $(B \lor C) \rightarrow D$ 3, 2 HS

R → ¬(S & T) ∴ ¬[R & (S & T)]

(1) R → ¬(S & T)   Prem
(2) ¬R v ¬(S & T)   1 MI
(3) ¬[R & (S & T)]   2 DM

¬¬H → ¬G ∴ ¬(G & H)

(1) ¬¬H → ¬G   Prem
(2) G → ¬H   1 TR
(3) ¬G v ¬H   2 MI
(4) ¬(G & H)   3 DM

11.1.2 TWO SIMPLIFYING MODIFICATIONS (OPTIONAL)[1]

One of the advantages of classifying equivalence rules separately is that we may now introduce the following simplifications:

1. Any statement may be replaced by another statement to which it is equivalent by an application of one of the Equivalence Rules (DN, DM, BE, TR, and MI), even if it is only a component of a compound statement. That is, unlike the other rules of inference, from now on *these do not have to be applied only to whole lines.*
2. Each of these equivalence rules can be applied simultaneously with, and on the same line as, one of the other rules of inference, e.g., 2, 3 MT, DN.

These two modifications can simplify certain proofs a lot. Here is an example of use of the first modification:

¬A → B ∴ ¬B → A

(1) ¬A → B   Prem
(2) ¬B → ¬¬A   1 TR
(3) ¬B → A   2 DN

Here we have applied DN within the conditional, to its component ¬¬A. Without the first modification we would instead have had to do a 5 line conditional proof, beginning with ¬B as the supposition.

---

[1] Some instructors may wish to defer this "relaxation" of the application of equivalence rules until later in the course. Accordingly, solutions for chapters 11-12 will be given both with and without these simplifying assumptions, and they will not be assumed to be in use until chapter 17.

Using the second modification we could save a further line in the same proof by combining TR and DN on one line:

(1) ¬A → B   Prem
(2) ¬B → A   1 TR, DN

But even greater economy can be achieved by using our first modification, as can be seen in the following example. Without it, we need to perform a *reductio*:

¬(A ↔ B), A → B ∴ ¬(B → A)
(1) ¬(A ↔ B)   Prem
(2) A → B   Prem
   |(3) B → A   Supp/RA
   |(4) (A → B) & (B → A)   2, 3 Conj
   |(5) A ↔ B   4 BE
   |(6) ⊥   5, 1 Conj
(7) ¬(B → A)   3-6 RA

But if instead we apply the equivalence rule BE within the negation, we save three lines:

¬(A ↔ B), A → B ∴ ¬(B → A)
(1) ¬(A ↔ B)   Prem
(2) A → B   Prem
(3) ¬[(A → B) & (B → A)]   1 BE
(4) ¬(B → A)   3, 2 CS

In some of the more complex proofs we shall consider later, particularly in Predicate Logic, the saving of writing allowed by these modifications will be considerable.

Caution: when applying the equivalence rules within compound statements, make sure that you are applying them to a *component*, not just an arbitrary string of symbols. For example, the following is *NOT* a valid application:

(1) ¬M → N   Prem
(2) ¬¬N → ¬M   1 TR   *INVALID!*

Here ¬N → ¬M has been substituted for M → N in line 1. This a mistake because M → N is *not* a component of ¬M → N. Compare with the following two valid applications of the above rules:

(1) ¬(M → N)   Prem
(2) ¬(¬N → ¬M)   1 TR

(1) ¬M → N   Prem
(2) ¬N → M   1 TR, DN

In the second of these we have subbed ¬M for p and ¬N for q in applying TR, and then applied DN to ¬¬M to save a line.

11.1.3 PROOF STRATEGIES

The strategies for constructing proofs using some of these rules of inference are reasonably obvious. In the case of the equivalence rules just considered, they can be used any time the replacement of some statement by its equivalent looks promising in the overall context of the proof. Likewise the strategy for Conj and Simp is straightforward: you apply Conj to form a conjunction, and Simp to get one of the conjuncts from a conjunction you already have. (But remember, these can only be applied to whole lines, not within a line. From ¬(A & B) you cannot infer ¬A by disjunction, since ¬(A & B) is a negation—the ¬ is the governing operator.)

Still, it is the overall strategy of a proof that may cause difficulty, and here some advice will be in order. The overall strategy is determined by whatever the *conclusion* is that you are trying to reach. That will be your initial goal. In order to get there you may then determine various *subsidiary goals*, which will then generate strategies for various sub-proofs. So strategies may be organized according to whatever statement it is you are trying to prove. Here you should keep in mind the governing operator which tells you the kind of statement you are dealing with. For example, ¬(F → ¬G) is not a conditional: the governing operator is ¬, indicating that it is a negation (the negation of a conditional, to be sure). This is why, if you are trying to prove such a statement, you should be thinking about applying RA, which is a rule that introduces a ¬. In fact, in working out how to solve a proof it is quite helpful to think of which rules will introduce the governing operator of the statement you are aiming to prove:

governing operator	¬	&	v	→	↔
rule that can introduce it	RA	Conj	Disj	CP	BE

This gives you a starting point. But the following table gives more detailed strategic tips:

Goal-Directed Strategies

TYPE OF STATEMENT YOU ARE TRYING TO PROVE	STRATEGY TO CONSIDER
conjunction	**Conj:** Search for the two conjuncts among your premises; if either one is not there, make deriving it a subsidiary goal.
disjunction	**Disj:** search for one of the two disjuncts among your premises; then apply Disj.
conditional	**CP:** suppose the antecedent of the conditional, and make deriving the consequent a subsidiary goal.
biconditional	**BE:** search your premises for the relevant conditional and its converse; if either is not there, make deriving it a subsidiary goal, and apply the **CP** strategy.
negation of a conjunction	**RA:** suppose the conjunction, and make a subsidiary goal of deriving a contradiction.
negation of a disjunction	**RA:** suppose the disjunction, and make a subsidiary goal of deriving a contradiction; or **DM:** apply DM to convert into a conjunction of negations, and apply **Simp**.
negation of a conditional	**RA:** suppose the conditional, and make a subsidiary goal of deriving a contradiction.
negation of a biconditional	**RA:** suppose the biconditional, and make a subsidiary goal of deriving a contradiction.

These are just rules of thumb: often they will work, but sometimes not. When no other goal-directed strategies seem to work, you can always do a reductio proof: suppose the opposite of what you are trying to prove, and aim for a contradiction.

Premise-directed Strategies

I would recommend always having some such overall goal-directed strategy. But it is only human nature to try proceeding in the opposite direction, namely by beginning with the premises, and seeing how far you can get towards your conclusion by applying rules to what you are given. For this you will need strategies for breaking down the premises in proofs or subproofs into their components.

In such premise-directed strategies, you will need to identify the governing operator of the statement you are starting from, and then look for ways to eliminate it. We can draw up a table similar to the one given above for strategies for proving statements, but this time a table for strategies for breaking down statements:

governing operator	¬	&	v	→	↔
rule that can eliminate it	RA + DN	Simp	DS, DL	MP, MT	BE

Again, we can give more detailed strategic tips:

TYPE OF STATEMENT YOU ARE WORKING FROM	STRATEGY TO CONSIDER
conjunction	**Simp:** detach either conjunct, as needed.
disjunction	**DS:** search for the negation of one of the disjuncts among your premises; then apply DS. **DL:** if the argument has a dilemma form, search for the conditionals which have one of the disjuncts as antecedent, the conclusion as consequent. If they are not there, derive them by a CP strategy.
conditional	**MP:** search for the antecedent of the conditional, and apply MP to get the consequent. **MT:** search for the negation of the consequent of the conditional, and apply MT to get the negation of the antecedent.
biconditional	**BE:** detach the conditional or its converse as needed.
negation of a conjunction	**CS:** search for one of the conjuncts, and apply CS to derive the negation of the other.
negation of a disjunction	**DM:** apply DM to convert into a conjunction of negations, and apply Simp strategy to detach either of the negations.

negation of a conditional	**MI:** apply MI to convert $\neg[p \rightarrow q]$ into $\neg[\neg p \vee q]$; then apply DM and DN together to get p & $\neg q$, then apply Simp.
negation of a biconditional	**BE:** apply BE to get a negation of the conjunction of the two conditionals, and proceed from there by the CS strategy.

Here is an example of application of these strategies. The proof in question has a conclusion that is a conjunction, but neither conjunct is given, so we set these as goals

$\neg F \vee \neg G, G \vee G \therefore \neg F$ & G

(1)	$\neg F \vee \neg G$	Prem
(2)	$G \vee G$	Prem

But now it is not easy to see where to proceed. Working forward from the premises, we cannot use a **DS** strategy on either one, and there is no obvious way to apply the **DL** strategy. So we resort to a reductio (**RA**). G should be provable from G $\vee$ G, so let's suppose the opposite and aim for a contradiction:

	(3) $\neg G$	Supp/RA	
	(4) G	2, 3 DS	
	(5) G & $\neg$G	4, 3 Conj	—*so $\neg$G must be false*
(6)	G	3-5 RA, DN	

Now what? We have G, and that is half the conclusion. And we haven't used premise (1). So this suggests combining G with $\neg F \vee \neg G$ by **DS**. But DS is "From $p \vee q$ and $\neg q$, infer p," so p is $\neg F$ and q is $\neg G$, so $\neg q$ is $\neg\neg G$, which we need first:

(7)	$\neg\neg G$	6 DN
(8)	$\neg F$	1, 7 DS
(9)	$\neg F$ & G	8, 6 Conj

A **DL**-type proof is possible, but by no means obvious. It depends on noticing that the conclusion is derivable on the supposition of G, and that *both* disjuncts (!) of the second premise are G:

(1)	$\neg F \vee \neg G$	Prem	
(2)	$G \vee G$	Prem	
	(3) G	Supp/CP	
	(4) $\neg\neg G$	3 DN	—*for correct DS subst'n instance*
	(5) $\neg F$	1, 4 DS	
	(6) $\neg F$ & G	3, 5 Conj	
(7)	$G \rightarrow (\neg F$ & G$)$	2-6 CP	
(8)	$\neg F$ & G	2, 7, 7 DL	

EXERCISES 11.1

Prove the validity of the following abstract arguments:

1. P v P ∴ ¬¬P

2. P ∴ Q → (P & Q)

3. ¬(F → ¬G) ∴ G

4. ¬(¬A & ¬B), ¬(B v C) ∴ A

5. A v (¬B → C), ¬(A v C) ∴ B

6. (P › Q) → P ∴ P

7. (P v Q) v R ∴ P v (Q v R)

8. P ↔ Q ∴ ¬P ↔ ¬Q

9. P → (Q → R) ∴ (P → Q) → (P → R)

10. P → Q ∴ (P → ¬Q) → ¬P

11. P → R ∴ (Q → R) → [(P v Q) → R]

12. M v N, N → (O → P), O, ¬P → ¬M ∴ P

13. ¬J ↔ K, ¬K v L, ¬(L & M) ∴ M → J

14. In the following quote, an argument is advanced by (then) Toronto Maple Leafs defenceman Bryan McCabe (a hockey player not usually noted for his logical expertise). What is he arguing for (what's the conclusion)? *Symbolize as indicated, fill in any premises that are implicit, and prove the argument valid:*
    "I've got Spezza and Schaeffer right on me in the crease. If I get a STICK on one of them, I get a PENALTY. If I don't, one of them pokes it IN. I LOSE either way."[2]

___

[2] From "Mistakes Begin to Upset Coach Quinn as Leafs Lose Again," Ken Campbell, *Toronto Star*, Tuesday, October 11, 2005, p. C2.

15. In an editorial for the Toronto *Globe and Mail* on the Canadian Government's cancelling of funding for the Law Commission, John Ibbitson argued:

> By eliminating the commission's funding, the Conservative government is strangling an agency it dislikes, without consulting Parliament, through fiscal trickery and sleight of hand.... If Justice Minister Vic Toews is unhappy with the sort of work that the Law Commission is doing, he has the authority to direct it to do other work. If the government believes the commission has outlived its usefulness,...then it should ask Parliament to repeal the act that created the commission. But the Conservatives know they would lose that vote. (Thursday September 28, 2006, p. 4)

This argument can be paraphrased:

> If the Conservative government is not CANCELLING the Law Commission through fiscal trickery and sleight of hand, then it should either DIRECT it to do other work, or it must believe the Commission has OUTLIVED its usefulness. But it has not directed it to do other work. If the government believes the commission has OUTLIVED its usefulness,...then it should ASK Parliament to repeal the act that created the commission. But the Conservatives cannot ask Parliament to repeal the act [since they would not have enough votes to repeal it]. It follows that the Conservative government is cancelling the Law Commission through fiscal trickery and sleight of hand.

Symbolize the paraphrased argument as indicated, and prove it valid.

16. (**CHALLENGE**) *Symbolize the following argument as indicated, and prove it valid:* "If the WHITE Sox are American League champions, then the YANKEES and BOSTON must both have been eliminated. Hence either Boston has been eliminated, or the White Sox are not American League champions."

17. (**CHALLENGE**) *Symbolize the following argument as indicated, and prove it valid:* "If the AMERICANS and BRITISH do not both stay in Iraq, there will be a CIVIL war or a DISSOLUTION of the state. But since the Americans will stay and there won't be a dissolution of the state, there will be civil war unless the British also stay in Iraq."

11.2 DERIVED RULES

It will prove useful in some abstract derivations to have a rule that allows us to repeat a statement already given or proved on a previous line. This is the rule of *Reiteration*:

Reiteration (R)

From a statement p, infer the same statement p (on another line of the derivation, with the same indentation or one to the right of the original statement).

It obviously stretches the meaning of "inference" or "argument" to call this an argument form. It is simply a rule that allows us to reiterate a statement already assumed or derived. (The qualification about indentation is needed only to prevent a statement that depends on an undischarged supposition being used later in a proof as if it does not.) Here is a simple (but admittedly contrived) example of its use:

To prove J, (J & J) → M ∴ M

(1) J	Prem
(2) (J & J) → M	Prem
(3) J	1 R
(4) (J & J)	2, 3 Conj
(5) M	2, 4 MP

The validity of this rule follows immediately from our definition, since whatever p stands for, you cannot validly deny it, having asserted it. But its validity can also easily be derived from the rules of inference we have already:

(1) p	Prem
(2) $\neg p$	Supp/RA
(3) ⊥	1, 2 Conj
(4) $\neg\neg p$	2-3 RA
(5) p	4 DN

As such, we can regard it as an example of a *derived rule of inference*: that is, it is a valid argument form derived from the set of rules that we have taken as basic or primitive. We do not strictly speaking need it, as we could always run a derivation similar to that just given in any proof in which we needed it: it simply makes such proofs shorter. We could say precisely the same thing about some of our other rules of inference. For example, we proved the Hypothetical Syllogism (From $p \rightarrow q$ and $q \rightarrow r$, infer $p \rightarrow r$) using CP, and obviously any proof in which we use HS could be replaced by a longer proof where p is supposed and r is derived, and then CP is applied.

In fact, as you may have realized by now, it is a bit arbitrary which of the various valid forms we dignify as rules of inference. We want to pick a set of forms that is sufficient to derive all the argument forms that are formally valid, and we certainly do not want a set of forms from which a contradiction is provable. If the first condition is satisfied, our system can be said to be *complete*; if the second is satisfied, it is said to be *consistent*.

As the above examples of R and HS show, we have more than enough rules in our system. So we could reduce the number of rules of inference that we must have to those sufficient to guarantee completeness and consistency of the system. These would be our *primitive rules* of inference. The remaining ones (which would be kept simply for making derivations more intuitive and shorter) would be *derived rules*. Thus, now that we have the rule RA, from this together with the other rules of inference we may derive rules such as Conjunctive Syllogism, Double Negation, and De Morgan's Laws (exercises 18, 19, 20, respectively). If you do all the exercises for this chapter and the last, you will see that there are some other redundancies in our system. In chapter 10, exercise 1, MT was proved using MP, Conj, and RA. On the other hand, in the next chapter, we will establish *reductio ad impossibile* using only CP, Simp, MP, MT, CS, and DN. So it appears we do not strictly need both MT and RA. Again, BE is strictly only a definition, giving a short form for a conjunction of conditionals, and so could be dispensed with. The following set would make a concise and adequate set of primitive rules, two rules for each main operator: MP, CP; Conj, Simp; Disj, DS; RA, DN. (Here the first form of DN, from *p* infer ¬¬*p*, is not strictly necessary, since it is derivable using RA: see exercise 19. But we do need the second form of DN: from ¬¬*p* infer *p*.)

Of course, if economy of rules and symbols is what is desired, we could do much better. Given De Morgan's Laws, we could translate any expression containing '&' into one containing '¬' and 'v.' And given MI, we could translate any disjunction into an expression involving only '→' and '¬.' So these last two operators could be the only two we used, and then the only rules we would need would be MP, CP, RA, and DN. This does not establish that these rules alone would be sufficient to prove every valid argument form valid, however, and the economy of expression would be bought at the cost of a tremendous loss of economy and intuitiveness in our proofs, which would be almost impossible to follow, and easy to make errors in.

Another concise way of presenting systems of logic is in terms of *axioms, rules of inference*, and *theorems*. We'll come back to that in the next chapter, when we have the wherewithal to define axioms and theorems.

EXERCISES 11.2

18. *Prove the CS rule by a reductio argument.*

19. *Show that* once we have the Reductio ad Absurdum rule, *the first form of DN may be derived in a four-line proof* by proving the substitution instance: P ∴ ¬¬P.

20. *Show that De Morgan's Laws may be derived from the other rules by proving*
    (a) ¬(A v B) ∴ ¬A & ¬B
    (b) ¬A & ¬B ∴ ¬(A v B)
    (c) ¬(A & B) ∴ ¬A v ¬B
    (d) ¬A v ¬B ∴ ¬(A & B)
    —without using DM, of course!

Using only the "primitive" rules of inference MP, CP, Conj, Simp, Disj, DS, RA, DN, *derive the following rules:*

21. Modus Tollens (MT): From $p \rightarrow q$ and $\neg q$, infer $\neg p$.

22. Dilemma (DL): From $p \lor q$, $p \rightarrow r$ and $q \rightarrow r$, infer r.

23. Two results that follow immediately from the rule MI (Material Implication) are the infamous Paradoxes of Material Implication: (i) $\neg p \therefore p \rightarrow q$ (ii) $q \therefore p \rightarrow q$.
    The first states that if we know a statement p is false, then if it is true, then q—i.e., anything—follows! The second, given that q is true, then if p—i.e., if anything at all!—then q follows. Each of these contradicts our normal understanding of a conditional. See Appendix 1 on the Paradoxes of Material Implication.
    (a) Prove these in three lines each using MI.
    (b) **(CHALLENGE)** Construct proofs without using MI.

24. **(CHALLENGE)** An alternative set of primitive rules would be MP, CP, Conj, Simp, Disj, DL, RA, DN. *Derive DS as a derived rule using this set of primitive rules only.*
    [Hint: Prove $\neg(\neg p \ \& \ \neg q)$ from $p \lor q$ first, before using the premise $\neg p$.]

Chapter Twelve

SL as a Formal System

12.1 RULES OF FORMATION

12.1.1 SYMBOLS, FORMULAS, AND WFFS

The logic we have pursued so far has been concerned with arguments and statements. We have also dealt with abstract arguments, where capital letters stand for statements, and with formulas representing compound statements, argument forms, proofs, and rules of inference. The latter were formulated in terms of statement variables, as were the argument forms we encountered in the last chapter and whose validity we proved, and there we even came across an argument form in which a conclusion was validly proved from no premises. Now it is time to bring some order to this zoo, by approaching it all systematically.

We already defined *argument* and *statement* above in chapters 1 and 2. But we did not define *formula*. A formula is just a string of logical symbols, and when these are ordered properly so they can represent a statement, the formula is said to be *well-formed*. So let's begin by listing our logical symbols, and then proceed to some definitions. Capital letters represent simple statements, or statements we choose not to analyze further. Then we have the statement operators, the unary one, '¬,' and the four binary operators, '&,' 'v,' '→,' and '↔.' In addition we have the groupers, i.e., (parentheses), [brackets], and {braces}. These divide into the left-hand groupers, '(', '[', '{', and the matching right-hand groupers, ')', ']', '}', each of which is a mirror-image of the corresponding left-hand one. Finally, we have the triple-dot sign representing therefore, '∴,' and the turnstile representing "entails," '⊢' (see section 2 below). In terms of these we may establish the following definitions:

*Each of the following is a **logical symbol**:*	
a capital letter	such as A, B, R, W

a unary or binary statement operator	$\neg; \&, \vee, \rightarrow, \leftrightarrow$	
a left-hand or matching right-hand grouper	(, [, {;	},],)
the triple-dot and turnstile	$\therefore$	$\vdash$

| A **formula** is a string of logical symbols | e.g., | $[\neg A \rightarrow (\} \vee$ |

Now since we know a *well-formed formula* must correspond to a statement, simple or compound, we may use the rules of statement formation from chapter 3 to define it. The standard abbreviation is "wff," as pronounced by dogs:

Well-formed Formulas (wffs)
1) (*simple statements*) Any capital letter is a **wff**.
2) (*unary compounds*) A **wff** preceded by a negation symbol is a **wff**.
3) (*binary compounds*) A left-hand grouper, followed by a **wff**, followed by a binary operator, followed by a **wff**, followed by a matching right-hand grouper, is a **wff**.
3*) (*convention regarding outermost groupers*) The outermost groupers are understood, and need not be explicitly written in (although they can be).
4) Only formulas that are constructible by application of the above three rules are **wffs**.

The above is what's called a *recursive definition*; once we have something that's a wff by clause 1) we can plug it into clause 2) or 3) wherever the word **wff** appears and generate another wff, and so on recursively. Conversely, if we have a formula and want to see whether it is a wff, we see if we can build it up by the above rules: it will be a wff if and only if it can be built up by these rules. Let's look at some examples to see how this works:

P → Q & R This cannot be a wff, because although P, Q, and R are wffs by clause 1), both → and & are binary operators, and by 3) each would come with associated groupers. Only the outermost groupers would remain unwritten by clause 3*). On the other hand, proceeding in this way we could form {P → Q} & R, as well as P → (Q & R), etc.

¬¬¬A ↔ B This is a wff, because A and B are wffs by clause 1), ¬¬¬A is a wff by repeated application of clause 2), [¬¬¬A ↔ B] is formable from these wffs by clause 3), and by 3*) we need not write in the outermost groupers.

[C ¬ F] This is a not a wff, because the only way to get the brackets is by clause 2); but '¬' is not a binary operator.

A, B ∴ C   This is not a wff, because the comma and triple-dot do not occur in the definition of wffs.

This definition of wffs can be useful in helping to properly identify statements as negations, conditionals, etc., and thus in applying rules of inference without making mistakes. Take, for instance, the following "proof" of an instance of one of De Morgan's Laws using only rules of inference other than DM:

(1) ¬(A ∨ B)	Prem	*THIS "PROOF" IS INVALID!!*
(2) A & ¬B	Supp/RA	
(3) A	2 Simp	
(4) ¬¬B	2, 3 DS	*YOW!*
(5) ¬B	2 Simp	
(6) ¬B & ¬¬B	5, 4 Conj	
(7) ¬A & ¬B	2-6 RA	*YOUCH!*

I leave the blunder on line (4) for you to identify. Here I'm interested in the error on line (7) of mistaking ¬A & ¬B for the negation of the supposition on line (2), A & ¬B. The statement ¬A & ¬B is a *conjunction of negations*; whereas what can validly be inferred on line (7) is the negation of the supposition, i.e., ¬(A & ¬B), which is a *negation of a conjunction*. The rules for wff formation help to distinguish statements like these, by looking at how the various wffs could be formed (not *inferred*, notice). The supposition A & ¬B could be formed (after getting A and ¬B by clauses (1) and (2)) by an application of the clause for binary operators, (3), which introduces groupers. The outermost groupers are implicit when A & ¬B stands alone (3*), but must be written in when it is used to form a compound, as in its negation, ¬(A & ¬B).

In looking at how wffs are formed in this way, we build them up from the inside out by application of the rules of formation. The last operator used in so building the wff is the ***governing operator*** for the compound statement. Thus ¬(A & ¬B) is a negation; but (¬A & ¬B) is a conjunction.

The formula in the last of the examples considered above, A, B ∴ C, is recognizable as what we have called an *abstract argument*: this is what we get when we take an argument in words (a *concrete argument*) and symbolize it. That is, each constituent statement of the argument is symbolized by representing it by a wff. It is then an interpreted statement. Thus

An **abstract argument** is what is obtained by symbolizing an argument. The premises are represented as wffs separated by commas; they are followed by the triple-dot symbol, and a wff symbolizing the conclusion, e.g., B → C, ¬A ∨ B ∴ C ∨ ¬A.

Analogously,

> An **abstract statement** is what is obtained by symbolizing a statement. It is simply an interpreted wff.[1]

Now, in analyzing arguments we found that certain patterns often recurred, and in stating these patterns we found it convenient to introduce *statement variables*, which stand for any abstract statements that we may consistently substitute for them. Thus

> A **statement variable** is any lower-case italicized letter from p to z that is used as a place-holder for statements, i.e., for which any abstract statement may be substituted.

We used these statement variables to express argument forms:

> An **argument form** is an array of logical symbols containing statement variables rather than statements, such that a single-inference argument is produced when statements are consistently substituted for the variables, e.g., $p \lor q, q \rightarrow r \therefore p \lor r$.

Obviously the components of such argument forms are likewise not statements, but are themselves forms:

> A **statement form** is an array of logical symbols containing statement variables such that an abstract statement or wff is produced when statements or wffs are consistently substituted for the variables, e.g., $p \lor q, \neg[q \rightarrow r]$.

Thus if the wff A & B is substituted for p, ¬C is substituted for q, and ¬A for r in the above statement form examples, we get (A & B) ∨ ¬C and ¬[¬C → ¬A]. If we make the same substitutions consistently in the argument form $p \lor q, q \rightarrow r \therefore p \lor r$, we get the abstract argument (A & B) ∨ ¬C, ¬C → ¬A ∴ (A & B) ∨ ¬A. This motivates the definition

> A **substitution instance** of an argument form is any argument that results when the same statement or wff is substituted for each occurrence of the same statement variable, e.g., (A & B) for each occurrence of p, ¬C for each occurrence of q, and so forth.

---

[1] The only point in defining wffs separately from abstract statements is that one can construct a formal system wholly in terms of *uninterpreted* wffs and then supply an interpretation later. Many logicians prefer this approach.

Now $p \lor q, q \to r \therefore p \lor r$ is a valid argument form; but it is not a rule of inference. As we have seen, only some argument forms are deemed sufficiently basic or memorable to be distinguished as rules of inference. But essentially, that's all a rule of inference is: a valid argument form elevated to the status of being usable to derive some statements from others in a proof. But what is a proof? Here we need to say something about the equivalence between proving an argument form valid and proving an argument formally valid.

If we can prove that an argument of a given form is valid, we have thereby proved that that form of argument is valid. For instance, if we can prove the formal validity of the abstract argument $\neg C \to B, \neg B \therefore C$ by applying our rules of inference, we know that the form $\neg p \to q, \neg q \therefore p$ is valid. We know that $\neg C \to B, \neg B \therefore C$ is formally valid because the denial of the conclusion is logically inconsistent with the acceptance of the premises: otherwise one of our rules of inference would have been formally invalid. Given all this, and bearing in mind proofs involving suppositions, we may define a proof of the validity of an argument form as follows:

A **proof** of the validity of an argument form is a numbered sequence of lines, each of which contains either a premise of an argument of this form, a supposition, or a statement derived from one of the preceding lines by a rule of inference; and whose last line is the conclusion of the argument, occurring after all suppositions have been discharged.

12.1.2 CONSISTENCY AND COMPLETENESS

Each of our rules of inference corresponds to a valid argument form, as we have argued in each case, either by proving validity through appeal to the definition of formal validity, or by proving its validity using the rules already proved valid by that means. It follows that any argument form that is provable using the rules of inference of statement logic is itself formally valid. That being so, we say that the set of rules of inference of statement logic—the "primitive" rules identified in the previous chapter as MP, CP, Conj, Simp, Disj, DS, RA, and DN, as well as all the rules of inference derived from them—is *consistent*.[2]

A system of rules of inference is said to be **consistent** if and only if any argument form that is provable using the rules is itself formally valid.

We have not, however, proved that any argument form that is valid according to the definition of formal validity is provably valid by these rules. If that is so, the set of rules is said to be *complete*.

---

[2] In approaches to logic depending on syntactical versus semantic interpretations of the rules of inference, what I have called here "consistency" is usually called "soundness." I prefer the older term so as to avoid confusion with the quite different concept of soundness of arguments. But if you go on to further studies in logic you will probably encounter this notion as "soundness."

A system of rules of inference is said to be **complete** if and only if any argument form that is formally valid is provably valid by these rules.

To demonstrate completeness is a little beyond the scope of a first course in logic. We will, however, prove the consistency and completeness of the closely related tree rules of chapter 14 below, as well as of the Truth Tree method itself.

EXERCISES 12.1

1. *Identify which of the following formulas are **wffs***, giving a brief explanation for your answer.

    EXAMPLE: ¬(¬B) v R; ANSWER: not a **wff**. B and R are wffs by clause (i), and ¬B and ¬¬B by clause (ii), but not ¬(¬B). Parentheses only come with binary operators.
    (a) ¬¬¬B
    (b) O ¬ P
    (c) L → M
    (d) B ∴ ¬A
    (e) ¬(p v R)
    (f) ¬(R → ¬R)
    (g) [¬(V ↔ ¬P] }
    (h) q ∴ p → q

2. Each of the following is either (i) an abstract statement, (ii) an abstract argument, (iii) an argument form, or (iv) a statement form. *Identify which each is*.
    (a) ¬¬¬B
    (b) ¬p ∴ p → q
    (c) L → M
    (d) B ∴ ¬A
    (e) ¬(p v q)
    (f) R → ¬R ∴ ¬R
    (g) q → (p → q)

3. *Determine the governing operator of each of the following wffs*, i.e., the last to be applied in building it up by the rules of formation. Use this to determine whether the corresponding abstract statement is (i) a simple statement; (ii) a negation; (iii) a conditional; (iv) a conjunction; (v) a disjunction; or (vi) a biconditional:
    (a) L → M
    (b) ¬¬¬B
    (c) ¬(V ↔ ¬P)
    (d) ¬A & ¬B

(e) ¬(A & ¬B)
(f) ¬(R → ¬R)
(g) {¬B → A}
(h) (¬[F & G] → H)

4. *State which of the following are correct substitution instances of* MT, DS, or CS:
    (a) B, R → ¬B ∴ ¬R
    (b) ¬(A & ¬B), ¬B ∴ ¬A
    (c) C → ¬B, ¬C ∴ ¬¬B
    (d) (¬B v R), B ∴ R
    (e) (¬B v R), ¬B ∴ R
    (f) (¬B v R), ¬¬B ∴ R
    (g) (A & B), ¬B ∴ A
    (h) ¬¬S v ¬R, ¬¬¬S ∴ ¬R
    (i) ¬[(A & B) & C], A & B ∴ ¬C

Identify the errors in the following incorrect "proofs":

5.   (1) ¬A & ¬B   Prem
       | (2) B   Supp/CP
       | (3) ¬¬B   2 DN
       | (4) ¬¬A   1, 3 CS
      (5) B → ¬¬A   2-4 CP

6.   (1) ¬A & ¬B   Prem
       | (2) A v B   Supp/RA
       | (3) A   2 DS
       | (4) B   2 DS
       | (5) ¬A   3 DN
      (6) ¬(A v B)   2-5 RA

7.   (1) ¬(A v B)   Prem
       | (2) ¬A   Supp/CP
       | (3) ¬B   1, 2 DS
      (4) ¬A & ¬B   2-3 CP

8.   (1) ¬(A v B)   Prem
       | (2) ¬(¬A & ¬B)   Supp/RA
       | (3) ¬¬A   2 Simp
       | (4) A   3 DN
       | (5) ¬A   1, 4 DS
       | (6) A & ¬A   4, 5 Conj
      (7) ¬A & ¬B   2-6 RA

9.   (1) ¬(A ∨ B)   Prem
         (2) A & ¬B   Supp/RA
         (3) A   2 Simp
         (4) ¬¬B   1, 3 DS
         (5) ¬B   2 Simp
         (6) ¬B & ¬¬B   5, 4 Conj
     (7) ¬A & ¬B   2-6 RA

12.2 SEQUENTS, THEOREMS, AND AXIOMS

12.2.1 SEQUENTS AND THEOREMS

In proving the Law of Excluded Middle in section 1 of chapter 10 we saw an example of a proof of a statement—or more accurately, a statement form—from no premises. This can occur because we can begin a proof with a supposition, which is discharged by the step of *reductio ad absurdum* at the end. It could also occur using a supposition and a Conditional Proof strategy, as in this example:

     (1) (P → Q) & (Q → R)   Supp/CP
     (2) P → Q   1 Simp
     (3) Q → R   1 Simp
     (4) P → R   2, 3 HS
   (5) [(P → Q) & (Q → R)] → (P → R)   1-4 CP

The existence of such proofs raises some interesting questions. First, we cannot have an argument with no premises, so what shall we say that such a proof has proved valid? Second, all we have done in this proof is to take a valid argument, show that the conjunction of all its premises entails its conclusion, and then conditionalize the conclusion on this conjunction. Couldn't we do that with *any* valid argument?

The answer to the second question is, yes, indeed we could. What this shows is that there is a very close relationship between an argument and the corresponding conditional whose antecedent is the conjunction of the argument's premises, and whose consequent is the argument's conclusion: if the conditional is logically true, the argument is formally valid; and if the conditional is logically false, the argument is formally invalid. Differently put, the argument is formally valid iff the conditional is true. (Can you prove that? Exercise 10). This is as we would expect, given the close relationship between P ∴ Q and P → Q, i.e., between inference and implication, explained in chapter 4, section 3.

It therefore proves useful to have some way of representing the notion of consequence, of "following from," that is involved in both asserting that P → Q, Q → R ∴ P → R and in summarizing this in a statement of the form [(P → Q) & (Q → R)] → (P → R). This can be done by introducing a symbol for *entailment*, the turnstile: ⊢. This is to be read as asserting that the statements on the left of the '⊢' *entail* the statement on the right, or equivalently, that the statement to the right of the '⊢' *follows from* those (if any) on the left.

> One statement or set of statements **entails** another statement if the latter **follows from** the former. Thus, in the case of a valid argument (where all the premises are asserted) such as $\neg C \rightarrow D, C \rightarrow E, \neg D \therefore E$, we say that the premises **entail** the conclusion, symbolized $\neg C \rightarrow D, C \rightarrow E, \neg D \vdash E$.

Thus the proof of the Hypothetical Syllogism (see chapter 7) establishes that

(1) $P \rightarrow Q, Q \rightarrow R \vdash P \rightarrow R$

whilst the above conditional proof establishes that

(2) $\vdash [(P \rightarrow Q) \& (Q \rightarrow R)] \rightarrow (P \rightarrow R)$

The formulas (1) and (2) are called *sequents*. The two formulas on the left of the '⊢' in (1) (which we may call the *premises of the sequent*) validly entail the one on the right (which we may call its *conclusion*); in such a case, we may call that sequent *valid*. By extension, we may also call the second sequent valid.

> A **sequent** is an assertion that one statement or wff (the *conclusion*, written to the right of a turnstile) follows from a sequence of zero or more statements or wffs (the *premises*, written to the left of the turnstile and separated by commas).

Again, we know that (1) and (2) are valid sequents whatever statements might be substituted for P, Q, and R, so long as they are consistently substituted. So, by analogy with the distinction between *argument* and *argument form*, we may define a *sequent form*:

> A **sequent form** is an array of logical symbols containing statement variables rather than statements, such that a sequent is produced when statements are consistently substituted for the variables. e.g., $p \vee q, q \rightarrow r \vdash p \vee r$.

Thus (1) is an *instance* of the valid *sequent form*

(3) $p \rightarrow q, q \rightarrow r \vdash p \rightarrow r$

and (2) is an instance of the valid sequent form

(4) $\vdash [(p \rightarrow q) \& (q \rightarrow r)] \rightarrow (p \rightarrow r)$

Thus we have extended the meaning of validity so that it not only applies to arguments and argument forms, but also to sequents and sequent forms.

In a sequent form like (4), with nothing to the left of the '⊢,' the statement form to the right of the '⊢' is *logically true*, or, in logicians' parlance, a *tautology*. (We shall examine tautologies in the next chapter, on truth tables.) The way we have set up statement logic, all such formulas are derivable by application of our rules of inference alone. They can therefore be regarded as *theorems*, as can any of the derived rules of inference.

A **theorem** is a sequent form with no premises, validly derived entirely by using the rules of inference.

12.2.2 AXIOMS AND THE PROPOSITIONAL CALCULUS (CHALLENGE LEVEL)

Another way of presenting the system of statement logic, perhaps modelled more closely on geometry, was pioneered by Gottlob Frege. Here one begins by taking a set of statement forms as *axiom schemas*. Each of these axiom schemas corresponds to what would be a theorem in a natural deduction system like ours, that is, the conclusion of a valid premise-less sequent. The idea is that each of these axiom schemas represents a true statement form, and all other true statement forms are then derivable from them by the application of very simple rules of inference. Thus any valid argument form corresponds to such a valid sequent form whose conclusion is a statement form provable from the axiom schemas. Statement logic presented in this manner is traditionally called *Propositional Calculus*.

An **axiom schema** is a statement form assumed without proof in the Propositional Calculus. A valid argument form is represented by a statement form derivable from these axiom schemas using certain rules of inference, understood as representing the conclusion of a valid premiseless sequent form.

In Frege's system for statement logic the only rules of inference are Modus Ponens and a Rule of Substitution allowing you to substitute one statement form for any other, so long as it is done consistently. Frege presented six axiom schemas, all involving only the operators '¬' and '→.' But as the eminent Polish logician Łukasiewicz showed in the 1920s, the following three will suffice:

(f1) $(p \rightarrow q) \rightarrow [(q \rightarrow r) \rightarrow (p \rightarrow r)]$
(f2) $p \rightarrow (\neg p \rightarrow q)$
(f3) $(\neg p \rightarrow p) \rightarrow p$

Apart from his elegant axiomatization of logic, Jan Łukasiewicz (1878-1956) is famous for having invented the so-called Polish notation for logical operators, the basis for the memory store used in many calculators and programming languages. He was also a pioneer of many-valued logics.

The first of these is the conclusion of our sequent form (4) above representing the Hypothetical Syllogism. The second represents one of the so-called Paradoxes of Material Implication, first discovered by Duns Scotus in the Middle Ages (on these paradoxes, see chapter 11, exercise 23; this chapter, exercise 12 below; and Appendix 1). The third represents a sequent with a fascinating history, the *consequentia mirabilis*, or marvellous consequence: see Appendix 2.[3]

Of course, in order to apply a system such as Frege's, all disjunctions and conjunctions would have to be expressed in terms of the operators '¬' and '→.' As explained in the previous chapter, this can be done by recourse to the equivalence of $p \vee q$ to $\neg p \to q$ by MI, and the equivalence of $p \& q$ to $\neg(\neg p \vee \neg q)$ by DM, and thus to $\neg(p \to \neg q)$ by MI. Using these equivalences, f2 is just a version of the Disjunction rule of inference. The argument form represented by the Conjunctive Syllogism rule, on the other hand, would have to be proved by proving from f1-f3 the statement form

$$p \to [\neg(p \& q) \to \neg q]$$

This in turn must be expressed as

$$p \to [(p \to \neg q) \to \neg q]$$

which is readily seen to be a version of MP.

Converting all disjunctions and conjunctions into conditionals and negations certainly gives an economy of expression. Actually, greater economy of expression still can be achieved through the use of either of two new operators, Peirce's Arrow Operator '↓,' and Sheffer's Stroke Operator '|,' in terms of either of which all the other operators can be defined.[4] Peirce's Arrow expresses the meaning of "neither...nor...," and is therefore sometimes called the NOR operator:

---

[3] See William and Martha Kneale, *The Development of Logic*, p. 525.

[4] C.S. Peirce introduced his statement operator in a paper of 1880, reproduced in vol. 4, §§12-20 of his *Collected Papers*, ed. C. Hartshorne, P. Weiss, and A.W. Burks (Cambridge: Cambridge, 1931-1958). H.M. Sheffer introduced his operator and the resulting simplified system in a paper in 1913, *Trans. Amer. Math. Soc.* xiv, pp. 181-88. See the Kneales, *Development*, p. 423ff.

The founder of pragmatism, the American philosopher Charles Sanders Peirce (1839-1914) was a polymath who wrote prolifically on his hugely varied interests. A practising chemist and geodesist, he was the founder of semiotics, an evolutionary metaphysician, and made numerous contributions to logic, including the theory of relations.

Photo courtesy of: National Oceanic and Atmospheric Administration/Department of Commerce; www.photolib. noaa.gov/historic/c&gs/theb3558.htm

Peirce's Arrow Operator: $(p \downarrow q) =_{\text{def}} \neg p \,\&\, \neg q$.

while Sheffer's Stroke expresses "not both... and...," and is therefore sometimes called the NAND operator:

Sheffer's Stroke Operator: $(p \mid q) =_{\text{def}} \neg (p \,\&\, q)$.

Thus, taking Peirce's Arrow as an example, negation can be expressed as follows: $\neg p$ is equivalent to $\neg p \,\&\, \neg p$, which = $(p \downarrow p)$, by the definition of $(p \downarrow q)$. Now conjunction: $p \,\&\, q$ is equivalent to $\neg\neg p \,\&\, \neg\neg q$, and this to $(\neg p \downarrow \neg q)$ by the definition. Given our representation of negation, this in turn can be expressed as $[(p \downarrow p) \downarrow (q \downarrow q)]$. Now disjunction: $p \lor q$ is equivalent to $\neg(\neg p \,\&\, \neg q)$ by DM, and thus to $\neg(p \downarrow q)$. This translates to $[(p \downarrow q) \downarrow (p \downarrow q)]$. The expressions for conditionals and biconditionals are more complex.

Similar expressions are obtainable for the Sheffer Stroke Operator (see exercise 14), and in 1917 J.G.P. Nicod showed that the whole of Propositional Calculus could be based on a single axiom and rule of inference expressed in terms of the Sheffer Stroke:

Nicod's axiom is

$$[p \mid (q \mid r)] \mid \{[t \mid (t \mid t)] \mid \{(s \mid q) \mid [(p \mid s) \mid (p \mid s)]\}\}$$

and the rule of inference is

From p and $[p \mid (q \mid r)]$, infer r.

As can be seen, this rule is equivalent to

From p and $p \rightarrow (q \,\&\, r)$, infer r.

Clearly, there is nothing intuitive about such a system, and it is almost impossible to create proofs in it except by converting the statements into the familiar operators and back.

EXERCISES 12.2

10. In the text it was stated "if the conditional is logically TRUE, the argument is formally VALID; and if the conditional is logically false, the argument is formally invalid. Differently put, the argument is formally valid iff the conditional is logically true." *Prove that the second statement follows from the first.*

11. According to an old tradition, there are three "Laws of Thought" (a term which gained ground after George Boole named his 1854 textbook *An Investigation of the Laws of Thought*, although today this is regarded as a misnomer). These are: (i) the Law of Identity, which we may represent $\vdash p \leftrightarrow p$; (ii) the Law of Non-contradiction: $\vdash \neg(p \ \& \ \neg p)$; and (iii) the Law of Excluded Middle: $\vdash p \lor \neg p$. The third law was proved in the text; *prove (i) and (ii).*

12. *Prove that each of the Paradoxes of Material Implication* (see Appendix 1) *may be derived as theorems using only the rules of inference* Supp, CP, Disj, and DS*:*
    (i) $\vdash p \rightarrow (\neg p \rightarrow q)$
    (ii) $\vdash q \rightarrow (p \rightarrow q)$

13. **(CHALLENGE)** As we saw in the text, Peirce's Arrow Operator is defined as $(p \downarrow q)$ $=_{\text{def}} \neg p \ \& \ \neg q$. *Find an expression for $p \rightarrow q$ in terms of the Arrow Operator.*

14. **(CHALLENGE)** The Sheffer Stroke is defined as $(p \mid q) =_{\text{def}} \neg(p \ \& \ q)$. We can express negation in terms of it as follows: $\neg p = \neg(p \ \& \ p) = (p \mid p)$. *Express the following in terms of it:*
    (a) $p \ \& \ q$
    (b) $p \lor q$
    (c) $p \rightarrow q$
    (d) $p \leftrightarrow q$

15. **(CHALLENGE)** As stated in the text, Nicod's Rule of Inference in his version of Propositional Calculus is, expressed in terms of the Sheffer Stroke: From p and $[p \mid (q \mid r)]$, infer r.
    Prove that this is equivalent to: From p and $p \rightarrow (q \ \& \ r)$, infer r.

16. **(CHALLENGE)** In Chrysippus's logical system, as far as we can reconstruct it, previously proved results, when conditionalized and expressed as tautological sequents, could be used in any subsequent proof. We may use this as a new Rule of Inference, the rule of Theorem Introduction, TI. Thus, for example, Modus Ponens may be conditionalized and expressed as a theorem: $\vdash [(p \rightarrow q) \ \& \ p] \rightarrow q$. This then allows the proof of $\vdash [(p \rightarrow \neg q) \ \& \ p] \rightarrow \neg(p \rightarrow q)$ as follows:

$$\begin{array}{lll} (1) \ (p \rightarrow \neg q) \ \& \ p & & \text{Supp/CP} \\ (2) \ p \ \ \rightarrow \neg q & & \text{1 Simp} \end{array}$$

$(3)\ p$ 1 Simp

$(4)\ [(p \to q)\ \&\ p] \to q$ TI (conditionalized Modus Ponens)

$(5)\ \neg q$ 2, 3 MP

$(6)\ \neg[(p \to q)\ \&\ p]$ 4, 5 MT

$(7)\ \neg(p \to q)$ 3, 6 CS

$(8)\ [(p \to \neg q)\ \&\ p] \to \neg(p \to q)$ 1-7 CP

By quoting *this* result in turn using TI (and without using RA), construct a similar proof for the *reductio ad impossibile*: $\vdash [(p \to q)\ \&\ (p \to \neg q)] \to \neg p$.

17. Despite his neglect of Statement Logic, Aristotle certainly used it. The following is an early instance of the *consequentia mirabilis* (see Appendix 2):

> Either we OUGHT to philosophize or we ought not. If we ought, then we ought. If we ought not, then also we ought [i.e., in order to justify this view]. Hence in any case we ought to philosophize.—Aristotle, *Protrepticus*

(a) *Symbolize and prove the formal validity of this argument.* (b) *Two of the premises are redundant. If your proof does not already show this, show it* by constructing a proof using only the non-redundant premise.

18. (**CHALLENGE**) St. Anselm of Canterbury (1033-1109) argued in his *Monologion*:

> Finally, if truth had a beginning or end, before the truth began it was true at that time that there was no truth; and after it is ended, it will be true at that time that there will be no truth. But something cannot be true without truth. Therefore there was truth before there was truth, and there will be truth after truth has ended, which is utterly self-contradictory. Therefore, whether truth is said to have a beginning or end, or is understood to have neither, truth cannot be circumscribed by beginning or end. Wherefore the same thing follows concerning the whole of nature, for the whole itself is truth.[5]

That this is an instance of *consequentia mirabilis* is brought out by St. Thomas Aquinas' apparent allusion to and summary of this argument:

> But truth follows on the destruction of truth, since, if there is no truth, then it is true that there is no truth, and nothing can be true without truth. Therefore truth is eternal.—*De veritate*, qu. 1, art. 5 (2)

(a) *Symbolizing* "there is truth" *by* T, "it is true that there is no truth" *by* U, and "truth follows on the destruction of truth" *by* $\neg T \to T$, *prove the validity of the inference stated in the first sentence.*

(b) *Interpreting "truth is eternal" by* T, *prove that this follows too.*

---

[5] My translation from the Latin text quoted by William and Martha Kneale in *Development*, p. 202; as is the passage from St. Thomas following.

Chapter Thirteen

Truth Tables

13.1.1 TRUTH TABLES

Up till now we have been concerned mainly with the validity of arguments. If a given argument whose validity depends on relationships between statements is valid, then we can prove it so (assuming the completeness of SL, statement logic). If an argument is an instance of one of the forms we have identified as fallacious, such as the Fallacy of Denying the Antecedent (FDA), then, assuming it is not an instance of a more specific valid form, we know it is invalid. But beyond that, we are stuck. We can prove arguments and their forms (and their corresponding sequents and forms) valid, if we have enough ingenuity; but if we can't prove them valid, we cannot conclude that they are invalid: it may be our lack of ingenuity. In this chapter we are going to examine techniques (originating with Gottlob Frege in 1879) that enable us to prove the validity or invalidity of any sequent (or sequent form). Given the sequent, we apply the technique and this itself will always yield the result: either valid, or invalid. Such a technique is known in the lingo as a *decision procedure*, a procedure that will always give you a yes-or-no answer for any choice of values of some input parameters.

We begin where we left off in chapter 3 where we introduced the five statement operators as *truth-functional*. Recall that this means that the *truth value* (T or F) of any compound statement formed using these operators depends only on the truth values of the component statements. We already exploited the particular ways each of these operators combine statements in formulating our rules of inference, so (with the exception, perhaps, of the pattern belonging to the conditional, which we will come to shortly) the particular patterns of truth values associated with each operator should come as no surprise. We may lay out these patterns in tables called *truth tables*, one for each operator. The first is the truth table for negation:

p	$\neg p$
T	F
F	T

This says that if a statement has one truth value, its negation will have the opposite one. Now in our truth tables for & and ∨ we need four rows, because the statement p stands for could be true or false, and for each of these values, the statement q stands for could be true or false. Their truth tables are just what you would expect:

p	q	$p \,\&\, q$
T	T	T
F	T	F
T	F	F
F	F	F

p	q	$p \vee q$
T	T	T
F	T	T
T	F	T
F	F	F

Finally there are the tables for conditionals and biconditionals

p	q	$p \to q$
T	T	T
F	T	T
T	F	F
F	F	T

p	q	$p \leftrightarrow q$
T	T	T
F	T	F
T	F	F
F	F	T

The first of these is something you should find a little perplexing. We'll come back to that later. The second is what we would expect intuitively. Now we may express the truth tables for all the operators together as follows:

p	q	$\neg p$	$p \,\&\, q$	$p \vee q$	$p \to q$	$p \leftrightarrow q$
T	T	F	T	T	T	T
F	T	T	F	T	T	F
T	F		F	T	F	F
F	F		F	F	T	T

For ease of recall, the essential information in this table can be summed up as follows:
- $\neg p$ F when p is T, and vice versa.
- $p \,\&\, q$ T if both conjuncts (p, q) are T, otherwise F.
- $p \vee q$ F if both disjuncts (p, q) are F, otherwise T.
- $p \to q$ F if the antecedent p is T and the consequent q is F; otherwise T.
- $p \leftrightarrow q$ T if the truth values of p and q match, otherwise F.

Now given these assignments, we can work out how the truth value of any truth-functional compound depends upon the various possible combinations of truth values for its components. Take for example the compound statement ¬[P ∨ (Q ↔ ¬P)]. Now P may be true, or it may be false; and in each of these cases, Q may also be true or false. So there are four cases to consider. Consequently, we set this out in a table with four rows, representing the four possible combinations. Now we work from the inside out, assigning the values for P and Q first, then working outwards. I have put numbers under the columns to show you the order in which I worked things out:

P	Q	¬	[P	∨	(Q	↔	¬	P)]
T	T	F	T	T	T	F	F	T
F	T	F	F	T	T	T	T	F
T	F	F	T	T	F	T	F	T
F	F	T	F	F	F	F	T	F
		5	1	4	1	3	2	1
		*						

In the column marked 2, I wrote in for ¬P the opposite values to P. In the column marked 3, I used the truth table for ↔ (remembering it as T if the truth values match, otherwise F); then in the column marked 4, I used the truth table for ∨ (remembering it as F only if both disjuncts are F, otherwise T). Finally, in the column marked 5, which is the column for the governing operator (denoted by an asterisk, *), I entered the opposite truth values to those in column 4. The result is that the compound statement ¬[P ∨ (Q ↔ ¬P)] is true only when both P and Q are false. All this will be the same no matter what statements might be substituted instead of P and Q, so we may say that the truth table for statements of the form ¬[p ∨ (q ↔ ¬p)] is given in the column marked 5 above. Generally,

The **truth table** for a truth-functional compound statement of a given form, involving component statements $p, q, r, \ldots$, is a complete listing of the truth values of that compound corresponding to each possible combination of truth values for the component statements represented by $p, q, r, \ldots$, written in a column under the governing operator.

For the first component statement there will be 2 possibilities, and for each of these a second component can be true or false, giving four combinations; and for each of these a third component can be true or false, giving ($2 \times 2 \times 2 =$) eight combinations; and so on. Writing $2 \times 2 \times 2$ as 2^3, we can see that in general,

A truth table involving n component statements will have 2^n rows.

13.1.2 MATERIAL IMPLICATION

Let's return to the truth table for '→,' which we promised to discuss. We know by the equivalence rule Material Implication that $p \to q$ is equivalent to $\neg p \lor q$. And indeed, when we do a truth table for that statement form it comes out the same as the table for $p \to q$:

p	q	$\neg\, p \lor q$
T	T	F T
F	T	T T
T	F	F F
F	F	T T
		*

p	q	$p \to q$
T	T	T
F	T	T
T	F	F
F	F	T
		*

What you may have found puzzling about the truth table is this. It says that a conditional is false only if the antecedent is true and the consequent false. From this it follows that (a) the conditional is true if the consequent is true, and (b) the conditional is true if the antecedent is false. This can also be seen by inspecting rows 1 and 2 for (a), and 2 and 4 for (b). Thus by either of these criteria, "If all philosophers are immortal, Socrates is dead" would count as a true conditional! But (a) corresponds to the argument form $q \therefore p \to q$, and (b) to the argument form $\neg p \therefore p \to q$, which we proved valid in exercise 23 of chapter 11, and 12 of chapter 12. As noted there, these highly counter-intuitive results are known as the *Paradoxes of Material Implication*. Other examples can easily be created: (a) makes true any conditional with a true consequent, such as "If your underwear is blue then Elvis sold a lot of records," while (b) makes true any conditional with a false antecedent, such as "If Brazil is in Europe then pigs can fly." These paradoxical results derive from the fact that when we symbolize a conditional, we do not take into account any relationship of meaning or other connection between the antecedent and consequent, save for the truth-functional one: a conditional is false if the antecedent is true and the consequent false; otherwise it is true. Almost all the conditionals occurring in ordinary language, on the other hand, are considered true because of some non-truth-functional relationship between the antecedent and consequent, such as the meaning connection in the above example between being immortal and being dead, or the causal connection between falling out of a window and breaking a leg. If such a connection is relevant to the validity of an inference, it needs to be made explicit as an extra implicit premise: here, something like "Someone who is dead cannot be immortal." This will then relieve the air of paradox. All this is discussed more fully in Appendix 1.

13.1.3 TAUTOLOGIES, CONTRADICTIONS, AND CONTINGENT STATEMENTS

The truth table of any given compound statement consists in a column of T's and F's written under the main operator. Some statements will have a column consisting only in T's:

that is, the truth value of such compound statements will be T no matter what values the components have. Here is an example: P → (Q → P):

P	Q	P	→	(Q	→	P)
T	T	T	T	T	T	T
F	T	F	T	T	F	T
T	F	T	T	F	T	T
F	F	F	T	F	T	F
		1	3	1	2	1
			*			

Such a statement with a row of T's below the governing operator is called a *tautology*, or *logical truth*:

> A **tautology** or **logical truth** is a truth-functional compound statement whose form is such that its truth value is T for each possible combination of truth values of its components: its truth table consists only in T's.

It is logically true because it is true whatever the truth values of its components are; any compound of this form will be true, no matter what its components. Thus

> A **tautologous form** is a statement form every instance of which is a tautology.

We saw examples of tautologous forms in the previous chapter, where they appeared as statement forms that could be proven true from no premises. For example, a 3-line reductio proves the theorem ⊢ *p* ∨ ¬*p* (by supposing its negation and applying DM). So we expect this to be tautologous. A truth table test demonstrates that it is:

p	*p*	∨	¬*p*
T	T	T	F
F	F	T	T
		*	

Similarly, if the column under the main operator of a compound is all F's, the statement is *logically false*, or, a *contradiction*.

> A **contradiction** or **logical falsehood** is a truth-functional compound statement whose form is such that its truth value is F for each possible combination of truth values of its components: its truth table consists only in F's.

It is logically false because it is false whatever the truth values of its components are; any compound of this form will be false, no matter what its components. Thus

A **self-contradictory form** is a statement form every instance of which is a contradiction.

Here's an example of a self-contradictory form: $(p \rightarrow q) \& (p \& \neg q)$

p	q	$(p$	$\rightarrow$	$q)$	$\&$	$(p$	$\&$	$\neg$	$q)$
T	T		T		F		F	F	
F	T		T		F		F	F	
T	F		F		F		T	T	
F	F		T		F		F	T	
			,		*			,	

In setting out this truth table, I have not repeated the columns under p and q on the right side of the table; instead, I have read them directly from the left to compile the columns under $p \rightarrow q$ and so on. You may always do this, for the sake of the clarity it achieves. I have also put a ' under the penultimate columns as an aid to calculation, as well as the * under the column for the main operator.

Now most propositions will not be either logically true or logically false. Instead, like the compound statement $\neg [P \lor (Q \leftrightarrow \neg P)]$ above, they will have a column of truth values underneath the governing operator that is a mix of T's and F's. Such statements are called *contingent* statements.

A **contingent statement** is a truth-functional compound statement that is neither a tautology nor a contradiction. Its truth table contains at least one F and at least one T.

13.1.4 LOGICAL EQUIVALENCE

In discussing material implication above, we saw that $p \rightarrow q$ and its equivalent $\neg p \lor q$ have the same truth table: that is, one is T in exactly the same rows the other is T, and F wherever the other is F. This is true also of the other equivalence rules of inference. Indeed, any two statements that mutually entail one another, and may therefore be substituted one for the other, will have the same truth table. We define statements possessing the same truth table to be *logically equivalent*:

Two statements p and q having the same truth table column under their governing operators are **logically equivalent**.

Alternatively, we may define it in terms of mutual entailment. Introducing some obvious shorthand, we write "p is entailed by q" as $p \dashv q$, and "p entails and is entailed by q" as $p \dashv\vdash q$. In these terms,

Two statements p and q are **logically equivalent** iff each entails the other, $p \dashv\vdash q$.

That these two definitions are equivalent can be shown as follows. Suppose p validly entails q, and q validly entails p. If p validly entails q, then we can conditionalize on the premise to get $\vdash p \rightarrow q$ as a theorem. Likewise, if q validly entails p, then $\vdash q \rightarrow p$ is a theorem. So from our supposition it follows that $\vdash (p \rightarrow q) \& (q \rightarrow p)$ is a theorem. Therefore, by the BE rule, $\vdash p \leftrightarrow q$ is a theorem, so that $p \leftrightarrow q$ will be a tautology. But this will be a tautology if and only if p and q have identical truth tables. (Here p and q do not stand for any statements at all, only any statements fulfilling the initial supposition.)

This will perhaps be clearer from a specific example. Let us take the two statement forms $\neg(p \rightarrow q)$ and $p \& \neg q$ (where p and q once more stand for any statements whatsoever). First let's establish that each validly entails the other

(1) $\neg(p \rightarrow q)$ Prem
(2) $\neg(\neg p \vee q)$ 1 MI
(3) $p \& \neg q$ 2 DM, DN

(1) $p \& \neg q$ Prem
(2) $\neg(\neg p \vee q)$ 1 DN, DM
(3) $\neg(p \rightarrow q)$ 2 MI

In the first case we could have conditionalized the conclusion on the premise, getting:

   (1) $\neg(p \rightarrow q)$ Supp/CP
   (2) $\neg(\neg p \vee q)$ 1 MI
   (3) $p \& \neg q$ 2 DM, DN
(4) $\neg(p \rightarrow q) \rightarrow (p \& \neg q)$ 1-3 CP

and similarly for the second. Thus $\vdash \neg(p \rightarrow q) \rightarrow (p \& \neg q)$ is a theorem, and so is $\vdash (p \& \neg q) \rightarrow \neg(p \rightarrow q)$. Therefore, by Conj and BE, $\vdash \neg(p \rightarrow q) \leftrightarrow (p \& \neg q)$ is a theorem, so that $\neg(p \rightarrow q) \leftrightarrow (p \& \neg q)$ is a tautology.

This is immediately clear from the truth table for the sequent form: $\vdash \neg(p \rightarrow q) \leftrightarrow (p \& \neg q)$:

p	q	¬(p	→	q)	↔	(p	&	¬	q)
T	T	F	T		T		F	F	
F	T	F	T		T		F	F	
T	F	T	F		T		T	T	
F	F	F	T		T		F	T	
		,			*			,	

That this is a tautology follows immediately from the fact that the two statement forms $\neg(p \to q)$ and $(p \,\&\, \neg q)$ have the same truth table.

Summarizing: we have proved $\neg(p \to q) \vdash (p \,\&\, \neg q)$ and $(p \,\&\, \neg q) \vdash \neg(p \to q)$, and thus $\neg(p \to q) \dashv\vdash (p \,\&\, \neg q)$. We also proved $\vdash \neg(p \to q) \to (p \,\&\, \neg q)$ and $\vdash (p \,\&\, \neg q) \to \neg(p \to q)$, and thus $\vdash \neg(p \to q) \leftrightarrow (p \,\&\, \neg q)$. This is true generally: for any two logically equivalent statements p, q, it can be proven that $p \dashv\vdash q$ and $\vdash p \leftrightarrow q$.

SUMMARY

- A **truth table** for a truth-functional compound statement of a given form is a complete listing of the truth values (T or F) of that compound corresponding to each possible combination of truth values for the component statements, written in a column under the governing operator.
- The truth tables for the various truth-functional operators may be summarized thus:

$\neg p$	F when p is T, and vice versa.
$p \,\&\, q$	T if both conjuncts (p, q) are T, otherwise F.
$p \lor q$	F if both disjuncts (p, q) are F, otherwise T.
$p \to q$	F if the antecedent p is T and the consequent q is F, otherwise T.
$p \leftrightarrow q$	T if the truth values of p and q match, otherwise F.

- A truth table involving n simple statements will have 2^n rows.
- A **tautology** or **logical truth** is a truth-functional compound statement whose form is such that its truth value is T for each possible combination of truth values of its components: its truth table consists only in T's.
- A **contradiction** or **logical falsehood** is a truth-functional compound statement whose form is such that its truth value is F for each possible combination of truth values of its components: its truth table consists only in F's.
- A **contingent statement** is a truth-functional compound statement that is neither a tautology nor a contradiction. Its truth table contains at least one F and at least one T.
- A **tautologous form** is a statement form every instance of which is a tautology.
- Likewise, a **self-contradictory form** is a statement form every instance of which is a contradiction.
- Two statements p and q are **logically equivalent** iff each entails the other, $p \dashv\vdash q$. Logically equivalent statements will have identical truth table columns under their governing operators.

EXERCISES 13.1

1. For each of the following abstract statements, *determine using a truth table* whether it is a *tautology*, a *contradiction*, or a *contingent* statement:
   (a) $\neg(A \to A)$
   (b) $(F \,\&\, G) \to G$
   (c) $P \to \neg P$

(d) P ↔ ¬P

(e) R & (¬R ∨ S)

Symbolize each of statements 2-5, and *determine using a truth table* whether it is a *tautology*, a *contradiction*, or a *contingent* statement:

2. A television reporter describing a dilemma facing government officials said:
   "They're DAMNED if they do [take a certain ACTION], or damned if they don't."

3. The reporter perhaps meant to say:
   "They're DAMNED if they do [take a certain ACTION], <u>and</u> damned if they don't."

4. The head of the Longshoreman's Union, when asked if his union should boycott shipments to England if that country did not give autonomy to Northern Ireland, said:
   "I don't think we'll HAVE to go that far unless we have to."

5. The famous English philosopher G.E. Moore regarded this statement as a contradiction—was he correct?:
   "If A had not HAD P, it would not have been true that A did not have P."

6. For each of the following abstract statements, *determine using a truth table* whether it is *contingent, tautologous,* or *self-contradictory*:
   (a) [P → (P→ Q)] → Q
   (b) (P & Q) & (P → ¬Q)
   (c) P → [P → (Q & ¬Q)]

7. *Using truth tables, prove the following logical equivalences:*
   (a) ¬(B ∨ ¬C) ⊣⊢ ¬B & C
   (b) ¬(A & B) ⊣⊢ A → ¬B
   (c) P ⊣⊢ P ∨ P
   (d) (P ∨ Q) ∨ R ⊣⊢ P ∨ (Q ∨ R)
   (e) A & (B ∨ C) ⊣⊢ (A & B) ∨ (A & C)
   (f) A ∨ (B & C) ⊣⊢ (A ∨ B) & (A ∨ C)

13.2 TRUTH TABLES AND VALIDITY

13.2.1 THE FULL TRUTH TABLE METHOD

In chapter 2 we said that an argument form is valid if and only if there can be no instance of it with all premises true and conclusion false: that is, iff it is impossible for an argument of this form to have all its premises true and its conclusion false. The method of truth tables gives a way of determining this, since what we are doing is exhausting all the possible combinations of truth values of statements. This can be applied to the statements that constitute the premises and conclusion of an argument, and we can see by inspection whether any assignment of truth values to the component statements gives us a row with all premises T and conclusion F.

An example: from the statement "You are dAMNED if you DO, or you are damned if you don't," can we infer that "you are damned"? Let's examine the corresponding sequent: $(D \rightarrow A) \vee (\neg D \rightarrow A) \vdash A$

D	A	(D	→	A)	v	(¬D	→	A)	⊢ A	
T	T		T		T	F	T	T	T	
F	T		T		T	T	T	T	T	
T	F		F		T	F	T	F	F	—*shows invalidity!*
F	F		T		T	T	F	F	F	—*shows invalidity!*
			,		*	,			*	

I have put an asterisk under the main operator of each premise (here there's only one) and another under the conclusion (which is here just A). Now we read across the rows to see if there are any where the premises are all true and conclusion false. There are two rows here, rows 3 and 4, where the premise is true and the conclusion false. This shows that, given this premise, whether or not "you do it," it could be false that you are damned.

If this result seems surprising, it's probably because you are subconsciously correcting the premise to the common adage, "You are dAMNED if you DO <u>and</u> damned if you don't"—which is presumably what the speaker meant to say. In that case we get the different sequent: $(D \rightarrow A) \& (\neg D \rightarrow A) \vdash A$. Now the truth table analysis gives:

D	A	(D	→	A)	&	(¬D	→	A)	⊢ A	
T	T		T		T	F	T	T	T	
F	T		T		T	T	T	T	T	
T	F		F		F	F	T	F	F	
F	F		T		F	T	F	F	F	—*valid!*
			,		*	,			*	

In this case we find that the premise on both rows 3 and 4 is now false: but so is the conclusion. Now there are no rows in which a true premise leads to a false conclusion. So, since we have exhausted all the possibilities, no argument of this form can have all premises true and the conclusion false, so the argument must be formally valid.

As a little light relief, let's return to our logic gurus, Monty Python. In a sketch about the gangster brothers Doug and Dinsdale Piranha, the presenter delivers the following biographical vignette as a spoof on television documentaries:

When the Piranhas left school, they were called up but were found by an Army Board to be too mentally unstable even for National Service. Denied the opportunity to use their talents in the service of their country, they began to operate what they called "The Operation." They would select a victim and then threaten to beat him up if he paid them the so-called protection money. Four months later they started another operation, which they called "The Other Operation." In this racket they selected another victim and threatened *not* to beat him up if he *didn't* pay them. One month later they hit upon "The Other Other Operation." In this the victim was threatened that if he didn't pay them they would beat him up. This, for the Piranha brothers, was the turning point.[1]

To analyze a joke is to kill it, but let's not let that deter us from logical mayhem! We can construe each operation as involving an inference by the Piranha brothers that their threat will deliver them the protection money: "The victim will pay us the PROTECTION money": P. This depends on the assumption that the victim does not want to be beaten up that is, they assume ¬B, "The victim is not BEATEN up." In each operation the other premise is the conditional delivering the threat. Thus the reasoning behind the first operation can be construed: P → B, ¬B ⊢ P. Is it valid?

P	B	P	→	B,	¬B	⊢ P
T	T		T		F	T
F	T		T		F	F
T	F		F		T	T
F	F		T		T	F
			*		*	*

—*demonstrates invalidity!*

The truth table shows that both premises could be true and the conclusion false even though the victim does not pay and does not get beaten up—as we should have expected. Similar analyses of "The Other Operation" and "The Other Other Operation" are left as exercises.

So far, we've been looking at examples of statements and arguments involving only two component statements. As we saw, if we have *n* component statements, we need 2^n rows in the truth table. Thus when there are three component statements in an argument, we need eight rows. Let's look at an example:

If 4 is LESS than 6 and all EVEN numbers less than 6 are prime, then 4 is PRIME. Therefore, if 4 is less than 6, it is prime.

---

[1] From *Monty Python's Flying Circus: Just the Words*, vol. 1 (London: Methuen, 1989), p. 186.

L	E	P	(L & E) →	P	L → P	
T	T	T	T	T	T	
F	T	T	F	T	T	
T	F	T	F	T	T	
F	F	T	F	T	T	
T	T	F	T	F	F	
F	T	F	F	T	T	
T	F	F	F	T	F	—*demonstrates invalidity!*
F	F	F	F	T	T	
			*		*	

Here line 7 shows that if "4 is LESS than 6" is true, but "all EVEN numbers less than 6 are prime" and "4 is PRIME" are both false, the premise would be true and the conclusion false. So it is possible for the premise to be true and the conclusion false. Therefore the argument is invalid. This is the Full Truth Table method of determining validity, or FTT method, for short.

13.2.2 INVALID ARGUMENT FORMS

Consider the argument:

SAMARKAND is in Uzbekistan.
<u>UZBEKISTAN is in Central Asia.</u>
∴ Samarkand is in CENTRAL Asia.

All these statements—premises and conclusion—are *simple statements*: they have no parts that are also statements, and therefore no components. So the symbolization of the argument in statement logic is: S, U ∴ C.

And suck it does. The truth table test for statement logic gives a thumbs down on its validity: since no truth-functional connection between the premises and conclusion is revealed, it certainly appears possible for S and U to have the values T whilst C has the value F. It is an instance of the invalid form *p, q* ∴ *r*. Nevertheless it does not seem possible for the original argument to have all true premises and false conclusion. So we judge the argument itself to be *valid*, even though it is an *instance of the invalid form p, q* ∴ *r*. Thus it is true to say

- An argument that is an instance of a valid argument form is *formally valid*.

but false to say

- An argument that is an instance of an invalid argument form is *formally invalid*.

Actually, on further reflection you can see that a very wide class of valid arguments are instances of the invalid form *p, q* ∴ *r*. For example, the argument symbolized as M → N, ¬N ∴¬M is such an instance—to see, sub M → N for *p*, ¬N for *q*, and ¬M for *r*— even though it is also an instance of *p* → *q*, ¬*q* ∴ ¬*p*, or Modus Tollens, a paradigm of validity.

Later in the book we shall see that our original argument about Samarkand can be symbolized in Relational Logic in such a way as to show that it, too, is an instance of a valid form.

What all this means, as explained in chapter 2, is that we cannot conclude that an argument is formally invalid simply because it is an instance of an invalid form. It has to be the case that it is also not an instance of any valid argument form:

> An argument is **formally invalid** if it is both (i) an instance of an invalid argument form and (ii) not an instance of any valid argument form.

Another example to drive the point home:

> If the old lady has any living relatives, her nephew is still alive. But she has no living relatives. Therefore her nephew is no longer alive.

This argument is an instance of the form *p* → *q*, ¬*p* ∴ ¬*q*, or the Fallacy of Denying the Antecedent. However, the denial of the conclusion yields "her nephew is still alive," and this is incompatible with the conjunction of the premises, the second of which asserts that the old lady has no living relatives. So the argument is valid. The conclusion follows from the second premise together with the implicit premise that her nephew is a relative of hers. We'll see what valid form this is an instance of when we study Predicate Logic.

That said, you may take it that none of the instances of invalid forms in the exercises is also an instance of a valid form (unless you are explicitly told otherwise. That is, unless instructed otherwise, you may assume that *instances of invalid forms are invalid*, as we have tacitly assumed until now.

On the other hand, if we are dealing not with an argument or sequent, but directly with an *argument form*, the Truth Table method will determine validity or invalidity straightforwardly:

> An argument form is *invalid* if and only if there is at least one instance of the form which is invalid.

For example, the Truth Table method conclusively establishes the invalidity of the form *p* → *q*, ¬*p* ∴ ¬*q*.

SUMMARY

- An argument is **formally invalid** if it is both (i) an instance of an invalid argument form and (ii) not an instance of any valid argument form.
- An **argument form** is *invalid* if and only if there is **at least one instance of the form which is invalid**.
- An argument or sequent is an instance of an invalid form iff there is at least one line in its truth table with all true premises and a false conclusion.

EXERCISES 13.2

Using the full truth table method, determine whether each of the following sequents is valid or invalid:

8. M ∨ N, M ⊢ ¬N

9. ¬(F & G) ⊢ G → ¬F

10. (P & ¬P) ⊢ Q

11. R & (¬R ∨ S) ⊢ ¬S

12. ¬A → M, A ⊢ ¬M

13. L → M, M → ¬L ⊢ ¬L

14. In the text I analyzed the inference involved in the first version of Monty Python's "Piranha Brothers'" protection racket, which they called "The Operation," showing by a truth table that the inference was invalid. Provide a similar analysis of (a) *the second and* (b) *the third versions*, "The Other Operation," and "The Other Other Operation." *Do they both involve invalid inferences too?*

"The Other Operation": In this racket they selected another victim and threatened *not* to beat him up if he *didn't* pay them. One month later they hit upon "The Other Other Operation." In this the victim was threatened that if he didn't pay them they would beat him up. This, for the Piranha brothers, was the turning point.

15. An argument is symbolized A → A, ¬A ∴ ¬A. *Show that this is a substitution instance of both Modus Tollens and the Fallacy of Denying the Antecedent. Is the argument valid or invalid?*

16. *Using the Full Truth Table method, prove the validity of the following sequents:*
    (a) (¬ D → ¬ B) & [D → (B → C)] ⊢ ¬ B ∨ (D & C)
    (b) P ↔ (Q ↔ R) ⊢ (P ↔ Q) ↔ R

17. (**CHALLENGE**) In the text to this chapter I wrote that the truth table for $p \rightarrow q$ "says that a conditional is false only if the antecedent is true and the consequent false. From this it follows that (a) the conditional is true if the consequent is true, and (b) the conditional is true if the antecedent is false." Using the symbol C for "the conditional is true," S for "the consequent is true," and A for "the antecedent is true," *symbolize the two arguments that the conclusions (a) and (b) follow from that premise, and prove that they do follow validly (i), (ii) by the truth table method, and (iii), (iv) by constructing two formal proofs.*

13.3 THE BRIEF TRUTH TABLE METHOD

If it's easy to make an error in an eight-row truth table like the one above for the argument (L & E) → P ∴ L → P involving three statements, it is even easier when there are four or more component statements involved, and thus sixteen or more rows of truth values. Indeed, the ease of using the full truth table method just described falls off exponentially—literally—as the number of components increases. This seems excessive, especially when you consider that all we need to prove invalidity is one line where the truth values of all the premises are T and that of the conclusion F. So why don't we aim for this directly? Why not suppose that the premises are T and the conclusion F, and see if we can get a consistent set of truth values for the components? If we can, the argument is invalid. If we can't, our supposition (that we could have all premises T and conclusion F) must be false, and then the argument would be proved valid. This forms the basis for the Brief Truth Table Method:

Brief Truth Table Method (BTT):
First assign T for each of the premises and F for the conclusion (this corresponds to supposing that the argument is invalid). Then work backwards, seeing whether there are any values for all the component statements that will result in these initial assignments—that is, whether there is a row in a completely filled-in truth table that gives us these values, premises T and conclusion F.
• If there is, then you have found a row that demonstrates invalidity, and the argument is *invalid.*
• If there isn't, that is, if every assignment of values produces *an inconsistent set* of truth values for the component statements, then the argument is *valid.*

In working back from the original assignment, you are working from the outside inwards, as opposed to how we have been proceeding so far, from the inside outwards. The general strategy is to take assignments that force values first. For instance, if P → Q is false, we know that P must be true and Q false. If P & Q is true, we know both P and Q must be true.

This is how the method would work applied to the above example:

L	E	P	(L & E) → P	L → P
T	F	F	T F F T F	T F F
[2]	[4]	[2]	[2][3][4] [1] [2]	[2] [1] [2]
			*	*

Here the number in square brackets denotes the step in the calculation: [1] is the step of assigning T to the premises and F to the conclusion; in step [2] the falsity of the conclusion forces L to be T and P to be F; and in step [3], we deduce that since (L & E) → P is T and its consequent F, its antecedent L & E must be F. Finally, [4], if L & E is false but L is true, E must be false. This gives us a consistent set. Therefore the argument is INVALID.

> • Remember a consistent set proves *invalidity* of the form, whereas showing that there is no such consistent set proves *validity*.

This is contrary to our unthinking instincts. But it is because a consistent set gives a row in a truth table with all premises T and conclusion F; whereas to show that there is no such consistent set of truth values for the components is to show that our original supposition of invalidity was false.

Here's an example of a valid argument. Sir Isaac Newton is often credited with a materialistic worldview in which matter directly acts on all other matter at a distance, through the mediation of the innate force of gravity. The real historical Newton would beg to differ. In a letter to Richard Bentley of February 1692/93, Newton wrote:

It is inconceivable that brute inanimate matter should, without the mediation of something else which is not material, operate upon and affect other matter without mutual contact, as it must be if gravitation, in the sense of Epicurus, be essential and inherent in it. And this is one reason why I desired you not ascribe innate gravity to me. That gravity should be innate, inherent, and essential to matter, so that one body may act upon another at a distance through a vacuum, without the mediation of anything else, by and through which their action and force may be conveyed from one to another, is to me so great an absurdity that I believe no man who has in philosophical matters a competent faculty of thinking can ever fall into it.[2]

---

[2] Quoted from H.S. Thayer (ed.), *Newton's Philosophy of Nature* (New York/London: Hafner, 1953), p. 54.

One interpretation of Newton's argument:

> If gravity is INNATE in matter and is not MEDIATED by something immaterial, then it can ACT on other matter only if there is mutual CONTACT. But there is no mutual contact, and it still acts on other matter. Hence, if gravity is innate, it is mediated by something immaterial.[3]

I	M	A	C	(I & ¬ M) → (A → C)	¬ C & A	I → M
T	F	T	F	T T T F T T F F	T F T T	T F F
[2]	[2]	[3]	[4]	[2][6][5][2][1][3][7][4]	[3][4][1][3]	[2] [1] [2]

inconsistent set: therefore the argument is valid

(Again I have put the numbers in square brackets so you can follow the reasoning. You do not need to put them in when giving an answer, although it will certainly help your instructor to find any mistakes you might make.)

One shortcoming of the BTT method is this. The truth values of the components do not always get forced by the initial assignment of T to the premises and F to the conclusion. In such cases, we have to run through the possibilities for the remaining unforced components' truth values ourselves. Thus we end up with at least 2, possibly 4 or more, lines of what would have been the full truth table.

Here is an example of a case where this happens: In a *Star Trek* episode, the crew of the starship *Enterprise* is held captive by a powerful computer. The crew escapes when one of them has the wit to try out a version of the Liar Paradox[4] on the computer, by telling it "I am lying." Presumably the computer, which consequently blows a fuse, reasons as follows:

> He SAYS he is lying. But if he says he is lying and he is indeed LYING, then he is not lying. On the other hand, if he says that he is lying and he's not lying, then he is lying. So he is lying if and only if he is not lying.
> Symbolized: S, (S & ¬L) → L, (S & L) → ¬L ∴ L ↔ ¬L

---

[3] This is not necessarily a very *good* interpretation of Newton's argument. In a final sentence of the same paragraph, Newton says he is leaving it up to the reader to judge whether the agent causing gravity is material or immaterial. Two other interpretations of the argument are considered in exercises 32 and 33.

[4] This is a paradox of ancient vintage, dating back to Eubulides of Miletus in the fourth century BCE.

S	L	S	(S & ¬L) → L	(S & L) → ¬L	L ↔ ¬L
T		T	T T	T T	F
[1]		[1]	[1] [1]	[1] [1]	[1]

These are all the values that get forced. To proceed any further, we must assign values of T or F to L. Let's try assigning a value T to L; i.e., *suppose* L *is true*:

S	L	S	(S & ¬L) → L	(S & L) → ¬L	L ↔ ¬L
T	T	T	T T F T T	T T T T F	T F F
[1]	[2]	[1]	[1][3][2] [1][2]	[1][3][2][1][2]	[2][1][2]

inconsistent set: therefore L is false

S	L	S	(S & ¬L) → L	(S & L) → ¬L	L ↔ ¬L
T	F	T	T F T T F	T F F T T	F F T
[1]	[2]	[1]	[1][3][2] [1][2]	[1][3][2][1][2]	[2][1][2]

again an inconsistent set: therefore
the argument is VALID

To recap: this is a reductio within a reductio. We tried supposing the argument is invalid. This did not force a conclusion. So we tried supposing that L is true. This led to a contradiction; therefore L is false. From this we derived a contradiction. Therefore the original supposition was incorrect: the argument is valid.

In general, if you are stuck in the BTT method, you have to take one component and try each of its values (T and F) on two different rows.

- If both rows are inconsistent, the argument is VALID.
- If one or both rows are consistent, the argument is INVALID.

This may seem complicated. If it seems too complicated, in a case like this we can easily do a full truth table, since it has only four rows. Alternatively, there is another method which applies to all cases, and which, like the FTT method, is a decision procedure (it always produces results up or down directly): the method of Truth Trees. But that is the subject of our next chapter.

SUMMARY

- In the Brief Truth Table method (BTT), we *suppose* the argument or sequent has an *invalid* form, writing T under each premise and F under the conclusion, and working backwards; if this leads to a *consistent* set of truth values for the constituent statements, it is indeed *invalid*; if not, it is valid.
- Sometimes this supposition does not force the values of all the component statements; in such a case, you must systematically exhaust the possible truth values for the remaining component statements to see whether it issues in a consistent set.

EXERCISES 13.3

For each of the following, *determine whether the argument is valid or invalid using the brief truth table method*:

18. L → M ⊢ M ∨ L

19. L → M ⊢ ¬(¬M & L)

20. ¬A → M, A ⊢ ¬M

21. ¬A → B, ¬B → C ⊢ ¬A → C

22. L → M, M → ¬L ⊢ ¬L

23. ¬A ∨ M, A → B ⊢ ¬M ∨ B

24. (E & L) → M, ¬M ∨ L ⊢ E

25. (P & Q) → R, ¬R & ¬Q ⊢ P

26. (P & Q) → R ⊢ (¬R & Q) → P

27. ¬M → (¬E ∨ ¬L) ⊢ (¬M & L) → E

For each of the following, *determine whether the argument is valid or invalid using either the full or the brief truth table method*:

28. I have already said that he must have gone to KING'S Pyland or to CAPELTON. He is not at King's Pyland, therefore he is at Capleton.—Arthur Conan Doyle, *Silver Blaze*

29. If this argument is an instance of the FALLACY of affirming the consequent, then it is not VALID. This argument is not an instance of the fallacy of affirming the consequent. Therefore it is valid.—adapted from Cohen and Copi's *Introduction to Logic*

30. And certainly if its ESSENCE and POWER are infinite, its GOODNESS must be infinite, since a thing whose essence is finite has finite goodness.—Roger Bacon, *Opus Majus*

31. The INSTRUMENTALIST interpretation of quantum mechanics is correct if POSITIVISM is true; but positivism is false; hence, since REALISM is true if instrumentalism is false, we must interpret quantum theory realistically.—a version of an argument in a student paper

32. This and the following problem are further different interpretations of the reasoning of Newton in his letter to Bentley quoted in the text:
    If gravity is INNATE in matter and is not MEDIATED by something immaterial, then it can ACT on other matter only if there is mutual CONTACT. But there is no mutual contact. Hence, if gravity is not mediated by something immaterial, it cannot be innate.

33. If gravity is INNATE in matter, matter acts on other matter without mutual CONTACT and without the MEDIATION of anything else. But matter acts on other matter either through mutual contact, or through the mediation of something else. Hence, gravity is not innate in matter. (C := matter acts by mutual contact, M := it acts through the mediation of something else.)

34. (**CHALLENGE**) (a) The Sheffer Stroke operator is defined as $(p \mid q) =_{\text{def}} \neg(p \ \& \ q)$. *Using this definition, determine the truth table for the Sheffer Stroke Operator.* In exercise 14 of the previous chapter, we determined the following *equivalences. Verify them using truth tables*:
    (b) $p \ \& \ q = [(p \mid q) \mid (p \mid q)]$
    (c) $p \rightarrow q = [p \mid (q \mid q)]$

35. (**CHALLENGE**) (a) Peirce's Arrow Operator is defined as $(p \downarrow q) =_{\text{def}} \neg p \ \& \ \neg q$. Using this definition, *determine the truth table for Peirce's Arrow Operator. Using truth tables, verify these equivalences* established in the previous chapter:
    (b) $\neg p = (p \downarrow p)$
    (c) $p \vee q = [(p \downarrow q) \mid (p \downarrow q)]$.

36. (**CHALLENGE**) The following passage from P.C.W. Davies's *God and the New Physics* contains an argument. *Using the key below, identify the argument, supplying any implicit premises you deem necessary, and prove its validity using a truth table method*:

> The biblical version of the creation of the universe 'on the first day' is vague about exactly what was involved. There are actually two accounts of creation, but neither explicitly mentions that the material from which the stars and planets, the Earth, and our own bodies are made, existed prior to the creation event. The belief that God created this cosmic material out of nothing is a longstanding part of Christian doctrine. Indeed, it seems to be demanded by the assumption of God's omnipotence, for if God did not create matter, it would imply that he was limited in his work by the nature of the raw material available to him.

> [M := God created MATTER out of nothing, O := God is OMNIPOTENT (all-powerful), L := God was LIMITED in his creation of the universe by the nature of the raw material available to him.]

Chapter Fourteen

Truth Trees for SL

14.1.1 THE TRUTH TREE METHOD

In this chapter we examine a different way of analyzing sequents and arguments (and their schemas) using a new format, called a "truth tree." The diagrams are called trees because they look like a kind of stick-figure tree turned upside down—or, as I prefer to think of them, a tree stump and roots right side up. Like the truth table methods we considered in the previous chapter, the truth tree method is a decision procedure, enabling us to determine formal invalidity as well as formal validity by entirely mechanical means, as well as to determine whether statements are tautologous, self-contradictory or contingent, or logically equivalent. Its advantages are its ease of use and visual appeal, the close correspondence of its rules with the rules of inference with which we are familiar, and its easy generalizability to predicate logic (see chapter 23 below). Also, unlike the truth table method, it may also be extended to some other more general kinds of arguments we'll be coming to later.

The basis of the Truth Tree method for determining formal validity is the same as that of the BTT method: *we suppose all the premises are true and the conclusion false.* If this supposition pans out, the argument is formally invalid, and as a bonus we find out what set of truth values for the components would make the premises true and conclusion false. If it does not pan out, that is, if every branch of the tree ends in an inconsistency, the argument is formally valid. The difference is that the "forcing" of values that are consistent with the initial assignments is explicit, and laid out vertically. Before introducing the method formally, let's run through a simple example to show the gist of the method. Take the sequent

(1) R, ¬R ∨ S ⊢ ¬S

First, we write out the premises, and beneath these, the negation of the conclusion. (These statements comprise the 'stump.') We draw a line under this (which you can think of as the ground), as follows:

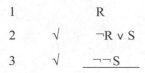

Then we proceed to derive what we can from this, branching every time we have a choice of options:

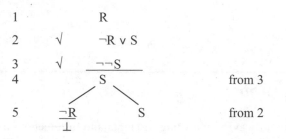

It's always best to treat those compound statements first that do not involve any branching possibilities. So first, on line 4 we note that S follows from ¬¬S by DN. Every time we decompose a compound statement we put a √ to the left of it to indicate that it has been decomposed. Now we have exhausted all the information except that contained in line 2, which entails two possibilities, so the tree (or root) *branches*. So on line 5 we write down the alternative possibilities, one in each branch, ticking line 2 as we do so. In the left hand branch of the tree we derived ¬R; but this is incompatible with R on line 1. So we have a logical contradiction, denoted by ⊥, and that branch *closes* (as indicated by the short line above the ⊥). The right hand branch does not close, but we have exhausted all the information: there are no compound statements that remain unticked, they have all been decomposed. So S's being true must be compatible with our starting assumptions. In other words, the premises are consistent with the denial of the conclusion, so the argument is formally INVALID. Moreover, the tree diagram shows us that it is the possibility of S's being true (as well as R's being true) that would render the premises true and the conclusion false.

Now let's see what happens if we investigate a valid sequent by this method. Let's take

(2) A, ¬(A & ¬B) ⊢ B

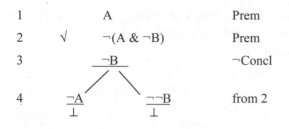

Here A (the first premise) and ¬B (the negation of the conclusion) cannot be decomposed any further. Regarding the second premise, ¬(A & ¬B) is equivalent to ¬A ∨ ¬¬B by one of De Morgan's Laws, which accounts for the branching alternatives of ¬A and ¬¬B. But ¬A contradicts A above it, so this branch closes. In the other branch, ¬¬B contradicts ¬B above it, so this branch also closes. We conclude that the premises are incompatible with the negation of the conclusion, so that the sequent is VALID. As for the validity of *arguments*, as opposed to sequents: If a given sequent is valid, this means the argument corresponding to it is *formally valid.*

Let's look at a couple more examples.

(3) A & B, ¬B ∨ C ⊢ A & C

1	√	A & B		Prem
2	√	¬B ∨ C		Prem
3	√	¬(A & C)		¬Concl
4		A		from 1
5		B		from 1
6	¬B		C	from 2
	⊥			
7		¬A	¬C	from 3
		⊥	⊥	

Here lines 4 and 5 represent the decomposition of A & B from line 1. When we decompose ¬B ∨ C from line 2 we get a branching into the two possibilities ¬B and C on line 6. ¬B, however, is inconsistent with B above it, so this path through the tree closes. Then we have to see what to do with line 3. If not both A and C, then by De Morgan's, it must be not one or not the other, so this gives us another branching into ¬A and ¬C on line 7. But ¬A is inconsistent with A on line 4, which lies on the path back up the tree to the premises. And ¬C is inconsistent with C on line 6, which also lies on the same path.

So both these remaining paths close. Again, we conclude that the premises are incompatible with the negation of the conclusion, so that the sequent is VALID.

Now let's look at an argument form:

(4) $\neg(p \lor q) \therefore \neg(r \& p)$

1	√	$\neg(p \lor q)$	Prem
2	√	$\neg\neg(r \& p)$	$\neg$Concl
3		$\neg p$	from 1
4		$\neg q$	from 1
5	√	$r \& p$	from 2
6		r	from 5
7		p	from 5
		$\bot$	

Here lines 3 and 4 exploit another of De Morgan's Laws, that *not either p* or *q* is equivalent to *neither p* nor *q*, i.e., not *p* (line 3) and not *q* (line 4). Line 5 follows from line 2 by a DN equivalence, so that both *r* and *p* must be true. But this is incompatible with $\neg p$ on line 3, so we have a contradiction. Thus the argument form is VALID.

To summarize the truth tree method of determining the validity of a sequent:

- Write each premise on a separate numbered line; then write the negation of the conclusion on the last line of the "stump," and underline (draw in the "ground").
- Now on succeeding lines, conclude what follows from each of the statements of the trunk and their consequences in terms of the truth or falsity of the component statements. Tick each compound statement when it has been decomposed.
- Once a tree has branched, if you apply a decomposition rule to a compound statement above the branching, you must do the decomposition in all the different branches on the same horizontal line.
- Statements that cannot be further decomposed are called **literals**; they will be either component statements or negations of component statements.
- A **path** through the tree is the collection of all the statements from the bottom of a branch up to the top of the trunk (first premise).
- Inspect each path of the tree as you proceed. If on the same path there occurs both a statement and the negation of that statement, then the **path closes**, as indicated by a short line at the bottom of the path with a $\bot$ under it. Any path that does **not close** is said to be **open**.
- Proceed in this way until all the statements on any remaining open paths are either ticked compounds or literals. Any such remaining open path is then said to be a **complete open path**.

- When all the paths of a tree are either closed or complete open paths, the **tree** is said to be **complete**.
- If **all** the paths of a complete tree are **closed**, then the **sequent** is **valid**.
- If there are **any complete open paths** in a tree, then the sequent is **invalid**. The combinations of literals that make the premises true and the conclusion false can be read off each complete open path of the tree: all positive component statements on the path have the value **T**, and all negations on the path yield the value **F** for the statements they negate.

14.1.2 DECOMPOSITION RULES

Now there is just one more thing we need to do to complete the formalization of the method: to make explicit the justification for breaking down the compound statements. On each line where a compound statement has been decomposed we have indicated this with a √ to the left of the compound in question. But now we need to make explicit the rules of decomposition over on the right. For Statement Logic there are **nine** rules in all, one for each of the four binary operators, and one for the denial of each of the five operators (including the unary one, ¬). Let's look first at those involving **&**, v, and ¬:

Decomposition Rules for Ampersand, Wedge and Not

&	¬**&**	v	¬v	¬¬
√p & q	√¬(p & q)	√p v q	√¬(p v q)	√¬¬p
p	/ \	/ \	¬p	p
q	¬p ¬q	p q	¬q	

The justification of these rules should be self-evident: **&** is a version of Simp, v simply gives a branch, ¬**&** and ¬v follow by De Morgan's Laws, and ¬¬ is DN.

Decomposition Rules for Arrow and Double-Arrow

→	¬→	↔	¬↔
√$p \to q$	√¬($p \to q$)	√$p \leftrightarrow q$	√¬($p \leftrightarrow q$)
/ \	p	/ \	/ \
¬p q	¬q	p ¬p	p ¬p
		q ¬q	¬q q

These rules call for a little more explanation. The first, →, is based on the fact that $p \to q$ is equivalent to ¬p v q by MI. So either ¬p or q, and the tree branches accordingly. In the second, $\neg(p \rightarrow q)$ is equivalent to $\neg(\neg p \lor q)$ by MI again, and this is equivalent to $\neg\neg p \& \neg q$ by DM, and thus to $p \& \neg q$ by DN. So both p and $\neg q$ are consequences of $\neg(p \rightarrow q)$—a fact closely related to the Paradoxes of Material Implication. The two rules for the biconditionals, on the other hand, are most naturally seen as following from the truth table: $p \leftrightarrow q$ is **T** iff both p and q are **T** or both are **F**, giving the rule $\leftrightarrow$. On the other hand, $p \leftrightarrow q$ is **F** iff one is **T** and the other **F**, giving the rule $\neg\leftrightarrow$.

It will be evident that some of the above rules involve branching, and some do not:

The **non-branching** rules are **&**, $\neg\lor$, $\neg\neg$, and $\neg\rightarrow$

The **branching** rules are $\neg$**&**, $\lor$, $\rightarrow$, $\leftrightarrow$, and $\neg\leftrightarrow$

As a rule of thumb, we should always try to use the non-branching rules first. This will minimize the branching, and thus the complexity, of the tree. As an example, let's analyze an abstract argument involving $\rightarrow$ and $\neg\rightarrow$.

(5) (E & L) $\rightarrow$ M $\therefore$ E $\rightarrow$ M

1	√	(E & L) $\rightarrow$ M	Prem
2	√	$\underline{\neg(E \rightarrow M)}$	$\neg$Concl
3		E	2 $\neg\rightarrow$
4		$\neg$M	2 $\neg\rightarrow$

Here we decompose $\neg(E \rightarrow M)$ first, because, unlike (E & L) $\rightarrow$ M, it does not involve branching. As we do so, we tick line 2 to show that it has been decomposed. Now we decompose line 1, ticking it as we do so, which yields two branches:

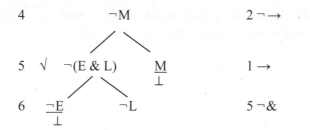

On line 5, M contradicts $\neg$M from line 4 so that branch closes. We then decompose the negation of the conjunction on line 6, involving a further branching. On line 6, $\neg$E contradicts E further up the branch on line 3. But when we trace $\neg$L up its branch, we find no L to contradict it, so it does not close. But every statement above it on that branch has either been ticked off, or is a simple statement or negation of one. So the branch is a **complete open** one. This means that the argument is formally INVALID.

The full tree is as follows:

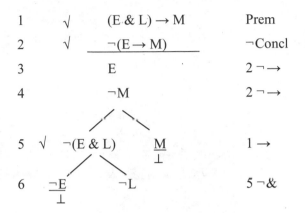

Compare this tree with the tree (also correct, but slightly more complicated) that we would have obtained by first decomposing line 1, involving a branching rule (remember, once the tree has branched, we must apply the same rule to a compound statement above the branch in each branch horizontally):

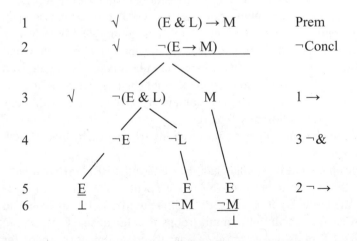

In both diagrams the literals on the remaining open path are ¬L, E, and ¬M, so that E's being true and L and M false are truth value assignments that make all the premises true and the conclusion false.

Now let's use the tree method to prove the validity of the following sequent, which establishes one half of the distributive law for 'v' over '&':

(6)   A v (B & C) ⊢ (A v B) & (A v C)

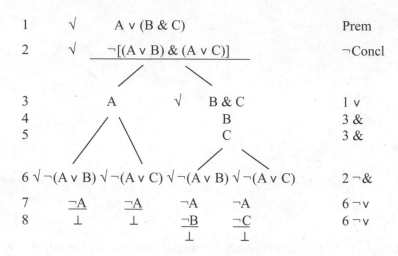

1	√ A v (B & C)	Prem
2	√ ¬[(A v B) & (A v C)]	¬Concl
3	A √ B & C	1 v
4	B	3 &
5	C	3 &
6	√ ¬(A v B) √ ¬(A v C) √ ¬(A v B) √ ¬(A v C)	2 ¬&
7	¬A ¬A ¬A ¬A	6 ¬v
8	⊥ ⊥ ¬B ¬C	6 ¬v
	⊥ ⊥	

Here we have two statements that require branching rules, but A v (B & C) appears simpler, so we do that first, using the decomposition rule v on line 3. Next we break down B & C using the rule for & on lines 4 and 5, before proceeding to analyze ¬[(A v B) & (A v C)]. Now when we apply the branching rule ¬& to it we already have two open branches, so we have to apply ¬& to each of these branches, giving us 4 branches on line 6. Applying ¬v to the compounds in both branches on the left, we immediately find that those paths close, because the ¬A in each of them contradicts A previously derived on that path. Applying ¬v to the two compounds on the right (line 8), ¬B contradicts B obtained above it on that path, and ¬C contradicts C obtained above it on that path. Thus all the paths **close**, so the sequent is formally VALID.

Here's a made-up example of an argument whose validity we can test by this method.

(7) If the UNITED States pulls out of Afghanistan then either the BRITISH will have to commit troops for the long term or the CANADIANS will. If the British do make such a commitment, the US will not pull out. But if it is put to a VOTE of Canadian public opinion, the Canadians will not commit troops to Afghanistan for the long term. Therefore, if the US pulls out its troops, Canada's commitment of troops for Afghanistan in the long term will not have been put to the vote.
Symbolized: U → (B v C), B → ¬U, V → ¬C ∴ U → ¬V

Again, applying the rule of thumb that we should use non-branching rules before branching ones, we decompose premise 4 first:

1	√	U → (B v C)	Prem
2	√	B → ¬U	Prem
3	√	V → ¬C	Prem
4	√	¬(U → ¬V)	¬Concl
5		U	4 ¬→
6	√	¬¬V	4 ¬→
7		V	6 ¬¬

```
7              V
             /  \
8          ·V    ·C          3 →
          ⊥   /  \
9           ¬B    ¬U         2 →
          /  \    ⊥
10     ¬U  √ B v C           1 →
       ⊥   /  \
11       B    C              10 v
         ⊥    ⊥
```

8 · 3 →

9 · 2 →

10 · 1 →

11 · 10 v

Here ¬V on line 8 contradicts V above it on line 7, ¬U in lines 9 and 10 is contradicted by U above them in the same path on line 5; B on line 11 is contradicted by ¬B above it in the same path on line 9, as is C by ¬C above it in the same path on line 8. Thus all the paths close. We have a VALID argument.

SUMMARY

- The **truth tree method** is a way of determining invalidity as well as validity of a sequent by entirely mechanical means. It can also be used to determine whether statements are tautologous, self-contradictory or contingent, or logically equivalent. An **argument** is formally valid or invalid if and only if its corresponding sequent is valid or invalid.
- The truth tree method proceeds by assuming the premises true and the conclusion false, and seeing whether a contradiction follows. You start out from the premises together with the negation of the conclusion, and derive whatever can be derived from them by the rules of decomposition.
- The rules of decomposition are of two kinds:
  the **non-branching** rules **&**, ¬ v, ¬¬, and ¬ →:

&	¬v	¬¬	¬→
√p & q	√¬(p v q)	√¬¬p	√¬(p → q)
p	¬p	p	p
q	¬q		¬q

and the **branching** rules $\lor$, $\neg$ **&**, $\rightarrow$, $\leftrightarrow$, and $\neg \leftrightarrow$:

$\lor$	$\neg$ **&**	$\rightarrow$	$\leftrightarrow$	$\neg \leftrightarrow$
$\sqrt{} p \lor q$	$\sqrt{} \neg (p \,\&\, q)$	$\sqrt{} p \rightarrow q$	$\sqrt{} p \leftrightarrow q$	$\sqrt{} \neg (p \leftrightarrow q)$
/ \	/ \	/ \	/ \	/ \
$p \quad q$	$\neg p \quad \neg q$	$\neg p \quad q$	$p \quad \neg p$	$p \quad \neg p$
			$q \quad \neg q$	$\neg q \quad q$

- If on the same path there occurs both a statement and the negation of that statement, then the branch **closes** (and with it the **path**), as indicated by a short line at the bottom of the path with a $\perp$ under it. Any path that does **not close** is said to be **open**.
- Statements that cannot be further decomposed are called **literals**; they will be either component statements or negations of component statements. If all the statements on a path that has not closed are either compounds that have been decomposed or literals, the path is said to be a **complete open path**.
- If **all** the paths of a complete tree are **closed**, then the **sequent** is **valid**.
- If there are **any complete open paths** in a tree, then the sequent is **invalid**.

EXERCISES 14.1

Apply the Method of Truth Trees to determine whether or not each of the following sequents is valid:

1. $L \rightarrow M \vdash M \lor L$

2. $L \rightarrow M \vdash \neg (M \lor L)$

3. $L \rightarrow M \vdash \neg (\neg M \,\&\, L)$

4. $\neg A \rightarrow M, A \vdash \neg M$

5. $(P \,\&\, \neg P) \vdash Q$

6. $\neg (F \,\&\, G) \vdash G \leftrightarrow \neg F$

7. $L \rightarrow M, M \rightarrow \neg L \vdash \neg L$

8. $\neg A \lor M, A \rightarrow B \vdash \neg M \lor B$

9. $(E \,\&\, \neg L) \rightarrow M, \neg (M \lor L) \vdash \neg E$

10. $(P \& Q) \rightarrow R, \neg R \& \neg Q \vdash P$

11. $R \& (\neg R \lor S) \vdash \neg S$

12. $(P \& Q) \rightarrow R \vdash (\neg R \& Q) \rightarrow P$

13. $\neg A \leftrightarrow B, \neg B \rightarrow C \vdash \neg A \rightarrow C$

14. $(E \& L) \rightarrow M \vdash (\neg M \& L) \rightarrow E$

For exercises 15-20 (= 28-33 of chapter 13), symbolize the argument contained in each passage, and then apply the Method of Truth Trees to determine whether it is formally valid:

15. I have already said that he must have gone to KING'S Pyland or to CAPLETON. He is not at King's Pyland, therefore he is at Capleton —Arthur Conan Doyle, *Silver Blaze*

16. If this argument is an instance of the FALLACY of affirming the consequent, then it is not VALID. This argument is not an instance of the fallacy of affirming the consequent. Therefore it is valid.—adapted from Cohen and Copi's *Introduction to Logic*

17. And certainly if its ESSENCE and POWER are infinite, its GOODNESS must be infinite, since a thing whose essence is finite has finite goodness.—Roger Bacon, *Opus Majus*

18. The INSTRUMENTALIST interpretation of quantum mechanics is correct if POSITIVISM is true; but positivism is false; hence, since REALISM is true if instrumentalism is false, we must interpret quantum theory realistically.

19. This and the following problem are further different interpretations of the reasoning of Newton in his letter to Bentley quoted in the text of chapter 13:
    If gravity is INNATE in matter and is not MEDIATED by something immaterial, then it can ACT on other matter only if there is mutual CONTACT. But there is no mutual contact. Hence, if gravity is not mediated by something immaterial, it cannot be innate.

20. If gravity is INNATE in matter, matter acts on other matter without mutual CONTACT and without the MEDIATION of anything else. But matter acts on other matter either through mutual contact, or through the mediation of something else. Hence, gravity is not innate in matter. (C := matter acts by mutual contact, M := it acts through the mediation of something else.)

21. *Using the Method of Truth Trees, prove the validity of the following sequents:*
    (a) $(\neg D \rightarrow \neg B) \& [D \rightarrow (B \rightarrow C)] \vdash \neg B \vee (D \& C)$
    (b) $P \leftrightarrow (Q \leftrightarrow R) \vdash (P \leftrightarrow Q) \leftrightarrow R$

22. The following is an argument given by Amicus in the 1620s:

> Before the creation of the world there was no POSITIVE being apart from God, since it would either be produced by ITSELF, and therefore be God; or it would be produced by ANOTHER: either by this God—but as it was supposed that this God produced nothing before this world, this settles the matter; or by a different God—but it is repugnant to natural reason that there be many Gods.

The main inference of this we symbolize: $P \rightarrow (I \vee A), \neg I, \neg A \therefore \neg P$. *Using a truth tree, prove the validity of this inference.*

14.2 STATEMENTS, CONSISTENCY, AND COMPLETENESS

14.2.1 TAUTOLOGIES, CONTRADICTIONS, AND LOGICAL EQUIVALENCE

It should now be fairly easy to see how to use the truth tree method to prove a given statement to be a contradiction or tautology. If a compound statement is a contradiction, we should be able to show by a truth tree that all paths downwards from it are closed. For this would show that every possibility consistent with it leads to a contradiction. Let us take the following example:

(8) To prove that $\neg[P \rightarrow (Q \rightarrow P)]$ is a contradiction:

1	√	$\neg[P \rightarrow (Q \rightarrow P)]$	Contr?
2		P	$\neg \rightarrow$
3	√	$\neg(Q \rightarrow P)$	
4		Q	$\neg \rightarrow$
5		$\neg P$	
		$\bot$	

This forlorn tree has no branches, and the only path ends in a contradiction. So the original statement is a contradiction.

By the same token, a statement would be a tautology if and only if every possibility consistent with its negation led to a contradiction. Therefore we would need to construct a truth tree whose only premise is its negation, and show that all paths are closed. Let's prove that the following is a tautologous statement form:

(9) To prove $p \rightarrow [(p \mathbin{\&} q) \vee \neg q]$ tautologous:

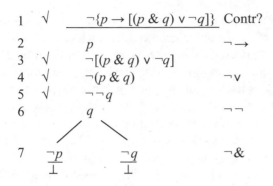

Here the negation of the original statement form is proved to be a contradiction, so that the original statement form is thereby proved tautologous.

Two statements P and Q, finally, are logically equivalent iff their truth tables are identical. As we have seen, this would mean that the biconditional formed from them, P $\leftrightarrow$ Q, would have to be a logical truth. So, to prove them logically equivalent, we would need to construct a tree whose only premise is the negation of the biconditional formed from them, $\neg$ (P $\leftrightarrow$ Q), and show that all its paths are closed. An example:

(10) To prove whether Z ⊣⊢ Z $\rightarrow$ (Z v Z):

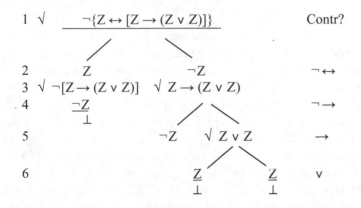

Here there is a complete open path, whose literals are both $\neg$Z. This shows that the statement Z is therefore not logically equivalent to Z $\rightarrow$ (Z v Z); and that the reason is that if Z is not true, this is compatible with Z $\rightarrow$ (Z v Z), but not, obviously, with Z; thus Z $\rightarrow$ (Z v Z) does not validly entail Z. This is perhaps not an obvious result, and shows well the power of the truth tree method.

14.2.2 CONSISTENCY AND COMPLETENESS (CHALLENGE LEVEL)

That the truth tree method is consistent with the rules of inference we have developed so far would seem to be self-evident. As we remarked in chapter 12.1, each of those rules corresponds to a valid argument form, thus establishing the *consistency* of the rules of inference of propositional logic: any sequent or argument form that is provable using the rules of inference of propositional logic is itself valid. We did not, however, prove that any argument form that is valid according to the definition of formal validity is provably valid by those rules, i.e., that the set of rules of inference of propositional logic is *complete*. [See the definitions of consistency and completeness in section 12.1.2 above.] It is easier, however, to prove the consistency and completeness of the truth tree method.

First let's consider the individual tree rules. We may define the consistency and completeness of truth tree rules as follows:

> A truth tree rule is **consistent** iff whenever the premise has the truth value T, all the statements derived from it by the rule on at least one branch also have the value T.

If this were not the case, it would be possible to derive a false statement from a true one by the rule, contrary to the definition of formal validity. Conversely,

> A truth tree rule is **complete** iff the premise also has the truth value T whenever all the statements derived from it by the rule on at least one branch have the value T.

Now, beginning with the non-branching rules, it is clear from its truth table that $p \& q$ has the value T iff both p and q have the value T. This establishes that the decomposition rule **&** is both consistent and complete. Similarly, the negation of a disjunction, $\neg(p \vee q)$, is T when and only when both disjuncts are F, i.e., iff $\neg p$ and $\neg q$ are T, thus establishing the consistency and completeness of $\neg \vee$. The consistency and completeness of $\neg\neg$ follow from the formal validity of the two versions of DN. As for of $\neg\rightarrow$, $p \rightarrow q$ is false when and only when p is T and q is F, so that $\neg(p \rightarrow q)$ is T iff p is T and $\neg q$ is T, establishing the consistency and completeness of $\neg\rightarrow$.

Turning now to the branching rules, $p \vee q$ is T when and only when either p is T or q is T. Thus there is a T on at least one of the branches iff the premise is T. The rule $\vee$ is therefore consistent and complete. Similarly, $\neg(p \& q)$ is T iff one or both of $\neg p$ and $\neg q$ are T, thus establishing the consistency and completeness of $\neg$**&**. $p \rightarrow q$ is T exactly when either p is F or q is T, i.e., when either $\neg p$ is T or q is T, so that again there is a T on at least one of the branches iff the premise is T. The rule $\rightarrow$ is therefore consistent and complete. Finally, $(p \leftrightarrow q)$ is T when and only when p and q have the same truth value, and $\neg(p \leftrightarrow q)$ is T when and only when p and q have opposite truth values, from which the consistency and completeness of the $\leftrightarrow$ and $\neg\leftrightarrow$ rules follow.

To establish the completeness of the truth tree method itself, we need first to assure ourselves that a complete truth tree always terminates. We note that according to the rules of formation for Statement Logic, any compound statement is formed by the five truth-functional operators (four binary and one unary) operating on simple statements. The decomposition rules—one for each of the four binary operators and one for each of the negations of them—will therefore be sufficient to reduce any finite compound statement to literals, statements of the form p or $\neg p$, where p is a simple statement. Since each decomposition rule results in at most a doubling of the number of branches, there will therefore be a finite number of paths in the complete tree.

Now we note that if the two premises and the negation of the conclusion—all the statements "above ground" in the tree—are consistent with one another, it will be possible to assign them all the truth value T. But now an application of any of the rules to any statement above it in the tree will result in all the statements derived from it on at least one branch also having the value T, by the definition of consistency of the rules. This shows that any tree beginning with all the above-ground statements T will have at least one open path. Because the number of such applications is finite, we are therefore guaranteed that the tree will be completed, and that in such a complete tree there will be at least one complete open path: one where all the literals in it are T. Contrarily, if the tree is closed, the premises together with the negation of the conclusion cannot be consistent. That is, *for any given argument form or sequent of Statement Logic, if the truth tree associated with it is closed, the argument form or sequent is valid.* The truth tree method is consistent.

A reversal of this kind of reasoning can now be used to establish the completeness of the truth tree method. If below the above-ground statements there is a complete open path consisting of only true literals, then, because this can only be reached by applying decomposition rules each of which is itself complete, the above-ground statements must all be true on that evaluation, and are therefore consistent. Thus if there is at least one complete open path in a complete tree corresponding to an argument or sequent, the premises together with the negation of the conclusion will be consistent. Conversely, *the truth tree associated with any valid argument or sequent of Statement Logic will be closed.* The truth tree method is complete.

SUMMARY

- If a compound statement is a **contradiction**, then all paths downwards from it in the corresponding truth tree are **closed**. If a compound statement is a **tautology**, then all paths downwards from its negation in the corresponding truth tree are **closed**.
- A truth tree rule is **consistent** iff whenever the premise has the truth value T, all the statements derived from it by the rule on at least one branch also have the value T.
- A truth tree rule is **complete** iff the premise also has the truth value T whenever all the statements derived from it by the rule on at least one branch have the value T.
- Since every argument form or sequent of Statement Logic that is associated with a closed truth tree is valid, the truth tree method is **consistent**, and since the truth tree associated with any valid argument form or sequent of Statement Logic is closed, the truth tree method is **complete**.

EXERCISES 14.2

23. *Determine using a truth tree* which of the following abstract statements is a *contradiction*. For each that is not a contradiction, is it a *tautology*, or a *contingent* statement?
    (a) ¬(A → A)
    (b) (F & G) → G
    (c) P → ¬P
    (d) P ↔ ¬P
    (e) R & (¬R ∨ S)

24. One of the following three statement forms is *tautologous*, and one *contradictory*. Use a truth tree method to *determine* which is which.
    (a) $p → (p → q)$
    (b) ¬[$(p \& q) \& (p → ¬q)$]
    (c) $p \& [p → (q \& ¬q)]$

25. *Determine using a truth tree* whether Z ↔ Z is logically equivalent to Z → (Z ∨ Z).

26. *Determine using a truth tree* whether ¬(¬A ∨ B) is logically equivalent to ¬A → ¬B.

27. (**CHALLENGE**) Give a detailed argument for the soundness and completeness of each of the following rules, making explicit the truth tables for the appropriate operators:
    (a) ¬¬
    (b) ¬→
    (c) →
    (d) ¬↔

28. (**CHALLENGE**) If the truth tree for each rule is *complete*, why is this not enough to prove the completeness of the truth tree method as a whole? What more is needed, and why?

PART III
PREDICATE LOGIC

Chapter Fifteen

Syllogistic Logic

15.1 CATEGORY LOGIC

15.1.1 ARISTOTLE'S LOGIC

Consider the argument:

All animals of the dog family are carnivores.
Foxes are animals belonging to the dog family.
Therefore foxes are carnivores.

Is it valid? Well, according to the root definition of validity, it is valid if the denial of the conclusion is incompatible with the truth of the premises. Clearly, you can't deny that foxes are carnivores while holding to the truth of both premises, so it is definitely valid. Yet when we try to analyze its validity using statement logic, we get nowhere. The premises and conclusion have no component statements (they do not even have any parts that are themselves statements). So they are *simple statements* (see the definitions in chapter 3). Nevertheless, the validity of the argument seems to depend on certain elements of these statements that get repeated in an identifiable pattern. If we replace "animals of the dog family" by D, "foxes" by F, and "carnivores" by C, we get an abstract argument of a clearly identifiable form:

All D are C.
All F are D.
Therefore all F are C.

Here the capital letters are not standing for statements but categories of things: if C instead stood for the category of things that are "descended from *Cynodictis*," we would have another valid argument, indeed another sound argument, since all the premises would again be true. If we use the Greek letters A, B, Γ to stand for any arbitrary categories of things, we may identify the following as a valid form:

All A are B.
All B are Γ.
———————————
Therefore all A are Γ.

This is exactly how Aristotle proceeded in setting up his logical system. He followed the practice of the other Ancient Greek logicians of analyzing complex arguments into a series of basic arguments or *syllogisms* (the Greek for argument), each of which consists of two premises and a conclusion. But he seems to have had a low opinion of the logic of statements begun by the Megarians (and completed after his death by the Stoics, especially Chrysippus). For him the real logical work in reasoning was done using arguments like the one above that involved connections among categories of things. So he proceeded to establish, apparently single-handed, a complete system for determining the validity or invalidity of arguments of this kind. Thus, in Aristotelian logic each of the premises and the conclusion is a *categorical statement*, i.e., one that asserts a connection between two categories or terms, the subject term and the predicate term; and each term appears in the argument twice. Such a syllogism is a *categorical syllogism*. Here's an example of a categorical syllogism with an invalid form:

Beans are vegetables.
Some vegetables are not legumes.
———————————
Therefore some beans are not legumes.

Here the categories are "beans," "vegetables," and "legumes." Denying the conclusion is the same as claiming that all beans are legumes. But this is true! Clearly it is also compatible with both premises (which are also true).

That Aristotle regarded categorical logic as the "real logic" was probably fostered by the prevalence of this kind of reasoning in field biology, his greatest passion. It is said that when his former pupil Alexander (soon to be "the Great") set off on his campaign of conquest, he was under instructions from his teacher to bring back specimens of exotic flora and fauna from distant lands. Now Aristotle was a keen biologist not just in the sense of an enthusiastic amateur, but, as the first to subject the chief biological categories to systematic study, the founder of the discipline of biology. Even his physics is cast in terms that seem more suitable to biology, with each elemental type of body having a natural place in the universe towards which it tends, like so many plants seeking the sunlight. At any rate, as soon as Aristotle's physics and logic were introduced to the West at the end of the so-called Dark Ages, they took root. In fact his thought dominated these subjects in the universities from their inception in Padua, Bologna, Paris, and Oxford in the thirteenth and fourteenth centuries till the Scientific Revolution in the case of physics, and till the twentieth century in the case of logic. (Actually, in the Middle Ages Logic, along with Rhetoric and Grammar, was part of the *Trivium*, the three-fold curriculum that you undertook prior to university studies: hence our word *trivial*—I thought you'd appreciate this bit of *trivia*!)

15.1.2 A-, E-, I-, AND O-STATEMENTS

One of the salient and enduring contributions Aristotle made to logic was his identification of four main types of statement that predominate in syllogistic reasoning. Two of them *affirm* that all or some individuals of one category belong to the other (the universal affirmative and particular affirmative types), while two of them *deny* that any or some individuals of one category belong to the other (universal negative and particular negative). In the Middle Ages they were dubbed A-, E-, I-, and O-statements:

FORM	EXAMPLE	TYPE	CODE
All A are B.	All foxes are dogs.	Universal affirmative	**A**
No A are B.	No rock stars are celibate.	Universal negative	**E**
Some A are B.	Some senators are corrupt.	Particular affirmative	**I**
Some A are not B.	Some snakes are not poisonous.	Particular negative	**O**

Tradition has it that the A and I are the first two vowels of the Latin *affirmo*, I affirm, while E and O are the two vowels of *nego*, I deny. The examples in the second column are all of categorical statements in *standard form*. Here are some examples in non-standard form, all of which are symbolized in the same way as the standard one of the same type:

Non-standard A-statements:	Symbolized:
Every CITIZEN loves FREEDOM.	All C are F.
GEESE are BIRDS.	All G are B.
MICE SQUEAK.	All M are S.
Each STOCKHOLDER is morally RESPONSIBLE.	All S are R.
A MANATEE is an ANIMAL.	All M are A.
Every single person in the AUDIENCE is UNDER age.	All A are U.
Any LIFE is PRECIOUS.	All L are P.

Points to note:

- Although "A manatee is an animal" seems to be equivalent to "All manatees are animals," not every statement of this form is an A-statement: for example, "A man is on the veranda" does NOT mean "All men are on the veranda!" In such cases, as always, you will need to use your judgement.

Non-standard E-statements:

PIKACHUs aren't REAL.	No P are R.
ABSTRACTIONS are all non-ENTITIES.	No A are E.
Professional BASKETBALL players are never LESS than six feet tall.	No B are L.
None of my OUTFITS still FITS me.	No O are F.

Non-standard I-statements:

There are PLANETS in OTHER solar systems.	Some P are O.
Many ACCOUNTANTS have a sense of HUMOUR.	Some A are H.
Most MOVIE-stars are WEALTHY.	Some M are W.
At least one OUTFIT still FITS me.	Some O are F.
PEOPLE are LEAVING.	Some P are L.
Somebody REMEMBERS me. [P := is a PERSON]	Some P are R.

Points to note:

- Just as in statement logic, the symbolizations do not capture all the information contained in the original statements. "Most" and "Many" tell us more than "Some"; but what more they tell us does not affect the validity of categorical syllogisms. "Some" will always be interpreted as "at least one."
- "People are leaving" seems to be equivalent to "*Some* people are leaving," not "*All* people are leaving." Contrast with "Geese are birds" above.
- Terms like "somebody," "someone," "any body," "no one" tacitly refer to people. In the exercises, you will be given an explicit hint, such as [P := is a PERSON].

Non-standard O-statements:

There are PHILOSOPHERS who are not ATHEISTS.	Some P are not A.
At least one SYSTEM is not Y2K-COMPLIANT.	Some S are not Y.
Not all REFEREES are BLIND.	Some R are not B.

Points to note:

- The last statement is clearly the contradictory of "All referees are blind." In fact, this is always the case: each O-statement is the contradictory of the corresponding A-statement.
- Likewise, "At least one OUTFIT still FITS me" is the contradictory of "None of my OUTFITS still FITS me." Again, every I-statement is the contradictory of the corresponding E-statement.

The Square of Opposition:

These last two facts are summarized in the following table:

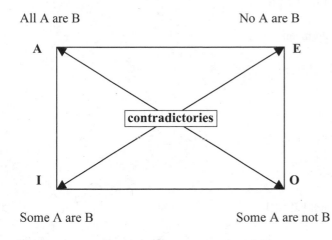

All A are B   No A are B

Some A are B   Some A are not B

There are several other relationships of opposition between A-, E-, I-, and O-statements that were included in the traditional square of opposition constructed by medieval logicians. However, these other relationships depended on interpreting all A- and E-statements as involving non-empty first categories, e.g., on interpreting a statement such as "All foxes are dogs" to imply that there are foxes, and likewise an E-statement such as "None of my outfits still fits me" as implying the existence of outfits. We won't be interpreting them in this way, as I shall explain further below.

15.1.3 AMBIGUOUS STATEMENTS

Finally, once more on the ambiguity of natural language and the importance of context. Consider the statement:

Some doctors have bad handwriting.

As it stands this is a simple I-statement. But suppose it were said in correction to someone's claim that "*All* doctors have bad handwriting," like this: "Well, *some* doctors have bad handwriting." Here it would have the force "*some, and not all*, doctors have bad handwriting": that is, as a conjunction of an I- and an O-statement: "Some doctors have bad handwriting, and some don't."

Here as before, we shall not try to guess at such conversational implications. *When we are asked to symbolize a statement, we will symbolize what we are given.* If a natural argument depends on such an implication, however, then we shall have to make explicit such implicit features. That said, there are some statements in English that are genuinely ambiguous even as they stand. The worst culprits are statements of this form:

(1) All PLANETS are not LIFELESS.

What does this mean? It could mean

(2) No PLANETS are LIFELESS.

or it could mean

(3) Not all PLANETS are LIFELESS.

i.e., by the square of opposition,

(4) Some PLANETS are not LIFELESS.

Statement (2) is an E-statement, whereas (4) is an O-statement. They mean different things. If someone said (1) to you, you would have to ask which she meant, (2) or (4). Consequently, we should try to avoid statements of the form (1), not just in a logic course, but generally, if we want to be understood.

SUMMARY

- In Aristotelian logic, each statement is a **categorical statement**, that is one that asserts a connection between two categories or terms, the subject term and the predicate term.
- A **categorical syllogism** is an argument consisting in two premises and a conclusion (all categorical statements), in which each term appears in the argument twice.
- The four main types of categorical statements are
  A-statement: All A are B.   I-statement: Some A are B.
  E-statement: No A are B.   O-statement: Some A are not B.
- A-statements and O-statements are contradictories. So are I-statements and E-statements.

EXERCISES 15.1

1. *Identify whether each of the following statements is an A-, E-, I-, or O-statement:*
   (a) Dolphins are mammals.
   (b) Many accountants have a sense of humour.

(c) No place in the world is empty.

(d) Some jokes are lost on him.

(e) Weaners suck.

2. *Put the following statements in standard form, and identify whether each is an A-, E-, I-, or O-statement:* e.g., (a) No G are W.—E-statement:

(a) GOURMETS don't eat their steaks WELL-done.

(b) Each TABLET contains 15 mg of CAFFEINE.

(c) There are airline PILOTS who have an ALCOHOL problem.

(d) Anybody who RACES horses must BELIEVE in miracles.

(e) The Vatican GUARDS are all SWISS.

(f) Not everyone who TRAINS WINS.

(g) Many BIRDS fly at HIGH altitudes.

(h) He who DEFILES an Egyptian tomb will PERISH.

(i) Not many ANIMALS cannot be TAMED.

(j) EXCEPTIONS must be MADE.

(k) NOBODY is PERFECT.

15.2 CARROLL DIAGRAMS

15.2.1 CARROLL'S DIAGRAMS

Lewis Carroll was the pen name of the Oxford professor and author Charles Dodgson (1832-98). Although he was a logician by profession, he became internationally famous for his whimsical children's books, *Alice's Adventures in Wonderland, Through the Looking Glass*, etc. His diagrams are contained in his posthumously published *Symbolic Logic*, ed. W.W. Bartley III, which also contained perhaps the earliest elaboration of the idea of truth trees or semantic tableaux (see chapters 14 and 23). This portrait of Carroll is from about 1860.

In the nineteenth century certain deep correspondences between mathematics and logic were discovered by thinkers familiar with abstract algebra. At around mid-century, building on pioneering work of the English logicians Augustus De Morgan and George Boole, John Venn systematized and popularized a way of presenting categorical logic by means of the diagrams now named after him. Shortly afterwards Lewis Carroll proposed a related system of diagrams that are in some respects superior to the familiar Venn diagrams, and it is a modified version of these that I shall present here.

The basic idea is that each category or predicate term, such as "foxes" or "animals of the dog family," corresponds to a class of individuals. The individuals in question are whatever we are talking about, and they belong to an all-encompassing class, the so-called *universe of discourse*. This may be a somewhat larger class—in this case, say, animals—or it may be supposed to be all individuals whatsoever.

The universe of discourse, (UD), is the class of all the individuals under discussion, those to which the predicates may or may not apply.

In the Carroll diagram technique, we represent the universe of discourse as a square, and then divide it into 4 distinct square regions. The top two squares represent, say, foxes (**F**), and the bottom two, animals that aren't foxes ($\overline{\text{F}}$). Similarly, the left two squares could represent animals of the dog family (**D**), and the right two, animals not of the dog family ($\overline{\text{D}}$). Thus the top left represents foxes that are animals of the dog family (**FD**), the top right foxes that are not animals of the dog family (**F$\overline{\text{D}}$**), the bottom left non-foxes that are animals of the dog family ($\overline{\text{F}}$**D**), the bottom right animals that are neither foxes nor members of the dog family ($\overline{\text{F}}\overline{\text{D}}$):

(Dogs) D $\overline{\text{D}}$ (Non-dogs)

(Foxes)   F

(Non-foxes) $\overline{\text{F}}$

Here it should be emphasized that we do not know whether any animals exist in any of these classes, and we shall assume them all to be empty unless told otherwise. Now we can fill in information in these diagrams to represent categorical statements, proceeding as follows. If we know there is an individual in a given region, we put an **x** (standing for an arbitrary individual) in this region. If we know there is no individual in a given region, we put a **0** (for zero) in that region.[1] This gives:

A-statements

e.g., All FOXES are DOGS.

---

[1] Carroll used 'I' to represent an arbitrary individual; the 'x' originates with Venn, and his diagrams. Venn used shading to indicate the absence of any individuals in a region; the **0** is Carroll's notation. See Appendix 3.

To say "All foxes are dogs" is to say that there aren't any fox/non-dogs, i.e., that the top right square **FD̄** is empty. So we put a **0** in that square:

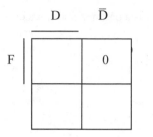

Note that this does not give us any information about non-foxes; nor does it tell us whether there are any foxes (more on this later!).

E-statements

e.g., No FROGS are WARM-blooded.

To say "No frogs are warm-blooded" is to say that there aren't any warm-blooded frogs, i.e., that the top left square is empty. So we put a **0** in that square:

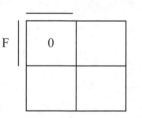

I-statements

e.g., Some BACTERIA are PARASITES.

Here we are asserting that there is at least one individual that is a bacterium and a parasite, so we put an **x** in the **BP** square:

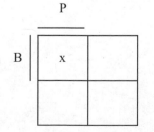

O-statements

e.g., Some BAGMEN are not CROOKS.

Here we are asserting that there is at least one individual that is a bagman and not a crook, so we put an **x** in the **BC̄** square:

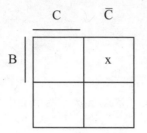

15.2.2 EXISTENCE AND NON-EXISTENCE

Now, suppose we have two categories, **A** and **B**, and we are told simply that "There are some **A**." If we are told nothing about whether these individuals are or are not **B**, we will not know whether to put the **x** in the top left square (**AB**) or the top right (**AB̄**). Thus we put it straddling both, using a line to join the two regions, thus:

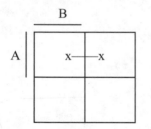

Similarly, if we were told that "There are some B," this would be represented:

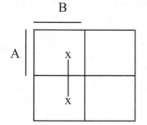

Now, suppose we have the same two categories, **A** and **B**, and we are told simply that "There are no **A**." This requires us to put a **0** in two regions: the top left square (**AB**) and the top right (**AB̄**):

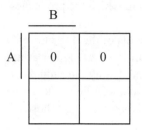

15.2.3 CONVERSION

One feature of Aristotle's logic that is represented very clearly by Carroll diagrams is the idea of *conversion*.

> The *converse* of a categorical statement is what you get when you switch the subject and predicate terms.

For instance, the converse of

(1) Some SOILS are not LOAMS.

is

(2) Some LOAMS are not SOILS.

We say that a statement is *validly convertible* iff it is logically equivalent to its converse. In the example given (1) is not validly convertible into (2). Indeed no O-statement is validly convertible, nor is any A-statement. This is obvious from their Carroll diagrams. If we switch the terms, this makes no difference if and only if the diagram is symmetrical about the diagonal from the top left to the bottom right. Thus the diagrams of both E- and I-statements are symmetrical, and therefore E-statements are validly convertible, and so are I-statements. For instance,

(3) No IMAMS are BA'ATHISTS.

is logically equivalent to

(4) No BA'ATHISTS are IMAMS.

SUMMARY

- The class to which all the individuals in question belong is called the **universe of discourse,** (UD). This class includes all those individuals to which the predicates may or may not apply.
- Each category or predicate term, such as "foxes" or "animals of the dog family," corresponds to a class of individuals. A **Carroll diagram** is a rectangular array in which statements involving categories may be represented. Any individuals of a given category **C**, or of which a given predicate **C** is true, will lie in the areas opposite the **C**. Any individuals of which the predicate is not true, i.e., those of category **not-C** or **C̄**, will lie in the remaining area.
- In such a diagram, a zero **0** in a region indicates that there are no individuals there, an **x** indicates that there is at least one individual there, and an **x** straddling two regions means that there is at least one individual in one or the other region, or both.
- The **converse** of a categorical statement is what you get when you switch the subject and predicate terms. A categorical statement is **validly convertible** iff it is logically equivalent to its converse. **I-statements** are validly convertible, and so are **E-statements**. A-statements and O-statements are not.
- A-statements and O-statements are contradictories of one another. So are **I**-statements and **E**-statements.

EXERCISES 15.2

3. (a)-(k): *Construct a Carroll diagram for each statement in exercise 2 above.*

4. *Identify* (i) *which pairs of the following statements are converses of each other*, and (ii) *which pairs are validly convertible into one other:*
   (a) All COMPUTERS are INTELLIGENT.
   (b) Some COMPUTERS are INTELLIGENT.
   (c) Some COMPUTERS are not INTELLIGENT.
   (d) There are INTELLIGENT things that are not COMPUTERS.
   (e) No MICROORGANISMS are SENTIENT beings.
   (f) No INTELLIGENT things are COMPUTERS.
   (g) No COMPUTERS are INTELLIGENT.
   (h) Some SENTIENT beings are MICROORGANISMS.

5. *Identify which pairs of statements in 4 are contradictories of each other.*

15.3 EVALUATING VALIDITY OF SYLLOGISMS

More than one categorical statement can be represented on the same diagram. For instance, the statements "All BA'ATHISTS are IRAQIS" and "Some IRAQIS are not BA'ATHISTS" can be represented on the same diagram thus:

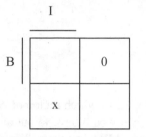

What happens when there are more than two predicate terms or categories? How do we represent them on the same diagram? Categorical statements involving three distinct predicates, **A**, **B**, and **C**, each of which may apply or not apply to a given individual, require 2^3 or eight distinct regions. Carroll has a neat way of representing this, but the following is a modification of his diagrams (see Appendix 3 on Logic Diagrams). Within the above square, we draw two horizontal lines bisecting the upper and lower rectangles of the square, creating a new region of 4 rectangles in the middle: individuals inside this region are those to which the third category **C** applies, those in the 2 rectangles above and 2 rectangles below it are those to which the third category does not apply, like this:

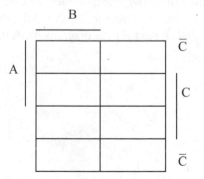

Thus the two statements "Some AFRICANS are BUDDHISTS" and "No CHEROKEES are Africans" can be represented as follows:

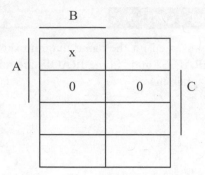

Note that if we'd filled in the first premise first we would not know which region of **AB** to put the **x** in: does it go in **ABC** or **ABC̄**? In such a case we would have to put an **x** straddling the two regions, only to find that there were none in **ABC**. But then when we enter the second premise, we see that the region **ABC** has a **0**, so the **x** must be in **ABC̄**. This motivates the following rule of procedure:

> **It always pays to do those statements involving '0's first and those involving 'x's last** —that is, to do the *universal* or A- and E-statements first, and the *particular* or I- and O-statements last.

Now we can evaluate validity as follows. According to our definition, if an argument is valid, then the denial of the conclusion will be incompatible with the truth of the premises. So if we have entered the premises of an argument on our diagram, then the denial of the conclusion will be incompatible with what we have entered; or, equivalently, the conclusion should be entailed by the information we can read off the diagram. Thus the above diagram shows that the argument

Some AFRICANS are BUDDHISTS.
No CHEROKEES are Africans.
Therefore some Buddhists are not Cherokees.

is VALID. But the argument

Some AFRICANS are BUDDHISTS.
No CHEROKEES are Africans.
Therefore no Cherokees are Buddhists.

is INVALID. The information in the diagram does not preclude there being non-African Cherokee Buddhists: in order to do that, the **ĀBC** region would have to have a **0**.

As another example, let's look at the following argument:

Some elementary PARTICLES are ELECTRONS.
All electrons are CHARGED.

Therefore there are charged particles.

After drawing our diagram of eight regions, we should enter the second premise first, since this is universal, while the first is particular: That all electrons are charged is equivalent to there being no electrons that are not charged, so we put a **0** in the two rectangles that are **E$\bar{\text{C}}$**:

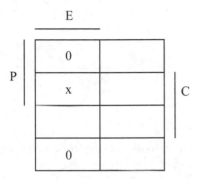

Now we see that it is impossible for the conclusion to be false: the **x** in the **EPC** region shows that there are charged particles. The argument is VALID.

Let's look at some more examples. In his *Monadology*, Leibniz argues:

No SIMPLE substances are DIVISIBLE.
No indivisible substances can come to an END naturally.

Hence, no simple substances can come to an end naturally.

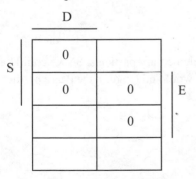

The second premise says that no $\bar{\text{D}}$ are **E**, so we put **0**'s in $\overline{\text{DE}}$ regions. Now, given the premises, we see that it is impossible to deny the conclusion. Therefore, by the definition of validity, the argument is VALID!

Some POLITICIANS are CORRUPT.
All SENATORS are politicians.

Hence, some senators are corrupt.

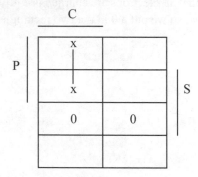

Here we do not know from the premises whether the individuals who are corrupt politicians are senators or not, so we have to put **x**'s joined by a line on either side of the $\text{S}\bar{\text{S}}$ divide. That is, the individuals could be on the $\bar{\text{S}}$, or non-**S**, side. Thus the premises are compatible with there being no corrupt senators (a **0** in **CSP** as well as $\text{CS}\bar{\text{P}}$), which is the denial of the conclusion. Therefore, by the definition of validity, the argument is INVALID!

Finally, we should note that sometimes we can simplify our analysis by *restricting the universe of discourse*. Thus returning to the argument concerning electrons,

Some elementary PARTICLES are ELECTRONS.
All electrons are CHARGED.

Therefore there are charged particles.

we note that the only things under discussion are elementary particles. So we could have restricted the UD to elementary particles. Then we would no longer have P as a predicate, but only E and C:

Some elementary particles are ELECTRONS.
All electrons are CHARGED.

Therefore there are charged particles.

This gives the simpler 2-predicate diagram:

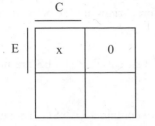

SUMMARY

- The **validity** of categorical syllogisms can be evaluated by a modified Carroll diagram for representing statements involving 3 categories. The premises are entered, and then the diagram is inspected. If **the denial of the conclusion is incompatible with what has been entered**, the argument is **valid**; if it is compatible with the entered premises, the argument is invalid.
- It pays to enter **universal premises first**, and particular ones later.
- Sometimes the analysis of an argument can be simplified by restricting the UD. Whenever one of the predicates in an argument applies to all the individuals under discussion, that predicate may be dropped and the UD restricted to those individuals to which the predicate applies.

EXERCISES 15.3

6. Ann Scott, discussing the military draft in 1972, commented that "as long as Congress intends to draft CITIZENS, and WOMEN are citizens, women will be DRAFTED."[2] *What categorical syllogism does this seem to involve? Determine whether it is valid using a Carroll diagram.*

For each of the following (7-17), put the argument in standard form (e.g., "All A are B"). (In cases where the predicates need clarifying, we will indicate them using the following notation: Hx := x is intense heat, Sx := x is a kind of painful sensation, etc.) *Then use the Carroll diagram method to determine whether it is VALID or INVALID:*

7. Some NEUTRINOS go FASTER than light. But no neutrinos have rest MASS. It follows that some things with no rest mass go faster than light.

---

[2] Ann Scott, "The Equal Rights Amendment: What's in It for You?," *Ms.* (July 1972): p. 85; quoted from Howard Pospesel, *Introduction to Logic: Predicate Logic*, 1st ed. (Prentice Hall), p. 80.

8. ARIANS do not BELIEVE in Christ's divinity. Therefore Arians are DEISTS, since no Deists believe in Christ's divinity.

9. All AARDVARKS are EDENTATES. Some animals that eat TERMITES are not edentates. Thus there are aardvarks which do not eat termites.

10. No WAFFLES sold here are HEALTH food. For they all contain TRANSFATS, and nothing that contains transfats is health food

11. A newspaper article reports consumer advocate Bess Myerson Grant as saying: FILET mignon is not a KOSHER cut of meat. Federal regulations define filet mignon as beef cut from the HIND quarter. But Jewish dietary laws forbid eating meat cut from the hind quarter of any animal [i.e., no such meat is kosher].[3]

12. An alleged argument against atheism:
Anyone is MORAL who UPHOLDS the teachings of a religious faith. Therefore, since no ATHEIST upholds the teachings of a religious faith, it follows that no atheist is moral.

13. From Monty Python's *Holy Grail*:
Anything MADE of wood BURNS. WITCHES burn. Therefore witches are made of wood.

14. From G.H. Hardy's *A Mathematician's Apology*:
…it is obvious that irrationals are uninteresting to engineers, since they are concerned only with approximations, and all approximations are rational.
(Ix := x is interesting to engineers, Rx := x is rational, Ax := x is an approximation)

15. (**CHALLENGE**) From Plato's *Ion*:
And no man can be a RHAPSODIST who does not UNDERSTAND the meaning of the poet. For the rhapsodist ought to INTERPRET the mind of the poet to his hearers, but how can he interpret him well unless he knows what he means?

16. (**CHALLENGE**) From George Berkeley's *Three Dialogues between Hylas and Philonous*:
…because intense HEAT is nothing else but a particular kind of painful SENSATION; and pain cannot exist but in a PERCEIVING being; it follows that no intense heat can really exist in an unperceiving corporeal substance.
(Hx := x is intense heat, Sx := x is a kind of painful sensation, Px := x exists in a perceiving being or substance)

---

[3] Modified from Pospesel, *Predicate Logic*, 1st ed., p. 83.

17. (**CHALLENGE**) The Scots philosopher David Hume wrote:
    All IDEAS are borrow'd from preceding PERCEPTIONS. Our ideas of OBJECTS, therefore, are deriv'd from that source [i.e., from preceding perceptions].

The following whimsical examples (18-23) are from Lewis Carroll's *Symbolic Logic*. *Determine by the method of Carroll diagrams whether they are valid or invalid*; if the latter, *what if anything could have been validly concluded* (i.e., assuming each term appears exactly twice in the argument, is there a categorical statement (involving only two terms) that follows validly from the premises)?

18. Some EPICURES are unGENEROUS. All my UNCLES are generous. ∴ My uncles are not epicures. (G :– are generous)

19. Some CANDLES give very LITTLE light. Candles are MEANT to give light. ∴ Some things that are meant to give light give very little.

20. All LIONS are FIERCE. Some lions do not drink COFFEE. ∴ Some creatures that drink coffee are not fierce. (Restrict the UD to creatures.)

21. (**CHALLENGE**) HIS songs never LAST an hour. A song that lasts an hour is TEDIOUS. ∴ His songs are never tedious. (Restrict the UD to songs.)

22. A PRUDENT man SHUNS hyenas. No BANKER is imprudent. ∴ No banker fails to shun hyenas. (Restrict the UD to men.)

23. (**CHALLENGE**) BORES are DREADED. No bore is ever begged to PROLONG his visit. ∴ No one who is dreaded is ever begged to prolong his visit. (UD: people.)

24. The English materialist philosopher Thomas Hobbes claimed:
    "The world (I mean the whole mass of all things that are), is corporeal, that is to say, body; and that which is not body is not part of the universe."
    That is, (i) "Everything in the UNIVERSE is BODY," and (ii) "everything which is not body is not in the universe." *Do these two statements say the same thing? Find out by representing each by a Carroll diagram, and see whether the diagrams are the same.*

Chapter Sixteen

Universal Quantification

16.1.1 UNIVERSAL QUANTIFICATION

The diagram methods we looked at in the last chapter were simple generalizations of Aristotle's category logic. But it was not extended to cover a significantly wider class of arguments. This situation changed radically in the late nineteenth century when Gottlob Frege introduced the notion of **quantifiers**. This gave him a way of symbolizing the categorical statements of traditional logic using statement connectives, thus enabling him to subsume all of Syllogistic Logic under an extended version of Statement Logic.

Friedrich Ludwig Gottlob Frege (1848-1925) was a German logician of great originality, who made important contributions to the foundations of mathematics and the philosophy of language. He recast traditional logic in terms of quantifiers and proofs of validity, thus establishing modern predicate logic. His lifelong project of reducing mathematics to logic came unstuck with Russell's discovery of an inconsistency at the heart of his axiomatic system.

This extended logic, called Quantifier Theory or just plain Predicate Logic, not only applies automatically to a much wider class of arguments than its predecessors, but is readily generalizable to predicates involving relations among several individuals, the Relational Logic we shall come to consider in chapter 20.

First we shall treat universal statements (A- and E-statements), postponing particular statements (I- and O-statements) till the next chapter. The basic idea is to treat universal statements as stating a conditional relationship between membership of the two categories or classes: the class of individuals to which the subject term applies, and the class of individuals to which the predicate term applies. Thus an **A-statement** "All M are N" is interpreted as saying: if an arbitrary individual is in class M, then it is in class N; whereas an **E-statement** "No M are N" says: if an arbitrary individual is in class M, then it is not in class N. Borrowing from algebra, we denote the arbitrary individual by the variable x, and symbolize the **A-statement** "All M are N" as:

$$\forall x(Mx \rightarrow Nx)$$

Here the symbol $\forall x$ stands for "for all x"; it is called a **universal quantifier** and the whole abstract statement that results is called a **universal quantification**. Mx stands for "x is an M" and Nx stands for "x is an N." Thus the whole formula reads:

For all x, if x is an M then x is an N.

Similarly the **E-statement** "No M are N" is symbolized:

$$\forall x(Mx \rightarrow \neg Nx)$$
For all x, if x is an M then x is not an N.

In both cases the 'x' is understood to range over all the individuals of the kind under discussion. This is the "Universe of Discourse," or UD for short, which we already met in the previous chapter. It is also called the **domain** of the quantifier.

> The **universe of discourse (UD)** is the set of individuals over which the individual variable 'x' (or 'y' or 'z') occurring in a quantifier is assumed to range.
> This is also known as the **domain** of the quantifier.

The UD is generally not specified, in which case it will be understood as including everything without qualification. But in certain cases where the kind of thing under discussion is some narrower class, say people, it will pay to restrict the UD accordingly, as we saw in the previous chapter.

One oddity of the Fregean way of symbolizing universal statements is that it is non-committal on whether there exist individuals in the classes mentioned. We already saw that in our treatment of universal statements in the previous chapter, where only I- and O-statements involved the assertion that there was an individual in the class denoted by the subject term (in the jargon, only I- and O-statements have *existential import*). For many statements this conflicts with our intuitions. If I said "All BACTRIAN camels have

TWO humps," you would certainly take this to imply that Bactrian camels exist—to the degree that you would accuse me of deliberately misleading you if there were no such things. On the other hand, though, a statement such as "All DODOS are EXTINCT" carries with it no such implication as to the existence of its subject—quite the contrary. This question is involved enough to deserve a thorough discussion, which I postpone to a section of chapter 18. For now, just take it as read that *A- and E-statements are interpreted as having no existential import.*

16.1.2 'ONLY' AND 'NOTHING BUT'

Finally, now that we know how to symbolize categorical statements, we are in a better position to understand the symbolization of two non-standard forms we have not yet looked at:

1. "None but A are B," "Nothing but A are B," or "No one except A is a B"; and
2. "Only A are B."

Some examples:

Nobody but a MISER would SAVE egg shells.
Nothing but GOLD will SILENCE him.
Only RUBBISH can be had for a SONG.

If none but misers save egg shells, this means no one except misers, i.e., only misers, save egg shells. But does this mean that "All misers save egg shells"? No. It means "Anyone who saves egg shells is a miser," i.e., All S are M. So

"Only M are S" is equivalent to "All S are M."

This is immediately understandable when we symbolize. For

$\forall x(Sx \rightarrow Mx)$

means

For all x, x is an S *only if* x is an M.

or, "only if someone is a miser does he save egg shells." So the kind of inversion we get with "only" with respect to "all" is the same as the inversion we got with "only if" in relation to "if." Similarly, the other two statements above come out as

Nothing but GOLD will SILENCE him. All S are G. $\forall x(Sx \rightarrow Gx)$
Only RUBBISH can be had for a SONG. All S are R. $\forall x(Sx \rightarrow Rx)$

16.1.3 SINGULAR STATEMENTS AND INDIVIDUAL NAMES

Suppose someone argues:

Of course Steve <u>Sharkey</u> is a MERCENARY. All BRITONS fighting in Angola are mercenaries, and he is a Briton fighting there.

We have two premises: one of them is an A-statement, "All Britons fighting in Angola are mercenaries"; but the other, "Steve Sharkey is a Briton fighting in Angola," is a simple statement of a different kind. It asserts that a given individual, Steve Sharkey, belongs in a given category. Expressions used to refer to individual things or people are called **singular terms** or **individual names**, and a statement containing one or more singular terms is called a **singular statement**. Individual names are symbolized by *lower case letters*. In general, we will symbolize a name by the first letter of the name or designating expression, which will be underlined; the letters *x*, *y*, and *z*, however, are reserved for the *variables* we have already encountered in universal and existential quantifications. (Variables are not names; they are placeholders for names; just as statement variables are not statements in statement logic.) In symbolizing simple singular statement, we write the PREDICATE **P** first, and the <u>name</u> **n** second, thus: **Pn**.

Thus in the above example, Steve Sharkey is symbolized as **s**, "is a mercenary" by **M**, and "is a Briton fighting in Angola" by **B**, "Sharkey is a mercenary" as **Ms**, etc., giving:

$\forall x(Bx \rightarrow Mx)$, Bs $\therefore$ Ms

Now a singular statement such as Bs is a statement—as indeed are the universal and particular statements we have already encountered. By our previous definitions, Bs is a simple statement: it has no components. Further examples of simple singular statements:

SINGULAR STATEMENT	SINGULAR TERM	PREDICATE	SYMBOLIZED
Amos <u>Judd</u> LOVES cold mutton.	Amos <u>Judd</u>	LOVES cold mutton	**Lj**
This <u>dish</u> is a PUDDING.	This <u>dish</u>	is a PUDDING	**Pd**
<u>Shakespeare</u> WROTE *Hamlet*.	<u>Shakespeare</u>	WROTE *Hamlet*	**Ws**

I always AVOID kangaroos.	I	always AVOID kangaroos	**Ai**
The <u>reader</u> will perhaps be PUZZLED.	The <u>reader</u>	will perhaps be PUZZLED	**Pr**

It should be noted here that not just names but also definite descriptions that are sufficient to pick out an individual, such as "The reader," are treated as singular terms. (We will give a more sophisticated treatment of definite descriptions in chapter 21.) Now we can make compounds from these simple statements using statement operators, just as with simple statements in statement logic. Thus Bs → Ms is a conditional statement, symbolizing "If Steve Sharkey is a Briton fighting in Angola, then he is a mercenary." ¬Bs symbolizes "Steve Sharkey is not a Briton fighting in Angola," and so forth.

Note also that we may symbolize a statement differently in a different argument context. If some inference we were making depended on Steve Sharkey's being a Briton, and another on his fighting in Angola, we would need to use the symbolization key: Bx := x is a Briton, Fx := x is fighting in Angola, and "Steve Sharkey is a Briton fighting in Angola" would be symbolized: Bs & Fs.

Traditionally, singular terms presented something of a difficulty for logicians. One way of dealing with them had been to treat them as classes with only one member. That way a singular statement could be represented as an A-statement. This is the approach adopted, for example, by Lewis Carroll in his *Symbolic Logic*, from which, incidentally, all the above examples are taken. Thus Carroll treated "Amos Judd loves cold mutton" as "All those who are Amos Judd love cold mutton," assimilating it to an A-statement. This works if, like him, one holds A-statements to have existential import. For from the fact that Amos Judd loves cold mutton, it clearly follows that someone loves cold mutton. But if, like Frege (and us), one denies that A-statements have such import or entail their corresponding I-statements, this option is foreclosed.

In fact, it is very easy to accommodate singular terms to the Fregean approach, and to Carroll's diagrams. For to assert that "Amos Judd loves cold mutton" is simply to assert that the class of those who LOVE cold mutton has as member the individual <u>Judd</u>. That is, the individual named **j** is to be found in the class **L**. This is diagrammed:

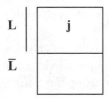

Similarly, if we diagram the premises of the "mercenary" argument with which we began this subsection, we obtain

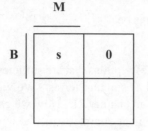

Entering the A-statement first, "All BRITONS fighting in Angola are MERCENARIES," the fact that Steve Sharkey is a Briton means that the **s** is in the **B**-region; the only place to enter it is in **BM**. Hence the conclusion follows: Sharkey is a mercenary.

SUMMARY

- The symbol ∀x stands for "for all x"; it is called a **universal quantifier**. It precedes a formula in the **variable** x, and the whole abstract statement that results is called a **universal quantification**.
- The **A-statement** "All M are N" is symbolized ∀x(Mx → Nx), which reads "For all x, if x is an M then x is an N."
- The **E-statement** "No M are N" is symbolized ∀x(Mx → ¬Nx), which reads "For all x, if x is an M then x is not an N."
- The **universe of discourse** (**UD**) or **domain** of a quantifier such as ∀x is the set of individuals over which x is assumed to range.
- If there is an individual in the class denoted by the subject term, a categorical statement is said to have **existential import**. On the interpretation adopted here, only I- and O-statements have existential import, and universal quantifications such as A- and E-statements do not.
- Expressions used to refer to individual things or people are called **singular terms** or **individual names**. They are symbolized by lower case letters from **a** to **w**; the letters **x**, **y**, and **z** are reserved for **variables**.
- The abstract statements "**Only M are S**" and "**None but M are S**" are each equivalent to "**All S are M**."
- A statement containing one or more singular terms and no variables is called a **singular statement**. A statement that the predicate **P** applies to an individual **m** is symbolized **Pm**. Such singular statements can be combined using the 5 truth functional operators to form compound statements.

EXERCISES 16.1

1. *Symbolize the following A- and E-statements:*
   (a) GOURMETS don't eat their steaks WELL-done.
   (b) Each TABLET contains 15 mg of CAFFEINE.
   (c) No WORLD Series is ever DULL.
   (d) Anybody who RACES horses has got to BELIEVE in miracles.
   (e) YEOMEN are all PETTY officers.
   (f) He who laughs LAST laughs LOUDEST. (A, O)

2. *Symbolize the following non-standard categorical statements:*
   (a) Only MEN go BALD.—J.R. Lucas
   (b) None but the BRAVE DESERVE the fair.—Lewis Carroll
   (c) Only those living along the COAST will have RAIN today.—TV weatherman
   (d) No one would DOUBT it but a SKEPTIC.

3. *Symbolize the following singular statements:*
   (a) Socrates is MORTAL.
   (b) That book is BORING.
   (c) Quentin Crisp was GAY and PROUD of it.
   (d) Pat TRAINED hard, but didn't WIN.
   (e) If Beeblebrox LAUGHED his head off, he would STILL have one head left.
   (f) If Eugene Hasenfus was not a CIA agent, he would not have worked for SOUTH-ERN AIR.
   (g) The experiment is WORTHWHILE only if it TESTS something.

The following syllogisms of Lewis Carroll (4-5) have one premise that is a singular state-ment. *Represent the premises using Carroll diagrams, and determine whether the stated conclusions follow:*

4. No DOCTORS are ENTHUSIASTIC. Alice is enthusiastic. Therefore Alice is not a doctor.

5. John is in the HOUSE. Everybody in the house is ILL. Therefore John is ill. [UD: people]

Assuming that every predicate or name is to appear exactly twice in the argument, use Carroll diagrams to work out the conclusions of the following arguments of Carroll's:[1]

---

[1] 4-8 are from Carroll's *Symbolic Logic*, p. 162. (In 4, I have put 'Alice,' where Carroll had 'you.')

6. All PUDDINGS are NICE. This <u>dish</u> is a pudding. No nice things are WHOLE-SOME. Therefore...

7. No EXPERIENCED person is incompetent. <u>Jenkins</u> is always BLUNDERING. No COMPETENT person is always blundering. Therefore...[UD: people]

8. (**CHALLENGE**) My <u>gardener</u> is well WORTH listening to on military subjects. No one can REMEMBER the Battle of Waterloo unless he is very OLD. Nobody is really worth listening to on military subjects unless he can remember the Battle of Waterloo. Therefore...[UD: people]

16.2 RULES OF INFERENCE: UI AND UG

We have proved the above argument about mercenaries valid using the Carroll diagram method. Now let us investigate how to deal with it in Predicate Logic. It seems obvious that if every x that is a B is an M, and s is a B, then s must be an M. Yet, by our definitions the A-statement "All Britons fighting in Angola are mercenaries" is a simple statement, not a conditional: no part of the original statement is itself a statement. Nonetheless, it seems perfectly valid to infer the conditional Bs → Ms from it. This is in effect our first rule of inference for Predicate Logic, **universal instantiation**. But to state it properly, we need to define a few terms. First we need a term for the part of the universal statement that is not the universal quantifier. In the above example, ∀x(Bx → Mx), this would be (Bx → Mx). We call this a *propositional function*:

> A **propositional function in x** (symbolically represented Φx) is a formula containing at least one variable x such that when an individual name is substituted throughout for x the result is a singular statement; e.g. (Mx → Nx), or (Px & ¬Qx) or (Pa & ¬Qx).

This definition (adapted from Bertrand Russell) will suffice for our purposes here, although we shall have to modify it in chapter 19 below when we come to statements involving more than one quantifier, and other variables, y and z.[2] With it we can define *universal quantification* and an *instance* of one:

> A **universal quantification** is a propositional function in x (or y, or z) preceded by a universal quantifier ∀x (or ∀y, or ∀z, respectively).

---

[2] In chapter 19 we will define quantifications first, and then define propositional functions in terms of them.

The variable x in a propositional function formed as above is no longer "bound" by the quantifier, and is thus called a "free variable." (A formal definition of "free variable" can wait until we have defined the *scope* of a quantifier in chapter 19.)

An **instance of a quantification** is what is obtained when the initial quantifier $\forall$x is dropped and all instances of the free variable x in the resulting propositional function are replaced by the same individual name **n**.

In all the above, what is stated in terms of x is tacitly understood to apply to expressions involving y and z too. Thus (Ma → Na) is an instance of $\forall$x(Mx → Nx), but it is also an instance of $\forall$y(My → Ny) or $\forall$z(Mz → Nz). Again, (Mi → Ni) is another instance of any of these quantifiers. But (Ma → Ni) is not an instance of any of them, because we have not used the same individual name in substituting for the variable.

Now we may define our rule of inference:

Universal Instantiation (**UI**)
From a universal quantification infer any instance of it.
From $\forall$xΦx derive Φ**n**, where **n** denotes any individual name.

Again, what is stated here in terms of x is tacitly understood to apply to expressions involving y and z too. Likewise, Φx can be any propositional function in x. So the rule allows us to go from $\forall$x(Mx → Nx) to (Ma → Na), as well as, for instance, from $\forall$x Px to Pi.

Now the proof of the "mercenary" argument's validity is straightforward:

(1) $\forall$x(Bx → Mx)   Prem
(2) Bs   Prem
(3) Bs → Ms   1 UI
(4) Ms   2, 3 MP

Other more complex arguments involving singular statements can be handled just as easily. Here's an example:

No PERFECT being is immoral. No MORAL being would punish AGNOSTICISM. It follows that if God is perfect, he will not punish agnosticism.
Symbolized: $\forall$x(Px → Mx), $\forall$x(Mx → ¬Ax) ∴ Pg → ¬Ag (UD: beings)

(1) $\forall$x(Px → Mx)   Prem
(2) $\forall$x(Mx → ¬Ax)   Prem
(3) Pg → Mg   1 UI
(4) Mg → ¬Ag   2 UI
(5) Pg → ¬Ag   3, 4 HS

Now what about categorical syllogisms? When I was listening to PBS one night while working away on some exercises for this book, I heard the following argument:

> Many people don't realize that MUSHROOMS are FUNGI and fungi are mICRO-OR-GANISMS, so that mushrooms are in fact micro-organisms.

This is the most basic valid categorical syllogism, expressed abstractly as:

All M are F.
All F are I.
$\overline{}$
∴ All M are I.

or, in terms of predicate logic: $\forall x(Mx \rightarrow Fx)$, $\forall x(Fx \rightarrow Ix)$ ∴ $\forall x(Mx \rightarrow Ix)$.

We could give a justification of the validity of this syllogism as follows. Suppose we take some arbitrary individual. Then the first premise tells us that if it is a mushroom, then it is a fungus, while the second premise tells us that if it is a fungus it's a micro-organism. From this we may infer by HS that if it is a mushroom, then it's a micro-organism. Now if the individual we chose was suitably arbitrary, then it seems we would be justified in generalizing from this to say that *any* mushroom is a micro-organism. This is what is involved in our next rule, **Universal Generalization**.

Notice that the argument we just gave is a *suppositional argument*, but one in which we suppose something *for the sake of example*, that is, for the sake of giving specific content to a general principle. That is, in effect, we are now showing how to formalize suppositional arguments of the second kind considered in chapter 7.3. What we need is the notion of an **arbitrary individual**. To this end let us reserve the letters **u**, **v**, and **w** for arbitrary individuals assumed in a proof by universal generalization. For our purposes here, an arbitrary individual is one that has not already been mentioned in the statement of the argument, and has been introduced in the proof solely in anticipation of general-izing from it later. (This means that it must be a distinct arbitrary name from the other arbitrary names we will be introducing in the next chapter for Existential Instantiations, for which we reserve the letters **i**, **j**, and **k**.) Then the above reasoning can be rendered as follows: suppose we have an arbitrary individual, say **u**. Then the first premise gives Mu → Fu, and the second gives Fu → Iu, from which we may infer Mu → Iu by HS. Now we need to have some way of legitimizing the step from the singular statement Mu → Iu, where u is an arbitrary individual, to the universal statement $\forall x(Mx \rightarrow Ix)$. This motivates the following rule:

Universal Generalization (**UG**)
Infer a universal quantification from a suitably arbitrary instance of it.
From **Φu** derive **∀xΦx**, provided
(i) **Φu** neither is nor depends upon an undischarged supposition involving **u**, and
(ii) **Φu** does not contain a name **i** (or **j** or **k**) introduced by an application of **EI** to a formula involving **u**.

The meaning of these two provisos will be spelled out in later chapters, and there will be no need to worry about them until then. The first comes into play in proofs involving suppositions for CP and RA, the second in multiple quantifications. Remember, u is an arbitrary name, rather than the name of some individual occurring in the argument. Thus Φu is an instance of the quantifier, and not a propositional function, as it would be if u were a variable. Again, since Φu is an instance of ∀xΦx, in applying the rule, *all* occurrences of u must be replaced by *x*. The rule also applies if instead of u we had used either of the other two arbitrary names, v and w.

Applying this rule we may prove the validity of the above syllogism ∀x(Mx → Fx), ∀x(Fx → Ix) ∴ ∀x(Mx → Ix) as follows:

(1) ∀x(Mx → Fx)	Prem	
(2) ∀x(Fx → Ix)	Prem	
(3) Mu → Fu	1 UI	*—here, anticipating a need for UG later, we use u*
(4) Fu → Iu	2 UI	
(5) Mu → Iu	3, 4 HS	
(6) ∀x(Mx → Ix)	5 UG	*—here, we have correctly generalized from u*

Here's another example. According to the Utilitarian moral philosopher John Stuart Mill, only acts that promote the GENERAL interest are RIGHT. But since no act that INTERFERES with someone acting in his own interest while not affecting others promotes the general interest, no such act can be right. This gives the syllogism ∀x(Rx → Gx), ∀x(Ix → ¬Gx) ∴ ∀x(Ix → ¬Rx), whose validity is proven as follows:

(1) ∀x(Rx → Gx)	Prem	
(2) ∀x(Ix → ¬Gx)	Prem	
(3) Ru → Gu	1 UI	*—again, anticipating UG later, we use u*
(4) Iu → ¬Gu	2 UI	
(5) ¬Gu → ¬Ru	3 TR	
(6) Iu → ¬Ru	4, 5 HS	
(7) ∀x(Ix → ¬Rx)	6 UG	

Finally, here are some examples of mistakes in applying the rules we have introduced. First, let's consider the following erroneous proof of the (invalid) abstract argument

Ea ∴ ∀x Ex

(1) Ea	Prem	
(2) ∀x Ex	1 UG	*—WRONG!*

This is wrong because we can only apply UG when we have a suitably arbitrary instance of the quantification, i.e., one involving an arbitrary individual **u** (or **v** or **w**). Here **a** could have been anything in the universe of discourse, so the argument could have been, say,

"Arthur is a cartoon ELEPHANT. Therefore everyone is a cartoon elephant," which is clearly not valid.

The same kind of mistake occurs in the following proof. It is less serious here, but still a mistake:

(1) ∀x(Fx → Gx)	Prem	
(2) ∀x(Gx → ¬Hx)	Prem	
(3) Fa → Ga	1 UI	—*this is an allowable application of UI* ...
(4) Ga → ¬Ha	2 UI	
(5) Fa → ¬Ha	4, 5 HS	
(6) ∀x(Fx → ¬Hx)	6 UG	—*...but this is not an allowable application of UG*

Because we can only apply UG to an instance involving **u** (or **v** or **w**), line 6 involves an error. On lines 3 and 4 we should have taken our instances as Fu → Gu and Gu → ¬Hu, anticipating the need for **u** when we got to line 6. These were *strategic errors* on lines 3 and 4, but not *errors in applying a rule of inference*, as is line 6.

SUMMARY

- A **propositional function in x** (symbolically represented Φx) is a formula containing at least one variable x such that when an individual name is substituted throughout for x the result is a singular statement; e.g., (Mx → Nx), or (Px & ¬Qx) or (Pa & ¬Qx).
- A **universal quantification** is a propositional function in x (respectively, y, z) preceded by a universal quantifier in x, ∀x (respectively, ∀y, ∀z).
- An **instance of a quantification** is what is obtained when the initial quantifier ∀x (respectively, ∀y, ∀z) is dropped and all instances of the free variable x (respectively, y, z) in the resulting propositional function are replaced by the same individual name **n**.
- The rule of inference **Universal Instantiation (UI)** is:
  From a universal quantification infer any instance of it.
  From ∀xΦx derive Φ**n**, where **n** is the name of any indivual in the UD.
- The rule of inference **Universal Generalization (UG)** is:
  Infer a universal quantification from a suitably arbitrary instance of it.
  From Φu derive ∀xΦx, provided
  (i) Φu neither is nor depends upon an undischarged supposition involving u, and
  (ii) Φu was not obtained by an EI step in the proof.

EXERCISES 16.2

Prove the formal validity of the arguments in 9-12 by giving proofs in predicate logic:

9. $\forall x(Cx \rightarrow Nx)$, $\neg Na$ $\therefore$ $\neg Ca$

10. $\forall x(Ex \rightarrow Fx)$, $\neg(Fb \,\&\, Gb)$ $\therefore$ $Eb \rightarrow \neg Gb$

11. $\forall x(Cx \rightarrow Dx)$, $\forall x(Dx \rightarrow \neg Ex)$, Em $\therefore$ $\neg Cm$

12. $\forall x(Lx \rightarrow \neg Ex)$, $\forall x(Hx \rightarrow Ex)$ $\therefore$ $\forall x(Lx \rightarrow \neg Hx)$

Instructions for exercises 13-16:
(i) *Using the Carroll diagram method, determine whether each of the following arguments is valid or invalid.* (ii) *If it is valid, prove its validity by a formal proof in predicate logic.*

13. "Also, what is sIMPLE cannot be sEPARATED from itself. The <u>soul</u> is simple; there-fore, it cannot be separated from itself."—Duns Scotus, *Oxford Commentary on the Sentences of Peter Lombard* [Ix := x is simple, Ex := x can be separated from itself, s := the soul]

14. "Barcelona <u>Traction</u> was UNABLE to pay interest on its debts; BANKRUPT compa-nies are unable to pay interest on their debts; therefore, Barcelona Traction must be bankrupt."—John Brooks, *The New Yorker* (May 28, 1979)

15. "…no NAMES come in CONTRADICTORY pairs; but all PREDICABLES come in contradictory pairs; therefore no name is predicable."—Peter Geach, *Reference and Generality*

16. "Since then fighting against NEIGHBOURS is an EVIL, and fighting against the THEBANS is fighting against neighbours, it is clear that fighting against the Thebans is an evil."—Aristotle, *Prior Analytics*

Prove the formal validity of the arguments in 17-23 by giving proofs in predicate logic:

17. "These WAFFLES are not HEALTH food. They contain TRANSFATS, and nothing that contains transfats is health food."

18. "Only AFRICANS are BANTUS, and no CARPATHIANS are Africans. So, it is obvious that no Carpathians can be Bantus."

19. "A person can BE rehabilitated in prison only if he or she WANTS rehabilitation. MARIJUANA users do not want rehabilitation. So they cannot be rehabilitated in prison." [UD: people]

20. "It seems that MERCY cannot be ATTRIBUTED to God. For mercy is a kind of SORROW, as Damascene says. But there is no sorrow in God; and therefore there is no mercy in him."—Thomas Aquinas, *Summa Theologia*, I, question 21, art. 3 [Mx := x is mercy, Sx := x is sorrow, Ax := x can be attributed to (is in) God]

21. "And no man is a RHAPSODIST who does not UNDERSTAND the meaning of the poet. For the Rhapsodist ought to INTERPRET the mind of the poet to his hearers, but how can he interpret him well unless he knows what he means?"—Plato, *Ion* [UD: people; Ux := x understands the poet's meaning]

22. "...it is obvious that irrationals are uninteresting to ENGINEERS, since they are concerned only with approximations, and all APPROXIMATIONS are RATIO-NAL."—G.H. Hardy, *A Mathematician's Apology* [Ex := x is interesting (or of concern) to engineers]

23. When the California Supreme Court ruled that the state's system of financing education was illegal, it based its decision on the following argument:
    California's system depends on LOCAL property taxes, and a system that depends on local property taxes DISCRIMINATES against the poor. Hence, California's system VIOLATES the Fourteenth Amendment, because any system that discriminates against the poor violates that amendment. [UD: systems of financing education]

24. (**CHALLENGE**) A news story written shortly before Pope Paul's 75th birthday reported:
    There have been recurrent rumors about a possible resignation since 1966, when he [Pope Paul] told Roman Catholic bishops around the world to hand in their resignations when they reach 75. By tradition the Pope is also Bishop of Rome.[3]
    (a) *Formalize the argument implicit in this story* using the abbreviations: [Bx := x is a bishop, Rx := x should resign when he reaches 75, p := Pope Paul]
    (b) *Give a proof of its formal validity.*

---

[3] From Howard Pospesel, *Introduction to Logic: Predicate Logic* (Englewood Cliffs, NJ: Prentice Hall, 1976), p. 82.

Chapter Seventeen

Existential Quantification

17.1.1 EXISTENTIAL QUANTIFICATION

Particular statements are interpreted as asserting the existence of at least one individual in the relevant category, or of which the relevant predicate is true. Thus the **I-statement** "Some P are Q" is symbolized:

$\exists x(Px \ \& \ Qx)$

Here the symbol $\exists x$ stands for "there is at least one x such that"; it is called an **existential quantifier**. Thus the formula reads:

There is at least one x such that x is a P and x is a Q.

Similarly, the **O-statement** "Some P are not Q" is symbolized

$\exists x(Px \ \& \ \neg Qx)$
There is at least one x such that x is a P and x is not a Q.

Thus universal statements involve a universal quantifier and an arrow, $\rightarrow$: particular statements involve an existential quantifier and an ampersand, &.

Some people are perplexed by this lack of symmetry. Granting the difference in quantifiers, why the difference in statement operators too? Why don't universal statements have an '&,' or existential ones an '$\rightarrow$'? The best way to answer this is to back-translate and see what Carroll diagrams (if any) correspond to statements of that kind. For instance, if Cx := x is a concept, and Mx := x is in the mind of God, and the UD (what's contained in the Carroll box) is everything in the universe, then the formula

$\forall x(Cx \ \& \ Mx)$

comes out as "Everything in the universe is a CONCEPT in the MIND of God." Its Carroll diagram is:

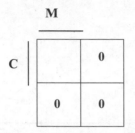

The difference between this and an A-statement diagram should be obvious at a glance. "All concepts are in the mind of God" rules out there being any concepts that are not divine ones ($C\overline{M}$); but it does not rule out, as this does, other things in the mind of God ($\overline{C}M$), and more importantly, other things in the universe ($\overline{C}$)!

But what about a statement like the following?

$\exists x(Px \rightarrow \neg Qx)$

This asserts that there is an individual in the universe of discourse which, if it is **P**, is not **Q**. We cannot represent this on a Carroll diagram. It's a bit easier to understand with a concrete example in which the Universe of Discourse (UD) is delimited. Suppose the UD is airbags in motor vehicles, **P** is "has been activated" and **Q** is "crushes small children." Then the statement would say

There are airbags which, if they have been activated, do not crush small children.

This is not the same as saying "There are airbags that have been activated and do not crush small children" (although it may be understood this way, in ordinary imprecise conversation), precisely in that it does not claim, as the latter does, that there are airbags that have been activated. It does not assert the existence of the subject term (or the predicate term, for that matter); it asserts the existence of airbags, but remains agnostic on whether any have been activated or have failed to crush small children. In fact, it would be true if there's at least one airbag that hasn't been activated.

In general, the existential-quantifier-with-conditional is made true by the existence of one thing of which the antecedent is false, or by one thing of which the consequent is true. So they're almost always true, but say what we hardly ever want to say. Similarly, the universal-quantifier-with-conjunction is made false by one thing of which either the first conjunct or the second is false, so they're almost always false, but say what we hardly ever want to say. EXERCISE: Try to think up (a) an interpretation of the predicates A and B, with any UD you wish, that would make a statement of the form ∃x(Ax → Bx) FALSE, or (b) an interpretation of the predicates C and D, with any UD you wish, that would make a statement of the form ∀x(Cx & Dx) TRUE.

SUMMARY

- the **I-statement** "Some P are Q" is symbolized ∃x(Px & Qx).
- the **O-statement** "Some P are not Q" is symbolized ∃x(Px & ¬Qx).
- statements of the form ∀x(Ax & Bx) and ∃x(Cx → Dx), while meaningful, are very rare.
- an existential quantification is a propositional function in x (respectively, y, z) preceded by an existential quantifier in x, ∃x (respectively, ∃y, ∃z).

EXERCISES 17.1

1. Symbolize the following as I- or O-statements:
   (a) Some ATHEISTS are MORAL.
   (b) Some DINOSAURS did not become EXTINCT.
   (c) There are airline PILOTS who have an ALCOHOL problem.
   (d) Many BIRDS fly at HIGH altitudes.
   (e) Not everyone who TRAINS WINS.
   (f) There are few ANIMALS that can not be TAMED.

2. Back-translate the following abstract statements into colloquial language using the following key: UD: people; Px := x is a politician, Ax := x is ambitious, h := Hillary:
   (a) ∃x(Px & Ax)
   (b) ∃x(Ax & ¬Px)
   (c) Ph & ¬Ah
   (d) Ah → ∃x(Px & Ax)

17.2 RULES OF INFERENCE

17.2.1 EXISTENTIAL INSTANTIATION

We now pass to rules of inference for particular statements, the first of which is Existential Instantiation, (EI). As in Universal Instantiation, it allows us to pass from the quantified statement to a particular instance of it. A little reflection will show that this, like UG, must have some restrictions. From the premises "There was a nineteenth century LOGICIAN who wrote CHILDREN'S books" and "George <u>Boole</u> was a nineteenth century LOGI-CIAN" we cannot infer the conclusion that George Boole wrote children's books. But if there were no restriction on EI, this is exactly what we could infer:

(1) $\exists x(Lx \ \& \ Cx)$ Prem
(2) Lb   Prem
(3) Lb & Cb   1 EI *—WRONG!*
(4) Cb   3 Simp

Note that the second premise hasn't even been used to reach the conclusion. But that is not the problem. The point is that if EI had no restrictions we could infer (3) that "George Boole was a nineteenth century LOGICIAN who wrote CHILDREN'S books" directly from (1), the fact that *someone* did. The instance of the existential quantification needs to involve an *arbitrary* individual, not someone we are already interested in. Given the existential statement, that is, we know it is true of someone or something, and we *suppose* an individual to which it applies. Just as with the case of proofs involving UG considered in the previous chapter, we assume it true of such an individual *for the sake of example.* That is, we are again showing how to formalize suppositional arguments of the second kind considered in chapter 7.3, ones that involve not statements assumed for the sake of argument, but individual cases assumed for the sake of giving specific content to a generalization.

As was the case in UG, in order for the name we use in EI to be arbitrary it cannot have occurred either in the symbolization of the argument or on any previous line of the proof. But the arbitrary individual we assume in an EI argument needs to be one of the individuals the existential generalization is true of, so we need to introduce distinct names for these arbitrary individuals to distinguish them from the ones assumed in UG arguments, **u**, **v**, or **w**. Let us reserve the letter **i** for the arbitrary individual in an EI; if **i** has already been used in a previous line or in the symbolization of the argument, we shall use **j**, and if this has been taken, **k**, as was the case for the arbitrary individuals **u**, **v**, or **w**. Of course, having assumed the existential generalization true for a specific instance, the individual name **i** we supposed cannot appear in the conclusion. But this is already taken care of by the rule that the name cannot have occurred in the symbolization of the argument: it could only appear in the conclusion if this rule had been violated. Now we may state the EI rule as follows:

Existential Instantiation (EI)
From an existential quantification infer a suitably arbitrary instance of it.
From $\exists x \Phi x$ derive Φi, where **i** denotes an arbitrary individual name (one that has not occurred either in the symbolization of the argument or on any previous line of the proof).

Again, what is stated here in terms of x is tacitly understood to apply to expressions involving y and z too, and what is said of **i** applies also to **j** and **k**.

First, let's look at some examples of derivations that fail to obey the restrictions on EI. Consider the following erroneous proof of the obviously invalid argument

Some ROCK stars are ENGLISH. So <u>Madonna</u> is English. ∃x(Rx & Ex) ∴ Em

(1) ∃x(Rx & Ex)   Prem
(2) Rm & Em   1 EI —*WRONG!* m occurred in the symbolization of the arg't
(3) Em   2 Simp

If some rock stars are English, we can take some arbitrary individual who is an English rock star and reason about him or her; but Madonna is clearly not such an arbitrary individual, since she is named beforehand.

Now here's an example involving a violation of the restriction that the name cannot occur on a previous line of a proof:

(1) ∃x(Sx & Rx)   Prem
(2) ∃x(Px & Rx)   Prem
(3) Si & Ri   1 EI
(4) Pi & Ri   2 EI   —*WRONG! i occurred on a previous line*
(5)...

On line (4) we should have used a different individual, **j**. But then we would not have been able to infer anything very interesting from Si & Ri together with Pj & Rj, since Ri and Rj are two different statements.

The EI rule enables us to prove certain arguments with negative conclusions, like this one:

It is false that there are MUONS composed of QUARKS. For all muons are LEPTONS, and no leptons are composed of QUARKS. [UD: elementary particles]

(1) ∀x(Mx → Lx)   Prem
(2) ∀x(Lx → ¬Qx)   Prem
　(3) ∃x(Mx & Qx)   Supp/RA
　(4) Mi & Qi   3 EI
　(5) Mi → Li   1 UI
　(6) Li → ¬Qi   2 UI
　(7) Mi   4 Simp
　(8) Li   5, 7 MP
　(9) ¬Qi   6, 8 MP
　(10) Qi   4 Simp
　(11) ⊥   10, 9 Conj
(12) ¬∃x(Mx & Qx)   3-11 RA

A few points to note about this proof:
- It is a standard *reductio* proof: we assume the contradictory of the conclusion and aim for a contradiction.
- The contradiction ⊥ reached on line 11 is Qi & ¬Qi, where Qi is the statement: "Elementary particle **i** is composed of quarks."
- It was vital that on line 4 we did EI before applying UI. Otherwise **i** would not have been arbitrary, for it would have occurred on a previous line of the proof:

> (3) ∃x(Mx & Qx)   Supp/RA
> (4) Mi → Li   1 UI
> (5) Li → ¬Qi   2 UI
> (6) Mi & Qi   3 EI   —*WRONG!* **i** *has already been used!*
> (7) Mi   6 Simp
> (8)…

On line (6) we could validly have used **j** instead, but that won't get us anywhere:

> (4) Mi → Li   1 UI
> (5) Li → ¬Qi   2 UI
> (6) Mj & Qj   3 EI   —*CORRECT. But this gets us nowhere!*
> (7) Mj   6 Simp??

This motivates the following procedural rule:

Always use EI before UI wherever possible.

Finally, here are two examples to show why we keep distinct the two kinds of arbitrary individual—**i** (or **j** or **k**) for EI, and **u** (or **v** or **w**) for UG.

> (1) ∃x Gx   Prem
> (2) ∀x(Gx → ¬Hx)   Prem
> (3) Gu   1 EI   —*this is NOT an allowable application of EI*
> (4) Gu → ¬Hu   2 UI
> (5) ¬Hu   4, 5 HS
> (6) ∀x ¬Hx   5 UG

Line (3) is an error: you must EI onto **i** (or **j** or **k**). Otherwise, line 6 would have been fine, since we have the **u** for UG. On the other hand, if on line (3) we EI onto **i**, we do not have the **u** (or **v** or **w**) we need for UG, as here:

(1) ∃x Gx	Prem
(2) ∀x(Gx → ¬Hx)	Prem
(3) Gi	1 EI —*this is an allowable application of EI*…
(4) Gi → ¬Hi	2 UI
(5) ¬Hi	4, 5 HS
(6) ∀x ¬Hx	5 UG —…*but this is not an allowable application of UG*

17.2.2 EXISTENTIAL GENERALIZATION

Now we come to *Existential Generalization*, EG. This rule, unlike EI, needs no restrictions. If we know Georgie is a space cadet, then we know that someone is a space cadet (UD: people)—i.e., at least one person is. This motivates the rule:

Existential Generalization (EG)
Infer an existential quantification from any instance of it.
From Φ**n**, where **n** is any individual name, derive ∃xΦx.

Here's a proof of the argument: Georgie is a SPACE cadet. Therefore someone is a space cadet. (UD: people): Sg ∴ ∃x Sx

(1) Sg	Prem
(2) ∃x Sx	1 EG

Here's a more interesting example:

All philosophers ALLOWED in Plato's Academy had to know GEOMETRY. Some philosophers did not know geometry. So some philosophers were not allowed in Plato's Academy. (UD: philosophers)

∀x(Ax → Gx), ∃x ¬Gx ∴ ∃x ¬Ax

(1) ∀x(Ax → Gx)	Prem	
(2) ∃x ¬Gx	Prem	
(3) ¬Gi	2 EI	
(4) Ai → Gi	1 UI	
(5) ¬Ai	4, 3 MT	
(6) ∃x ¬Ax	5 EG	—…*no restrictions on EG*

Summarizing, UI and EG are generally applicable, with no restrictions. But in order to do UG, we need to have introduced an arbitrary individual **u**, **v**, or **w** (either in a UI step, or in a supposition for CP or RA), supposed for the sake of example. Thus if the letter **u** has already occurred in the symbolization of the argument or on a previous line, we should use **v** or **w** instead. Likewise when we employ EI on an existential quantification $\exists x \Phi x$, we are supposing for the sake of example that the individual **i**, **j**, or **k**, of which Φ is true, is indeed arbitrary. Again, if the letter **i** has already occurred in the symbolization of the argument or on a previous line, we should use **j** or **k** instead. The following table encapsulates this:

Letter designations:

LETTERS	FUNCTION	INTRODUCED IN	RESTRICTIONS
a, b, c, … w	proper names	symbolization of argument	–
x, y, z	variables	(quantifications in) symbol'n of arg't, UG, EG, or Supp	cannot occur "free": must always be in scope of a quantifier
u, v, w	arbitrary names for UI/UG proofs	UI or Supp (in anticipation of a later UG) —but NOT EI	must not occur in symbolization of arg't or on a previous line
i, j, k	arbitrary names for EI proofs	EI or UI	must not occur in symbolization of arg't or on a previous line

Now with these four quantifier rules in place, we can prove a wide variety of arguments, including categorical syllogisms like the following:

All BATS can FLY. Some animals that are ALMOST blind are bats. Therefore some flying animals are almost blind. [UD: animals]

(1) $\forall x(Bx \rightarrow Fx)$	Prem	
(2) $\exists x(Ax \,\&\, Bx)$	Prem	
(3) Ai & Bi	2 EI	—N.B. EI before UI!
(4) Bi $\rightarrow$ Fi	1 UI	
(5) Bi	3 Simp	
(6) Fi	4, 5 MP	
(7) Ai	3 Simp	
(8) Fi & Ai	6, 7 Conj	
(9) $\exists x(Fx \,\&\, Ax)$	8 EG	

Another example of the use of EG: the reasoning of an Israeli fighter pilot as he watched a man eject from an Egyptian fighter plane he had just shot down:

> The <u>downed</u> pilot who flew the Egyptian FIGHTER had BLOND hair. EGYPTIAN pilots don't have blond hair. Any non-Egyptian pilot would have to be a RUSSIAN. Hence there are Russians flying Egyptian fighters. [UD: pilots]
> *Symbolized:* Fd & Bd, $\forall x(Ex \rightarrow \neg Bx)$, $\forall x(\neg Ex \rightarrow Rx)$ $\therefore$ $\exists x(Rx \& Fx)$

(1) Fd & Bd	Prem
(2) $\forall x(Ex \rightarrow \neg Bx)$	Prem
(3) $\forall x(\neg Ex \rightarrow Rx)$	Prem
(4) Ed $\rightarrow \neg$Bd	2 UI
(5) $\neg$Ed $\rightarrow$ Rd	3 UI
(6) Bd	1 Simp
(7) $\neg\neg$Bd	6 DN
(8) $\neg$Ed	4, 7 MT
(9) Rd	5, 8 MP
(10) Fd	1 Simp
(11) Rd & Fd	9, 10 Conj
(12) $\exists x(Rx \& Fx)$	11 EG

Finally, you'll remember from the Square of Opposition (p. 237) that an A-statement is the contradictory of an O-statement, and so entails its negation, and also that an I-statement is the contradictory of an E-statement, and so entails its negation. Here are proofs of those entailments:

(1) $\forall x(Sx \rightarrow Px)$	Prem
(2) $\exists x(Sx \& \neg Px)$	Supp/RA
(3) Si & $\neg$Pi	2 EI
(4) Si $\rightarrow$ Pi	1 UI
(5) Si	3 Simp
(6) Pi	4, 5 MP
(7) $\neg$Pi	3 Simp
(8) $\bot$	6, 7 Conj
(9) $\neg\exists x(Sx \& \neg Px)$	2-8 RA

(1) $\exists x(Sx \& \neg Px)$	Prem
(2) $\forall x(Sx \rightarrow Px)$	Supp/RA
(3) Si & $\neg$Pi	1 EI
(4) Si $\rightarrow$ Pi	2 UI
(5) Si	3 Simp
(6) Pi	4, 5 MP

$$\begin{array}{lll} & (7)\,\neg Pi & 3\ \text{Simp} \\ & (8)\,\bot & 6,7\ \text{Conj} \\ (9)\,\neg\forall x(Sx \to Px) & & 2\text{-}8\ \text{RA} \end{array}$$

17.2.3 PROOF STRATEGY

We have seen that in a predicate logic proof you must do any **EI**s that are required before any **UI**s. But you may not know whether any **EI**s are required until after you have worked out whether you are going to need any suppositions, as in the proof of the "Muon-Quark" argument above. Remember, if you try to do **EI** late in a proof, it must be an instance involving an arbitrary individual (**i**, **j**, or **k**), one that has not already been used; and now, this may no longer work. With this in mind, it may be useful to have a set of guidelines on how to proceed in a predicate logic proof:

I.   Write down the premises as the first lines of your proof.
II. Work out whether you need to make any supposition involving a quantification: in particular, if your conclusion is the negation of a quantification, this suggests supposing the quantification and trying a **reductio**.
III. If you have an existential quantification, apply **EI** with arbitrary individual **i**.
IV. If you have universal quantifications, apply **UI** with an appropriate individual: **i** if you already have it above; a particular name if that occurs in the premises or conclusion of the argument; **u** if you are aiming to prove a universal quantification with a **UG** at the end.
V.   Now you are in *statement logic* territory! Work out your strategy accordingly.
VI. Finally, if your conclusion is a universal quantification, apply **UG** to your instance of **u**; if it is an existential quantification, apply **EG**. If your proof is a reductio, apply **RA** to derive the negation of your supposition.

SUMMARY

- The rule of inference **Existential Instantiation (EI)** is
  From an existential quantification infer a suitably arbitrary instance of it.
  From $\exists x\Phi x$ derive Φi, where **i** is an arbitrary individual name, i.e., one that has not occurred either in the symbolization of the argument or on any previous line of the proof).
- The rule of inference **Existential Generalization (EG)** is
  Infer an existential quantification from any instance of it.
  From Φn, where **n** is any individual name, derive $\exists x\Phi x$.

> EXERCISES 17.2

In each of the following incorrect proofs, there are **two errors** *in applying rules of infer-*
ence (we are not counting strategic errors). (i) *Identify and describe the errors.* (ii) *Give
a correct proof of validity of the sequent.*

3. (1) Pf   Prem   ⊢ ∃x(Mx & Px)
    (2) ∀x(Px → Mx)   Prem
    (3) ∃xPx   1 EG
    (4) ∃xMx   2, 3 MP
    (5) ∃x(Mx & Px)   3, 4 Conj

4. (1) ∃x(Ax & Bx)   Prem   ⊢ ∃x(Ax & Cx)
    (2) ∀x(Bx → Cx)   Prem
        (3) ¬∃x(Ax & Cx)   Supp/RA
        (4) ¬Ai & Ci   3 EI
        (5) Ai & Ci   1 EI
        (6) Ai   5 Simp
        (7) ¬Ai   4 Simp
        (8) ⊥   6, 7 Conj
    (9) ¬∃x(Ax & Cx)   4-8 RA, DN

5. (1) ∀x(Mx → Lx)   Prem   ⊢ ¬∀x(Lx → ¬Qx)
    (2) ∃x(Qx & Mx)   Prem
        (3) ∀x(Lx → ¬Qx)   Supp/RA
        (4) Mi → Li   1 UI
        (5) Li → ¬Qi   3 UI
        (6) Mi → ¬Qi   4, 5 HS
        (7) ¬Mi v ¬Qi   6 MI
        (8) ¬(Mi & Qi)   7 DM
        (9) Qi & Mi   2 EI
        (10) ⊥   9, 8 Conj
    (11) ¬∀x(Lx → ¬Qx)   3-10 RA

6. (1) ∀x(Sx → Px)   Prem   ⊢ ∃x(Mx & ¬Sx)
    (2) ∃x(Mx & ¬Px)   Prem
    (3) Sa → Pa   1 UI
        (4) Sa   Supp/RA
        (5) Pa   3, 4 MP
        (6) Ma & ¬Pa   2 EI
        (7) ¬Pa   6 Simp
        (8) Pa & ¬Pa   5, 7 Conj

(9) ¬Sa	4-8 RA
(10) Ma	6 Simp
(11) Ma & ¬Sa	10, 9 Conj
(12) ∃x(Mx & ¬Sx)	11 EG

Prove the validity of each of arguments 7-13 using predicate logic.

7. At least some WALLOONS are BILINGUAL, since <u>Isabel</u> is a Walloon who is bilingual. [UD: people]

8. All KAZAKHS are Central ASIAN. <u>Borat</u> is morally RETARDED, although he is not really a Central Asian. So at least some moral retards are not Kazakhs.

9. Some DINOSAURS have FEATHERS. But only BIRDS have feathers. Therefore some dinosaurs are birds. [UD: creatures]

10. No FAT creatures RUN well. Some GREYHOUNDS run well. Therefore some greyhounds are not fat. [UD: creatures]

11. All POLITICIANS tell LIES. So there's no such thing as a politician who does not tell lies.

12. Whoever engages in INTERCOURSE is EVIL. MINISTERS are not evil. Some ministers have CHILDREN. Therefore some who have children have never had intercourse. [UD: people]

13. PARTICULAR statements have EXISTENTIAL import. But the CONTRADICTORIES of particular statements do not have existential import. Now UNIVERSAL statements are contradictories of particular statements. Therefore universal statements do not have existential import. [UD: statements; Cx := x is the contradictory of a particular statement, Ex := x has existential import]

Using Carroll diagrams, determine whether each of arguments 14-18 is valid. For each that is, prove its validity using predicate logic.

14. <u>Borat</u> is a KAZAKH who often SLEEPS with his sister. Anyone who sleeps with his sister commits INCEST. So all Kazakhs commit incest.

15. No FROGS are POETICAL. Some DUCKS are unpoetical. Therefore some ducks are not frogs.

16. No EMPERORS are DENTISTS. All dentists are dreaded by CHILDREN. Therefore no emperors are dreaded by children.[1]

17. Some VALID arguments have FALSE premises. Therefore some valid arguments are not SOUND, because no sound argument has false premises. [UD: arguments]

18. No arguments with a FALSE conclusion are SOUND. But some VALID arguments are not sound. Therefore some arguments with a false conclusion are not valid. [UD: arguments]

19. A clever Englishman, on learning that British law prohibits taxes being collected from animals, avoided paying taxes by investing in stocks in his dog's name.[2] A syllogism based on this case:
    No ANIMALS may be TAXED. So, since some animals may INVEST in stocks, some individuals who may invest in stocks cannot be taxed. [UD: individuals]
    Give a formal proof of the validity of this argument.

20. *Prove that I- and E-statements are logically inconsistent* by deriving a contradiction from their conjunction: $\exists x(Px \ \& \ Qx) \ \& \ \forall x(Px \rightarrow \neg Qx)$.

21. (**CHALLENGE**) A filler in the *Washington Star-News* goes:
    Not all of TODAY'S women DEVOTE all their waking thoughts to pleasing men. Some are MARRIED. [UD: women; Tx := x is one of today's women]
    (a) *Supply what seems to be the intended implicit premise.*
    (b) *Symbolize the resulting argument, and prove its validity by a formal proof.*

22. (**CHALLENGE**) In *Being and Time*, Martin Heidegger argues:
    Every reference is a relation, but not every relation is a reference. Every 'indication' is a reference, but not every referring is an indicating. This implies at the same time that every 'indication' is a relation, but not every relation is an indicating. The formally general character of relation is thus brought to light.[3]
    Use a Carroll diagram to determine whether Heidegger's inference is valid. [Let E := is a reference or a referring, A := is a relation, I := is an indication or indicating.]

23. (**CHALLENGE**) *Symbolize Heidegger's argument in #22, and demonstrate its validity by a formal proof in predicate logic.*

---

[1] 15 and 16 are from Lewis Carroll, *Symbolic Logic*, p. 158.
[2] A television story reported without attribution by Howard Pospesel in his *Predicate Logic*, p. 44.
[3] Martin Heidegger, *Being and Time*, trans. John Macquarrie, Edward Robinson (Oxford: Blackwell, 1962), p. 108; my thanks to Sheldon Hanlon for finding this argument.

Chapter Eighteen

Advanced Class Logic

18.1 ARGUMENTS WITH MORE THAN 3 PREDICATES

18.1.1 CARROLL DIAGRAMS FOR 4 OR 5 CATEGORIES

Traditionally, arguments were treated by the theory of the syllogism. This involved putting each constituent statement into standard form, i.e., finding the equivalent A-, E-, I-, or O-statement, and then breaking the argument down into a series of syllogisms, each one with two premises and a conclusion involving each of three predicate terms twice. These syllogistic inferences were then compared with known valid forms, and there were a series of rules involving "mood" and "figure" for conversion into such forms. If an inference was not convertible by these rules into a valid form, then it was invalid.

The algebraic class logic invented in the nineteenth century by Boole, Venn, Carroll, and others was already considerably more general than this, as well as much easier to use. For example, as we have already seen, it could deal as well with those individuals not falling under a category as those that did. Consider, for instance, the following example of Carroll's:

No country that has been EXPLORED is infested with DRAGONS.
Unexplored countries are FASCINATING.

Therefore any country infested with dragons is fascinating. (UD: countries)

The first premise is an E-statement, No E's are D's. But what of the second? This is All non-E's are F. But that is not equivalent to any A-, E-, I-, or O-statement. The Carroll diagram, nevertheless, is straightforward:

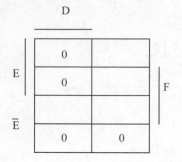

There are no countries in the $\overline{\text{E}},\overline{\text{F}}$ overlap, so we insert **0**'s there; and the conclusion follows: any country which is **D** must also be **F**.

Another advantage of Venn's and Carroll's approach is that it can be extended to arguments containing more than three predicates.[1] Our diagram for a 4-predicate argument is a very simple extension of the diagrams we have used for 2 and 3 predicates. The fourth category is put in the middle at the bottom, dividing the original square into 16 cells. Let's illustrate it with one of Carroll's whimsical examples:

BABIES are ILLOGICAL.	$\forall x(Bx \rightarrow Ix)$
Nobody is DESPISED who can manage a CROCODILE.	$\forall x(Cx \rightarrow \neg Dx)$
Illogical persons are despised.	$\forall x(Ix \rightarrow Dx)$
Therefore no babies can manage a crocodile.	$\forall x(Bx \rightarrow \neg Cx)$

We make the top 2 rows all **B**'s, the 2 columns on the left all **I**'s, the 2 rows in the middle all **D**'s, and the 2 columns in the middle all **C**'s, like this:

```
              I
       ┌───┬───┬───┬───┐
       │ 1 │ 2 │ 3 │ 4 │
    B  ├───┼───┼───┼───┤
       │ 5 │ 6 │ 7 │ 8 │
       ├───┼───┼───┼───┤  D
       │ 9 │10 │11 │12 │
       ├───┼───┼───┼───┤
       │13 │14 │15 │16 │
       └───┴───┴───┴───┘
              C
```

---

[1] Actually, Venn's diagram for 4-predicate arguments involves drawing 4 overlapping ellipses, which is extremely hard to draw, whereas Carroll's consists in a twelve-sided figure enclosed in a square, which is hard to use without making errors (see Appendix 3).

The three premises require **0**'s in, respectively, the $\overline{B}I$ region (in squares 3, 4, 7, and 8), the **DC** region (6, 7, 10, 11), and the $I\overline{D}$ region (1, 2, 13, 14). In marking them in we see that the **BC** region (2, 3, 6, 7) has already been filled with **0**'s, so the denial of the conclusion is incompatible with the acceptance of the premises. The argument is VALID.

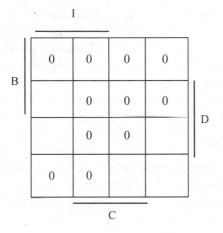

As a second example, we can look at the argument from the last chapter concerning the pilot of the Egyptian fighter plane:

> The <u>downed</u> pilot who flew the Egyptian FIGHTER had BLOND hair. EGYPTIAN pilots don't have blond hair. Any non-Egyptian pilot would have to be a RUSSIAN. Hence there are Russians flying Egyptian fighters. [UD: pilots]

In such a case we must do any universal statements first, putting **0**'s the areas in which there are no individuals, and then entering any particular or singular statements. This gives us **0**'s in the four cells of the **EB** region, and also in the four corner cells representing $\overline{E}\,\overline{R}$. It only remains to put in the first premise, that **d** has to be both F and B, so we put a **d** in the only non-empty square in the **FB** quadrant:

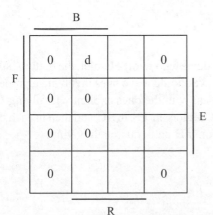

We see that the conclusion, that some R are F, is represented on the diagram as required. Alternatively put, the denial of the conclusion—which would be the assertion that there are no Russians flying Egyptian fighters—is incompatible with the premises. So the argument is VALID by our definition of validity.

Venn's diagrams are hard to extend to 5-predicate arguments, and here Carroll saw a decisive advantage of his methods. His technique for such arguments was to take the Carroll diagram for a 4-predicate argument and divide each square by a diagonal slash. But we can improve on this in a more natural way by dividing each square horizontally into two. This is a natural generalization of the diagrams we have been using, and it has the added advantage that it generalizes upwards for any number of predicates. Let's illustrate it using another of Carroll's examples. The problem here is to determine the conclusion assuming every name or predicate appears exactly twice:

> All writers who UNDERSTAND human nature are CLEVER. No one who cannot STIR people's hearts is a TRUE poet. <u>Shakespeare</u> wrote HAMLET. No writer who does not understand human nature can stir people's hearts. Only a true poet could have written Hamlet.

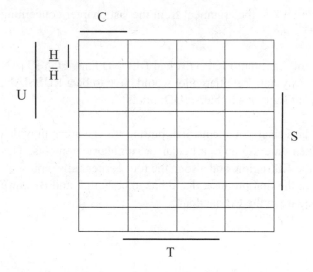

In this diagram the top half of each cell represents those who wrote Hamlet, the bottom half those who did not write it. Filling in the premises, we should leave ones involving a proper name (Shakespeare) till last. Also, it is easier to deal with the ones explicitly involving **H** after all the others. Doing this, we get **0**'s in the **U$\bar{\text{C}}$** region, in **T$\bar{\text{S}}$**, in **S$\bar{\text{U}}$**, and then in each of the upper half-squares **H$\bar{\text{T}}$**, and finally an **s** in the only **H** half-square left, giving:

C

0	0	0	0
	0	0	0
0	s	0	0
		0	0
0	0	0	0
0	0	0	0
0	0	0	0
	0	0	

U   H / H̄   (left)   S (right)

T

The only predicates and names to appear only once so far are <u>Shakespeare</u> (**s**) and "is clever" (**C**), so (assuming every name or predicate appears exactly twice) we see that the desired conclusion is "Shakespeare is clever."

We can generalize this method of diagrams further. A sixth predicate, such as **E**, "is English," could split each of the cells vertically, **E|Ē** producing 64 cells:

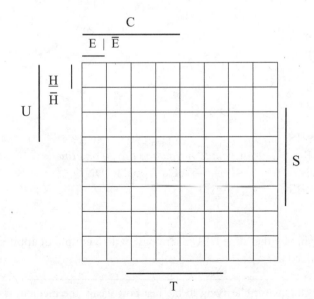

In fact, this method may be generalized to accommodate further predicates as desired, doubling the number of cells for each new predicate.[2]

18.1.2 SORITES

The second and the last arguments above are instances of a kind of argument called the **sorites** (pronounced so-RIGHT-eez). A sorites (plural: also, sorites) is a string of categorical statements, of which the predicate of one is the subject of the next (or the same in reverse order). As Lewis Carroll pointed out, traditional logic only recognized two sorts of sorites: "the *Aristotelian*, whose premises are a series of Propositions in *A*, so arranged that the Predicate of each is the Subject of the next, and the *Goclenian*, whose premises are the very same series written backwards."[3] With biting sarcasm he says of Goclenius that "we may apply to him what somebody (Edmund Yates, I think it was) said of Tupper, viz: 'Here is a man who, beyond all others of his generation, has been favoured with Glimpses of the Obvious!'" (*ibid.*). It was in contrast to these "puerile— not to say infantile—forms of a Sorites" that Carroll presented us with the whimsical examples above.

Clearly, though, it is very easy to make a mistake in filling in the above diagram for five or more categories. In contrast, these sorites are all easy to prove valid using the UI/UG strategy of chapter 16. For instance, the baby-crocodile syllogism is provable as follows:

(1) $\forall x(Bx \rightarrow Ix)$	Prem	
(2) $\forall x(Cx \rightarrow \neg Dx)$	Prem	
(3) $\forall x(Ix \rightarrow Dx)$	Prem	
(4) $Bu \rightarrow Iu$	1 UI	
(5) $Cu \rightarrow \neg Du$	2 UI	
(6) $Iu \rightarrow Du$	3 UI	
(7) $Bu \rightarrow Du$	4, 6 HS	
(8) $\neg\neg Du \rightarrow \neg Cu$	5 TR	*—we could have done this in one line:*
(9) $Du \rightarrow \neg Cu$	8 DN	(8) $Du \rightarrow \neg Cu$ 5 TR, DN
(10) $Bu \rightarrow \neg Cu$	7, 9 HS	
(11) $\forall x(Bx \rightarrow \neg Cx)$	10 UG	

The Shakespeare sorites is provable by the same UI/UG strategy, with a couple of applications of TR. It may be symbolized as

---

[2] I am indebted to Jim Monier-Williams for clarifying to me just how easily the method of modified Carroll diagrams can be extrapolated to accommodate further predicates.

[3] Lewis Carroll, *Symbolic Logic*, ed. W.W. Bartley III (New York: Potter, 1977), p. 250.

$\forall x(Ux \rightarrow Cx),\ \forall x(\neg Sx \rightarrow \neg Tx),\ Hs,\ \forall x(\neg Ux \rightarrow \neg Sx),\ \forall x(Hx \rightarrow Tx) \vdash Cs$

Here's another example, this time a proof devised by Gottfried Leibniz at the age of 23 for the immortality of the mind. This is set out as a long sorites with lots of subsidiary arguments for the various premises. He begins with the following characterization of the human mind: the HUMAN mind is a thing, one of whose activities is THINKING. He then proceeds to prove that a thing, one of whose activities is thinking, is not a body. From here the argument to the immortality of the mind proceeds as follows:

> Whatever is not a BODY is not in SPACE; for to be in space is the definition of body. Whatever is not in space is not MOVABLE, for motion is change of space. Whatever is immovable is inDISSOLUBLE, for dissolution is the motion of a part. Whatever is indissoluble is inCORRUPTIBLE, for corruption is internal dissolution. Everything incorruptible is IMMORTAL, for death is the corruption of the living, or dissolution of its fabric, through which self-moving things obviously move themselves. Therefore the human mind is immortal.[4]

Thus (ignoring the subsidiary arguments for each premise) we can symbolize the whole argument as follows: $\forall x(Hx \rightarrow Tx),\ \forall x(Tx \rightarrow \neg Bx),\ \forall x(\neg Bx \rightarrow \neg Sx),\ \forall x(\neg Sx \rightarrow \neg Mx),\ \forall x(\neg Mx \rightarrow \neg Dx),\ \forall x(\neg Dx \rightarrow \neg Cx),\ \forall x(\neg Cx \rightarrow Ix)\ \therefore\ \forall x(Hx \rightarrow Ix)$.

Its validity is obvious, and can be proven by 7 applications of UI and 7 applications of the Chain Rule, with a concluding step of UG.

SUMMARY

- The method of Carroll diagrams applies just as easily to statements involving things **not** falling in a given category, such as "Unexplored countries are fascinating," (All non-**E** are **F**)
- and can be extended to apply to arguments containing **4** or more distinct predicates.
- A **sorites** is a sequence of universal categorical statements, of which the predicate of one is the subject of the next (or the same in reverse order);
- they are generally best proved valid using a **formal proof** and the **UI/UG** strategy.

---

4 Gottfried Leibniz, "The Immortality of the Human Mind, Demonstrated in a Continuous Sorites," quoted from Leroy Loemker, ed., *Gottfried Wilhelm Leibniz: Philosophical Papers and Letters* (Dordrecht: D. Reidel, 1969), p. 113.

| EXERCISES 18.1 |

Using Carroll diagrams, determine whether each of arguments 1-5 is valid. For each that is, prove its validity using predicate logic.[5]

1. None of HIS stories are PROBABLE. Improbable stories are not easily BELIEVED. So none of his stories are easily believed. [UD: stories]

2. WARMTH RELIEVES pain. Nothing that does not relieve pain is useful for TOOTH-ACHE. So warmth is useful for toothache.

3. UNIVERSITY students are all EDUCATED. All uneducated people are SHALLOW. Therefore no university students are shallow. [UD: people]

4. No WHEELBARROWS are COMFORTABLE. No uncomfortable vehicles are POPULAR. Therefore no wheelbarrows are popular. [UD: vehicles]

5. Some HEALTHY people are OVERWEIGHT. No unhealthy people are good INSURANCE risks. Therefore some overweight people are not good insurance risks. [UD: people]

Assuming that every predicate or name is to appear exactly twice in the argument, use Carroll diagrams to work out what conclusion may be validly inferred for each of the following 4-predicate arguments:

6. My SAUCEPANS are the only thing I have that are made of TIN. I find all the PRESENTS you gave me USEFUL. None of my saucepans are of the slightest use. [UD: things of mine; S := is a saucepan, T := is made of tin, P := is a present you gave me, U := is useful]

7. None of the NEW potatoes have been BOILED. All the potatoes in this DISH are FIT to eat. No unboiled potatoes are fit to eat. [UD: potatoes]

8. No DUCKS WALTZ. No OFFICERS ever decline to waltz. All my POULTRY are ducks.

9. No TERRIERS wander among the signs of the ZODIAC. Nothing that does not wander among the signs of the zodiac is a COMET. Only terriers have cURLY tails. [U := has a curly tail]

---

[5] Numbers 1-9 are based on examples from Carroll's *Symbolic Logic*, p. 162. Number 10 is invented by me using Carrollian material.

10. No BOOJUM can be FOUND. No SLITHY things are TOVES. Some toves are boojums.

Use Carroll diagrams to work out what conclusion may be validly inferred for each of the following 4-predicate arguments:[6]

11. All things that are HARMFUL ought always to be AVOIDED. Some SNARKS do all manner of harm. Only BOOJUMS ought always to be avoided. [conclusion to involve S and B]

12. CONGENIAL SNARKS do no HARM. Some snarks are BOOJUMS. Boojums always do harm. [conclusion to involve B and C]

Instructions for exercises 13-15: *Determine the conclusion of each of the following valid sorites arguments* invented by Lewis Carroll,[7] either by a five-predicate diagram (in the case of 13), by informal reasoning, or by a formal proof:

13. (**CHALLENGE**) There is no box of mine HERE that I DARE open.
My <u>writing-desk</u> is made of ROSE-wood.
All my boxes are PAINTED except what are here.
There is no box of mine that I dare not open, unless it is full of live SCORPIONS.
All my rose-wood boxes are unpainted. [UD: boxes of mine, incl. writing desk]

14. (**CHALLENGE**) No husband who is always giving his wife new DRESSES can be a CROSS-grained man.
A METHODICAL husband always comes HOME for his tea.
No one who hangs up his hat on the gas-JET can be a man who is kept in proper ORDER by his wife.
A GOOD husband is always giving his wife new dresses.
No husband can fail to be cross-grained if his wife does not keep him in proper order.
An unmethodical husband always hangs up his hat on the gas-jet. [UD: husbands]

15. (**CHALLENGE**) All the policemen on this BEAT SUP with our cook.
No man with LONG hair can fail to be a POET.
<u>Amos Judd</u> has never been in JAIL.
Our cook's "COUSINS" all love cold MUTTON.

---

[6] Numbers 11 and 12 are based on Carroll's *The Hunting of the Snark*: "'For although some snarks do all manner of harm, / Yet I feel it my duty to say, / Some are boojums—' The Bell-man broke off in alarm. / For the baker had fainted away." Lewis Carroll, *The Annotated Snark* (New York: W.W. Norton, 1962), p. 60.

[7] These are from Carroll's *Symbolic Logic*, p. 169, 172, 135-36.

None but policemen on this beat are poets.
None but her "cousins" ever sup with our cook.
Men with short hair have all been in jail. [UD: men]

16. The Clown in Shakespeare's *All's Well that Ends Well* offers the following humorous syllogism:

> [H]e that COMFORTS my wife is the cHERISHER of my flesh and blood; he that cherishes my flesh and blood LOVES my flesh and blood; he that loves my flesh and blood is my FRIEND: ergo, he that KISSES my wife is my friend. (Act 1, Scene III, lines 45-49)[8] [UD: men]

Supply the missing premise. What kind of argument is this, specifically? (No need to prove it.)

18.2 EXISTENTIAL IMPORT

18.2.1 ON GIVING UNIVERSAL STATEMENTS EXISTENTIAL IMPORT

The principal difference between the traditional Aristotelian logic of the medieval schools and the modern approach we have followed above lies in the treatment of universal statements. For according to traditional logic, an **A**-statement entails the corresponding **I**-statement, and an **E**-statement entails the corresponding **O**-statement. For instance, "All pro HOCKEY players have high DENTAL bills" entails that "Some pro hockey players have high dental bills"; similarly, "No one who HEARS the joke can FAIL to laugh" is understood to entail that there are people who hear the joke who will not fail to laugh. Getting from an **A**- to an **I**- or from an **E**- to an **O**-statement like this was called **conversion by limitation**, and the relationship between corresponding **A**- and **I**-statements and between **E**- and **O**-statements, was known as **subalternation**.

Moreover, if I say "Surely, all electrons are composed of quarks," and you reply, "On the contrary, no electrons are composed of quarks," you are certainly correcting me. On the traditional view, this was interpreted as follows: both statements cannot be true (although they can both be false). If one is true, the other is false. Two corresponding categorical statements having this relationship were said to be **contraries**.

A fourth kind of opposition—in addition to *contradiction*, *contrariety*, and *subalternation*—is that between **I**- and **O**-statements. If I say "Some raccoons are rabid," and you say "Some of them aren't," you are opposing me in a way. But although both of us could be right, it is not the case that both of us could be wrong. Corresponding categorical

---

[8] *The Complete Works of William Shakespeare*, ed. W.G. Clark and W. Aldis Wright (New York: Halcyon House, n.d.), p. 690.

statements which are such that both cannot be false are called **subcontraries**. These various relationships are encapsulated as follows in the Square of Opposition of traditional Aristotelian Logic:

The Traditional Square of Opposition:

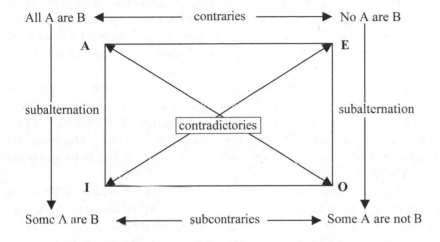

All this may seem eminently reasonable. But there are problems. First, it seems very difficult to deny that particular (i.e., **I**- and **O**-) statements have *existential import*, that is, that they assert the existence of the individuals falling in the subject category. If I say "Some of David CRONENBERG's movies are OVER the top," then I am saying that there exists at least one Cronenberg movie of that kind. Likewise, "Some species of insects do not have wings" commits me to the existence of at least one species of insect. In our Carroll diagrams this was represented by an **x** in the appropriate section of the box representing the subject term. But here's the rub. If an **I**-statement is entailed by an **A**-statement and involves the existence of things in the subject category, then so must the corresponding **A**-statement. But then how can an **A**-statement be the contradictory of an **O**-statement, if both assert the existence of things in the subject category? For example, if "All students who are ABSENT in the exam will FAIL the course" commits us to the existence of at least one student who is absent in the exam, and so does its contradictory "There are students ABSENT in the exam who will not FAIL the course," then both these statements will be false if there are no students absent in the exam. But then they cannot be contradictories! (The truth of a statement entails the falsity of its contradictory, and vice versa.)

When Lewis Carroll faced this dilemma, he wrote (in Humpty Dumpty vein):

I maintain that any writer of a book is fully authorised in attaching any meaning he likes to any word or phrase he intends to use.[9] If I find an author saying at the beginning of his book "Let it be understood that by the word *black* I shall always mean *white*, and by the word *white* I shall always mean *black*," I meekly accept his ruling, however injudicious I may think it.

And so, with regard to the question of whether a Proposition is or is not to be understood as asserting the existence of its Subject, I maintain that every writer may adopt his own rule, provided of course that it is consistent with itself and with the accepted facts of logic. —Lewis Carroll, *Symbolic Logic*, 4th edition, p. 166

Unfortunately, however, Carroll went on to beg precisely the question at issue, claiming that given that **I**-statements assert the existence of their subjects, "we must regard a Proposition in *A* [i.e., an **A**-statement] as making the *same* assertion [of existence of its subject], since it necessarily *contains* a Proposition in *I* [i.e., an **I**-statement]." This prevented him from seeing the best way out of this impasse, which is to *deny* that **I**-statements are always entailed by the corresponding **A**-statements.[10]

This last option is the one favoured by modern logicians. It is often called the Boolean approach, even though Boole himself did not assume that universal propositions have no existential import. It was forcefully promoted as the best solution by John Venn in his influential textbook *Symbolic Logic*.[11] As Venn explains, it consists in taking the following line. (i) Particular statements seem clearly to have existential import. ii) But if they

---

[9] As Carroll's editor W.W. Bartley notes, this is more than a little reminiscent of Carroll's Humpty Dumpty in *Through the Looking-Glass*: "When *I* use a word it means just what I choose it to mean—neither more nor less." When Alice questions "whether you *can* make words mean so many different things," Humpty Dumpty replies, "the question is, which is to be master—that is all." Chapter VI, "Humpty Dumpty."

[10] Carroll took the view that A- and I-statements have existential import, but E- and O-statements do not. This is odd, to say the least: "Some BABIES are ILLOGICAL" could as easily be interpreted as "Some **B** are **not L**" (with **L** = Logical) as "Some **B** are **I**" (with **I** = Illogical)" so one would think that I- and O-statements should receive the same treatment. On the other hand, it should be said that one of the consequences of adopting the modern view is that certain forms of syllogisms traditionally regarded as valid, such as *Darapti*, no longer come out valid. (*Darapti* is All **M** are **P**. All **M** are **S**. Some **S** are **P**.) But see below.

[11] According to William and Martha Kneale the first logician to assume that universal propositions have no existential import was "Franz Brentano, in his *Psychologie vom empirischen Standpunkt* (1874), ii, ch. 7, and the consequences were developed in detail by his pupil F. Hildebrand in *Die neuen Theorien der kategorischen Schlüsse* of 1891" (*Development*, 411, fn. 1). Bertrand Russell, in his 1905 article in *Mind* on existential import, adopted this interpretation while attributing it to Giuseppe Peano. But I surmise that it prevailed above all because of John Venn's advocacy of it in his *Symbolic Logic* (New York: Franklin, 1881), pp. 141-72; this is the most thorough and lucid treatment of the problem of existential import of which I am aware.

John Venn (1834-1923) was an English logician and philosopher, famous for his invention of Venn diagrams (*Symbolic Logic*, 1881), which are now widely used in set theory, logic, statistics, and computer science. He had earlier pioneered the frequency interpretation of probability in *The Logic of Chance*, 1866.

do, then their contradictories cannot. (iii) But the contradictory of a particular statement is a universal statement. (iv) This means that **A-** and **E-statements do not have existential import**. (v) This in turn means that the traditional notion called "conversion by limitation" fails: A-statements do not entail I-statements, and E-statements do not entail O-statements. As further consequences, as we shall see, (vi) contrariety fails too, and (vii) so does subcontrariety.

But what of our intuitions about **A-** and **E-**statements? The short answer is that in most contexts we do presuppose that they have existential import. If I say "All the camels I have ridden had two humps," you take this to imply that I have ridden some camels. On the other hand, though, if I say "All trespassers will be prosecuted," then, far from presupposing that there are trespassers, I am hoping the effect of the threat will be to prevent there being any. So existential import seems to depend on context. It is *conversationally implied*, to use Grice's term, in certain situations, but not in others. Thus we can deal with this problem in the same way we have dealt with others in this book: we will say that universal statements do not logically imply existential import. But in certain contexts they can be taken to presuppose it. Thus we will symbolize **A-** and **E-**statements in such a way that no existential import is involved; but if the validity of an argument depends upon an existential import that is implicit in the context, we will treat this as an implicit existential premise that must be made explicit.

18.2.2 PENEVALID ARGUMENTS

Let's now have a look at such cases, where the validity of an argument depends upon an existential import that is implicit in the context. These arguments are sometimes called *penevalid* (from the Latin for "almost valid"), although we shall be treating them as *valid enthymemes*. The most typical form of such an argument is the following:

All A are B.
All A are Γ.
_____
Therefore some Γ are B.

This form was known as *Darapti* in medieval logic. To Lewis Carroll its validity was obvious, and he used this as a main argument against rival interpretations of existential import. On our interpretation the form Darapti is invalid, but certain arguments apparently having that form are valid when an obvious implicit premise is made explicit. A specific example:

> All VERMONT-made beers taste GREAT.
> All Vermont-made beers are MICRO-BREWED.
>
> Therefore at least some micro-brewed beers taste great.

The obvious validity of this argument depends on the implicit premise that "there are Vermont-made beers." Thus when we diagram the argument, we see that when this premise is added, we get an **x** in the **V**-region. But the only part of **V** that is not empty is **VGM**, so we must insert the **x** there. That is, the implicit premise also guarantees that there are great tasting micro-brewed beers (and the world is the better for it!):

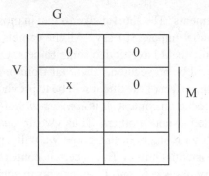

Now we symbolize the argument and prove its validity as follows:

$\forall x(Vx \rightarrow Gx), \forall x(Vx \rightarrow Mx), \exists x Vx$ (implicit) $\therefore \exists x(Mx \& Gx)$

(1) $\forall x(Vx \rightarrow Gx)$ Prem
(2) $\forall x(Vx \rightarrow Mx)$ Prem
(3) $\exists x Vx$ Prem (implicit)
(4) Vi 3 EI
(5) $Vi \rightarrow Gi$ 1 UI
(6) $Vi \rightarrow Mi$ 2 UI
(7) Gi 4, 5 MP
(8) Mi 4, 6 MP
(9) $Mi \& Gi$ 8, 7 Conj
(10) $\exists x(Mx \& Gx)$ 9 EG

Perhaps you are not convinced, and think that the traditional approach of interpreting A-statements as having existential import might be the correct one, so that Darapti is always valid. If so, consider the following argument:

> All ALIEN spacecraft can CLOAK themselves to avoid detection.
> All alien spacecraft are PILOTED by aliens.
> _____
> Therefore there are spacecraft piloted by aliens that can cloak themselves to avoid detection.

This also has the form Darapti: All A are C. All A are P. Therefore some P are C; with UD: spacecraft, A := is alien, C := can cloak itself to avoid detection, P := is piloted by aliens. *But this argument is not valid!* For it is possible to accept the truth of both premises, and yet deny the truth of the conclusion: one only needs to deny that there are any alien spacecraft! This should help to convince you that Darapti cannot be regarded as generally valid; and that valid arguments having this form are better regarded as enthymemes with an implicit existential premise.

18.2.3 NON-EMPTINESS OF THE UD

One final consideration: we have said that universal statements do not in general entail the corresponding existential statements, although in many and perhaps most contexts it is presumed that the class denoted by the subject term is not empty. A similar analysis applies to cases where we have restricted the UD so that it includes only individuals from the class denoted by what was the subject term. This is easier to explain by examples. Take Leibniz's famous Principle of Sufficient Reason: "Nothing happens without a sufficient reason why it should be thus rather than otherwise," or more briefly,

> "Everything that HAPPENS has a SUFFICIENT reason."

This could be symbolized:

$$\forall x(Hx \rightarrow Sx) \qquad (1)$$

From (1) we cannot get to the corresponding I-statement, "Something that happens has a sufficient reason"

$$\exists x(Hx \ \& \ Sx) \qquad (2)$$

without making the assumption ∃xHx an implicit premise in our reasoning. But that's fine, since obviously Leibniz is presuming that some things do happen! This corresponds to the fact that in our logic diagram we have to assume that there is at least one thing that **H**'s, an **x** in the **H** region, in order for it to follow:

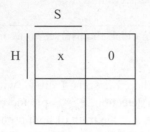

But what if we restrict the UD to things that happen? In that case, we *can* derive "Something that happens has a sufficient reason" from "Everything that happens has a sufficient reason" as follows:

(1) ∀xSx   Prem
(2) Si   1 UI
(3) ∃xSx   2 EG

(Since there are no restrictions on UI or EG, in this proof any individual at all could have served for the instance in line (2).)

It is therefore not the case that we can never derive an existential quantification from a universal one, nor even that we cannot derive an **I**-statement from the corresponding **A**-statement. We can if we assume that there is at least one individual satisfying the original subject term of the **A**-statement, or equivalently, once we have restricted the UD, if we assume that the restricted UD is non-empty.[12]

---

[12] There seems to be a lot of confusion on this subject in the literature. Introductory textbooks routinely state that a particular conclusion can never validly be derived from a universal premise, or that an existential statement can never be derived from a universal quantification, both of which claims are shown to be wrong by this simple example. Also, the existence in question is simply logical: the existential operator is not a magic wand conferring real existence on the individuals concerned, but asserts their existence only in the context of the reasoning concerned. Thus there is no paradox in deriving the conclusion ∀x(Ux → Cx) "All UNICORNS use CELL phones" from the premise ¬∃xUx (there are no unicorns), since the latter is not a statement of indisputable ontological fact, but simply an assertion that the class of the subject term is empty; and on that premise, it does indeed follow that anything in the resultant UD, if it is a unicorn, has whatever property we want to assign it.

This can be seen when we do a Carroll diagram for this case: in order for the conclusion to follow, we have to make the assumption that the restricted UD is non-empty. In other words, in the diagram, we must put an x somewhere in the UD, which means in the region **S**. The argument is valid if and only if we can assume, as an added implicit assumption, that the restricted UD is non-empty, i.e., that there is at least one thing that happens.

UD: things that happen

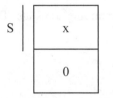

We can summarize this by saying that in any case where an existential conclusion is being derived from universal premises, it is presupposed that the class denoted by the subject term is not empty, or equivalently, when we have restricted the UD to members of that class, that the UD itself is non-empty. The argument will be valid only on that assumption; if making explicit on the diagram that there is an **x** somewhere in the restricted UD makes the argument valid, then it is penevalid. (In such a case the **x** must be entered last, and must straddle any remaining empty regions of the diagram.)

As an example, let's investigate the validity of the following argument:

No foods containing TRANSFATS are GOOD for your health.
Nothing that isn't good for your health is RECOMMENDED by the nutritionist.

Therefore some foods recommended by the nutritionist are good for your health.

Here it is natural to take the UD to be foods, and the Carroll diagram of the premises is:

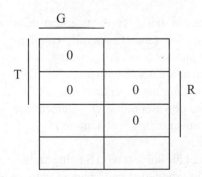

No existential conclusion is validly derivable as it stands. But is it penevalid? If the non-empty subject term is taken to be "foods containing transfats," we should enter an 'x' in the top right hand corner $T\overline{G}\overline{R}$. Applying the Principle of Charity, it seems reasonable to think this is being presupposed. But this will not allow us to infer the conclusion. What if what is being presupposed is that there are foods that are not good for your health? In that case the 'x' will have to straddle the top and bottom right squares, $T\overline{G}\overline{R}$ and $\overline{T}\overline{G}\overline{R}$. But these will not be foods recommended by the nutritionist, so it still will not yield a valid argument. This exhausts what we can allow by applying the Principle of Charity, and we conclude that the argument is **invalid**.

The same result is obtained if we restrict the UD to foods containing transfats. The resulting Carroll diagram is **UD**: foods containing transfats

R

G

0	0
0	

If we grant that it is being presupposed that there are foods that are not good for your health, this puts an 'x' in the bottom right hand corner. But this does not entail that some R are G, so the argument is invalid.

SUMMARY

On the interpretation adopted here
- **Universal (A- and E-) statements have no existential import**.
- **Particular (I- and O-) statements do have existential import**.

Consequently:
- The traditional notion of **conversion by limitation** fails: An A-statement does not generally entail an I-statement, nor does an E-statement generally entail an O-statement. They are not *subalternates* of one another.
- An A-statement and its corresponding E-statement are not *contraries*.
- An I-statement and its corresponding O-statement are not *subcontraries*.
- But it remains true that **an** A-statement and its corresponding O-statement are *contradictories*, as are an I-statement and its corresponding E-statement.

Finally:
- Arguments whose validity depends on the class of the subject term S being known to be non-empty are called *penevalid*. They are interpreted as enthymemes with an implicit premise ∃xSx.

- In order to test the validity of such an argument by the Carroll diagram method, the non-emptiness of the class of the subject term S must be represented explicitly on the diagram by placing an 'x' (disjunctively) in any remaining non-empty cells in S; if the argument comes out valid when that is done, then it is penevalid.
- When an argument is symbolized by restricting the UD to the members of the subject class S of one of the universal quantifications in the original argument, the argument will be penevalid if and only if the restricted UD is assumed to be non-empty. On a logic diagram, the non-emptiness of the UD must be represented explicitly on the diagram by placing an 'x' (disjunctively) in any remaining non-empty cells of the restricted UD.

EXERCISES 18.2

The arguments in 17-21 are penevalid. (i) *Using Carroll diagrams, determine in each case the one-predicate existential premise that would render it valid*, (ii) *symbolize the argument together with this implicit premise*, and (iii) *prove its validity using predicate logic*.

17. Some philosophers have held that every meaningful word is a name. The following argument is offered in refutation:
    PREPOSITIONS are not NAMES, but they are MEANINGFUL. This proves that some meaningful words are not names. [UD: words]

18. No HORNED dinosaurs are FLESHEATERS. All flesheaters SCARE children. Therefore some dinosaurs that scare children are not horned. [UD: dinosaurs]

19. All BIRDS are MAMMALS. But birds have HOLLOW bones. Therefore some mammals have hollow bones.

20. No FUNDAMENTALISTS are ATHEISTS. No non-atheists argue RATIONALLY. Therefore some fundamentalists do not argue rationally.

21. All BIRDS are WARM-blooded. OSTRICHES cannot FLY. No creatures but birds are ostriches. Therefore some warm-blooded creatures cannot fly.

22. Lewis Carroll declares the following argument valid. *Show that it is penevalid:*
    No MONKEYS are SOLDIERS. All monkeys are mISCHIEVOUS. Therefore some mischievous creatures are not soldiers. [UD: creatures]

23. *Re-analyze argument 19 above, restricting the UD to BIRDS. That is, prove it is penevalid by* (i) *representing the argument with this restricted UD on a Carroll diagram*, (ii) *representing the non-emptiness of the UD on the diagram*, and (iii) *showing that the conclusion cannot now be denied*.

24. *Re-analyze argument 20 above, restricting the UD to FUNDAMENTALISTS.* That is, *prove it is penevalid* by (i) *representing the argument with this restricted UD on a Carroll diagram*, (ii) *representing the non-emptiness of the UD on the diagram*, and (iii) *showing that the conclusion cannot now be denied.*

For exercises 25-28 use Carroll diagrams to determine whether the argument given is valid, penevalid, or invalid:

25. No DINOSAURS are ALIVE today. Some REPTILES are alive today. Therefore some dinosaurs are not reptiles.

26. No VEGANS eat MEAT. All VEGANS refuse DAIRY foods. Therefore some people who refuse dairy foods are Vegans.

27. Only BELIEVERS are FUNDAMENTALISTS. Some non-believers are ATHEISTS. Therefore some atheists are not fundamentalists.

28. Only BELIEVERS are FUNDAMENTALISTS. All non-believers are ATHEISTS. No fundamentalists argue RATIONALLY. Therefore some atheists argue rationally.

29. Two statements are said to be *contraries* if they cannot both be true, i.e., if the truth of one entails the falsity of the other. Traditionally, an A-statement and its corresponding E-statement were held to be contraries. But on the modern interpretation of existential import, an A-statement and its corresponding E-statement can both be true if there are no individuals in the subject category. *Prove this by proving that*
$$\forall x(Sx \rightarrow Px), \forall x(Sx \rightarrow \neg Px) \vdash \neg \exists x Sx$$

30. **(CHALLENGE)** Two statements are said to be *subcontraries* if they cannot both be false, i.e., if the falsity of one entails the truth of the other. Traditionally, an I-statement and its corresponding O-statement were held to be subcontraries. But on the modern interpretation the falsity of an I-statement entails the corresponding O-statement if and only if there are individuals in the subject category. *Prove that existence of the individuals in the subject category is a sufficient condition by proving that*
$$\neg \exists x(Sx \& Px), \exists x Sx \vdash \exists x(Sx \& \neg Px)$$

31. **(CHALLENGE)** In a letter to T. Fowler, author of a well-known nineteenth-century logic book, Lewis Carroll wrote objecting against Fowler's interpretation of the copula "are" as not connoting any actual existence: "According to this view the Propositions 'all *x* are *y*,' 'some *x* are *y*,' mean '*if any x exist*, all of them are *y*,' '*if any x exist*, some of them are *y*.'"

Now suppose my (empty) purse to be lying on the table, and that I say
"All the sovereigns in that purse are made of gold;
All of the sovereigns in that purse are my property;
∴ Some of my property is made of gold."
Carroll takes this to be a valid syllogism, and objects that on Fowler's interpretation "though these two premises are *true*, the conclusion may very easily be *false*: it might easily happen that I *had* much 'property,' but that none of it was 'made of gold.'" [On Carroll's own interpretation, A- and I-statements have existential import, but E- and O-statements do not.] *Explain how the interpretation of existential import offered in the text could resolve this dispute.*

Chapter Nineteen

Asyllogistic Arguments

19.1.1 NON-CLASSICAL STATEMENTS

So far we have been using predicate logic to treat the material traditionally amenable to the theory of syllogisms: first what was dealt with in Aristotle's theory of the syllogism, then with the additional material (singular statements, negative predicates in the subject, arguments with more than 3 predicates, non-standard sorites, and so on) amenable to the methods introduced by Boole, Venn, and company in the nineteenth century. But it should be obvious that we can do very much more with the predicate logic that we have generalized from modern statement logic. For example, if the universe of discourse (UD) is people, Bx := x is a backwoodsman, and Hx := x has heard of Sigmund Freud, we have not only

(1) ∃x(Bx & ¬Hx)   Some backwoodsmen have not heard of Freud.

and

(2) ∀x(Bx → ¬Hx)   No backwoodsman has heard of Freud.

but also

(3) ∃x¬Hx   Some people have not heard of Freud.
(4) ∀x¬Hx   No one has heard of Freud.
(5) ¬∃xHx   There isn't anyone who has heard of Freud.
(6) ¬∀xHx   Not everyone has heard of Freud.
(7) ∀x(¬Hx → Bx)   Anyone who has not heard of Freud is a backwoodsman.

(8) ∀x(Hx ∨ Bx)	Everyone has either heard of Freud or is a backwoodsman.
(9) ∃xHx & ∃x¬Hx	Some people have heard of Freud, and some haven't.
(10) ∀x(Bx ↔ ¬Hx)	All and only backwoodsmen have not heard of Freud.

Statements (3) to (6) are worth a bit of reflection. It is tempting to translate (5) "There isn't anyone who has heard of Freud" by ∃x¬Hx. But this is (3), "There are *some* people who haven't heard of Freud." We want (5), "there are *no* people who have heard of Freud...," so the ¬ negates the existential quantifier, not the predicate. However, (5) seems to say exactly the same as (4). Likewise, (3) seems to say exactly the same as (6). This is indeed the case, and we shall prove the equivalence of (3) and (6), and of (4) and (5), in due course.

Also, note that statement (9), ∃xHx & ∃x¬Hx, is *not a contradiction*. That some people have heard of Freud is perfectly compatible with some having not heard of him. What is a contradiction is ∃xHx & ¬∃xHx, since it has the form p & $\neg p$ with $p := $ ∃xHx.

Predicate logic can even deal with some quite complex statements, such as the following from the envelope of a Delta Airlines ticket:

(11) PASSENGERS presenting themselves at the airport loading gate LESS than 10 minutes before scheduled departure will not be ACCEPTED if boarding them will DELAY the flight.

This has the overall structure of an A-statement, "All...are...": "Everyone who is P and L will not be A if D," giving

(11F) ∀x[(Px & Lx) → (Dx → ¬Ax)]

The symbolization is simplified if we are allowed to assume that we are only concerned with passengers, so that this constitutes the universe of discourse:

(12) Passengers presenting themselves at the airport loading gate LESS than 10 minutes before scheduled departure will not be ACCEPTED if boarding them will DELAY the flight. (UD: passengers)

(12F) ∀x[Lx → (Dx → ¬Ax)]

19.1.2 'ANY'

This little word is surprisingly problematic. You were probably thinking that it should always be translated by a universal quantifier, as in the first of the following statements:

(13) Anything CONCERNING the theatre INTERESTED Diderot.
(13F) $\forall x(Cx \rightarrow Ix)$

(14) If anyone was a GREAT guitar player, <u>Hendrix</u> was. [UD: guitar players]

But what about the second statement, (14F)? $\forall xGx \rightarrow Gh$ would symbolize

(15) If *everyone* was a GREAT guitar player, <u>Hendrix</u> was.

This is trivially true, because it is false that everyone was a great guitar player, whereas (14) makes a substantive claim for Hendrix's lasting glory. What it seems to mean is that if there was *someone* who was a great guitar player, then Hendrix was. So it could be symbolized as

(14F) $\exists xGx \rightarrow Gh$

Thus as a general rule of thumb, we may note:

> **If 'any' can be replaced by 'some' without altering the meaning of a statement, then it should be translated by an existential quantifier.**

Good examples of this are provided by negative statements involving 'any.' For instance,

(16) There aren't any books on RESERVE for this course. [UD: books for this course]
(16F) $\neg \exists xRx$

whereas $\neg \forall xRx$ would symbolize "Not all books for this course are on reserve"—i.e., that some are not on reserve.

But, going back to the previous example, what about $\forall x(Gx \rightarrow Gh)$? (Notice the arrangement of parentheses here.) This seems to say that, for each guitar player, if that player was a great guitar player, then Hendrix was. Isn't that the same thing as $\exists xGx \rightarrow Gh$? If it is, we should be able to prove one abstract statement from the other, and vice versa. We'll do this in the next section.

SUMMARY

- A wide range of statements can be symbolized with the resources we already have, going well beyond the traditional categorical logic. For instance $\exists x \neg Hx$ translates "There are some people who haven't heard of Freud," and $\forall x(Hx \lor Bx)$ translates "Everyone has either heard of Freud or is a backwoodsman" (with Hx := x has heard of Freud, Bx := x is a backwoodsman; UD: people).

- $\exists x G x \rightarrow Gh$ translates "If anyone was a GREAT guitar player, <u>Hendrix</u> was" (UD: people), implying the rule of thumb:
- If **'any'** can be replaced by **'some'** without altering the meaning of a statement, then it should be translated by an existential quantifier.

EXERCISES 19.1

1. *Symbolize the following statements:*
   (a) Everybody is GUILTY.—Albert Camus [UD: people]
   (b) There are WEREWOLVES.
   (c) There are pilots with an ALCOHOL problem. [UD: pilots]
   (d) There is no such thing as SOCIETY.—Margaret Thatcher [UD: things]
   (e) Not all PROSTITUTES are JUNKIES.—Newspaper
   (f) He LIVES well who is well HIDDEN.—Descartes' motto [UD: people]
   (g) Only those who are well HIDDEN LIVE well. [UD: people]
   (h) All non-TICKET-holders should LINE up at the booth.
   (i) No one without TICKETS should LINE up at the booth.
   (j) No MURDERED child or DYING father POISONED his love of the Lord.— Marshall Sella, 1997
   (k) A member of PARLIAMENT who behaves as a strictly HONEST man is regarded as a FOOL.—James Boswell
   (l) Paul <u>Revere</u>, American HERO and PATRIOT, was also a MIDDLECLASS BUSI-NESSMAN who had mouths to FEED.—Marcella Bombardieri, *Boston Globe*
   (m) Everything GOOD in Christianity comes from either PLATO or the STOICS.— Bertrand Russell
   (n) Some HUSBANDS are IMPERIOUS and some WIVES PERVERSE.—Samuel Johnson
   (o) Any pilot, MUSLIM or CHRISTIAN, who sees he is heading toward TROUBLE, will say religious PRAYERS.—Yusri Hamid, Egypt Air pilot [UD: pilots]
   (p) WOMEN with long FINGERNAILS never make MEAT loaf, and they have HUSBANDS who make over $50,000 a year.—Erma Bombeck [Mx := x some-times makes meatloaf]
   (q) A crime is a MISDEMEANOR if and only if it is not punishable by DEATH or IMPRISONMENT in a state penitentiary.—Webster's Dictionary [UD: crimes]
   (r) If anyone's to BLAME, <u>I</u> am. [UD: people; Bx := x is to blame, i := I]
   (s) There isn't anyone in this ROOM. [UD: people; Rx := x is in this room]
   (t) There isn't anyone in this ROOM who has never SINNED. [UD: people; Rx := x is in this room, Sx := x has sinned at some time]
   (u) No one whose TESTICLES are crushed or whose male MEMBER is cut off shall ENTER the assembly of the Lord.—Holy Bible, Deuteronomy 23:1 [UD: men]
   (v) Every man I meet is either MARRIED, too YOUNG, or he wants to do my HAIR.—Doris Day [UD: men; Dx := x is met by Doris Day]

2. *Using the symbolizations suggested, **translate (a) from English into Predicate Logic**, and then use the same interpretations of the symbols to **render (b) from Predicate Logic into colloquial English***:
   (a) If there are no UNICORNS, then all unicorns use BLACKBERRIES.
   (b) $\neg \forall x(Ux \rightarrow Bx) \rightarrow \exists x \neg Bx$

3. *Using the dictionary provided, **translate (a)-(c) from English into Predicate Logic**, and then use the same interpretations of the symbols to **render (d)-(f) from Predicate Logic into colloquial English***:
   (a) Only logicians who wrote CHILDREN's books are FAMOUS.
   (b) All logicians who wrote children's books with an INSPIRED imagination are famous.
   (c) The necessary and sufficient conditions for Lewis <u>Carroll</u>'s being FAMOUS are that he was a logician who wrote CHILDREN's books and had an INSPIRED imagination.
   (d) $\neg \forall x(Ix \rightarrow Cx)$
   (e) $\exists x(\neg Ix \& Fx) \& Cc$
   (f) $\forall x(\neg Ix \rightarrow \neg Cx)$
   [**Dictionary**: UD: logicians; C := wrote children's books, F := is famous, I := had an inspired imagination]

19.2 ASYLLOGISTIC PROOFS: QN

Now let's turn to some proofs. I promised in chapter 16 to say more in explanation of the restrictions on our quantifier rules. Our UG rule (in terms of u and x) is as follows:

From Φu derive $(\forall x)\Phi x$, provided
(i) Φu neither is nor depends upon an undischarged supposition involving **u**, and
(ii) Φu does not contain a name **i** (or **j** or **k**) introduced by an application of **EI** to a formula involving **u**.

The second restriction does not come into its own until we get to relational logic with formulas involving both **u** and **i**. In our system **UG** cannot otherwise be validly applied to a formula derived by **EI** because the letters **i**, **j**, and **k** are reserved for **EI**, and **u**, **v**, and **w** are reserved for **UG**. Here are two examples of short, invalid proofs that illustrate this:

(1) $\exists xAx$ Prem
(2) Au 1 EI   *—MISTAKE! EI must be to an instance involving the*
(3) $\forall xAx$ 2 UG   *arbitrary name i!*

(1) ∃xAx   Prem
(2) Ai   1 EI
(3) ∀xAx   2 UG   —*MISTAKE! UG must be on an instance involving the arbitrary name **u**!*

For example, without that restriction we could have proved from the true statement "Some movies are *AVANT garde*" (UD: movies) that "All movies are *avant garde*"!

But why the first restriction? Well, we do not want to allow proofs like the following:

(1) ∃xAx   Prem
  (2) Au   Supp/CP
  (3) ∀xAx   2 UG   —*MISTAKE! violates first restriction on UG!*
(4) Au → ∀xAx   2-3 CP
(5) ∀y[Ay → ∀xAx]   4 UG
(6)...

Notice that the problem here is not getting to line (5) from line (4): there we have correctly generalized from an instance involving **u** that **no longer depends** on a supposition involving **u**—the supposition was correctly discharged on line 4 by the CP move. It is the move from line (2) to line (3) that violates the restriction, as indicated by (3)'s having the same indentation as (2), the line on which the supposition was made. If that were not a mistake and (5) were validly derived, the proof could continue:

(6) Ai   1 EI   —*it's OK not to do EI first so long as i has not*
(7) Ai → (∀x)Ax   5 UI   *occurred on a previous line.*
(8) ∀xAx   7, 6 MP

Again we would have proved that *all* x's are A's from the assumption that only *some* are. So this first restriction is made precisely to preclude invalid proofs of this sort.

Now let's prove (as we promised to) that statements (3) and (6) of section 1, "Some people have not heard of Freud" and "Not everyone has heard of Freud," mutually entail one another:

(1) ∃x¬Hx   Prem   ⊢ ¬∀xHx
  (2) ∀xHx   Supp/RA
  (3) ¬Hi   1 EI
  (4) Hi   2 UI
  (5) Hi & ¬Hi   4, 3 Conj
(6) ¬∀xHx   2-5 RA

(1) ¬∀xHx   Prem   ⊢ ∃x¬Hx
  (2) Hu   Supp/RA
  (3) ∀xHx   2 UG   —*MISTAKE! violates first restriction on UG!*

The first restriction is that "Φu neither is nor depends upon an undischarged supposition involving u." Here the instance we are generalizing from, Hu, *is* an undischarged supposition involving u. We need to try something subtler:

(1) ¬∀xHx	Prem	⊢ ∃x¬Hx
│ (2) ¬∃x¬Hx	Supp/RA	
│ (3) ¬Hu	Supp/RA	
│ (4) ∃x¬Hx	3 EG	
│ (5) ∃x¬Hx & ¬∃x¬Hx	4, 2 Conj	
│ (6) Hu	3-5 RA	
│ (7) ∀xHx	6 UG	*—no longer violates restriction!*
│ (8) ∀xHx & ¬∀xHx	7, 1 Conj	
(9) ∃x¬Hx	2-8 RA, DN	

The reason that line (7) no longer violates the first restriction on UG is that by line (6) the supposition involving **u** has been discharged. As a result, Hu neither is nor depends on a supposition involving **u**, even though it contains the name **u**.

Similar proofs will establish the mutual equivalence of statements (4) and (5) above: ∀x¬Hx ⊣⊢ ¬∃xHx. I leave this as an exercise.

In the same way we could prove the logical equivalence of any statement beginning ∃x¬... with the same statement beginning instead ¬∀x..., and the same with statements beginning ∀x¬... and ¬∃x... That is, the same proofs could have been performed whatever propositional function of x followed the quantifiers in x. This means that we have effectively proved the following, our only derived rules in Predicate Logic:

Quantifier Negation (QN)

From the negation of a universal quantification infer the existential quantification whose propositional function is the negation of the original one, and vice versa.
From ¬∀xΦx, derive ∃x¬Φx, and vice versa.

From the negation of an existential quantification infer the universal quantification whose propositional function is the negation of the original one, and vice versa.
From ¬∃xΦx, derive ∀x¬Φx, and vice versa.

As usual, this rule is also understood to apply to the variables y and z too.

Here's an example of a use of this rule of inference:

If <u>Gorbachev</u> was TELLING the truth about Stalin's purges, then <u>Brezhnev</u> DECEIVED the Soviet people. But if Gorbachev was not telling the truth, then he himself deceived the Soviet people. Thus it is certain that someone deceived the Soviet people.

This is symbolized as follows: Tg → Db, ¬Tg → Dg ∴ ∃xDx. The proof is a reductio:

(1) Tg → Db	Prem	
(2) ¬Tg → Dg	Prem	
(3) ¬∃xDx	Supp/RA	—*the negation of our conclusion*
(4) ∀x¬Dx	3 QN	—*if it's false that someone D'd, then nobody did*
(5) ¬Db	4 UI	—*if that's so, Brezhnev didn't D*
(6) ¬Tg	1, 5 MT	—*if that's so, Gorby was lying*
(7) Dg	2, 6 MP	—*if that's so, Gorby D'd the Soviet people*
(8) ¬Dg	4 UI	—*but nobody D'd the Soviet people, so G didn't!*
(9) Dg & ¬Dg	7, 8 Conj	—*but this is a contradiction, so…*
(10) ∃xDx	3-9 RA	

Notice the two uses of UI on 4 in lines (5) and (8) to two different instances. We could also have obtained a contradiction by EG as follows:

(8) ∃xDx	7 EG	—*so somebody D'd the Soviet people*
(9) ∃xDx & ¬∃xDx	8, 3 Conj	—*but this is a contradiction, so…*
(10) ∃xDx	3-9 RA	

This illustrates why we can use the general symbol ⊥ for any explicit contradiction: they are all equivalent.

Finally, let's look at the promised "Hendrix" proof, i.e., ∃xGx → Gh ⊢ ∀x(Gx → Gh):

(1) ∃xGx → Gh	Prem	
(2) Gu	Supp/CP	
(3) ∃xGx	2 EG	
(4) Gh	1, 3 MP	
(5) Gu → Gh	2-4 CP	
(6) ∀x(Gx → Gh)	5 UG	

Again, this does not break the first restriction on UG, because the dependence on **u** has been discharged by the step of CP. To prove logical equivalence, we also need to prove ∀x(Gx → Gh) ⊢ ∃xGx → Gh. I leave this as an exercise. Notice, though, that the following won't do:

(1) ∀x(Gx → Gh)	Prem	
(2) Gi → Gh	1 UI	
(3) ∃xGx → Gh	2 EG	—*WRONG!*

The reason is not that any restrictions on quantifiers have been violated: there aren't any on UI or on EG. The problem is that the abstract statement ∃xGx → Gh **is not an existential quantification**! It is a **conditional** whose **antecedent is an existential quantification**. And you cannot get to a conditional by EG; to prove a conditional you would use CP.

But granting the equivalence of these two abstract statements, it must be admitted that all this raises a lot of questions. If ∀x(Gx → Gh) is a universal quantification, why is there an 'h' in it? What does it mean to say that 'h' lies within the scope of the quantifier ∀x? Why doesn't the 'h' in ∃xGx → Gh lie within its scope? To address these and similar perplexities, we need to define the scope of a quantifier, and this requires setting up predicate logic in a systematic way. We'll do this in section 3 below.

SUMMARY

- The restrictions on the UG rule are there to prevent proofs of invalid arguments. In deriving ∀xΦx from Φu, (i) the latter must neither itself be nor depend upon an undischarged supposition involving **u**, and (ii) it must not involve a letter **i** introduced by an application of **EI** to a formula involving **u**. In non-relational predicate logic, **UG** cannot be invalidly applied to a formula obtained by **EI** because **i**, **j**, and **k** are reserved for **EI**, and **u**, **v**, and **w** are reserved for **UG**.
- The rule of inference **Quantifier Negation (QN)** is:
  From the negation of a universal quantification infer the existential quantification whose propositional function is the negation of the original one, and vice versa. From ¬∀xΦx, derive ∃x¬Φx, and vice versa.
  From the negation of an existential quantification infer the universal quantification whose propositional function is the negation of the original one, and vice versa. From ¬∃xΦx, derive ∀x¬Φx, and vice versa.

EXERCISES 19.2

*Identify the mistakes in the following proofs (4-8). In each one there is **one** major gaffe or type of error (if repeated) that renders the proof invalid.*

4. (1) ¬∀y[Fy & Gy]   Prem   ⊢ ∀x[Fx → ¬Gx]
    (2) ∃y¬[Fy & Gy]   1 QN
    (3) ¬[Fi & Gi]   2 EI
       | (4) Fi   Supp/CP
       | (5)¬Gi   3, 4 CS
    (6) Fi → ¬Gi   4-5 CP
    (7) ∀x[Fx → ¬Gx]   6 UG

5. (1) ∀xFx → ∀xGx   Prem   ⊢ ∀x[Fx → Gx]
    (2) Fu → Gu   1 UI
    (3) ∀x[Fx → Gx]   2 UG

6. (1) ∀x[Fx → Gx]   Prem   ⊢ ∀xFx → ∀xGx
    │(2) ∀xFx   Supp/CP
    │(3) Fx   2 UI
    │(4) Fx → Gx   1 UI
    │(5) Gx   3, 4 MP
    │(6) ∀xGx   5 UG
    (7) ∀xFx → ∀xGx   2-6 CP

7.   │(1) Fu   Supp/CP   ⊢ ∀y[Fy → ∀xFx]
        │(2) ∀xFx   1 UG
    (3) Fu → ∀xFx   1-2 CP
    (4) ∀y[Fy → ∀xFx]   3 UG

8. (1) ∃x(Ax & Bx)   Prem   ⊢ ∀x(Ax → Bx)
    │(2) ¬∀x{Ax → Bx}   Supp/RA
    │(3) ∃x¬{Ax → Bx}   2 QN
    │(4) ¬(Ai → Bi)   3 EI
    │(5) ¬(¬Ai ∨ Bi)   4 MI
    │(6) ¬¬Ai & ¬ Bi   5 DM
    │(7) ¬Bi   6 Simp
    │(8) Ai & Bi   1 EI
    │(9) Bi   8 Simp
    │(10) ⊥   9, 7 Conj
    (11) ∀x(Ax → Bx)   2-10 RA, DN

9. *Give a correct proof of* 6 above, ∀x[Fx → Gx] ⊢ ∀xFx → ∀xGx.

Prove the validity of the arguments occurring in exercises 10-16:
10. On my 21st birthday an editorial appeared in the *Miami Herald*, "Never Forget What's-His-Name," in which it was asserted that no biography has ever been written of my namesake, the 21st President of the United States. This prompted a letter to the editor from a certain E.F.B. Fries, who pointed out that one had been written, *Chester A. Arthur: A Quarter Century of Machine Politics*, by George Frederick Howe in 1934. Fries's implicit argument:

> It is false that there has never been a BIOGRAPHY of Chester Arthur. For Howe's book is just such a biography. [UD: books; Bx := is a biography of Chester Arthur]

11. Here is another interpretation of the probable reasoning of the tax-evading English-man of exercise 19 of chapter 17:

No TAXES may be collected from ANIMALS. My dog <u>Glory</u> is an animal. Therefore, if Glory INVESTS in stocks, some individual who invests in stocks cannot be taxed. [UD: individuals; Tx := can be taxed]

12. Psychologists at a state prison in Connecticut in the 1970s ran a behaviour-modification program for child-molesters, who were given electric shocks as they watched slides of naked children. The psychologist in charge claimed that "the program is entirely voluntary"; to which the director of the Connecticut Civil Liberties Union replied with the following argument:

It's inherently coercive—there's no such thing as a real volunteer in a prison, especially when a prisoner knows participating may enhance his chances for parole.[1]

Symbolize and prove the validity of this paraphrase of the CCLU director's argument:

Any prisoner who KNOWS participating in a program may enhance his chances for parole is not a VOLUNTEER. Since all prisoners know this, there is no such thing as a real volunteer in a prison. [UD: prisoners; Kx := x knows participating in a program may enhance his chances for parole, Vx := x is a real volunteer]

13. Responding to a proposed constitutional amendment that would permit non-denominational prayer in public schools, Congressman Drinan (then the sole Catholic priest in congress) attacked the amendment with an argument paraphrased by Howard Pospesel (*Predicate Logic*, 54) as follows:

The proposed amendment sanctions only nondenominational prayer. Therefore, since there is no such thing as a nondenominational prayer, it sanctions nothing. [UD: prayers; Sx := x is sanctioned by the proposed amendment, Dx := x is denominational]

14. The following is a paraphrase of an argument by the French philosopher René Descartes:

Everything that is EXTENDED is a SUBSTANCE. But nothing is both a substance and a VACUUM. Yet every vacuum is extended. Therefore there is no vacuum.

15. Prove that if the statement "Beauty is in the eye of the beholder" is interpreted to mean "Everything that is BEAUTIFUL is in the EYE of the beholder," then it follows that "if there are things that are not in the eye of the beholder, then not everything is beautiful." [Bx := x is beautiful, Ex := x is in the eye of the beholder]

---

[1] Quoted from Howard Pospesel, *Predicate Logic* (1st ed., Upper Saddle River, NJ: Prentice Hall), p. 55. My paraphrase, however, is quite different from Pospesel's.

16. Sarah knows that her friend Alice is holding a party for people of one sex only, but does not know which. But then she learns that Alice herself will be at the party, and concludes that everyone invited is female. Her reasoning:
> Either all those invited are MALE or they are all FEMALE. At least one of them is female. No one can be both male and female. Therefore all those invited are female. [UD: those invited to the party]

17. *Prove* $\forall x(Gx \rightarrow Gh) \vdash \exists x Gx \rightarrow Gh$ (the other side of the "if any" equivalence).

18. *Prove* that from "If anything is CERTAIN, this is," and "Not everything fails to be certain," it follows that "This is certain" (whatever "this" may happen to be).

19. (**CHALLENGE**) Since they are contradictories, an E-statement entails the negation of the I-statement with the same subject and predicate terms. Construct a 6 line proof.

20. (**CHALLENGE**) Construct a nine-line formal proof for the sequent
$\exists x(Sx \lor Px) \vdash \exists x Sx \lor \exists x Px$

19.3 PREDICATE LOGIC AS A FORMAL SYSTEM

19.3.1 SYMBOLS, FORMULAS, AND WFFS

As we saw in Statement Logic, we can discuss validity at varying levels of abstraction. On the one hand, we have the unreconstructed natural arguments, occurring in their original wordings. Then, when we have supplied missing premises and/or conclusions, discarded inessential elements, and perhaps even paraphrased, we have a system of one or more inferences, whose validity we can investigate. Each single-inference argument, expressed in words, is a *concrete* argument,[2] whose form we can proceed to investigate. In doing so, we make certain judgements about whether the form depends on a pattern of statements related by our statement connectives, or a pattern of predicates ascribed to individuals (or, in relational logic, a pattern of predicates relating two or more individuals). We then represent the statements by letters: *capitals* for statements and their components, *capitals followed by lower case letters* for singular statements; and we represent combinations of these statements using statement operators and quantifiers. These are now *abstract* statements. They are represented by strings of symbols or *formulas*, not arbitrary strings of symbols, but ones that can be interpreted as abstract statements according to our conventions. We can then look at these patterns of abstract statements, our abstract arguments, and see whether they conform to *forms of inference* that are valid.

---

[2] This follows the usage of Lewis Carroll in his *Symbolic Logic*: "A *concrete* Proposition is one that is expressed in words, and an *abstract* Proposition is one expressed in terms of letters."

The forms of inference are expressed as *argument forms*, patterns into which the symbols representing abstract statements can be substituted. So a given inference may be valid or invalid; but the inference may be expressed concretely or abstractly; and the form of a valid inference corresponding to a rule of inference is expressed as an argument form.

To express Predicate Logic as a formal system we need only to generalize a little on our definitions for Statement Logic. As before, we concentrate on the abstract statements, which will be represented by *well-formed formulas* or *wffs*. For these, we can give rules of formation by a simple extension of the rules of formation for statements we examined in chapter 12. First, we list our symbols:

WHAT IS SYMBOLIZED	SYMBOLS FOR IT
Statements or predicates:	the capital letters: A, B, C, etc.
Individual names:	the lower-case letters: a, b, c, ... v, w
Individual variables:	the lower-case letters: x, y, z
Groupers: parentheses, brackets, and braces:	(,), [,], {, }
Unary statement operators:	negation symbol: ¬
Binary statement operators:	arrow, ampersand, wedge, and double arrow: →, &, ∨, ↔
Quantifiers:	reverse-E and inverted-A: ∃, ∀

We can define a *formula* as before:

A formula is a string of (one or more) logical symbols, e.g., [¬, A → (}∨.

Thus the following are formulas by this definition:

¬¬Me
∀x(Tx → Qx)
Fx ↔ Gx
∃m[Tm & Vm]
x∀→
aZo & ∀x → Bx
∃x[Tx → (Qx & Rx}

Of these, only the first two are well-formed. Clearly we need to define what strings represent well-formed statements. These may be the singular statements of statement logic, such as F or B, or those of predicate logic, such as Fa or Bm. But we will set up our definitions so that they also accommodate the statements in relational logic that we will need in chapters 20-23. There we will meet statements involving predicates that link two or more individuals, such as "Angelina MARRIED Brad," which we will symbolize aMb.

In addition, we will also need to have groupers only occurring in corresponding pairs, and for quantifications we also need to define quantifiers:

Simple (abstract) singular statement:	a capital, a capital followed by a lower-case letter a-w, or a capital followed and preceded by 1 or more lower-case letters a-w.
Left grouper:	any of the symbols (, [, and {.
Matching right grouper:	the mirror image of a left-hand grouper.
Universal quantifier:	an ∀, followed by a variable: ∀x, ∀y, or ∀z.
Existential quantifier:	an ∃, followed by a variable: ∃x, ∃y, or ∃z.

Now we can give a *recursive definition* of a **well-formed formula** as follows:

The following, and only the following, formulas are wffs:

(i) a simple singular statement   or
(ii) a negation symbol followed by a wff   or
(iii) a left grouper, followed by a wff, followed by a binary operator, followed by a wff, followed by a matching right grouper   or
(iv) a formula that can be generated from a wff by prefixing a quantifier (whose variable does not occur in the wff) and replacing one or more occurrences of an individual name by the same variable.[3]

As in statement logic, we will append the convention that:

(v) Matching left and right groupers at the left and right extremes of a wff formed by applying clause (iii) last are *understood* to be there even when they are not explicitly written in.

Let's see how this definition works by exploring some examples. First the symbol

(1) A

is a wff by clause (i). It is an abstract statement, and could stand for any statement at all (whose internal structure we have declined to investigate further). Similarly,

---

[3] Alternatively: (iv) a quantifier in x followed by a wff in which one or more individual names has been replaced by the variable x (where the variable x did not occur in the wff prior to that replacement).

(2) Fe, aCr, sEs, and aBth

are all wffs by clause (i). 'Fe' could stand for "<u>Erica</u> has a FEAR of flying." 'aCr' could stand for "<u>Angela</u> CARES for <u>Rodney</u>," 'sEs' for "The preceding <u>statement</u> is EQUIVA-LENT to itself," and 'aBth' for "The <u>ambulance</u> station is BETWEEN the <u>theatre</u> and the <u>hospital</u>." In practice, you are unlikely to see wffs with more than three individual names.

(3) ¬Fe, ¬¬Fe, ¬¬¬aCr

are all wffs by clause (ii), and so will be an infinity of others such as ¬(So & Do), provided (So & Do) is itself a wff.

(4) (Fe → Ge), (So & Do), (Am ∨ Bm), (P ↔ Ge), [aCa → (rCa ∨ aCr)]

are all wffs by clause (iii), and by convention (v) may be written as

(5) Fe → Ge, So & Do, Am ∨ Bm, P ↔ Ge, aCa → (rCa ∨ aCr)

Finally, by clause (iv) the following are wffs:

(6) ∀x(Fx → Gx), ∀x(Fx → Ge), ∃x(Sx & Dx), ∀y(Ay ∨ By), ∀x∀y∀z[xCz → (yCx ∨ zCy)]

The first of these is an A-statement obtained by replacing every **e** in the first wff of (4) by **x**. The second is obtained by replacing only the first name **e** by an **x**. The result is a statement like the "Hendrix" one above. The last of these would be obtained from the last of the wffs in (4) in three stages: first, replace the second and fourth occurrences of **a** by **z** and put an ∀z in front; then replace all occurrences of **r** by **y** and put a ∀y in front; then replace the remaining occurrences of **a** by **x** and put a ∀x in front. **N.B. These are rules of formation, not rules of inference.** No rule of inference legitimates these moves: they are simply ways of determining whether the formula is a wff. It is if we can construct it by following these rules. If we cannot so construct it, it is not a wff. For example, since groupers are only introduced by clause (iii) with binary operators, a string such as ∃x(Bx) is not a wff. Notice that a *quantification* may now be defined as follows:

> **A quantification is a formula that is a wff according to the above rules of formation when (and only when) clause (iv) is applied last.**

It is not just any wff beginning with a quantifier. Remember ∃xGx → Gh is not an existential quantification, but a conditional. This corresponds to the fact that it would be generated as a wff as follows: Ge is a wff by (i), so ∃xGx is by clause (iv). Gh is a wff by (i), so ∃xGx → Gh is a wff by clause (ii) (applying the convention (v) to drop the outermost groupers). The last connective used in forming a wff according to clauses (ii) and (iii) is the governing connective of the wff. Here it is the arrow, so the wff as a whole is a conditional. If clause (iv) is applied last, the wff is a quantification, as we just saw.

19.3.2 PROPOSITIONAL FUNCTIONS AND QUANTIFIER SCOPE

With a quantification defined, we may now define a *propositional function* in terms of it. This will replace the provisional definition we gave in chapter 16, which is adequate only to the single-quantifier quantifications we were considering there. Our new definition is:

A propositional function Φx is a formula containing at least one variable x that results when one or more quantifiers are deleted from the front of a quantification.

A quantification, as defined on the previous page, is a wff generated by application of clause (iv) last. As usual, this definition is also understood to apply to the variables y and z too. Here are some examples:

(1) (Px & ¬Qx) is a propositional function obtained from the wff ∃x(Px & ¬Qx) by deleting the quantifier ∃x.
(2) (My → Ny) is a propositional function obtained from the wff ∀y(My → Ny) by deleting the quantifier ∀y.
(3) [xMy → Nx] is a propositional function obtained from the wff ∃x∀y[xMy → Nx] by deleting the quantifiers ∃x and ∀y.
(4) ∀z(Mz ∨ xNb) is a propositional function obtained from the wff ∃x∀z(Mz ∨ xNb) by deleting the quantifier ∃x.

We used the notion of a propositional function, it will be remembered, in stating our rules of inference for predicate logic. We could have stated them without it, though, at the cost of a little elegance. But where the notion of a propositional function is really useful is in helping to clarify the idea of quantifier scope:

The scope of a quantifier in variable x is the shortest propositional function immediately following the quantifier that is not itself immediately followed by either a variable or a name.

Thus the scope of ∃x in ∃xGx → Gh is just Gx; whereas the scope of ∀x in ∀x(Gx → Gh) is (Gx → Gh). The reason for this is that ∀x(Gx → Gh) is a wff by the application of clause (iv) last, making it a universal quantification, and thus making (Gx → Gh) the shortest propositional function in x following the quantifier. '∀x(Gx' is not a wff, so '(Gx' is not a propositional function. It now clearly follows from these definitions that

> **A formula is a wff only if each variable in it occurs within the scope of a quantifier in the same variable.**

We may rephrase this by giving the definitions of *free* and *bound* variables promised earlier:

> **A variable x occurring within the scope of a quantifier ∀x or ∃x is said to be *bound* by the corresponding quantifier.**

and

> **A variable x not occurring within the scope of any quantifier is said to be *free*.**

Thus any formula in which a variable occurs free—e.g., a propositional function—is not a wff. Again, no variable in a wff can be bound by more than one quantifier.

EXERCISES 19.3

21. *Identify which of the following formulas are wffs*, giving a brief explanation for your answer. E.g., (An & Bm); ANSWER: wff by clauses (iii) and (i). E.g., ∀y[(Ax & Px) → ¬Dy]; ANSWER: not a wff because x is not bound by a quantifier in x.
    (a) ¬¬¬Ba
    (b) Oa ¬ Ob
    (c) ∃x(Lx)
    (d) ∃zQz
    (e) ∀xAg
    (f) ∀x(Rx → Rs)
    (g) ∀xIx → Tx
    (h) A_G ∨ B_G
    (i) (Ae ↔ ∀xRx)
    (j) ∃x(Bx → ¬∀xQx)
    (k) (Bx & Px) ∨ ¬Dx
    (l) (∀x)Ag
    (m) ∃x(Ax & Px) → ¬Qx)

22. *Which of the following are propositional functions, according to the above definition?*
    (a) Px
    (b) (Rx ∨ ¬Qx)
    (c) (Pa & ¬Qa)
    (d) (Ba → Cx)

(e) (Mx → Nx)
(f) (Mi → Ni)
(g) ∀y[Fx → Gay]
(h) ∃y(Fxy → Gx)
(i) (Mx ↔ xNb)
(j) (Mx ↔ Nz)

23. (**CHALLENGE**) *Identify the scope of the quantifier ∃x in each of the following wffs:*
(a) ∃y(By → ¬∃xQx)
(b) ∃x[(Ax & Px) → ¬Qx]
(c) ∃x(Rx → Rs)

Chapter Twenty

Relational Logic

20.1.1 RELATIONS

Consider the argument:

(1) Earth is bigger than Venus, but Venus is bigger than Mars. So Earth is certainly bigger than Mars.

Assuming the premises are true, there is no way for the conclusion to be false. Thus the argument is definitely valid. But how could we represent this using predicate logic? If we represent 'Earth' by the individual name **e**, and 'bigger than Venus' by the predicate **V**, then the first premise is **Ve**. Similarly, in the second premise, **v** can denote 'Venus,' but now 'bigger than Mars' is a different predicate than in the first premise, which we must represent with a different letter, **M**, giving **Mv**. But now the conclusion comes out as **Me**, yielding the symbolization:

(F1) Ve & Mv ∴ Me

The problem is, of course, that what accounts for the validity of the inference is not the repetition of the predicate **M**, but that of the phrase "is bigger than," occurring in all three statements, linking together different *pairs of individuals*. Predicates of this kind that link two or more individuals are called *relations*. In this case, then, we can symbolize "is bigger than" by B, a predicate relating two names, and our two premises become eBv, vBm, and the argument is symbolized as:

(F2) eBv & vBm ∴ eBm

321

This appears to capture the form. If we substitute another relation for B, say "is the brother of," and interpret **e**, **v**, and **m** as Harpo, Chico, and Groucho respectively, we get the valid argument:

(2) Harpo is Chico's brother, but Chico is Groucho's brother. Therefore Harpo is Groucho's brother.

But here's a problem: what if we interpret B as "is the son of"? Then we would get, applying this to the Darwins: Charles, Robert, and Erasmus:

(3) Charles Darwin is Robert Darwin's son, but Robert Darwin is Erasmus Darwin's son. Therefore Charles is Erasmus Darwin's son.

But this is invalid! The premises are true, but the conclusion is false: Charles should be (and was) Erasmus's *grandson*, not his son. What's gone wrong? The problem is this. The Marx brothers[1] argument's validity depends on a property of the relation "is bigger than," a property it shares with the relation "is the brother of": namely that if the relation holds between x and y, and between y and z, then it must hold between x and z. This is the property of *transitivity*. Formally, we may represent it by:

(F3) $\forall x \forall y \forall z \ \{(xBy \ \& \ yBz) \rightarrow xBz\}$

It is this property that is not shared by the relation "is the son of." So the validity of the arguments (1) and (2) depends on this property implicitly, and it has to be made explicit in the formalization of the argument:

(F2') $eBv \ \& \ vBm, \ \forall x \forall y \forall z \{(xBy \ \& \ yBz) \rightarrow xBz\} \ \therefore \ eBm$

The validity of this argument may now be proved without having to add any new rules of inference to those we have learned so far, but simply by extending predicate logic to apply also to relations. (Our formalization of wffs in chapter 19 already anticipated this extension.) Here is the proof:

(1) $eBv \ \& \ vBm$ Prem

(2) $\forall x \forall y \forall z \ \{(xBy \ \& \ yBz) \rightarrow xBz\}$ Prem .

(3) $\forall y \forall z \ \{(eBy \ \& \ yBz) \rightarrow eBz\}$ 2 UI   *—instantiating **e** for **x***

(4) $\forall z \ \{(eBv \ \& \ vBz) \rightarrow eBz\}$ 3 UI   *—instantiating **v** for **y***

---

[1] For the record there were five Marx brothers: "Chico" (Leonard Marx: 1887-1961), "Harpo" (Adolf Marx: 1888-1964), "Groucho" (Julius Marx: 1890-1977), "Gummo" (Milton Marx: 1897-1977), and "Zeppo" (Herbert Marx: 1901-79).

(5) (eBv & vBm) → eBm   4 UI   —*instantiating **m** for **z***
(6) eBm   1, 5 MP

20.1.2 SYMBOLIZING RELATIONS

The above relations were each between two individuals, and indeed these are the most common kind. Such relations are called *dyadic predicates*, from the Greek for two, or *binary relations* (from the Latin for two), in contrast to the ones we have been dealing with up till now, *monadic* or *unary* predicates involving one individual. Symbolizations of such predicates will be suggested by capitalizing as usual, but by adding a suffixed subscript$_2$ to denote that they are dyadic (binary), thus:

Abbie is TALLER$_2$ than Duncan.   **aTd**

There are relations among more than two individuals, such as something's being between two things. We denote a tryadic relation with a subscript$_3$ and so on:

Montreal is BETWEEN$_3$ Quebec City and Toronto.   **mBqt**

Also, we adopt the convention that all relations in the passive mood are re-expressed in the active mood before symbolizing. Thus

Maria is LOVED$_2$ by Carlos.

is interpreted as the equivalent statement in active mood:

Carlos LOVES$_2$ Maria.   **cLm**

Here's a less boring example from Groucho Marx (*Horse Feathers*, 1932):

(4) Whatever it is, I'm AGAINST$_2$ it.

Taking g = Groucho, we have in "Loglish" that for all x, g is against x, giving

(F4) ∀x gAx

Noam Chomsky seems to be giving a variant on this joke when he tells John Horgan

(5) Whatever the ESTABLISHMENT is, I'm AGAINST$_2$ it.
(F5) ∀x(Ex → nAx)   [n := Noam Chomsky]

20.1.3 NESTED QUANTIFIERS

Even though the order of the quantifiers is not significant in a statement like (F3) above, which begins with three universal quantifiers, it can be. In fact, when we have a mix of existential and universal quantifications, their order is crucial. For example, suppose we have the statement

(6) Everyone NEEDS$_2$ someone.   (UD: people)

We can take the process of symbolization in two steps: "x needs someone" is "there is a y such that x needs y": $\exists y\ xNy$; and this is so for all x:

(F6) $\forall x\ \exists y\ xNy$

Thus here the universal quantifier has a scope of the propositional function to its right, $\exists y\ xNy$: there is someone x needs. The existential quantifier in y has as its scope "x needs y." On the other hand, the abstract statement

(F7) $\exists y\ \forall x\ xNy$

although it differs from (F6) only in the order of the quantifiers, it symbolizes a very different statement. Here $\exists y$ has as its scope the propositional function $\forall x\ xNy$, "everyone needs y." So the whole statement back-translates as "there is a y such that everyone needs y," i.e.,

(7) There is someone everyone NEEDS$_2$.

Whereas in (6) who the 'someone' is will generally differ in each case, (7) asserts the existence of some uniquely useful person whom everyone needs! And while (6) is possibly true, (7) is surely by contrast false. Make sure you understand why.

20.1.4 RELATIONAL PROOFS

Returning to our proof of the planet/brother argument with which we began this section, it would have been shorter (by two lines) had we been allowed to instantiate all three of the quantifiers (over **x**, **y**, and **z**) in one fell swoop:

(1) eBv & vBm	Prem
(2) $\forall x\ \forall y\ \forall z\{(xBy\ \&\ yBz) \rightarrow xBz\}$	Prem
(3) (eBv & vBm) $\rightarrow$ eBm	2 UI —*instantiating e, v, m for x, y, z*
(4) eBm	1, 3 MP

This is generally the case with proofs involving relational properties. So in applying proofs involving quantifiers, we allow a telescoping of successive applications of UI, so that they may be performed all in one go on one line. This is licensed by

Telescoped UI:
For any abstract statement beginning with several consecutive universal quantifiers $\forall x \, \forall y \, \forall z \ldots \Phi xyz \ldots$, successive applications of UI may be performed in order on a single line of proof.

In fact, it will prove convenient to telescope all the rules involving quantifiers for relational proofs in the same way:

Telescoped EI:
For any abstract statement beginning with several consecutive existential quantifiers $\exists x \, \exists y \, \exists z \ldots \Phi xyz \ldots$, successive applications of EI to distinct arbitrary names **i, j, k** respectively may be performed in order in a single line of proof.

Telescoped EG:
For any abstract statement involving several individual names **i, j, k**, successive applications of EG may be performed in order in a single line of proof.

Telescoped UG:
For any abstract statement involving several distinct arbitrary names **u, v, w**, successive applications of UG may be performed in order in a single line of proof.

Finally there is also the Quantifier Negation rule:

Telescoped QN:
For the negation of any abstract statement beginning with several consecutive quantifiers successive applications of QN may be performed in order on a single line of proof.
E.g., from $\neg \forall x \, \exists y \, \forall z \, \Phi xyz$, infer $\exists x \, \forall y \, \exists z \, \neg \Phi xyz$, and vice versa.

I call these rules "telescoped" to signify that you are applying them as usual (e.g., with all the usual restrictions on EI and UG), but one within the other. Here is an example of a proof using some of these telescoped rules:

(1) $\forall x \forall y \, xHy$	Prem	$\vdash \exists x \exists y \, (xHy \, \& \, yGx)$
(2) $\neg \forall x \forall y \, \neg xGy$	Prem	
(3) $\exists x \exists y \, \neg\neg xGy$	2 QN	
(4) $\exists x \exists y \, xGy$	3 DN	

(5) iGj	4 EI
(6) jHi	1 UI
(7) jHi & iGj	6, 5 Conj
(8) ∃x∃y (xHy & yGx)	7 EG

Notice that in applying EI on line 5, we had to take two different names, **i** and **j**, just as we would if we had done the rule on 2 separate lines. On line 6 I can choose any names for instances of UI, so I choose **j** and **i** in that order just because I have looked ahead to the conclusion and see that I need an instance like jHi & iGj in order to get the conclusion by EG.

SUMMARY

- **Relations** are predicates linking together more than one individual, **polyadic predicates**. Most relations are **dyadic** or **binary**, linking together two individuals. An example is "is greater than" in the statement "<u>Four</u> is GREATER$_2$ than <u>three</u>," symbolized **fGt**. (The subscript $_2$ indicates that it is a binary relation.)
- We adopt the convention that all relations in the passive mood are re-expressed in the active mood before symbolizing: "<u>Maria</u> is LOVED$_2$ by <u>Carlos</u>" becomes "<u>Carlos</u> LOVES$_2$ <u>Maria</u>," symbolized **cLm**.
- The order of quantifiers can be crucial: "Everybody LOVES$_2$ somebody" (∀x∃y xLy) is a very different proposition than "There is somebody who is loved by everybody" (∃y∀x xLy).
- The **telescoped rules of inference** allow successive applications of the predicate logic rules UI, EI, EG, UG, and QN to be performed in order in a single line of proof.

EXERCISES 20.1

1. *Symbolize the following statements* [UD: planets]:
    (a) <u>Jupiter</u> is BIGGER$_2$ than <u>Saturn</u>.
    (b) There is a planet BIGGER$_2$ than <u>Saturn</u>.
    (c) <u>Jupiter</u> is BIGGER$_2$ than at least one planet.
    (d) No planet is BIGGER$_2$ than itself.
    (e) Not all planets are BIGGER$_2$ than <u>Mars</u>.
    (f) If <u>Mars</u> is BIGGER$_2$ than <u>Pluto</u>, then not all planets are BIGGER$_2$ than <u>Mars</u>.

2. *Using the symbolizations suggested,* **translate (a) through (c) from English into Relational Logic**, *and then use the same interpretations of the symbols to* **render (d) through (f) from Relational Logic into colloquial English**:

(a) No one LOVES$_2$ him- or herself. [UD: people; Lxy := x loves y]
(b) Everybody loves somebody.
(c) No one loves everybody.
(d) ∃x∀y xLy
(e) ∃x∀y yLx
(f) ∀x∃y (Lxy & ¬Lyx)

3. "One morning, I shot an elephant in my pajamas. How an elephant got into my pajamas I'll never know." (Groucho Marx in *Animal Crackers*, 1930) (Another problem in the "ruin a joke by analyzing it" series.) *Show how Groucho's joke trades on an amphiboly* (a sentence ambiguous because of its construction) *by giving the two alternative symbolizations of the first sentence on which the joke depends.* [g := Groucho (i.e., 'I'), xSy := x shot y, Ex := x is an elephant, Px := x is in my pajamas; ignore the "one morning"]

Use the telescoped quantification rules of inference to prove the following sequents:

4. ∀x∀y xFy ⊢ ∃x∃y xFy

5. ¬∃x∃y xFy ⊢ ¬∀x∀y xFy

6. ∀x∀y(xFy & yFx) ⊢ ¬∀x∀y ¬xFy

20.2 PROPERTIES OF BINARY RELATIONS

20.2.1 TRANSITIVITY, SYMMETRY, AND REFLEXIVITY

We saw in the previous section that the relations of 'being BIGGER$_2$ than' and of 'being a BROTHER$_2$ of' have the property of *transitivity*. 'Being FATHER$_2$ of,' on the other hand, lacked this property. In fact, if Erasmus is the father of Robert and Robert is the father of Charles, we are able to infer that Erasmus is NOT the father of Charles. A relation having this property is said to be *intransitive*. Symbolically:

(F8) ∀x∀y∀z {(xFy & yFz) → ¬xFz}

Using this fact of the intransitivity of the relation of 'being FATHER$_2$ of,' we can symbolize and prove the inference as follows:

eFr & rFc, ∀x∀y∀z {(xFy & yFz) → ¬xFz} ⊢ ¬eFc

(1) eFr & rFc	Prem	
(2) ∀x∀y∀z {(xFy & yFz) → ¬xFz}	Prem	
(3) (eFr & rFc) → ¬eFc	2 UI	—*instantiating e, r, c for x, y, z*
(4) ¬eFc	1, 3 MP	

Not all binary relations are either transitive or intransitive, however. Consider the relation of 'being $EAST_2$ of,' applied to cities. If Moscow is to the east of Reykjavik, and Reykjavik is east of Montreal, then Moscow is east of Montreal. But Tokyo lies east of Paris, and Paris is east of Seattle, yet Tokyo is west (by our usual conventions), not east, of Seattle. So for some triples of cities 'being east of' appears to be transitive, for other triples it is not. A relation of this kind is said to be *nontransitive* on its domain or UD:

(F9) ∃x∃y∃z{(xRy & yRz) & xRz} & ∃x∃y∃z{(xRy & yRz) & ¬xRz}

It is the same with the relations "is afraid of" and "seeks advice from" on people, "is four miles away from" applied to places, and a host of others. There are, however, no other possibilities. A binary relation is either transitive, intransitive, or neither, and in that case nontransitive. We may represent this family of properties in a table:

TRANSITIVITY:	∀x∀y∀z{(xRy & yRz) → xRz}
INTRANSITIVITY:	∀x∀y∀z {(xRy & yRz) → ¬xRz}
NONTRANSITIVITY:	∃x∃y∃z{(xRy & yRz) & xRz} & ∃x∃y∃z{(xRy & yRz) & ¬xRz}

A second property of the relation "is the brother of" is that it is symmetric: if Harpo is the brother of Gummo, then Gummo is the brother of Harpo, and so for all brothers:

(F10) ∀x∀y (xBy → yBx)

Again, this is not shared by "is the father of," nor "is the mother of." Minnie Schoenberg Marx is the mother of Chico, but if that is so, Chico is not Minnie's mother; and so for any other pair of individuals:

(F11) ∀x∀y (xMy → ¬yMx)

This is called *asymmetry*. Other examples of asymmetric relations are "is earlier than" on events, "is greater than," and "is to the north of" for places on the Earth's surface. But again, there are relations that are neither: e.g., "is less than or equal to" on the domain of rational numbers: $3/3 \leq 1$ and $1 \leq 3/3$, whereas $1/2 \leq 1$ but it's not the case that $1 \leq 1/2$. Here is the symmetry family:

SYMMETRY:	$\forall x \forall y (xRy \rightarrow yRx)$
ASYMMETRY:	$\forall x \forall y (xRy \rightarrow \neg yRx)$
NONSYMMETRY:	$\exists x \exists y (xRy \,\&\, yRx) \,\&\, \exists x \exists y (xRy \,\&\, \neg yRx)$

Some relations are such that every individual in the domain bears the relation to itself: such a relation is said to be *reflexive*. Examples are mostly relations of identity and equality: "is the same height as," "is equal to," "is as smart as," "is simultaneous with" (on events in classical physics), "implication" on the domain of statements. Many others are irreflexive on their domain: "is the brother of" on male siblings, and "is the sister of" on female siblings, are both examples, since no one is his own brother or her own sister. Others still are neither: some doctors may treat themselves, and some may not. This gives us a third family of relational properties, the reflexivity family:

REFLEXIVITY:	$\forall x \; xRx$
IRREFLEXIVITY:	$\forall x \; \neg xRx$
NONREFLEXIVITY:	$\exists x \; xRx \,\&\, \exists y \; \neg yRy$

Every binary relation can be classified according to these families, since it must have (at least) one property from each table. Not all these properties are independent, though. For example, every asymmetric relation is irreflexive, as you will prove in the exercises, and no relation can be intransitive and reflexive. The latter can be proved by showing that simultaneously asserting the two properties of a relation leads to contradiction. The proof will give us another example of the use of our telescoped UI:

(1) $\forall x \forall y \forall z \{(xRy \,\&\, yRz) \rightarrow \neg xRz\}$	Prem	
(2) $\forall x \; xRx$	Prem	
(3) $(aRa \,\&\, aRa) \rightarrow \neg aRa$	1 UI	*—no restrictions on UI!*
(4) aRa	2 UI	
(5) $\neg\neg aRa$	4 DN	
(6) $\neg(aRa \,\&\, aRa)$	3, 5 MT	
(7) $\neg aRa$	4, 6 CS	
(8) $\perp$	4, 7 Conj	

20.2.2 EQUIVALENCE RELATIONS

Of particular interest are relations that are *transitive*, *reflexive*, and *symmetric*. In fact, these are important enough to be given their own name:

An ***EQUIVALENCE RELATION*** is a relation that is *transitive*, *reflexive*, and *symmetric*.

The class of all individuals standing in an equivalence relation to one another is called an **EQUIVALENCE CLASS**.

These relations are particularly efficacious in clearing up controversies about what is meant by certain terms. A very early example occurs in Euclid's elements. To explicate what he meant by the term *ratio* of magnitudes he set out certain conditions that must be satisfied for one pair of magnitudes to have *the same ratio* as another (*Elements*, V, 5). Taking his cue from this, Leibniz, in his famous correspondence with Clarke, attempted to throw light on the concept of place by explicating what is meant by one body being *at the same place* as another. A body A has certain relations of situation to all bodies co-existing with it. Supposing some subset of these (C, E, F, G, etc.) maintain the same relation among themselves for a given time, a second body B can be said to be *in the same place as A* iff it has the same relations of situation with C, E, F, G, etc. that A formerly had. "*Place*," says Leibniz, "is that which is said to be the same for A and for B, when the relation of co-existence between B and C, E, F, G, etc. entirely agrees with the relation of co-existence that A previously had with those bodies, supposing there to have been no cause of change in C, E, F, G, etc." Given this, it clearly follows that if any body A is in the same place as a body B, and B is in the same place as C, then A is in the same place as C (*transitivity*); if A is in the same place as a B, then B is in the same place as A (*symmetry*), and every body is in the same place as itself (*reflexivity*). Thus *being in the same place as* is an equivalence relation. Since the class of all individuals standing in an equivalence relation to one another is an *equivalence class*, Leibniz has in effect defined place as an equivalence class of all bodies standing in this relation of sameness of place to one another.

Gottfried Leibniz (1646-1716) was a German philosopher noted for his invention of the differential calculus (independently of Newton), his relational theories of space and time, and his metaphysics of monads. Although he did not publish them, he devised several symbolic systems for logic, clearly defining conjunction, disjunction, negation, identity, and anticipating De Morgan's Laws and much of Boolean algebra.

Equivalence relations have the interesting effect of dividing up the domain of individuals in question. Supposing we arrange all members of a given class of students by putting together each of those born in the same month. (As you can easily verify for yourself, "being born in the same month as" is an equivalence relation.) Each subset will be an equivalence class of students under this relation; some may be empty, some may have only one member, some may have many. Notice that these subsets themselves will be orderable: the subset of all those born in September of a given year, say, will precede that of all those born in October of the same year, just because all members of the September subset will be OLDER$_2$ than all those of the October one. We will return to the notion of orderings in the next chapter.

SUMMARY

- There are three main families of properties of binary relations: the **transitivity** family, the **symmetry** family, and the **reflexivity** family.
- A binary relation may be **transitive** [$\forall x \forall y \forall z \{(xRy \ \& \ yRz) \to xRz\}$], **intransitive** [$\forall x \forall y \forall z \{(xRy \ \& \ yRz) \to \neg xRz\}$], or **nontransitive** [$\exists x \exists y \exists z \{(xRy \ \& \ yRz) \ \& \ xRz\} \ \& \ \exists x \exists y \exists z \{(xRy \ \& \ yRz) \ \& \ \neg xRz\}$].
- A binary relation may be **symmetric** [$\forall x \forall y (xRy \to yRx)$], **asymmetric** [$\forall x \forall y (xRy \to \neg yRx)$], or **nonsymmetric** [$\exists x \exists y (xRy \ \& \ yRx) \ \& \ \exists x \exists y (xRy \ \& \ \neg yRx)$].
- A binary relation may be **reflexive** [$\forall x \ xRx$], **irreflexive** [$\forall x \ \neg xRx$], or **nonreflexive** [$\exists x \ xRx \ \& \ \exists y \ \neg yRy$].
- An **equivalence relation** is one that is **transitive, symmetric,** and **reflexive**. The class of all individuals standing in an equivalence relation to one another is called an **equivalence class**.

EXERCISES 20.2

7. *On the domain (UD) of natural numbers, only one of the following relations is intransitive. Which?*
(a) 'is GREATER$_2$ than'; (b) 'is EQUAL$_2$ to'; (c) 'is greater than OR$_2$ equal to'; (d) 'is the immediate SUCCESSOR$_2$ of'; (e) 'is LESS$_2$ than.'

8. *State whether each of the following relations is (i) symmetric, (ii) asymmetric, or (iii) nonsymmetric on the domain (UD) in question:*
(a) 'is GREATER$_2$ than' (UD: natural numbers); (b) 'is SISTER$_2$ of' (UD: siblings); (c) 'is SISTER$_2$ of' (UD: the Andrews sisters); (d) 'is EQUAL$_2$ to' (UD: natural numbers); (e) 'is GREATER$_2$ than or equal to' (UD: the four rational numbers 1/2, 1, 2/2, 2/1).

9. *State whether each of the following relations is (i) reflexive, (ii) irreflexive, or (iii) nonreflexive on the domain (UD) in question:*
(a) 'is GREATER$_2$ than' (UD: natural numbers); (b) 'is BROTHER$_2$ of' (UD: the Marx brothers); (c) 'is genetically RELATED$_2$ to' (UD: people); (d) 'LOOKS$_2$ after' (UD: people).

Prove the formal validity of each of arguments 10-13. Some depend for their validity on a property or properties of the relation involved. In those cases you will need to treat those properties as implicit premises that must be included in the symbolization of the argument:

10. Mars must be SMALLER$_2$ than Earth, since Mars is smaller than Venus, and Venus is smaller than Earth. [UD: planets]

11. Three is EQUAL$_2$ to the square root of nine, and pi does not equal three. So the square root of nine does not equal pi. [UD: numbers]

12. Shaquille O'Neal is not TALLER$_2$ than everyone on his team, since he is not taller than himself. [UD: players on Shaquille's team]

13. Vancouver is NORTH$_2$ of Seattle, which is north of Chicago. So Chicago is not north of Vancouver. [UD: cities]

14. *Prove that any binary relation* R *that is neither* reflexive *nor* irreflexive *must be* non-reflexive.

15. *Prove that any binary relation* R *that is* asymmetric *is also* irreflexive.

16. *The relation 'is the* FATHER$_2$ *of' is* intransitive. *Prove that from this property alone it follows that it is* irreflexive.

17. *Prove that if a relation* R *does not hold on any pair of individuals in a domain, then the relation is* symmetric: *i.e., prove* $\forall x \forall y \ \neg xRy \vdash \forall x \forall y (xRy \rightarrow yRx)$.

18. *Prove that any binary relation* R *that is* irreflexive *and* transitive *is* asymmetric.

19. *Prove that no binary relation* R *can be* transitive, nonsymmetric, *and* irreflexive, *i.e., show that these properties are inconsistent.*

A binary relation R is said to be *Euclidean* iff $\forall x \forall y \forall z \ \{(xRy \ \& \ xRz) \rightarrow yRz\}$.
A binary relation R is said to be *serial* iff $\forall x \exists y \ xRy$.
A binary relation R is said to be *partially reflexive* iff $\forall x [\exists y (xRy \ v \ yRx) \rightarrow xRx]$.

20. *Prove that any* symmetric *and* transitive *relation* R *is also* Euclidean.

21. *Prove that any* reflexive *and* Euclidean *relation* R *is also* symmetric.

22. (**CHALLENGE**) *Prove that any* reflexive *and* Euclidean *relation* R *is also* transitive.

23. (**CHALLENGE**) *What do the results of 20-22 tell you about a relation* R *that is* Euclidean *and also* reflexive*?*

24. (**CHALLENGE**) *Prove that any* symmetric, Euclidean, *and* serial *relation* R *is also* reflexive.

25. (**CHALLENGE**) *Prove that any* symmetric, transitive, *and* serial *relation* R *is also* reflexive.

26. (**CHALLENGE**) *Prove that any* transitive *and* symmetric *relation* R *is* partially reflexive.

Chapter Twenty-One

Logic with Identity

21.1.1 SYMBOLIZING IDENTITIES AND QUANTITIES

Consider the following argument:

> It is not true that no famous AUTHORS like LOGIC. Charles <u>Dodgson</u> certainly likes logic. And Lewis <u>Carroll</u> is a famous author. But Lewis Carroll and Charles Dodgson are one and the same person.

The last statement could also be expressed:

> Lewis Carroll *is* Charles Dodgson.

But the 'is' here has a different status from the 'is' in the previous statement, "Lewis Carroll is a famous AUTHOR." For this is just the "**is of predication**," and we symbolize this statement Ac. In contrast, the 'is' in the last statement is the "**is of identity**": it expresses the fact that the two names Carroll and Dodgson refer to one and the same individual. Using an obvious notation, we express this identity of Carroll and Dodgson by

c = d

Some other examples:

<u>Santorini</u> and <u>Thera</u> are one and the same island.   s = t
The philosopher <u>Cicero</u> is the same person as the statesman <u>Tully</u>.   c = t
<u>Superman</u> is Clark <u>Kent</u>.   s = k

Likewise we can express non-identity or distinctness:

Stephen <u>Harper</u> is not Pierre <u>Trudeau</u>. $\neg h = t$

Note that the '$\neg$' in '$\neg h = t$' negates the statement $h = t$—it does not negate h, which would be meaningless (unless perhaps Stephen Harper is a non-entity, but we won't go into politics here). '$\neg$' is a unary statement operator. '$\neg h = t$' can be thought of as '$\neg(h = t)$,' though it isn't written that way (remember, parentheses only get introduced along with the binary statement operators). We may also write $\neg h = t$ as $h \neq t$. Thus

Clark <u>Kent</u> is not <u>Batman</u>. $\neg k = b$
or $k \neq b$
<u>Pi</u> is not the Golden <u>Mean</u>. $\neg p = m$
or $p \neq m$

Actually, identity is a **relation** between individuals (more precisely, the same individual under two different names), and we considered the logic of relations in the previous chapter. In fact, we could have symbolized "x is identical to y" by xIy, and "x is distinct from y" by $\neg$xIy; and we will see in due course that this relation is an equivalence relation. But the relation of identity is a special case, because in making valid inferences like the Carroll-Dodgson one above we depend on being able to substitute one individual name for another denoting the same individual. For this we will introduce a rule of inference governing how we reason about questions of identity. But we will postpone treatment of that topic to the next section.

Using this new notation, we will now show how to treat various kinds of statements that do not obviously involve identity, especially those concerning how many individuals of a particular type there are. Let's treat them on a case-by-case basis.

Only i ...
Only Yogi <u>Berra</u> would SAY that. [UD: people; Sx := would say that]

$Sb \,\&\, \forall x\{Sx \to x = b\}$

Analysis: Yogi Berra would say that, and anyone who said it would be him.

The only i ..., None but i ...
The only person who can SPEAK for all Canadians is Pierre <u>Trudeau</u>. [UD: people; Sx := can speak for all Canadians]

$St \,\&\, \forall x\{Sx \to x = t\}$

Analysis: Pierre Trudeau can speak for all Canadians, and anyone who can speak for all Canadians is Trudeau. The same symbolization takes care of

No one but Pierre <u>Trudeau</u> can SPEAK for all Canadians.

A slightly harder example involving a binary relation:

<u>Jung</u> is the only PSYCHIATRIST who TREATED$_2$ <u>Freud</u>. [UD: people]
(Pj & jTf) & $\forall$x[(Px & xTf) → x = j]

All except i...

All the network news anchors were AMERICAN except for Peter <u>Jennings</u>. [UD: network news anchors]

$\forall$x{x $\neq$ j → Ax} & $\neg$Aj

Analysis: Any network news anchor who was not Peter Jennings was American, and Peter Jennings was not American.

Superlatives

The LARGEST$_2$ planet is Jupiter. [UD: planets; xLy := x is larger than y]

$\forall$x(x $\neq$ j → jLx)

Analysis: Jupiter is larger than any planet except itself.

Note that if the UD were not restricted to planets, and instead we had Px := x is a planet, the symbolization would have been:

Pj & $\forall$x[(Px & x $\neq$ j) → jLx]
Analysis: Jupiter is a planet, and it is larger than any planet different from it.

There is no GREATEST prime number. [UD: prime numbers; xGy := x is greater than y]
$\forall$x $\exists$y[y $\neq$ x → yGx]
Analysis: For any prime x there exists at least one prime number y distinct from it that is greater than it.

Another example:

There is a LEAST positive integer. [UD positive integers; xLy := x is less than y]

$\exists$x $\forall$y{y $\neq$ x → xLy}

Analysis: There exists a positive integer x which is less than any positive integer y distinct from it.

Notice the crucial difference from the previous example in the order of the quantifiers. Notice, too, that if we had tried to symbolize it without identity, by

∃x∀y xLy

this would not do, since it would allow the deduction of iLi for some arbitrary integer i. But no integer can be less than itself.

At least one, two, ...
There is at least one EVEN prime. [UD: primes]

∃x Ex

Analysis: This is just our standard interpretation of the existential quantifier: 'some' means 'at least one.'

There are at least two HUMAN species. [UD: species]

∃x∃y{(Hx & Hy) & y ≠ x}

Analysis: There is at least one human species x, and at least one human species y, such that y is distinct from x.

At most one, two, ...
There is at most one EVEN prime. [UD: primes]

∀x∀y{(Ex & Ey) → x = y}

Analysis: For any primes x and y, if they are both even then x is identical to y.

There are at most two HUMAN species. [UD: species]

∀x∀y∀z{[(Hx & Hy) & Hz] → z = x ∨ z = y}

Analysis: For any species x, y, and z, if they are all human species, then z is either the same as x or the same as y.

Exactly one, two, ...
There is exactly one EVEN prime. [UD: primes]

∃x{Ex & ∀y(Ey → y = x)}

Analysis: There is at least one even prime x, such that any even prime y is identical to x.

Notice that this is just a more succinct formulation than what we would get by conjoining the symbolizations of 'there is at least one' and 'there is at most one':

∃xEx & ∀x∀y{(Ex & Ey) → x = y}

There are exactly two HUMAN species. [UD: species]

∃x∃y{[(Hx & Hy) & y ≠ x] & ∀z[Hz → (z = x ∨ z = y)]}

Analysis: There are two distinct human species x and y such that any human species z will be identical either with x or with y.

Notice that this is just a more succinct formulation than what we would get by conjoining the symbolizations of 'there are at least two' and 'there are at most two':

∃x∃y{(Hx & Hy) & y ≠ x} & ∀x∀y∀z {[(Hx & Hy) & Hz] → z = x ∨ z = y}

As can be seen, the above analysis can in principle be applied to any statement of the form "There are exactly *n* objects" where *n* is any natural number. Even though it is already looking fearsomely complicated for *n* > 2, the fact that it is possible in principle has suggested to some philosophers that by means such as this, mathematics could be reduced to logic. You can always eliminate the reference to *n* in the statement "There are exactly *n* objects." But there are difficulties; it is not obvious how to eliminate the references to numbers when they appear as individual names rather than adjectives, in statements such as '5 is prime.' Still, this discussion is an example of the potential of mathematical logic to contribute to philosophical analysis.

21.1.2 RUSSELL'S THEORY OF DEFINITE DESCRIPTIONS

Bertrand Russell (1872-1970) was one of the most influential philosophers of the twentieth century, publishing widely on politics, metaphysics, theory of knowledge, and mathematical logic. Born into a British aristocratic family, he was a social activist with radical views on morality and education. He was also an accomplished essayist, winning the Nobel Prize for literature in 1950. His classic works in logic are *Principles of Mathematics* (1903) and, with Alfred North Whitehead, *Principia Mathematica* (1910-13).

Bertrand Russell was one of the foremost champions of the "logicist" approach to the foundations of mathematics, the attempt to reduce all mathematics to logic and set theory.

So it is no accident that he was also one of the pioneers of the merits of quantificational logic for the analysis of problems in philosophy, particularly ones that seemed to depend on some linguistic formulation. In particular, Russell was the first to analyze sentences called *definite descriptions*. These are so called because they begin with a definite article—'the' in English—which picks out an individual by the accompanying description. An example would be:

The CARDINAL who OPPOSED Galileo was <u>Bellarmine</u>.

If we try to symbolize this by Cb & Ob (Cx := x was a Cardinal, Ox := x opposed Galileo), this fails to distinguish it from

<u>Bellarmine</u> was a CARDINAL who OPPOSED Galileo.

What we have failed to capture here is the uniqueness implicit in the definite article: the original statement connotes not only that Bellarmine was *a* Cardinal who opposed Galileo, but that he was the unique one (in some respect) who did so. Russell's famous example of a definite description was:

The present KING of France is BALD.

Russell's way of bringing out the logic of such sentences is to use the identity relation to capture uniqueness. On his view, the statement connotes that there is a present King of France, that there is only one such King, and he is bald. Thus he parses it as follows:

$\exists x\{(Kx \,\&\, Bx) \,\&\, \forall y(Ky \rightarrow y = x)\}$ [UD: (presently) living people]

Analysis: "There is a living person who is King of France and bald, and such that any living person we pick who is king will be that same person."

Using this kind of analysis, our original statement about Bellarmine,

The CARDINAL who OPPOSED Galileo was <u>Bellarmine</u>.

is symbolized

$(Cb \,\&\, Ob) \,\&\, \forall y[(Cy \,\&\, Oy) \rightarrow y = b]$

Analysis: "Bellarmine was a Cardinal who opposed Galileo, and any Cardinal who opposed Galileo was he."

A word of warning: not every statement beginning with the definite article is a definite description. We have already seen and dealt with examples like this:

The CARDINAL is a bird with a RED breast. (UD: birds, not clergymen!)

This is not referring to some unique cardinal, but to all birds that are cardinals. The 'is' is an 'is' of predication, giving

$$\forall x(Cx \rightarrow Rx)$$

Also some definite descriptions in English lack the definite article. For example,

Liza Minelli's MOTHER$_2$ is Judy Garland.

This means *the* person who is MOTHER$_2$ of Liza Minelli is Judy Garland, yielding

$$jMl \ \& \ \forall x(xMl \rightarrow x = j)$$

SUMMARY

- The "**is of identity**" expresses the fact that two individual names, say Carroll and Dodgson, refer to one and the same individual: $c = d$.
- If 2 individual names, say Batman and Clark Kent, refer to distinct, i.e., non-identical individuals, this is symbolized $b \neq k$, which is short for $\neg b = k$.
- "Only b is S" is symbolized $Sb \ \& \ \forall x(Sx \rightarrow x = b)$.
- "Everyone except j is an A" is symbolized $\forall x\{ x \neq j \rightarrow Ax \} \ \& \ \neg Aj$. [UD: people]
- "Jupiter is the largest planet" is symbolized $\forall x (x \neq j \rightarrow jLx)$. [UD: planets]
- "There is a LEAST positive integer": $\exists x \forall y \{ y \neq x \rightarrow xLy \}$. [xLy := x is less than y]
- "There are at least two FIRETRUCKS here": $\exists x \exists y \{(Fx \ \& \ Fy) \ \& \ y \neq x\}$.
- "There is exactly one EVEN prime": $\exists x \{Ex \ \& \ \forall y(Ey \rightarrow y = x)\}$. [UD: primes]
- On Russell's analysis of definite descriptions, "The present king of France is bald" is symbolized $\exists x \{(Kx \ \& \ Bx) \ \& \ \forall y(Ky \rightarrow y = x)\}$. The identity relation is used to capture the uniqueness of the individual picked out by the definite article 'the.'

EXERCISES 21.1

Symbolize the following statements:

1. (a) Superman is Clark Kent.
   (b) Francis Bacon is not Roger Bacon.

(c) Christopher <u>Marlowe</u> was <u>Shakespeare</u>.

(d) D.H. Lawrence was not Lawrence of Arabia. [d := D.H. Lawrence, a := Lawrence of Arabia]

2. Only <u>Saddam</u> would KILL his own sons-in-law. [UD: people; Kx := would kill his own sons-in-law]

3. All except <u>Einstein</u> had COMBED their hair. [UD: people; Cx := x had combed his or her hair]

4. <u>Paul</u> and <u>Ringo</u> are the only Beatles still ALIVE. [UD: Beatles]

5. There is only one GOD. [Gx := x is a god]

6. Nothing PRECEDED$_2$ the Big <u>Bang</u>. [UD: events]

7. <u>Everest</u> is not the TALLEST$_2$ mountain. [UD: mountains; xTy := x is taller than y]

8. George <u>Best</u> was the most SKILFUL$_2$ soccer player ever born in the <u>UK</u>. [UD: soccer players; Ux := x was born in the UK; xSy := x is more skilful at soccer than y]

9. There is no more POPULAR$_2$ RESTAURANT in the universe than the Big Bang <u>Burger</u> Bar. [xPy := x is more popular than y]

10. There's at least one ODD PRIME. [Ox := x is odd, Px := x is prime]

11. At most one SIGHTING of the Loch Ness Monster can be VERIFIED. [Sx := x is a sighting of the Loch Ness Monster, Vx := x can be verified]

12. If there are more than two PEOPLE, there's a CROWD. [Px := x is a person]

13. <u>Shaquille</u> O'Neal is TALLER$_2$ than everyone else on his team. [UD: the Lakers team; xTy := x is taller than y]

14. <u>Shaquille</u> O'Neal is the TALLEST$_2$ basketball player. [UD: basketball players; xTy := x is taller than y]

15. The MOUSE over there is SMALL.

16. He's the HORSE that EATS a lot. [Ex := x eats a lot]

17. The only cowboy FASTER$_2$ than <u>Doc</u> Holliday is the <u>Kid</u>. [UD: cowboys: xFy = x is faster than y]

18. (**CHALLENGE**) The CAT SAT$_2$ on the MAT. [xSy := x sat on y]

21.2 INFERENCES INVOLVING IDENTITY

21.2.1 THE RULE OF INFERENCE SI

Some arguments involving identity are provably valid without any addition to our rules of inference. Take, for instance, the following argument:

> The only person who can SPEAK for all Canadians is Pierre <u>Trudeau</u>. Stephen <u>Harper</u>, you are no Pierre Trudeau. [UD: people; Sx := x can speak for all Canadians]

The inference we are expected to draw is that Stephen Harper cannot speak for all Canadians. This argument may be symbolized and proved as follows:

St & ∀x{Sx → x = t}, ¬h = t ∴¬Sh
(1) St & ∀x{Sx → x = t}   Prem
(2) ¬h = t   Prem
(3) St   1 Simp
(4) ∀x{Sx → x = t}   1 Simp
(5) Sh → h = t   4 UI
(6) ¬Sh   2, 5 MT

In fact, in order to tackle this example we did not need the special notation for identity either. We could have treated it as an ordinary relation, xIy := x is identical with y, and proceed as follows:

St & ∀x{Sx → xIt}, ¬hIt ∴¬Sh
(1) St & ∀x{Sx → xIt}   Prem
(2) ¬hIt   Prem
(3) St   1 Simp
(4) ∀x{Sx → xIt}   1 Simp
(5) Sh → hIt   4 UI
(6) ¬Sh   2, 5 MT

Other arguments, though, depend on the fact that if certain properties are true of a given individual **a**, and **a** is identical to another individual **b**, those properties must be true of **b** too. A good example is the argument with which we began the previous section:

It is not true that no famous AUTHORS like LOGIC. Charles <u>Dodgson</u> certainly likes logic. And Lewis <u>Carroll</u> is a famous author. But Lewis Carroll and Charles Dodgson are one and the same person.

Such arguments are impossible to prove valid without a new rule of inference legitimizing the above principle, which we formulate as:

> **Substitution of Identicals (SI)**
> If two individuals **i** and **k** are identical, then **k** can be substituted for **i** anywhere it occurs in any statement involving **i**:
> From **i = k**, Φ**i**, infer Φ**k**.
> e.g., from a = b, Sa → ¬aLc, infer Sb → ¬bLc.

This new rule may now be put to use in proving the above argument valid:

Ld, Ac, c = d ∴ ¬∀x(Ax → ¬Lx)

(1) Ld		Prem
(2) Ac		Prem
(3) c = d		Prem
	(4) ∀x(Ax → ¬Lx)	Supp/RA
	(5) Ac → ¬Lc	4 UI
	(6) ¬Lc	2, 5 MP
	(7) Lc	1, 3 SI
	(8) ⊥	7, 6 Conj
(9) ¬∀x(Ax → ¬Lx)		4-8 RA

This rule of inference is sometimes called "Leibniz's Law," after Gottfried Leibniz (1646-1716). Leibniz was famous for his principle of the Identity of Indiscernibles (which we will revisit in chapter 24), according to which any two things which are in principle indiscernible must be identical. If we interpret indiscernible things as those with exactly the same properties, this says that any two things with all the same properties must be identical. The Substitution of Identicals is the converse of this: any two things which are identical must share all the same properties.

Here's another example illustrating use of this rule of inference:

The only SURVIVING Beatles are <u>Paul</u> and <u>Ringo</u>. Neither Paul nor Ringo is interested in INDIAN philosophy. So there is no one among the surviving Beatles with an interest in Indian philosophy.

(Sp & Sr) & ∀x[Sx → (x = p v x = r)], ¬Ip & ¬Ir ∴ ¬∃x(Sx & Ix)

(1) (Sp & Sr) & ∀x[Sx → (x = p ∨ x = r)]   Prem
(2) ¬Ip & ¬Ir   Prem
(3) ∀x[Sx → (x = p ∨ x = r)]   1 Simp
   | (4) ∃x(Sx & Ix)   Supp/RA   —*suppose there is an S who is I*
   | (5) Si & Ii   4 EI   —*let i be the S who is I*
   | (6) Si   5 Simp
   | (7) Ii   6 Simp
   | (8) Si → (i = p ∨ i = r) 3 UI   —*if i is an S, he must be Paul or Ringo*
   | (9) i = p ∨ i = r   6, 8 MP   —*then i must be Paul or Ringo*
     | (10) i = p   Supp/RA   —*suppose he is Paul*
     | (11) Ip   7, 10 SI
     | (12) ¬Ip   2 Simp
     | (13) ⊥   11, 12 Conj —*contradiction*
   | (14) i ≠ p   10-13 RA   —*he can't be Paul*
   | (15) i = r   9, 14 DS   —*then he must be Ringo*
   | (16) Ir   7, 15 SI
   | (17) ¬Ir   2 Simp
   | (18) ⊥   16, 17 Conj —*contradiction*
(19) ¬∃x(Sx & Ix)   4-18 RA   —*so there is no S who is I*

21.2.2 PROPERTIES OF IDENTITY

Now, it is intuitively obvious that identity is an *equivalence relation*: that is, it is *reflexive*, *symmetric*, and *transitive*.

The first of these properties, the **reflexivity of identity**, is something we will simply assume as an implicit premise wherever it's necessary for the validity of an argument. This is consistent with what we did in some of the relational arguments of the previous chapter where, if the validity of an argument depends on a certain property, that property can just be assumed as an implicit premise. Thus if we need the reflexivity of identity in a proof, we make ∀x x = x an implicit premise. Here's an example:

The Pope is speaking LATIN. Therefore there is someone speaking Latin and he is the Pope.

Lp ∴ ∃x(Lx & x = p)
  (1) Lp   Prem
  (2) ∀x x = x   Impl. Prem
  (3) p = p   2 UI
  (4) Lp & p = p   1, 3 Conj
  (5) ∃x(Lx & x = p)   4 EG

Interestingly, though, we do not have to posit the symmetry and transitivity of the identity relation, since these can be proven by application of SI. Here is a proof of symmetry:

⊢ ∀x∀y(x = y → y = x)

(1) ¬∀x∀y(x = y → y = x)	Supp/RA	—*suppose no symmetry*
(2) ∃x∃y¬(x = y → y = x)	1 QN	
(3) ¬(i = j → j = i)	2 EI	—*note, must use j on second EI*
(4) ¬(i ≠ j v j = i)	3 MI	
(5) i = j & j ≠ i	4 DM, DN	
(6) i = j	5 Simp	
(7) j ≠ i	5 Simp	
(8) j ≠ j	6, 7 SI	—*subbing j for i in (7)*
(9) ∀x x = x	Impl. Prem	—*Reflexivity of Identity*
(10) j = j	9 UI	
(11) ⊥	10, 8 Conj	—*contradiction*
(12) ∀x∀y(x = y → y = x)	1-11 RA	—*so symmetry follows*

Now here's a proof of transitivity. This time we will use the UG strategy, being careful to make sure that the statement in **u**, **v**, and **w** that we UG from does not depend on an undischarged supposition in **u**, **v**, or **w**:

⊢ ∀x∀y∀z[(x = y & y = z) → x = z]   —aim to prove (u = v & v = w) → u = w...

(1) u = v & v = w	Supp/CP	—*suppose the antecedent*
(2) u = v	1 Simp	
(3) v = w	1 Simp	
(4) u = w	2, 3 SI	—*subbing w for v in (2)*
(5) (u = v & v = w) → u = w	1-4 CP	—*completes the CP*
(6) ∀x∀y∀z [(x = y & y = z) → x = z]	5 UG	—*(5) does not depend on (1)*

SUMMARY

- The rule of inference **Substitution of Identicals (SI)** is:
  If two individuals **i** and **k** are identical, then **k** can be substituted for **i** in any statement involving **i**.
  From **i = k**, **Φi**, infer **Φk**—e.g., from **a = b, Sa → ¬aLc**, infer **Sb → ¬bLc**.
- The identity relation is an **equivalence relation**: i.e., it is **symmetric**, **transitive**, and **reflexive**. Its symmetry and transitivity are derivable; its reflexivity may be assumed as an implicit premise: ∀x x = x.
- If the validity of an argument depends on this reflexivity property, ∀x x = x is included as an additional implicit premise.

EXERCISES 21.2

Symbolize and prove valid the following arguments:

19. The only EVEN prime is two. Therefore there is an even prime. [UD: prime numbers; Ex := x is even]

20. Hesperus is the EVENING star. Phosphorus is the MORNING star. But the Morning Star is identical with the Evening Star. Therefore Phosphorus and Hesperus are one and the same heavenly body. [UD: heavenly bodies]

21. Karl Marx was a REVOLUTIONARY. Harpo Marx was one of the Marx BROTH-ERS. None of the Marx brothers was a revolutionary. So Karl is not the same person as Harpo Marx. [UD: people]

22. The FOUNDER of Marxism was GERMAN. Chico Marx was not German, so he did not found Marxism. [UD: people; Fx := x founds Marxism]

23. God HELPS$_2$ all those who do not help themselves. This entails that God helps him- or herself. [UD: beings]

24. God HELPS$_2$ only those who do not help themselves. This entails that God does not help him- or herself. [UD: beings]

25. Rasputin is not the devil. The devil is the most EVIL$_2$ of beings. Hence there is a being more evil than Rasputin. [UD: beings; Exy := x is more evil than y]

26. The PRINCE of Wales is BALDING. So Charles must be balding, as he is Prince of Wales.

27. Descartes can't be a SOLIPSIST, because he's not me. I am one, and there is only one solipsist. [UD: people; Sx := x is a solipsist, m := me, I (the speaker)]

28. (**CHALLENGE**) The actress who played DOROTHY in The Wizard of Oz is not Liza Minelli; that role was played by her MOTHER$_2$, and no one is her own mother. [UD: actresses; Dx := x played Dorothy in The Wizard of Oz, Mxy := x is the mother of y]

21.3 ORDERING RELATIONS

A paradigm example of an ordering relation is the relation ≤ (is less than or equal to) on the domain of rational numbers. As we noted in the previous chapter, this relation is not asymmetric, since, for example, 3/3 < 1 but it is not the case that ¬1 ≤ 3/3. This is because

3/3 and 1 are counted as *the same* rational number: $3/3 = 1$, where here "=" is our relation of identity, not just equality. But on each pair of distinct rational numbers, ones for which $x \neq y$, the relation $\leq$ will be asymmetric. Any such relation R that is asymmetric on all pairs of distinct objects on a domain, is called *antisymmetric*:

A binary relation R is *antisymmetric* iff $\forall x \forall y \{ x \neq y \rightarrow (xRy \rightarrow \neg yRx) \}$

An equivalent definition of antisymmetry is:

A binary relation R is *antisymmetric* iff $\forall x \forall y \{ (xRy \,\&\, yRx) \rightarrow x = y \}$

Another characteristic feature of this relation is that any pair of rational numbers x and y are related by it: either $x \geq y$ or $y \geq x$. Any relation having this property is said to be *totally connexive*[1] on its domain:

A binary relation R is *totally connexive* iff $\forall x \forall y (xRy \lor yRx)$

Now one might think that this is a common property, shared for instance by the relation > on rationals, or the alphabetical ordering of the letters of the alphabet. But a little further reflection (!) shows that this cannot be, for if x and y are the same individual u, then total connexivity would give $uRu \lor uRu$, i.e., uRu, allowing a proof of reflexivity. But asymmetric relations cannot be reflexive: no number can be greater than itself, and no letter can precede itself in the alphabet. Things are otherwise if we are talking about pairs of *different* numbers or letters, however; for if $x \neq y$, the relation $x > y$ or $y < x$ will hold for rational numbers, and similarly for distinct letters in alphabetical order. In such cases the relation R is said to be *simply connexive*:

A binary relation R is *simply connexive* iff $\forall x \forall y \{ x \neq y \rightarrow (xRy \lor yRx) \}$

Of course, a given relation R could also fail to be connexive. This would happen if there were pairs of individuals in the domain that were not related by R. For example, the relation "is a COUSIN$_2$ of" on all the individuals who are cousins of mine is nonconnexive. An individual who is a cousin of mine on my mother's side of the family is not a cousin of someone who is a cousin of mine on my father's side. We therefore have a fourth family of relational properties, the *connexivity* family:

TOTAL CONNEXIVITY: $\forall x \forall y (xRy \lor yRx)$
SIMPLE CONNEXIVITY: $\forall x \forall y \{ x \neq y \rightarrow (xRy \lor yRx) \}$
NONCONNEXIVITY: $\exists x \exists y \neg (xRy \lor yRx)$

---

[1] The terminology among logicians is not very uniform here. A *totally connexive* relation is also called *strongly connexive* or just plain *total*.

Meanwhile the full symmetry family is:

> **SYMMETRY:** $\forall x \forall y(xRy \rightarrow yRx)$
> **ASYMMETRY:** $\forall x \forall y(xRy \rightarrow \neg yRx)$
> **ANTISYMMETRY:** $\forall x \forall y\{x \neq y \rightarrow (xRy \rightarrow \neg yRx)\}$
> **NONSYMMETRY:** $\exists x \exists y(xRy \ \& \ yRx) \ \& \ \exists x \exists y(xRy \ \& \ \neg yRx)$

Unlike the groups of properties of relations in the last chapter, however, it is not the case that a relation may have only one property from each of these groups. As we have already noted, $\geq$ is both nonsymmetric and antisymmetric. Also, any binary relation that is totally connexive is also simply connexive (exercise below), and any binary relation that is asymmetric is also simply antisymmetric (exercise below).

A relation that is *antisymmetric* and *transitive* on a given domain is said to induce an *ordering* on that domain. If the relation is also *reflexive* it is a *(weak) partial ordering*; if it is in addition *totally connexive*, this is a *(weak) total ordering*. If the relation is *asymmetric* and *transitive*, and therefore *irreflexive*, the ordering is a *strict partial ordering*. If in addition it is *simply connexive*, it is a *strict total ordering*. In sum,

> An *ORDERING RELATION* is a relation that is *transitive* and *antisymmetric*.
> A *WEAK PARTIAL ORDERING* relation is *transitive, antisymmetric,* and *reflexive*.
> A *WEAK TOTAL ORDERING* relation is *transitive, antisymmetric,* and *totally connexive*.
> A *STRICT PARTIAL ORDERING* relation is *transitive, asymmetric,* and *irreflexive*.
> A *STRICT TOTAL ORDERING* relation is *transitive, asymmetric,* and *simply connexive*.

There are further relations between these orderings. For example, every weak total ordering, such as $\leq$ on the rational numbers, has associated with it a strict total ordering, such as $<$, on the same domain. The relation is that $x \leq y$ iff $x < y$ or $x = y$; and correlatively, $x < y$ iff $x \leq y$ and $x \neq y$.

EXERCISES 21.3

29. *Prove that any binary relation R that is* totally connexive *is* reflexive.

30. *Prove that any binary relation R that is* totally connexive *is also* simply connexive.

31. *Prove that any binary relation R that is* asymmetric *is also* antisymmetric.

32. *Prove that the two definitions of* antisymmetry *given in the text are logically equivalent.*

33. (**CHALLENGE**) One sometimes finds a *strict total ordering* defined as one that is transitive, asymmetric, and totally connexive. Prove, however, *that no relation R that is* asymmetric *can be* totally connexive.

34. (**CHALLENGE**) Show that if R is reflexive, symmetric, and antisymmetric then it is the relation of identity: i.e., that $\forall x \forall y(xRy \leftrightarrow x = y)$.

35. (**CHALLENGE**) For any number there is a GREATER$_2$. It follows that there is no greatest number. (*Hint*: You will need to supply an implicit premise giving an important property of "is greater than.") [UD: numbers; xGy := x is greater than y]

Chapter Twenty-Two

Relational Arguments

22.1.1 A METHOD FOR SYMBOLIZING

One of the things that can make great difficulties when it comes to symbolizing relational statements is the tacit assumption that there is a unique way of symbolizing a given statement. This is a very natural assumption, particularly since the formulas have all the appearance of mathematical formulas, and we are used to there being unique correct formulas in mathematical problems. But it is mistaken. Consider, for example, the statement:

(S1) "Every animal in the wild kingdom is an expert at something."

What is the most appropriate way of translating it into symbolic logic? It all depends on the context in which it is embedded. Suppose it were the first premise in an argument that continued: "If this is so, then the lion is expert at something. Therefore there must be something the lion is expert at," then we have a simple Modus Ponens, and the most appropriate symbolization would be in terms of statement logic. We would have

(A1) Every animal in the wild kingdom is an EXPERT at something. If this is so, then the LION is expert at something. Therefore there must be something the lion is expert at.

With an obvious choice of symbols, the symbolization (F1) of (S1) would simply be E and that of the argument would be:

E, E → L ∴ L

But suppose the argument had continued instead: "But cows are expert at nothing, so they cannot be wild animals." Now the reasoning depends on links between the predicates, so that the most appropriate way to symbolize it would be by using predicate logic. With W := is a wild animal, E := is an expert at something, C := is a cow, our statement (S1) becomes the A-statement

(S2) "Every animal in the WILD kingdom is an EXPERT at something."

whose symbolization (F2) is $(\forall x)(Wx \rightarrow Ex)$. Now we have the argument

(A2) Every animal in the WILD kingdom is an EXPERT at something. But COWS are expert at nothing, so they cannot be wild animals.

and it gets symbolized as:

$\forall x(Wx \rightarrow Ex)$, $\forall x(Cx \rightarrow \neg Ex)$ ∴ $\forall x(Cx \rightarrow \neg Wx)$

We can take this still further. For now suppose the argument had instead continued: "Frank is an expert at Judo. Therefore either some wild animal is expert at Judo or Frank is not a wild animal." In this case the reasoning depends not just on *who* are experts at whatever, but on *what* they are expert at. The expression "...is an expert at..." is a dyadic relation, and we symbolize "x is an EXPERT$_2$ at y" as xEy. Thus "Frank is an EXPERT$_2$ at Judo" is symbolized: fEj. "A WILD animal is EXPERT$_2$ at Judo," i.e., "There is at least one thing that is a wild animal and is expert at judo," is symbolized: $\exists x(Wx \,\&\, xEj)$, so that the conclusion of this argument is: $\exists x(Wx \,\&\, xEj) \lor \neg Wf$. But what about our original statement, which now involves two quantifications?

(S3) "Every animal in the WILD kingdom is an EXPERT$_2$ at something."

Let's take this in two stages. "Every animal in the WILD kingdom is an EXPERT$_2$ at y" is a kind of generalized but incomplete A-statement, which we can symbolize as we did (S2) above:

$\forall x(Wx \rightarrow xEy)$

On the other hand, "x is an EXPERT$_2$ at something" is the same as "there is at least one y such that x is an EXPERT$_2$ at y," so this is:

$\exists y\ xEy$

Putting these two complementary parts together gives:

(F3) $\forall x[Wx \rightarrow \exists y\, xEy]$

So our third (relational) argument is:

(A3) Every animal in the WILD kingdom is an EXPERT$_2$ at something. <u>Frank</u> is an expert at <u>Judo</u>. Therefore either a wild animal is expert at Judo or Frank is not a wild animal.

(A3) $\forall x[Wx \rightarrow \exists y\, xEy]$, fEj $\therefore$ $\exists x(Wx\ \&\ xEj) \lor \neg Wf$

So we see that the same statement in English gets symbolized quite differently in each context. Each of the three arguments above has the same first premise, but it gets symbolized respectively as

(F1) E   (F2) $\forall x(Wx \rightarrow Ex)$ (F3) $\forall x[Wx \rightarrow \exists y\, xEy]$

accordingly as it occurs in the three different arguments

(A1) E, E $\rightarrow$ L $\therefore$ L
(A2) $\forall x(Wx \rightarrow Ex)$, $\forall x(Cx \rightarrow \neg Ex)$ $\therefore$ $\forall x(Cx \rightarrow \neg Wx)$
(A3) $\forall x[Wx \rightarrow \exists y\, xEy]$, fEj $\therefore$ $\exists x(Wx\ \&\ xEj) \lor \neg Wf$

Exercise: Although we're primarily considering translation here and will get onto proofs later, you might try proving the validity of (A3) now as an exercise. You will find that its conclusion follows from the second premise alone: although this seems odd intuitively, the first premise is extraneous to the proof.

To summarize the method for symbolizing multiply-quantified statements just outlined:

> When **symbolizing relational statements**, it is best to break them down into complementary parts. Thus "No HUMAN being has ever SEEN$_2$ a DINOSAUR" is analyzable into "No HUMAN being has ever SEEN$_2$ y": $\forall x(Hx \rightarrow \neg xSy)$ and "x has SEEN$_2$ a DINOSAUR," i.e., "there is at least one thing that is a DINOSAUR and x has SEEN$_2$ it": $\exists y(Dy\ \&\ xSy)$. Combining gives: $\forall x\,[Hx \rightarrow \neg \exists y(Dy\ \&\ xSy)]$.

This method works for most if not all relational statements, and I would recommend that you apply it whenever you can. It is the safest way to ensure that you have the right quantifiers in the right order. A further example:

(S4) "Every CHARACTER HAS$_2$ at least one FLAW."

Step 1: (Quantifying x) "Every CHARACTER HAS_2 y" would be $\forall x(Cx \rightarrow xHy)$.
Step 2: (Quantifying y) "x HAS_2 at least one FLAW," i.e., "there is at least one thing that is a FLAW and x HAS_2 it," would be $\exists y(Fy \ \& \ xHy)$.
Step 3: Combining steps 1 and 2 gives:

(F4) $\forall x[Cx \rightarrow \exists y(Fy \ \& \ xHy)]$

22.1.2 PRENEX FORMS (CHALLENGE LEVEL)

It is important to realize that many equivalent alternative symbolizations of these statements are possible. For instance, (S4) above could have been symbolized as:

(F4a) $\forall x \exists y[Cx \rightarrow (Fy \ \& \ xHy)]$
—for all x there is at least one y such that if x is a character then y is a flaw and x has it.

On inspection, we see that (F4a) is the same as (F4) except that all the quantifiers are out in front in the same order. An expression with all the quantifiers governing it lined up in front like this is said to be in *Prenex Normal Form* (or just *prenex form* for short).[1]

This raises two questions: (i) is it always possible to symbolize a statement in prenex form—or equivalently, can any symbolized statement be put into prenex form? (The answer is yes!); and (ii) does converting a statement that isn't in prenex form into one that is just involve pulling all the quantifiers out of the middle and putting them in front? Let's see. Consider:

(S5) "If <u>Hilda</u> RESIGNS, then everyone will." [UD: people]

A natural symbolization would be:

(F5) $Rh \rightarrow \forall x Rx$

In prenex form:

(F5a) $\forall x(Rh \rightarrow Rx)$

---

[1] The term "Prenex Normal Form" was introduced in its current meaning by Alonzo Church in 1944: "Thus we have that a w.f.f. is in prenex normal form if and only if all its quantifiers are initially placed, no two quantifiers are upon the same variable, and every variable occurring in a quantifier occurs at least once within the scope of that quantifier" (*Ann. Math. Stud.* xiii., p. 60). As he notes (*ibid.*, p. 61) "Use of the prenex normal form was introduced by C.S. Peirce, although in a different terminology and notation."

Here (F5a) has been obtained from (F5) simply by pulling out the quantifier in front of the consequent and then putting it in front to quantify the whole conditional. But is this legal? Are the two statements logically equivalent? You can use two RA proofs, or the following two proofs using the UI/UG strategy, to establish that they are equivalent:

(1) Rh →∀xRx		Prem
	(2) Rh	Supp/CP
	(3) ∀xRx	1, 2 MP
	(4) Ru	3 UI
(5) Rh → Ru		2-4 CP
(6) ∀x(Rh → Rx)		5 UG

(1) ∀x(Rh → Rx)		Prem
	(2) Rh	Supp/CP
	(3) Rh → Ru	1 UI
	(4) Ru	1, 2 MP
	(5) ∀xRx	4 UG
(6) Rh → ∀xRx		2-5 CP

(Check to make sure that no restrictions on UI have been violated.) You should try:

Rh → ∃xRx ⊣⊢ ∃x(Rh → Rx)

¬[Rh & ∀xRx] ⊣⊢ ¬∀x(Rh & Rx)

But what about this statement:

(S6) "If anything will CAUSE Hilda to resign, this will."

We know that in statements like this the "anything" in the antecedent stands for "something," so (S6) is symbolized as:

(F6) ∃xCx → Ct

But we know this is *not* logically equivalent to

(F6a) ∃x(Cx → Ct)

but to

(F6b) ∀x(Cx → Ct)

Now this holds generally: when the antecedent of a conditional is an *existential* quantification, then we must change this to a *universal quantifier* when sticking it in front to convert the statement to prenex form. More examples:

$\forall x[\exists y(Py \rightarrow Cx)]$ ⊣⊢ $\forall x \forall y(Py \rightarrow Cx)$
$\exists xFx \rightarrow \forall xGx$ ⊣⊢ $\exists xFx \rightarrow \forall yGy$ ⊣⊢ $\forall x \forall y(Fx \rightarrow Gy)$

Note that $\forall x(Fx \rightarrow Gx)$ is *not* logically equivalent to any of the three latter statements. "If someone finds the net, everyone goes home" is not the same as "Anyone who finds the net goes home." Also note that $\forall x \forall x(Fx \rightarrow Gx)$ is not a wff, since no variable in a wff is bound by—occurs within the scope of—more than one quantifier.

Again, when the antecedent of a conditional statement is a *universal quantification*, when we pull the quantifier out in front it changes to an *existential quantifier*. Examples:

$\forall xCx \rightarrow Ct$ ⊣⊢ $\exists x(Cx \rightarrow Ct)$
$\forall xFx \rightarrow \exists yGy$ ⊣⊢ $\exists x[Fx \rightarrow \exists yGy]$
$\exists x[Fx \rightarrow \exists yGy]$ ⊣⊢ $\exists x \exists y(Fx \rightarrow Gy)$

Here's a proof of the first of these equivalences:

(1) $\forall xCx \rightarrow Ct$ Prem
  | (2) $\neg Ct$ Supp/CP
  | (3) $\neg \forall xCx$ 1, 2 MT
  | (4) $\exists x \neg Cx$ 3 QN
  | (5) $\neg Ci$ 4 EI
(6) $\neg Ct \rightarrow \neg Ci$ 2-5 CP
(7) $Ci \rightarrow Ct$ 6 TR
(8) $\exists x(Cx \rightarrow Ct)$ 7 EG

(1) $\exists x(Cx \rightarrow Ct)$ Prem
(2) $Ci \rightarrow Ct$ 1 EI
  | (3) $\forall xCx$ Supp/CP
  | (4) Ci 3 UI
  | (5) Ct 2, 4 MP
(6) $\forall xCx \rightarrow Ct$ 3-5 CP

Finally, remember that if there is a $\neg$ in front of the quantifier, what you have is a negation and not a quantification: you must do a step of QN first. Thus "No HUMAN being has ever SEEN₂ a DINOSAUR," $\forall x[Hx \rightarrow \neg \exists y(Dy \, \& \, xSy)]$, becomes

$\forall x[Hx \rightarrow \forall y \neg(Dy \, \& \, xSy)]$ and hence
$\forall x \forall y[Hx \rightarrow \neg(Dy \, \& \, xSy)]$

SUMMARY

- When **symbolizing relational statements**, it is best to break them down into complementary parts. Thus "No HUMAN being has ever SEEN$_2$ a DINOSAUR" is analyzable into "No HUMAN being has ever SEEN$_2$ y": $\forall x(Hx \rightarrow \neg xSy)$ and "x has SEEN$_2$ a DINOSAUR," i.e., "there is at least one thing that is a DINOSAUR and x has SEEN$_2$ it": $\exists y(Dy \ \& \ xSy)$. Combining gives: $\forall x \ [Hx \rightarrow \neg \exists y(Dy \ \& \ xSy)]$.

- To convert a statement to its logical equivalent in **prenex form**, you may extract the quantifiers occurring within it and set them in front *provided that*:
  (i) you do not change the order in which the quantifiers occur;
  (ii) there is no $\neg$ to the left of any quantifier you are extracting (if there is, apply QN);
  (iii) when the quantifier you are extracting governs the antecedent of a conditional, you change an *existential quantifier* governing the antecedent to a *universal quantifier* governing the whole, and vice versa.

EXERCISES 22.1

1. *Symbolize the following statements:*
   (a) Whatever it is, I'm AGAINST$_2$ it.—Groucho Marx [g := Groucho, I]
   (b) Whatever the ESTABLISHMENT is, I'm AGAINST$_2$ it.—Noam Chomsky [c := Chomsky, I]
   (c) <u>God</u> HELPS$_2$ them that help themselves.—Poor Richard
   (d) All LIVING humans are DESCENDED$_2$ from <u>Eve</u>. [Lx := x is a living human]
   (e) No one DECEIVES$_2$ you unless you deceive yourself.—Goethe
   (f) One does not LIKE$_2$ those whom one has greatly INJURED$_2$.—Boswell

2. *Using the symbolizations suggested, translate the following statements:*
   (a) Every MECHANIC can FIX$_2$ some CAR.
   (b) There is a mechanic who can fix every car.
   (c) No mechanic can fix every car.
   (d) No car can be fixed by every mechanic.
   (e) No mechanic can fix any car.
   (f) No car can fix itself.

3. *Using the symbolizations suggested [concerning the 1983 film "Liquid Sky"], translate (a)-(c) from English into wffs of relational logic, and then use the same interpretations of the symbols to render (d)-(f) from wffs into colloquial English:*
   (a) <u>Margaret</u> will ATTRACT$_2$ some alien SPACECRAFT to land nearby. [xAy := x will attract y to land nearby, Sy := y is an alien spacecaft]

(b) Only those who are highly stimulated EROTICALLY will ATTRACT$_2$ an alien SPACECRAFT to land nearby. [Ex := x is highly stimulated erotically]
(c) No alien SPACECRAFT have been ATTRACTED$_2$ to land nearby by <u>Margaret</u>.
(d) ¬∀x(Sx → mAx)
(e) Em & ¬∃x(Sx & mAx)
(f) ∀x[Sx → ¬∃y(Ey & yAx)]

(**CHALLENGE**) *Prove the equivalence of each of the following abstract statements with its counterpart in prenex form by constructing two proofs in each case:*
4. Rh → ∃xRx ⊣⊢ ∃x(Rh → Rx)
5. ¬[Rh & ∀xRx] ⊣⊢ ¬∀x(Rh & Rx)
6. ∀x[∃yPy → Cx] ⊣⊢ ∀x∀y(Py → Cx)
7. ∃xFx → ∀yGy ⊣⊢ ∀x∀y(Fx → Gy)

For each of statements 8-10 give (without proof) its equivalent in prenex form:
8. ∃x[Tx & ∀y(Ly → xPy)]
9. ∀x[Tx → ∀y(Ly → xPy)]
10. ∀x[Tx → ¬∀y(Ly → xPy)]

11. In his *Predicate Logic*, Howard Pospesel has symbolized the statement "No HUMAN being has ever SEEN$_2$ a DINOSAUR" as ∀x∀y[(Hx & Dy) → ¬xSy)]. We symbolized it as ∀x∀y[Hx → ¬(Dy & xSy)]. These two will be equivalent iff the following logical equivalence in statement logic holds: (H & D) → ¬S ⊣⊢ H → ¬(D & S). *Prove that it does.*

22.2 RELATIONAL ARGUMENTS

22.2.1 ARGUMENTS BEYOND THE SCOPE OF TRADITIONAL LOGIC

Notoriously, Aristotelian logic could not deal with arguments of the following form:

(A4) ADULTERY is a SIN. Therefore anyone who COMMITS$_2$ adultery commits a sin.

We have all the means at our disposal to deal with such arguments. With Px := x is a person, this would be symbolized:

∀x(Ax → Sx) ∴ ∀x{Px → [∃y(Ay & xCy) → ∃z(Sz & xCz)]}

In "Loglish," the conclusion says: For any person x, if there is some adultery y such that x commits it, then there is a sin z such that x commits it. A proof would go as follows:

(1) ∀x(Ax → Sx)	Prem
| (2) Pu	Supp/CP
| (3) ∃y(Ay & uCy)	Supp/CP
| (4) Ai & uCi	3 EI
| (5) Ai	4 Simp
| (6) uCi	4 Simp
| (7) Ai → Si	1 UI
| (8) Si	5, 7 MP
| (9) Si & uCi	8, 6 Conj
| (10) ∃z(Sz & uCz)	9 EG
| (11) ∃y(Ay & uCy) → ∃z(Sz & uCz)	3-10 CP
(12) Pu → [∃y(Ay & uCy) → ∃z(Sz & uCz)]	2-11 CP
(13) ∀x{Px → [∃y(Ay & xCy) → ∃z(Sz & xCz)]}	12 UG

Here is another example. Groucho Marx said famously:

(S7) I would never JOIN$_2$ any CLUB that would HAVE$_2$ me as member.

Here if we symbolize Cx := x is a club, yJx := y joins x, xHy := x has y as member, and g := Groucho, this would be symbolized:

(F7) ∀x[(Cx & xHg) → ¬gJx]

The joke turns on the fact that Groucho recognizes that any club that would accept him would be disreputable. But then since a club has someone as member if and only if he or she joins the club—an implicit premise here—we infer that *no* club will have Groucho as member! The symbolization of the implicit premise "a club has someone as member if and only if he or she joins the club" is:

(F8) ∀x∀y[(Cx & Py) → (xHy ↔ yJx)]

where again Px := x is a person. We also have the implicit premise that "Groucho is a person" (just about!). So we have the argument

(A5) Groucho would never JOIN$_2$ any CLUB that would HAVE$_2$ him as member. Since a club has someone as member only if he or she joins the club, and Groucho is a person, it follows that *no* club will have Groucho as member!

(S5) ∀x[(Cx & xHg) → ¬gJx], ∀x∀y[(Cx & Py) → (xHy → yJx)], Pg ⊢ ∀x(Cx → ¬xHg)

Proof:
(1) ∀x[(Cx & xHg)→ ¬gJx]	Prem	
(2) ∀x∀y[(Cx & Py)→ (xHy → yJx)]	Prem	
(3) Pg	Prem	
(4) (Cu & uHg) → ¬gJu	1 UI	—*we UI onto **u**, anticipating UG*
(5) (Cu & Pg) → (uHg → gJu)	2 UI	
(6) Cu	Supp/CP	—*suppose **u** is a club*
(7) Cu & Pg	6, 3 Conj	
(8) uHg → gJu	5, 7 MP	
(9) uHg	Supp/RA	—*suppose u will have*
(10) gJu	8, 9 MP	*Groucho and aim for ⊥*
(11) Cu & uHg	6, 9 Conj	
(12) ¬gJu	4, 11 MP	
(13) ⊥	10, 12 Conj	
(14) ¬uHg	9-13 RA	—***u** won't have Groucho*
(15) Cu → ¬uHg	6-14 CP	—*if u is a club, it won't have g*
(16) ∀x(Cx → ¬xHg)	15 UG	—*so no club will!*

Two rather artificial features of this proof are our having to assume that Groucho is a person, and having to suppose that **u** is a club, when x only ranges over individuals that are clubs. It would clearly be simpler if we split the UD accordingly, letting x range over clubs and y over people. This will save us from having to have the predicates C and P, and simplify both the symbolization and the proof. Doing this is a version of the restricting of the UD we encountered earlier, except that we are doing a different restriction for each of the variables. The technique will often simplify proofs, but you have to make it explicit that you are doing this. So with [UD for x: clubs; UD for y: people; g := Groucho, yJx := y joins club x, xHy := x has y as member] we get the following as a symbolization of the argument:

(S5a)   ∀x[xHg → ¬gJx], ∀x∀y[xHy → yJx] ⊢ ∀x ¬xHg

Proof:
(1) ∀x[xHg → ¬gJx]	Prem	
(2) ∀x∀y[xHy ↔ yJx]	Prem	
(3) uHg → ¬gJu	1 UI	—*take an arbitrary club **u***
(4) uHg → gJu	2 UI	
(5) uHg	Supp/RA	
(6) gJu	4, 5 MP	
(7) ¬gJu	3, 5 MP	
(8) ⊥	6, 7 Conj	
(9) ¬uHg	5-8 RA	—*even **u** won't have Groucho*
(10) ∀x ¬xHg	9 UG	—*so no club will!*

22.2.2 AMBIGUITIES AND THE QUANTIFIER SHIFT FALLACY

One of the most interesting applications of the analysis of relational statements is to reveal certain fallacies. These range from humorous examples concerning ambiguous terms to some quite subtle and historically important examples turning on a mistake concerning quantifier scope.

First let's look at some examples involving ambiguous terms (such an argument is technically called an *amphiboly*). Here's one from Lewis Carroll's *Through the Looking Glass*

> "I see nobody on the road," said Alice. "I only wish I had such eyes," the King remarked in a fretful tone. "To be able to see Nobody! And at the distance too! Why, it's as much as I can do to see real people, by this light!"[2]

Illustration by Sir John Tenniel (1820-1914)
from *Through the Looking Glass*.

The faulty inference made by the King is roughly this:

(A6) Alice can see Nobody. I cannot see anybody. So Alice can see someone I cannot see.

This has the same grammatical form as

(A7) Alice can see Noel. I cannot see anybody. So Alice can see someone I cannot see.
[UD: people; a := Alice, n := Noel, k := 'I,' the King, xSy := x can see y]

This is symbolized: aSn, $\forall x \neg kSx \therefore \exists x(aSx \, \& \, \neg kSx)$

---

2 *Through the Looking Glass*, Lewis Carroll, ch. 7: The Lion and the Unicorn; quotation and illustration taken from the website <http://www.sabian.org/Alice/lgchap07.htm>.

But since 'nobody' is not a proper name, the correct symbolization of (A6) is

∀x ¬Sax, ∀x ¬kSx ∴ ∃x(aSx & ¬kSx)

and this is clearly an invalid inference. A similar (apocryphal) example (not very popular with logic students) is:

(A8) Logic is better than nothing. Nothing is better than sex. Therefore logic is better than sex!

Again, this amphiboly trades on treating "nothing" as if it were a proper name.

Turning now to the history of logic, there is an argument form much beloved of the Stoics, of which the following argument invented by Zeno of Citium[3] is an instance:

(A9) What is rational is better than what is not rational. Nothing is better than the cosmos. Therefore the cosmos is rational.

At first sight it may appear as though this is a similar kind of amphiboly, since few people these days would believe (as the Stoics did) that the cosmos (ordered universe) was animate, and therefore could be rational. When we subject this to logical analysis, though, the results are quite surprising. Using Rx := x is rational, xBy := x is better than y, and c := the cosmos, we get

∀x∀y[(Rx & ¬Ry) → xBy], ∀x ¬xBc ∴ Rc

It turns out that this is a *penevalid* argument. When we include as an implicit premise that there is at least something that is rational—surely an innocuous addition—we can prove the validity of this argument as follows:

(1) ∀x∀y[(Rx & ¬Ry) → xBy]   Prem
(2) ∀x ¬xBc   Prem
(3) ∃xRx   Impl. Prem
(4) Ri   3 EI
(5) ¬iBc   2 UI
(6) (Ri & ¬Rc) → iBc   1 UI
(7) ¬(Ri & ¬Rc)   5, 6 MT
(8) ¬¬Rc   4, 7 CS
(9) Rc   8 DN

---

[3] Zeno of Citium was the founder of the Stoic school, and is not to be confused with the earlier philosopher Zeno of Elea, whose paradoxes we encountered earlier.

I think it is genuinely surprising that this argument comes out valid. If we do not accept the conclusion, which premise should we reject? One candidate is "Nothing is better than the cosmos," especially if we believe in a Creator-God. But then it would seem natural to substitute 'God' for the cosmos in this argument. Whether this was the reasoning of St. Anselm of Canterbury, one of the early Christian fathers, I do not profess to know. But Anselm's argument is sufficiently similar to Zeno's to suggest some kind of influence (whether or not he was aware of it):

(A10) What exists is better than what does not exist. Nothing is better than God. Therefore God exists.

If we allow 'x exists' as a predicate, then this argument has precisely the same (valid!) form as Zeno's, and it is perhaps even harder to deny the premises. (Those who reject it claim there is an ambiguity: the sense in which existence is 'better' than non-existence does not seem to be the same as the sense in which God is 'best.' Later criticisms of the argument thus focussed on whether 'existence' can be regarded as a perfection.)

A second famous argument for the existence of God was given by another philosophical saint, this time St. Thomas Aquinas:

(A11) That which is contingent is not in existence at some time. Therefore, since there could not have been a time when nothing was in existence, not everything can be contingent.

It follows, reasons Aquinas, that there must be something non-contingent, i.e., not dependent for its existence on anything else, and this being is identified with God.

The same argument is alluded to by John Locke, when he reasons

Bare nothing cannot produce any real being. Whence it follows with mathematical evidence that something existed from all eternity.[4]

But there is a logical slippage in this argument, ably pointed out by Gottfried Leibniz in his rejoinder to Locke's book:

I find an ambiguity here. If it means that there has never been a time when nothing existed, then I agree with it...But...it does not follow that if there has always been something then one particular thing has always been, i.e., that there is an eternal being. (Leibniz, *New Essays*, 436)

---

[4] Leibniz, *New Essays on Human Understanding*, trans. and ed. Peter Remnant and Jonathan Bennett (Cambridge: Cambridge UP, 1981), p. 435; quoted from Locke, *Essay*, Bk. IV, ch. x, §3.

What Leibniz is pointing out is that if one of Locke's and Aquinas' premises is that "there has never been a time when nothing existed," then all that validly follows from this is that at any time one thing or another is in existence, not that there is a thing that is in existence at every time. Letting xEy := x exists at time y, UD for x: things, UD for y: times, we have:

$$\neg\exists y\forall x \neg xEy \vdash \forall y\exists x\ xEy \qquad \text{by QN and DN}$$

But from $\forall y\exists x\ xEy$ you cannot validly infer $\exists x\forall y\ xEy$: as we saw above, the order of the quantifiers is all-important. This would be the same as inferring from the fact that everyone has a mother—$\forall y\exists x\ xMy$—that there is someone who is everyone's mother—$\exists x\forall y\ xMy$—an inference that is obviously invalid. This erroneous inversion of the order of universal and existential quantifiers is known as the Quantifier Shift Fallacy. It illicitly changes the scope of both quantifiers.

SUMMARY

- Relational logic is competent to handle numerous arguments that traditional logic could not, for instance: "ADULTERY is a SIN. Therefore anyone who COMMITS$_2$ adultery commits a sin."
- One of the most interesting applications of relational logic is to reveal certain fallacies. Some of these are arguments involving a term being used ambiguously, such as "nobody" being treated as a proper noun in the expression "I can see nobody." Such a fallacious argument involving the ambiguous use of a term is called an **amphiboly**.
- Another type of fallacy revealed by relational logic is the **quantifier shift fallacy**. This consists in the inversion of the order of existential and universal quantifiers in an expression, thus illicitly changing their scope; for example, fallaciously inferring from "Everyone has a mother"—true if it means that "for each person there is someone who is their mother" ($\forall y\exists x\ xMy$, with a UD of people)—that "there is someone who is everyone's mother" ($\exists x\forall y\ xMy$).

EXERCISES 22.2

12. *Symbolize and prove the validity of the "Frank-Judo" argument from the text:*
Every animal in the WILD kingdom is an EXPERT$_2$ at something. <u>Frank</u> is an EXPERT$_2$ at <u>Judo</u>. Therefore either a wild animal is expert at Judo or Frank is not a wild animal. [Wx := x is an animal in the wild kingdom]

13. In an episode of *The Simpsons*, Principal Seymour Skinner is accused by the school superintendent Chalmers of having had sexual relations with the teacher Edna Krabappel, but is adamant that he is a virgin. Chalmers replies: *"Well, Seymour, it is clear you have been falsely accused, because no one anywhere ever would pretend to be a 44-year-old virgin."* *Symbolize and prove the validity of this paraphrased version of the argument:*
   > No one who is FORTY-FOUR and is not a VIRGIN would CLAIM to be one. No one who is a virgin has had SEX₂ with anyone. <u>Seymour</u> is forty-four and claims to be a virgin. Therefore he has not had sex with <u>Edna</u>. [UD: people]

14. R.D. Laing has a poem that begins:
   > I don't RESPECT₂ <u>myself</u>.
   > I can't respect anyone who respects me.
   Prove that the first line follows from the second. [UD: people; m := I, me, myself]

15. In his ballad "Like a Rolling Stone" Bob Dylan sings: "When you got nothing, you got nothing to lose." *Prove that this follows from the truism that* "You can LOSE₂ something only if you have GOT it." [UD for x: people; UD for y: things; xLy := x loses y, xGy := x has got y]

16. *The following is a penevalid argument. Supply the implicit premise and prove the validity of the resulting argument:*
   > PLATYPUSES are MAMMALS that LAY₂ EGGS. Therefore some eggs are laid by mammals.

17. *The following argument is an amphiboly. Explain what ambiguity or ambiguities the fallacy depends on.*
   > No cat has eight lives. Therefore, since any cat has one more life than no cat, any cat must have nine lives.

18. *In a Dilbert cartoon, Dilbert has the following conversation with a female friend:*
   > *She:* "I believe there is one true soul mate for every person." *He replies:* "He must be very busy." *She:* "I meant one per person."
   Explain the quantifier scope confusion that the joke trades on, symbolizing both the intended interpretation and the mistaken one.

19. *Prove the validity of Leibniz's modified version of Aquinas' argument (using "exists at a time" as a relational predicate):*
   > There is never a time when nothing exists. So at all times, there is something in existence. [xEy := x exists at time y; UD for x: things; UD for y: times]

Chapter Twenty-Three

Truth Trees for PL

23.1.1 TRUTH TREE RULES FROM STATEMENT LOGIC

In introducing truth trees for statement logic, we used the following rules:

&	**¬&**	**∨**	**¬∨**	**¬¬**
√p & q	√¬$(p$ & $q)$	√$p \lor q$	√¬$(p \lor q)$	√¬¬p
p	/ \	/ \	¬p	p
q	¬p ¬q	p q	¬q	

→	**¬→**	**↔**	**¬↔**
√$p \to q$	√¬$(p \to q)$	√$p \leftrightarrow q$	√¬$(p \leftrightarrow q)$
/ \	p	/ \	/ \
¬p q	¬q	p ¬p	p ¬p
		q ¬q	¬q q

These rules may also be used to determine the validity of certain arguments in Predicate Logic. Let's have a look at one to refresh our memories of how the method works. Recall that we state the premises and the negation of the conclusion, drawing a line under this part. Then we apply these rules, trying to use non-branching rules first (the non-branching rules are **&**, ¬∨, ¬¬, and ¬→) to break the statements down into their components. Every time we decompose a compound statement, we put a check mark by it. If the tree has already branched when we decompose a compound premise by a branching rule, then the results must be written in on every branch. A path becomes closed when a statement is directly contradicted by another statement above it on the same path. The tree is complete either when all the paths close (this is a complete closed tree); or when, on at least one path, every compound statement has been decomposed leaving only literals (this is a complete open path). A complete tree with all its paths closed proves that the negation of the conclusion contradicts the conjunction of the premises, so that the argument is VALID. Otherwise—i.e., if one or more paths are still open and complete—the argument is INVALID.

As an example of an argument in Predicate Logic that can be treated with these rules alone, consider, for instance, this variation of the "Gorbachev-Brezhnev" argument we considered above:

> If <u>Gorbachev</u> was TELLING the truth about Stalin's purges, then <u>Brezhnev</u> DECEIVED the Soviet people. But if Gorbachev was not telling the truth, then he himself deceived the Soviet people. Thus either Gorbachev or Brezhnev deceived the Soviet people.

This is symbolized as follows: Tg → Db, ¬Tg → Dg ∴ Dg v Db. A truth tree analysis gives:

1	√	Tg → Db	Prem
2	√	¬Tg → Dg	Prem
3	√	<u>¬(Dg v Db)</u>	¬Concl
4		¬Dg	3 ¬v
5		¬Db	

```
                / \
6        ¬Tg   Db          1 →
         / \    ⊥
7    ¬¬Tg   Dg              2 →
      ⊥      ⊥
```

The tree is complete, because all the paths result in contradictions, and are therefore closed. So the argument is, as expected, valid. Now let's proceed to examples that require new rules.

23.1.2 ADDITIONAL TRUTH TREE RULES FOR QUANTIFICATIONS

As things stand, we have no rules for decomposing universal or existential quantifications. This motivates our first two rules, which correspond to the rules of inference UI and EI:

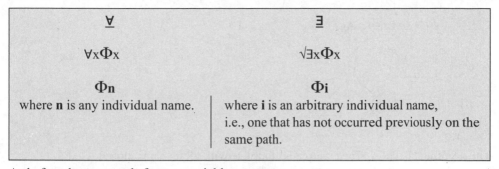

As before, here **x** stands for any variable, x, y, or z.

Points to note:
- When the ∀ rule is applied to decompose a universal quantification, that statement does not get checked off. The reason is that a universal quantification entails *any* instance, not just an instance involving one name. So in principle ∀ can be applied over and over, just as was UI in the original rule-of-inference proof of the Gorbachev-Brezhnev argument (see example in chapter 19, pp. 309-10).
- When the ∃ rule is applied to decompose an existential quantification, we check it off, since we know only that there is at least one individual instance of it. The name **n** will be **i**, **j**, or **k**, as before; if **i** occurs previously on the same path, use **j**; if that is taken, use **k**, and so on.
- The ∃ rule must be applied before the ∀ rule, for the same reason that **EI** had to be applied before **UI** in proofs: in order to guarantee that the **i** is indeed arbitrary.

These rules will allow us to determine the validity of arguments like the "moral God" argument considered in chapter 16, p. 261:

No PERFECT being is immoral. No MORAL being would punish AGNOSTICISM. It follows that if <u>God</u> is perfect, he will not punish agnosticism. [UD: beings]

Symbolized: $\forall x(Px \rightarrow Mx)$, $\forall x(Mx \rightarrow \neg Ax)$ ∴ $Pg \rightarrow \neg Ag$

1		$\forall x(Px \rightarrow Mx)$	Prem
2		$\forall x(Mx \rightarrow \neg Ax)$	Prem
3	√	$\underline{\neg(Pg \rightarrow \neg Ag)}$	¬Concl
4		Pg	3 ¬→
5	√	$\neg\neg Ag$	
6		Ag	5 ¬¬
7	√	$Pg \rightarrow Mg$	1 ∀

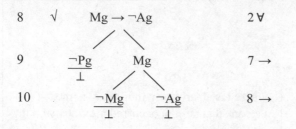

The argument is valid, since its tree is complete with all its paths closed.
Now an example involving ∃:

$$\forall x(Ax \rightarrow Bx), \exists x(Ax \ \& \ Cx) \therefore \neg \forall x(Bx \rightarrow \neg Cx)$$

1		$\forall x(Ax \rightarrow Bx)$	Prem
2	√	$\exists x(Ax \ \& \ Cx)$	Prem
3		$\underline{\forall x(Bx \rightarrow \neg Cx)}$	¬Concl
4	√	Ai & Ci	2 ∃
5		Ai	4 &
6		Ci	
7	√	Ai → Bi	1 ∀
8	√	Bi → ¬Ci	3 ∀

9   ¬Ai   Bi   7 →
          ⊥

10   ¬Bi   ¬Ci   8 →
             ⊥   ⊥

Here note that, just as in our proofs, we must treat the existential statement first, i.e., apply ∃ before ∀. Note also that the universal quantifications do not get checked off when ∀ is applied.

23.1.3 NEGATED QUANTIFIER DECOMPOSITION RULES

Our second two rules are almost mirror images of the first. ¬∀ is effectively a combination of QN and ∃, so that it has the same restrictions as did ∃; whereas ¬∃ is effectively a combination of QN and ∀, and so it has no restrictions:

$$\frac{\neg \forall}{\sqrt{\ } \neg \forall x \Phi x}$$
$$\neg \Phi i$$

$$\frac{\neg \exists}{\neg \exists x \Phi x}$$
$$\neg \Phi \mathbf{n}$$

where **i** is an arbitrary individual name, i.e., one that has not occurred previously on the same path.

where **n** is any individual name.

- Here it is ¬∃ that does not get checked off. Since ¬∃x Φx is equivalent to ∀x¬Φx by QN, we can apply UI as many times as we like without restriction.
- On the other hand, since ¬∀x Φx is equivalent to ∃x¬Φx by QN, the same restrictions as with the ∃ rule apply. This means that the ¬∀ rule cannot be instantiated by the same individual name more than once in the same path, and we should therefore apply it before the ∀ or ¬∃ rules.

As an example, let's determine the validity of the sequent:

∃x(Sx ∨ Px) ⊢ ∃xSx ∨ ∃xPx

1	√	∃x(Sx ∨ Px)	prem
2	√	¬[∃xSx ∨ ∃xPx]	¬concl
3	√	¬∃xSx	2 ¬∨
4	√	¬∃xPx	
5	√	Si ∨ Pi	1 ∃

```
6        Si      Pi          5 ∨
         |       |
7       ¬Si     ¬Si          3 ¬∃
        ⊥        |
8               ¬Pi          4 ¬∃
                 ⊥
```

Notice that here we applied the ¬∨ rule to line 2 first, since this is a non-branching rule. So is ¬∃; but had we applied that before ∃ (which branches), then we would not have been able to apply ∃ without either breaking the restriction on it that we cannot have used the same name previously on the same path, or using a different name, which would have got us nowhere. The economy of the Truth Tree method can be seen by comparing the succinct 8 line tree-proof above with a rule-of-inference proof of the same sequent:[1]

(1) ∃x(Sx ∨ Px)	Prem ⊢ ∃xSx ∨ ∃xPx
(2) ¬[∃xSx ∨ ∃xPx]	Supp/RA
(3) ¬∃xSx & ¬∃xPx	2 DM
(4) ¬∃xSx	3 Simp
(5) ¬∃xPx	3 Simp
(6) ∀x¬Sx	4 QN
(7) ∀x¬Px	5 QN
(8) Si ∨ Pi	1 EI
(9) ¬Si	6 UI
(10) Pi	8, 9 DS
(11) ¬Pi	7 UI
(12) ⊥	10, 11 Conj
(13) (∃x)Sx ∨ (∃x)Px	2-12 RA, DN

23.1.4 EFFECTIVE COMPLETENESS

Finally, we need to say something about the feature of the ∀ and ¬∃ rules that they may be applied as many times as we wish, each time instantiating with a different name. For it is a consequence of this that trees involving them are never complete. Now for most trees representing arguments this is not a problem. For as soon as we have applied the rules to all the names appearing in the argument—that is, to any proper names that may be mentioned in the premises or conclusion, or any instances **i**, **j**, or **k**, etc., that have occurred through application of the ∃ and ¬∀ rules—the tree is effectively complete. There is simply no point in applying the ∀ and ¬∃ rules to individuals that have nothing to do with the argument. So we need to augment our definitions, by defining **effective completeness**, and adjusting the definition of proof of invalidity:

An **open path** of a truth tree involving application of ∀ or ¬∃ or both is **effectively complete** when these rules have been instantiated with all the names appearing in the argument—that is, any proper names occurring in the premises or conclusion, or any names **i**, **j**, **k**…resulting from any previous applications of ∃ and ¬∀ rules on the path—the path being otherwise complete.

This complements our definition of a complete open path:

---

[1] Actually, it is possible to construct a shorter proof than this by noting the equivalence of the conclusion to the conditional ¬∃xSx →∃xPx, and constructing a conditional proof.

An **open path** of a truth tree is **complete** when all the statements on the path have been decomposed, i.e., are either ticked compounds or literals.

Now we can characterize the truth tree method for determining validity as follows:

A sequent is **valid** when all the paths of its truth tree are closed.

A sequent is **invalid** when at least one **open path** of its truth tree is **complete or effectively complete**.

Here's an example of an argument involving effective completeness:

$\forall x(Ax \rightarrow Fx) \therefore \exists xAx \rightarrow \forall xFx$

1		$\forall x(Ax \rightarrow Fx)$	Prem
2	√	$\neg[\exists xAx \rightarrow \forall xFx]$	¬Concl
3	√	$\exists xAx$	$2 \neg\rightarrow$
4	√	$\neg\forall xFx$	
5		Ai	$3 \exists$
6		$\neg Fj$	$4 \neg\forall$
7	√	$Ai \rightarrow Fi$	$1 \forall$

| 8 | | $\neg Ai$ $\quad$ Fi | $7 \rightarrow$ |
| | | $\perp$ | |

| 9 | √ | $Aj \rightarrow Fj$ | $1 \forall$ |

| 10 | | $\neg Aj$ $\quad$ Fj | $9 \rightarrow$ |
| | | $\perp$ | |

Here we use the $\exists$ and $\neg\forall$ rules before applying the $\forall$ rule, in accordance with the restrictions on the predicate logic rules. This means that we had to use a different name **j** in applying $\neg\forall$ on line 6, since we had already used **i** in applying $\exists$ on line 5. But this entails that when we come to apply $\forall$ at line 7, we have two choices for the name we use. When we have exhausted both, the path is effectively complete. But it remains open, so the argument is invalid. This is what we should have expected: it is hardly valid to reason from "All photos of ALIENS are FORGERIES" to "If there are any photos of aliens, all photos are forgeries"! (Here I have applied an interpretation to the abstract argument, with a UD of photos, Ax := x is a photo of an alien, Fx := x is a forgery.) The open path shows why: if there's some example i of an alien photo (Ai), then it is a forgery (Fi). But this is consistent with there being some photo j that is not a forgery (¬Fj) and not an alien photo (¬Aj).

SUMMARY

In predicate logic, our truth tree rules for statement logic need supplementing by decomposition rules for universal and existential quantifications:

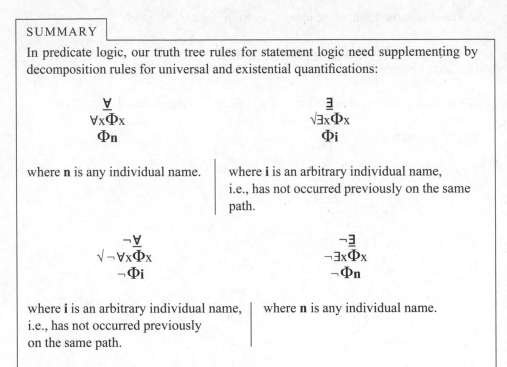

$$\frac{\forall}{\forall x \Phi x}$$
$$\Phi n$$

where **n** is any individual name.

$$\frac{\exists}{\sqrt{} \exists x \Phi x}$$
$$\Phi i$$

where **i** is an arbitrary individual name, i.e., has not occurred previously on the same path.

$$\frac{\neg \forall}{\sqrt{} \neg \forall x \Phi x}$$
$$\neg \Phi i$$

where **i** is an arbitrary individual name, i.e., has not occurred previously on the same path.

$$\frac{\neg \exists}{\neg \exists x \Phi x}$$
$$\neg \Phi n$$

where **n** is any individual name.

- ∃ and ¬∀ should be applied before ∀ or ¬∃.
- Note that the ∀ and ¬∃ rules may be applied as many times as we wish, each time instantiating with a different name. But when all the names occurring in the argument have been used the tree is effectively complete. This necessitates a definition of effective completeness, and a modification of proof of invalidity:
- An **open path** of a truth tree involving application of ∀ or ¬∃ or both is **effectively complete** when these rules have been instantiated with all the names appearing in the argument—that is, any proper names occurring in the premises or conclusion, or any names **i, j, k**...resulting from any previous applications of ∃ and ¬∀ rules on the path—the path being otherwise complete.
- A sequent is **invalid** when at least one **open path** of its truth tree is **complete or effectively complete**.

EXERCISES 23.1

Prove the validity of the following sequents using the truth tree method:

1. ∃x(Ax & ¬Bx) ⊢ ¬∀x(Ax → Bx)

2. ¬∃x(Ax & ¬Bx) ⊢ ∀x(Ax → Bx)

3. ⊢ ¬ ∃xFx ↔ ∀x¬Fx

4. ⊢ ¬∀xFx ↔ ∃x¬Fx

5. ∃xGx → Gh ⊢ ∀x(Gx → Gh)

6. ∀x(Gx → Gh) ⊢ ∃xGx → Gh

Using the truth tree method, determine whether each of the following abstract arguments is formally valid or invalid:

7. ∀x(Fx → Gx) ∴ ∀xFx → ∃xGx

8. ∀x(Fx → Gx) ∴ ∃xFx → ∃xGx

9. ∃x(Fx & ¬Gx) ∴ ∃x(Fx → ¬Gx)

10. ∃xFx & ∃x¬Gx ∴ ∃x(Fx → ¬Gx)

11. ∃xSx ∨ ∃xPx ∴ ∃x(Sx ∨ Px)

12. ∃x(Sx ∨ Px) ∴ ∃xSx ∨ ∃xPx

13. ∀x(Sx ∨ Px) ∴ ∀xSx ∨ ∀xPx

Using truth trees, determine whether each of arguments 14-18 (= ch. 18, 1-5) is valid. For those that are instances of invalid forms, give a set of possible truth values that makes the form invalid.

14. None of HIS stories are PROBABLE. Improbable stories are not easily BELIEVED. So none of his stories are easily believed. [UD: stories]

15. WARMTH RELIEVES pain. Nothing that does not relieve pain is useful for TOOTH-ACHE. So warmth is useful for toothache.

16. UNIVERSITY students are all EDUCATED. All uneducated people are SHALLOW. Therefore no university students are shallow. [UD: people]

17. No WHEELBARROWS are COMFORTABLE. No uncomfortable vehicles are POPULAR. Therefore no wheelbarrows are popular. [UD: vehicles]

18. Some HEALTHY people are OVERWEIGHT. No unhealthy people are good INSURANCE risks. Therefore some overweight people are not good insurance risks. [UD: people]

19. *Using a truth tree, show that the following penevalid argument is valid* by supplying the obvious *implicit premise* that there are Vermont-made beers:
    All VERMONT-made beers taste GREAT. All Vermont-made beers are MICRO-BREWED. Therefore at least some micro-brewed beers taste great.

20. *Using a truth tree, show that the following penevalid argument is valid* by supplying the obvious *implicit premise:*
    No SLOTHS throw CURVE balls. All sloths eat LEAVES. Therefore some creatures that eat leaves do not throw curve balls. [UD: creatures]

Prove the invalidity of the following sequents using truth trees:

21. $\exists x(Ax \ \& \ Bx) \vdash \forall x(Ax \rightarrow Bx)$

22. $\exists xGx \rightarrow Gh \vdash \forall x(Fx \rightarrow Gx)$

23.2 TREES FOR RELATIONAL LOGIC AND IDENTITY

23.2.1 TRUTH TREE RULES IN RELATIONAL LOGIC

In Statement Logic the Truth Tree Method is a decision procedure: it will always give us a decision whether a given argument is valid or invalid. Every tree will be complete: that is, will either be closed or contain at least one complete open path. As we saw in the previous section, in Predicate Logic we need to modify the definition of completeness of trees to incorporate effectively complete paths in trees:

A **truth tree** is **complete** if and only if either (i) every path is closed, or (ii) there is at least one open path that is either complete or effectively complete.

With this modification, the method will also be a decision procedure in Predicate Logic, but *only provided it is restricted to arguments involving predicates with only one individual*—the **unary** or **monadic predicates**. That is, in Monadic Predicate Logic every tree will be complete: i.e., either all its paths will close, or at least one of the open paths will be either complete or effectively complete. Unfortunately, however, when we turn to arguments involving predicates with more than one individual—relational or **polyadic predicates**—the method of truth trees no longer guarantees a decision on whether an argument is valid. This is because the trees associated with some arguments in relational logic there are open paths in trees that do not even become effectively complete. As we shall see, this occurs when we have to decompose certain quantifications over more than one variable—for instance, $\forall y \exists x\, xLy$ or $\neg\exists x \forall y\, xDy$. In such cases our demand that $\forall$ or $\neg\exists$ be instantiated with "all the names appearing in the argument" can never be met, and the tree becomes infinite. So the method of truth trees is not a decision procedure in relational logic. Nevertheless it does work for a large class of relational arguments. Some examples should make this clear.

First let's prove that any *totally connexive* relation R is also *reflexive*:

$\forall x \forall y(xRy \lor yRx) \vdash \forall x\, xRx$

1	$\forall x \forall y(xRy \lor yRx)$	Prem
2	$\sqrt{}$ $\underline{\neg\forall x\, xRx}$	$\neg$Concl
3	$\neg iRi$	$2\ \neg\forall$
4	$\sqrt{}$ $iRi \lor iRi$	$1\ \forall$
5	$iRi \quad iRi$	$4\ \lor$
	$\perp \quad\ \ \perp$	

All the paths close, so the sequent is **valid**. Again, the truth tree method yields a very economical proof. One point worth mentioning is that we interpret the $\forall$ rule as automatically licensing many applications in the same line, i.e., as analogous to our telescoped quantifier rules. The same goes for multiple existential quantifications: we may do repeated applications of $\exists$ in the same line, provided we are careful to use different names for each application.

As another example, let's investigate whether a *symmetric* relation can be *irreflexive*, that is whether

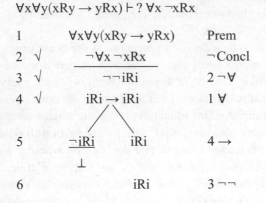

∀x∀y(xRy → yRx) ⊢ ? ∀x ¬xRx

1		∀x∀y(xRy → yRx)	Prem
2	√	¬∀x ¬xRx	¬Concl
3	√	¬¬iRi	2 ¬∀
4	√	iRi → iRi	1 ∀
5		¬iRi iRi	4 →
		⊥	
6		iRi	3 ¬¬

Here we have a tree with one path remaining open. But it is effectively complete—the only name occurring on previous lines is i, and we have found an instance, iRi, that makes the premise true and the conclusion false. So the sequent is **invalid**.

But, as mentioned, the Truth Tree Method does not always yield results for relational arguments, since sometimes the tree never meets the condition of becoming effectively complete. Consider the following example: from the fact that everyone has a mother ∀y∃x xMy, it does not follow that there is someone who is the mother of everyone, ∃x∀y xMy. We know this to be invalid: it is an instance of the Quantifier Shift Fallacy, ∀y∃x xMy ⊬ ∃x∀y xMy. But look what happens when we try using the truth tree method to prove its invalidity:

∀y∃x xMy ⊬ ∃x∀y xMy

1		∀y∃x xMy	Prem
2		¬∃x∀y xMy	¬Concl
3	√	∃x xMu	1 ∀
4		iMu	3 ∃
5	√	¬∀y iMy	2 ¬∃
6		¬iMj	5 ¬∀
7	√	∃x xMj	1 ∀
8		kMj	7 ∃
9	√	¬∀y kMy	2 ¬∃
10		¬kMl	9 ¬∀

···

On line 6, we could not get ¬iMu to obtain a contradiction with iMu because the rule ¬∀ requires us to instantiate with a letter that has not been used already: hence the instance iMj. But since the expression on line 1 is a universal quantification, we may use it again, this time taking j as an instance. But then when we apply ∃ on line 8 we again need a different letter, this time k, giving kMj. Again, there are no restrictions on ¬∃, so we can use k as an instance on line 9. But then when we apply ¬∀ on line 10 we will again need a new letter. This process will repeat indefinitely, and we will never arrive at a contradiction, nor at a path that is effectively complete. The sequent is definitely invalid; but we cannot prove this using truth trees.

23.2.2 ADDITIONAL TRUTH TREE RULES FOR IDENTITY AND DIVERSITY

Now we turn to rules for dealing with identity and diversity. The rule for identity is the analogue of our rule of inference SI: if there is an identity $a = b$ between two names of an individual on one line, and a statement Φa (or Φb) involving a or b one or more times on some other line in the same path, then one or more occurrences of the first name can be replaced by the other. The rule for diversity simply acknowledges the fact that identity is reflexive: this means that any path that eventuates in the statement $a \neq a$ for any individual a automatically closes:

$=$	$\neq$
Φa	
$a = b$	$n \neq n$
Φb	$\perp$

where a and b are any distinct names in the path, Φa is a formula involving at least one occurrence of a, and Φb is the same formula with at least one occurrence of a replaced by b.	where n is an arbitrary individual name.

(Note that the $=$ rule can be applied again and again, so that it does not get checked off.)

Some examples will suffice to demonstrate how to use these rules. First, let's take a simple one, a proof that every individual is self-identical: $\vdash \forall x\, x = x$.

$$1 \quad \neg \forall x\, x = x \qquad \neg\text{Concl}$$

$$2 \;\; \surd \quad \neg i = i \qquad 1\,\neg\forall$$

$$\perp$$

Now let's prove that the statement $\neg\exists x\ x = x$ is a contradiction:

1    $\neg\underline{\exists x\ x = x}$ Prem

2      $\neg u = u$ $1\ \neg\exists$

       $\bot$

Here's a slightly harder example, the Harper-Trudeau argument from chapter 21:

> The only person who can SPEAK for all Canadians is Pierre <u>Trudeau</u>. Stephen <u>Harper</u>, you are no Pierre Trudeau.

which we symbolized as:
St & $\forall x\{Sx \rightarrow x = t\}, \neg h = t\ \therefore \neg Sh$

1	St & $\forall x\{Sx \rightarrow x = t\}$	Prem
2	$\neg h = t$	Prem
3	$\neg\neg Sh$	$\neg$Concl
4 $\checkmark$	Sh	$3\ \neg\neg$
5 $\checkmark$	St	1 &
6	$\forall x\{Sx \rightarrow x = t\}$	
7	$Sh \rightarrow h = t$	$6\ \forall$
$\checkmark$		
8	$\neg Sh$ $h = t$	$7 \rightarrow$
	$\bot$ $\bot$	

Another proof that looks quite forbidding at first, but turns out to be simple, is exercise 20 from chapter 21.

> <u>Hesperus</u> is the EVENING star. <u>Phosphorus</u> is the MORNING star. But the Morning Star is identical with the Evening Star. Therefore Phosphorus and Hesperus are one and the same heavenly body. [UD: heavenly bodies]

This is symbolized:

Eh & ∀x{Ex → x = h}, Mp & ∀x{Mx → x = p}, ∀x∀y{(Mx & Ey) → x = y} ∴ p = h

1		Eh & ∀x{Ex → x = h}	Prem
2		Mp & ∀x{Mx → x = p}	Prem
3		∀x∀y{(Mx & Ey) → x = y}	Prem
4		¬ p = h	¬Concl
5	√	Eh	1 &
6	√	Mp	2 &
7		(Mp & Eh) → p = h	3 ∀

8 √   ¬(Mp & Eh)   p = h   7 →
                        ⊥

9   ¬Mp   ¬Eh   8 ¬&
        ⊥   ⊥

Here we see that the definite descriptions aspect of the first two statements was not nec-essary for validity.

For a proof involving our = rule, we can take this sequent as a simple example:

a = b, b ≠ c ∴ a ≠ c

1		a = b	Prem
2		b ≠ c	Prem
3		¬a ≠ c	¬Concl
4	√	a = c	3 ¬¬
5		b = c	1, 4 =

⊥

Here having a = b on the first line and a = c on the fourth, our = rule licenses us to sub b for a in the latter, giving b = c. As a final example, consider this argument:

Mrs. Peacock was the only person in possession of a CANDLESTICK. Someone with a candlestick was the MURDERER. Logically, therefore, we must conclude that Mrs. Peacock was the murderer. [UD: people]

$Cp \& \forall x \{Cx \rightarrow x = p\}, \exists x(Cx \& Mx) \therefore Mp$

1		$Cp \& \forall x \{Cx \rightarrow x = p\}$	Prem
2		$\exists x(Cx \& Mx)$	Prem
3		$\neg Mp$	$\neg$Concl
4	√	Cp	1 &
5	√	$\forall x \{Cx \rightarrow x = p\}$	1 &
6	√	$Ci \& Mi$	2 $\exists$
7	√	Ci	6 &
8	√	Mi	
9		$Ci \rightarrow i = p$	5 $\forall$
10	√	$\neg Ci \qquad i = p$	9 $\rightarrow$
11		$\perp \qquad\; Mp$	6, 10 =
		$\perp$	

EXERCISES 23.2

Prove the validity of the following sequents using the truth tree method:

23. $\forall x \forall y (xRy \rightarrow \neg yRx) \vdash \neg \forall x\, xRx$

24. $\forall x \forall y\, xFy \vdash \exists x \exists y\, xFy$

25. $\neg \exists x \exists y\, xFy \vdash \neg \forall x \forall y\, xFy$

26. $\forall x \forall y (xFy \& yFx) \vdash \neg \forall x \forall y \neg xFy$

27. *Using truth trees, show that the following two symbolizations of* "No HUMAN being has ever SEEN₂ a DINOSAUR" *are equivalent:* $\forall x \forall y [(Hx \& Dy) \rightarrow \neg xSy]$ and $\forall x \forall y [Hx \rightarrow \neg(Dy \& xSy)]$.

Using the truth tree method determine whether each of the following sequents is valid or invalid:

28. $\vdash \exists x\, x = x$

29. $\vdash \neg \exists x\, x \neq x$

30. $\vdash \neg \forall x \; x = x$

31. $\vdash \forall x \exists y \; x = y$

32. $\vdash \forall x \forall y \; x = y$

33. $\vdash \forall x \exists y \; x \neq y$

Using the truth tree method determine whether each of the following arguments (34-39) is formally valid or invalid:

34. The only EVEN prime is <u>two</u>. Therefore there is an even prime. [UD: prime numbers; Ex := x is even]

35. The <u>Pope</u> is speaking LATIN. Therefore there is someone speaking Latin and he is the Pope.

36. It is not true that no famous AUTHORS like LOGIC. Charles <u>Dodgson</u> certainly likes logic. And Lewis <u>Carroll</u> is a famous author. But Lewis Carroll and Charles Dodgson are one and the same person.

37. The only SURVIVING Beatles are <u>Paul</u> and <u>Ringo</u>. Neither Paul nor Ringo is interested in INDIAN philosophy. So there is no one among the surviving Beatles with an interest in Indian philosophy.

38. The PRINCE of Wales is BALDING. So <u>Charles</u> must be balding, as he is Prince of Wales.

39. <u>Descartes</u> can't be a SOLIPSIST, because he's not <u>me</u>. I am one, and there is only one solipsist. [UD: people; Sx := x is a solipsist, m := me, I (the speaker)]

40. (**CHALLENGE**) *Prove that an asymmetric relation cannot be totally connexive.*

41. (**CHALLENGE**) *Prove that if two individuals are related by both simple connexivity and nonconnexivity, then they are identical.*

42. (**CHALLENGE**) The following is a news report from the *National Post* (October 27, 2000):

> On Wednesday, Jim Flaherty, the Ontario Attorney-General, contacted officials at the federal immigration and justice departments to see whether Eminem could be barred from the country. However, Derik Hodgson, a spokesman for the Ministry

of Immigration, said officials found no reason to block Eminem, who takes his "Anger Management Tour" to Montreal's Molson Centre tonight. "We aren't the thought police," said Mr. Hodgson, adding "if all people who made bad music were kept out of Canada, we could have stopped disco."

[Bx := x makes bad music, Kx := x could be kept out of Canada, Dx := x could have stopped disco, m := the Ministry of Immigration, e := Eminem]

What is Hodgson's argument? Supplying the implicit premises "If some people who make bad music could not be kept out of the country, then Eminem could not be kept out," *and* "The Ministry could not have stopped disco," *and using the dictionary provided, determine the conclusion of the argument using a truth tree.*

Chapter Twenty-Four

Other Logics

You now have behind you a course in elementary symbolic logic and its application to argument. The purpose of this chapter is to give a taste of where logic goes from here. To this end, we will go over briefly a number of different topics in non-elementary logic: second order logic, modal logic, deontic logic, quantum logic, and intuitionistic logic.

24.1 SECOND ORDER LOGIC

This extension of logic generalizes it so that we can quantify over predicates themselves. For example, in treating identity above, we made use of the principle that if two individuals were identical, then they should have all their properties in common. (This was the foundation of our rule of SI, the Substitution of Identicals.) But to express this in a properly general way, we need to be able to generalize not only over all individuals, but also over all predicates. If we are allowed this extension, we can express both this and Leibniz's famous Principle of the Identity of Indiscernibles as follows:

> The Identity of Indiscernibles:
> $\forall x \forall y \{\forall \Psi(\Psi x \leftrightarrow \Psi y) \rightarrow x = y\}$
> Any two individuals having all their properties in common are identical.
>
> The Indiscernibility of Identicals:
> $\forall x \forall y \{x = y \rightarrow \forall \Psi(\Psi x \leftrightarrow \Psi y)\}$
> Any two identical individuals have all their properties in common.

The Indiscernibility of Identicals is encapsulated in the rule SI introduced in chapter 21. But it is a theorem we can prove in second order logic. Likewise the Identity of Indiscernibles:

$$(1)\ \forall\Psi(\Psi u \leftrightarrow \Psi v) \qquad\qquad \text{Supp/CP}$$
$$(2)\ u = u \leftrightarrow u = v \qquad\qquad \text{1 UI (\textit{making} }\Psi x := \text{'}u = x\text{')}$$
$$(3)\ (u = u \rightarrow u = v)\ \&\ (u = v \rightarrow u = u) \qquad \text{2 BE}$$
$$(4)\ u = u \rightarrow u = v \qquad\qquad \text{3 Simp}$$
$$(5)\ (\forall x)x = x \qquad\qquad \text{Reflexivity of Identity}$$
$$(6)\ u = u \qquad\qquad \text{5 UI}$$
$$(7)\ u = v \qquad\qquad \text{4, 6 MP}$$
$$(8)\ \forall\Psi(\Psi u \leftrightarrow \Psi v) \rightarrow u = v \qquad\qquad \text{1-7 CP}$$
$$(9)\ \forall x \forall y\{\forall\Psi(\Psi x \leftrightarrow \Psi y) \rightarrow x = y\} \qquad \text{8 UG}$$

EXERCISE 24.1

(a) Derive the Indiscernibility of Identicals as a theorem in second order logic.

(b) Symbolize the statement: "There is no object that has no properties."

24.2 MODAL LOGIC

We considered above (and in Appendix 1) the Paradox of Material Implication. This worries many philosophers, although teachers of first year logic are largely reconciled to it. As we saw, one way of expressing the paradox is this: $p \rightarrow q$ is logically equivalent to $\neg p \vee q$ (by MI), which is in turn equivalent to $\neg(p\ \&\ \neg q)$ (by DM and DN). And this is counterintuitive, since it says that $p \rightarrow q$ holds just in case it is not the case that p is T and q is F. But many people would expect it to be equivalent, not to its simply not being the case that p is T and q is F, but to its being *impossible that p* is T and q is F. For in that case, if p is true, it is impossible for q to be false, which seems to capture better the idea that q follows from p. This motivates us to look at the whole question of possibility and necessity, which are the subject of Modal Logic.

The basis of this extension of logic is the introduction of two more statement operators, not truth functional ones this time:

It is possible that p: $\Diamond$p
It is necessary that p: $\Box p$

Actually each of these may be defined in terms of the other as follows:

$$\Box p =_{\text{def}} \neg \Diamond \neg p$$
$$\Diamond p =_{\text{def}} \neg \Box \neg p$$

The first says that something is necessarily the case iff it is impossible for it not to be the case; the second says that something is possibly the case iff it is not necessary for it to not be the case. These are logically equivalent, and we'll take the first as a rule of inference for Modal Logic:

> **Modal Inference (Mod)**
> From the negation of the possibility that a given statement is not so, infer that it is necessary that it is so; and vice versa.
> *In symbols:*
> *From* $\neg \Diamond \neg p$ *infer* $\Box p$, *and vice versa.*

This allows us to get a handle on implication by defining a new notion of *strict implication*, $p \strictif q$, which captures the intuition mentioned above. p strictly implies q just in case *it is impossible that p is T and q is F*:

$$p \strictif q: =_{\text{def}} \neg \Diamond (p \mathbin{\&} \neg q)$$

EXERCISE 24.2

Prove that that definition is equivalent to this: $p \strictif q: =_{\text{def}} \Box (p \rightarrow q)$.

24.3 DEONTIC LOGIC

This is the branch of logic that investigates the logic of obligation, with particular application to moral theory. For example, suppose we define xAy to mean that person x performs action y. And now we define two new operators as follows:

> $Op =_{\text{def}}$ it is obligatory that p
> $Pp =_{\text{def}}$ it is permissible that p

Now we may articulate some precepts of moral theory as follows (with x implicitly taken to range over persons and y over actions):

$\forall x \forall y (\neg \mathbf{O}xAy \rightarrow \mathbf{P}\neg xAy)$
i.e., if it is not obligatory for a person to perform an action, then it is permissible for that person not to perform that action.

$\forall x \forall y (\mathbf{O}xAy \rightarrow \Diamond xAy)$
i.e., it is obligatory for a person to perform an action only if it is possible for that person to perform that action.

$\forall x \forall y \neg \Box(xAy \rightarrow \mathbf{O}Axy)$

i.e., it is not necessarily the case that if a person performs an action, that person is obliged to perform that action.

EXERCISE 24.3

Symbolize the following statements in deontic logic:
  (a) Some permissible actions are not necessary.
  (b) It is not necessary for everyone to perform every action that is obligatory.

24.4 QUANTUM LOGIC

One of the more curious features of Quantum Theory is that certain variables that physicists standardly use to define the state of a system, such as position, energy, momentum, angular momentum, etc., do not always have determinate values in certain situations. A certain elementary particle coming out of some interaction of particles, for instance, might have two and only two possible values of spin along the x-direction: spin-up and spin-down. (This is what it means for the spin to be *quantized*.) And yet if the particle is in a certain state there may be no fact of the matter which direction its spin is in. On a certain proportion of experiments on similarly prepared particles, it will be found in the spin-up state, and in the remainder, spin-down. Nevertheless, to suppose that each particle is either in the spin-up or in the spin-down state prior to the experiment is incompatible with the state description according to quantum theory. And experiment shows that quantum theory makes the right predictions, and that the alternative of supposing that the particle is or is not in the spin-up state, and it was just a question of our not knowing which, turns out to be incompatible with the experimental statistics.[1] There is no fact of the matter.

One way of expressing this state of affairs is to say that while it is true that the particle is in either spin-up or in spin-down—the disjunction is true—neither disjunct can be asserted to be true or false without contradiction. This has led some philosophers to experiment with the idea that in quantum theory, nature exhibits a non-classical logic, in a word, a *Quantum Logic*.

Hans Reichenbach was the first to offer a theory along these lines. He speculated that the Law of Bivalence—the principle that every statement is either true or false—should be abandoned. In place of the usual 2-valued logic, one should have for quantum theory a three-valued logic: true (T), false (F), and indeterminate ($\ddagger$). The statement that the particle mentioned above is in a state of spin-up would have the truth value $\ddagger$. Here is a table

---

[1]   This result, when made suitably precise, is the content of Bell's Theorem, subsequently verified by the experiments of Alain Aspect and others.

of the proposed truth values for this three-valued system for three standard truth-functional operators:

p	q	$p \& q$	$p \vee q$	$p \to q$
T	T	T	T	T
T	‡	‡	T	‡
T	F	F	T	F
‡	T	‡	T	T
‡	‡	‡	‡	‡
‡	F	F	‡	‡
F	T	F	T	T
F	‡	F	‡	T
F	F	F	F	T

The rationale for picking these values is as follows: whenever p and q have the classical values of T or F, the statement operators have the same values as classically: T if both p and q are T, F otherwise, etc. If p is T and q ‡ (indeterminate), however, there is insufficient reason to assign T or F to $p \& q$, so it also receives the value ‡ (indeterminate). Similarly, as classically, $p \to q$ is T if p is F (whatever the value of q), and T if q is T (whatever the value of p), and this conditional is only F if p is T and q is F; otherwise ‡. A similar reasoning explains all the other assigned values.[2]

In another system of three-valued logic invented by Kleene, '&,' '∨,' and '→' all have the values assigned above and the truth table for negation is:

p	$\neg p$
T	F
‡	‡
F	T

As can easily be seen, in Kleene's system (K_3) the law of excluded middle does not hold: if the value of p is ‡, then $p \vee \neg p$ also has the value ‡.

EXERCISE 24.4

(a) Prove that $p \to p$ also does not hold in K_3.
(b) Show that this can be fixed by altering the truth table for '→' so that it has the value T when both p and q are ‡.

---

[2] Reichenbach also distinguished three different types of negation, and an Alternative Implication and a Quasi-implication. These are all somewhat unintuitive, however, and I will not duplicate them here.

More recent theories, inspired by Hilary Putnam's paper "Is Logic Empirical?," have tried to develop an interpretation of quantum mechanics based on the idea that, just as Einstein's General Relativity reveals that geometry is not Euclidean, so Quantum Mechanics reveals that logic is not Boolean—i.e., that there are certain propositions that are neither true nor false. The general consensus, however, is that the Quantum Logic approach has failed to convince its critics that a new system of logic is needed to express what is going on in the theory, nor has it solved any of the interpretational problems that its devisers had hoped it would address.

24.5 INTUITIONISTIC LOGIC

Another interesting attempt to generalize from classical logic that denies the Law of Bivalence is that of the *Intuitionists*, who deny the applicability of the Law of Excluded Middle: $\vdash p \lor \neg p$. Here the motivation comes from within mathematics, and the desire to avoid the Platonist doctrine that mathematical propositions are true or false independently of whether any person knows them to be so. In opposition to this the Intuitionists held that a mathematical proposition is not true until a direct construction for it has been found whereby its truth may be exhibited. Brouwer, the originator of the idea,[3] wanted to set mathematics on a new and firmer foundation—free from the paradoxes discovered by Russell and others—by abandoning the idea that a proposition in mathematics could be proved by "Indirect Proof"—that is, by the form of *reductio ad absurdum* that derives p from the derivation of a contradiction from its negation, $\neg p$. (This would involve applying RA—from the derivation of $\bot$ from $\neg p$, derive $\neg\neg p$—this is still valid in intuitionistic logic—and then, by an application of the second form of DN—from $\neg\neg p$ derive p—this is what is denied by the intuitionists.) Indirect proof only works if you assume that each proposition has a determinate truth value in advance of being discovered or invented by human ingenuity; then p must be either true or false, so that proving its negation false leaves its truth as the only other option. If bivalence is rejected, then to have proved $\neg p$ false is to have proved $\neg\neg p$, but this is NOT the same as having established p directly. If no construction of p has been given, its possibility has not been established. (For this reason, Intuitionism in this form is often called *Constructivism*.) Thus Intuitionism denies the second form of Double Negation (DN), and with it the validity of indirect proof,

---

[3] Brouwer himself did not provide (or even encourage) a formal system of this logic, but soon afterwards it was shown by Heyting that a perfectly consistent set of rules could be given for an Intuitionistic Logic. Heyting took an axiomatic approach, giving his system as a set of 11 axioms for Statement Logic. It is possible to simplify his system and add axioms for predicate logic with identity, giving 12 axioms and three rules of inference, MP, UG, and EI.

involving RA together with this rule, as well as the theorem that can be established from this rule together with RA: the Law of Excluded Middle, $\vdash p \lor \neg p$. Correspondingly, in Predicate Logic only three of the four forms of Quantifier Negation are permissible:

From $\exists x \neg \Phi x$, derive $\neg \forall x \Phi x$.
From $\neg \exists x \Phi x$, derive $\forall x \neg \Phi x$, and vice versa.

But the following form is not valid:

From $\neg \forall x \Phi x$, derive $\exists x \neg \Phi x$.

EXERCISE 24.5

Prove that the first three forms of QN above are derivable without assuming DN.

An interesting application of this to mathematics is given by John Bell, who argues that infinitesimals (which we'll describe in a moment) can be justified if one accepts an intuitionistic foundation for them.[4] He gives the following example to illustrate this point. Suppose we take two points on the real line, a and b, and call them distinguishable if they are not identical, i.e., if $a \neq b$. Now two points a and b will be *indistinguishable* if they are not distinguishable, i.e., if $\neg a \neq b$, i.e., if $\neg \neg a = b$. But in intuitionistic logic the law of double negation does not hold, so that from this we cannot infer $a = b$: *indistinguishability does not entail identity*, in contradiction to Leibniz's principle described above. As a result, if we take all the points x that are indistinguishable from 0, and call this the *infinitesimal neighbourhood* of 0, $I(0)$, then this does not reduce to the set of points containing only 0. Thus if we call all those numbers that are so close to 0 as to be indistinguishable from it *infinitesimals*, then from the fact that

It is not the case that all infinitesimals in I (i.e., points that are indistinguishable from 0) are identical with 0. $\neg \forall x(\neg x \neq 0 \to x = 0)$

we cannot infer that

There exists an infinitesimal in I (i.e., a point indistinguishable from 0) that is not identical with 0. $\exists x(\neg x \neq 0 \,\&\, x \neq 0)$

---

[4] John Bell, *A Primer of Infinitesimal Analysis* (Cambridge: Cambridge UP, 1998), pp. 6-7.

This inference would be provable if we allowed the form of QN that was declared invalid above, namely, from $\neg \forall x \Phi x$, derive $\exists x \neg \Phi x$. But any point **i** satisfying $\exists x (\neg x \neq 0$ & $x \neq 0)$ would be such that $\neg \mathbf{i} \neq 0$ & $\mathbf{i} \neq 0$, an evident contradiction. Thus the example illustrates nicely how the jettisoning of DN requires a concomitant jettisoning of the form of QN that applies to $\neg \forall x \Phi x$.

As mentioned above, Heyting gave a set of axioms for Intuitionistic Logic (hereafter IL). These can be recast as a natural deduction system like the one in this book. In chapter 11 above we outlined the rules of Statement Logic that are necessary and sufficient for a formal system in which all correct proofs in classical logic can be performed (assuming biconditionals are re-expressed as conjunctions of conditionals): MP, CP; Conj, Simp; Disj, DS; RA, DN. We noted there that one form of the DN rule, $p \vdash \neg\neg p$, can be derived by RA, and thus need not be included among the primitive rules. Thus the converse DN rule, $\neg\neg p \vdash p$, together with the other seven primitive rules, constitute a complete system. Now Heyting's system of axioms is provably equivalent to this set of rules minus the converse DN rule: MP, CP; Conj, Simp; Disj, DS; and RA. To this set we may now add UI, UG, EI, EG; this set constitutes IL. What then is the status of this system vis-à-vis classical logic?

One way to regard IL is as a generalization of classical logic; on this reading it stands in the same relation to classical logic as non-Euclidean Geometry stands to Euclidean Geometry. In each case we drop one classical axiom; in each case, too, the resulting system can be proven to be consistent in the sense that the classical system can be modelled in it, so that the non-classical system is consistent if the classical one is. But then the meaning of at least some of the statement operators must be different. Just as the points and lines of non-Euclidean Geometry are implicitly defined by the four axioms of that geometry (without the parallel postulate), and so do not necessarily mean the same thing as in classical geometry, so 'and,' 'not,' 'if...then...,' and 'or' will also have slightly altered meanings without the principle of bivalence. This is particularly true of negation, since the law of double negation does not hold in the intuitionists' system; and as we have seen, to say that a proposition is negated in the intuitionists' sense is to say that it can be (constructively) proven that it is not (constructively) provable. It is possible, though, that all the signs have different meanings, and indeed Heyting insisted that his signs are all to be taken as undefined primitives.[5] In keeping with this, if all the operators are defined implicitly by the axioms and rules, we may introduce new symbols for the intuitionistic statement operators: '$\sim$' in place of '$\neg$,' '$\bullet$' in place of '&,' '$\cup$' in place of 'v,' and '$\supset$' in place of '$\rightarrow$.' The rules of inference of IL will then be MP, CP; Conj, Simp; Disj, DA; and RA, but all expressed in terms of the new operators.

---

[5] See Kneale and Kneale, *Development*, p. 675.

EXERCISE 24.6

Suppose we define two further new operators in IL as follows:

$$p \oplus q =_{\text{def}} \sim(\sim p \bullet \sim q) \quad \text{and} \quad p \Rightarrow q =_{\text{def}} \sim(p \bullet \sim q)$$

Clearly $p \oplus q$ is an analogue of classical disjunction, and $p \Rightarrow q$ an analogue of classical implication. Show that the following analogues of the law of excluded middle and of double negation can be derived as theorems in IL: (a) $p \oplus \sim p$; and (b) $\sim\sim p \Rightarrow p$. (It is by such devices that we can model classical logic within IL.)

Following Gödel, however, we may take this reasoning further.[6] If negation in the intuitionists' sense, $\sim p$, means that it is (constructively) provable that p is not (constructively) provable, and $p \bullet q$ likewise means that p is demonstrable (= constructively provable) and q is demonstrable, why not make this explicit? Let us therefore introduce a new (non-truth-functional) operator Δ, so that

Δp means "it is demonstrable that p."

Then Heyting's *not, and, or,* and *if... then...* can be interpreted as follows:

$\sim p$	$\equiv$	$\Delta \neg \Delta p$
$p \bullet q$	$\equiv$	$\Delta p \,\&\, \Delta q$
$p \cup q$	$\equiv$	$\Delta p \vee \Delta q$
$p \supset q$	$\equiv$	$\Delta p \rightarrow \Delta q$

EXERCISE 24.7

Prove that given these equivalences and assuming that $\Delta\Delta p \equiv \Delta p$, the Law of Excluded Middle in IL, $p \cup \sim p$, is equivalent to the claim that $\neg\Delta\neg\Delta p \rightarrow \Delta p$. (This means "if it is not demonstrable that p is undemonstrable, then p is demonstrable"; it's hardly surprising that Brouwer would want to reject such a strong claim!)

On the above interpretation of Gödel's, the meaning of intuitionism has been made explicit: it concerns provability by constructive methods, and Heyting's system can be

---

[6] See Kurt Gödel, "Zur intuitionistischen Arithmetik und Zahlentheorie," and "Eine Interpretation des intuitionistischen Aussagenkalküls," *Ergebnisse eines mathematischen Kolloquiums*, Heflt iv (1932), pp. 34-38 and 39-40; Kneale and Kneale, pp. 678-80.

regarded as an axiomatic theory of provability by such constructive methods. But then, as the Kneales astutely observe, "Heyting's calculus is not a system of logic in the strict sense," since "it presupposes classical logic, and has only been mistaken for an alternative logic because of the intuitionists' unfortunate custom of talking of theorems as statements of provability" (*Development*, p. 681).

The Paradoxes of Material Implication

MATERIAL IMPLICATION

"Material Implication" is the traditional name for the kind of implication we have been discussing in this book, symbolized by the '→'; that is, the relation between p and q in a conditional statement of the form $p \rightarrow q$. (Another name for this type of conditional is the "Philonian Conditional," after the philosopher Philo, a pupil of Diodorus Cronus of the fourth century BCE.) The neatest way of describing this kind of conditional is by stating its equivalence to the disjunction $\neg p \vee q$: this is what is expressed in our equivalence rule Material Implication. And as explained in chapter 13, when we do a truth table for $\neg p \vee q$ it comes out the same as the table for $p \rightarrow q$:

p	q	¬p ∨ q
T	T	F T
F	T	T T
T	F	F F
F	F	T T

p	q	p → q
T	T	T
F	T	T
T	F	F
F	F	T

Philo is reported by Sextus Empiricus to have claimed that "A conditional is false only when it begins with a truth and ends with a falsehood" (*Against the Mathematicians*, viii, 113; Kneale and Kneale, p. 130). A rival view reported by Sextus is that of Chrysippus, where a conditional is true "when the contradictory of its consequent is incompatible with its antecedent" (*Outlines of Pyrrhonism*, ii, 110-12; Kneale and Kneale, 129). The former view parallels our definition of formal validity, the latter Chrysippian view parallels our general definition of the validity of an argument.

This says that a conditional is false only if the antecedent is true and the consequent false. From this it follows that (a) the conditional is true if the consequent is true, and (b) the conditional is true if the antecedent is false. (You can see this by inspecting rows 1 and 2 for (a), and 2 and 4 for (b).) To see what is paradoxical about this, take the following statement:

(A1) "If all philosophers are immortal, Socrates is dead."

This has been chosen because it is evidently a false statement. Yet by the above criterion, it would count as a true conditional! For it not only satisfies (a), since the consequent is certainly true; it also satisfies (b), since the antecedent is clearly false. The sense of paradox is heightened by the fact that (a) corresponds to the argument form $q \therefore p \rightarrow q$, and (b) to the argument form $\neg p \therefore p \rightarrow q$, which we proved valid in Exers. 23 (ii) and (i) resp. in the exercises for chapter 11. Let's symbolize "all philosophers are immortal" by I, and "Socrates is dead" by D. Then (A1) is symbolized by I $\rightarrow$ D. Now D is true, so I $\rightarrow$ D follows by (a); and I is false, but from $\neg$I we can prove I $\rightarrow$ D by (b).

Perhaps the result that brings out this paradox the best is that if we interpret (A1) as a Philonian conditional, then its denial, $\neg(I \rightarrow D)$, entails I & $\neg$D: that is, asserting the evident falsity of (A1) produces the result that we can infer that all philosophers are immortal and Socrates is not, after all, dead! Or, to give another example, if you claim that

(A2) "If I FALL out of the window, I won't break my LEG," F $\rightarrow \neg$L,

and I deny it and thus assert $\neg$(F $\rightarrow \neg$L), I would hardly be taken to be asserting that F & L, that you will fall out of the window and break your leg!

As noted in chapter 11, these highly counterintuitive results are known as the *Paradoxes of Material Implication*. They derive from the fact that when we symbolize a conditional, we do not take into account any relationship of meaning or other connection between the antecedent and consequent, save for the truth-functional one. Many (if not most) of the conditionals occurring in ordinary language, on the other hand, are considered true because of some non-truth-functional relationship between the antecedent and consequent, such as the meaning connection in the above example between being immortal and being dead. If such a connection is relevant to the validity of an inference, it needs to be made explicit as an extra implicit premise. In the above example concerning immortal philosophers and the dead Socrates, we would need to make explicit that "Someone who is immortal cannot be dead" (and also that Socrates is a philosopher). This is the reason we regard (A1) as false. If all philosophers are immortal, then, since Socrates is a philosopher and someone who is immortal cannot be dead, it cannot be true that Socrates is dead. Likewise, if I deny that when you fall out of the window you won't break your leg it is because I believe there is a causal relationship between your falling out of the window and your possibly breaking your leg.

As a result of this situation, many philosophers have been motivated to try a different approach to the conditional. One famous attempt is the attempt by C.I. Lewis (1883-1964) to replace material implication by what he called "strict implication" (see chapter 24). There is a whole literature on Relevance Logic, in which one is precisely not allowed to assert a conditional if there is no relevant connection between antecedent and consequent; and likewise one is not allowed to infer a disjunction from a statement if the second disjunct is not relevant to the first. (This prevents the proof of the Paradoxes of Material Implication using the Disjunction rule of inference.) There is also much written on the causal conditional, and on counter-factual conditionals ("If you were to fall out of the window, your leg would not get broken"). All these attempts, however, give us a different kind of logic than the classical one. Strict Implication is a case in point, as I will now briefly discuss.

Lewis identified the problem underlying the paradoxes of material implication as being that it involves too liberal a notion of implication.[1] From the mere fact that p is false, it implies any other statement q (this is the sequent form $\neg p \therefore p \to q$, i.e., (b) above); and from the mere fact that q is true, it is implied by any other statement p (this is the sequent form $q \therefore p \to q$, i.e., (a) above). He held, on the other hand, that one statement p implies another q if and only if it is *impossible* for p to be true and q to be false. This he called *strict implication*, and symbolized it by $p \dashv q$. Using the symbol from modal logic '$\Diamond$' to denote "it is possible that," Lewis's strict implication may be defined as

$p \dashv q =_{\text{def}} \neg \Diamond (p \,\&\, \neg q)$

That one statement *strictly implies* another is defined as meaning that it is impossible for the first to be true and the second false.

Lewis's intention in introducing this kind of implication was to use it as the basis for Modus Ponens. The trouble with this is that it is not the use of material implication in Modus Ponens that leads to any kind of difficulty in logic, but rather the kind of argument represented by (a) and (b) above, where the conditional is derived from the denial of the antecedent or from the truth of the consequent. But as William and Martha Kneale observe, "No one would dream of putting forward an argument of the form

$p, p \to q \therefore q$

if he had established the truth of the second premise either by discovering the falsity of the other premise or by establishing the truth of the conclusion. For in the first case he would not be able to assert the other premise, and in the second case he would not need an argument to reach the conclusion" (Kneale and Kneale, p. 554).

---

[1] In what follows I am following the account of Lewis's strict implication given in Kneale and Kneale, pp. 549-59.

This is a profound observation, and explains very neatly why, contrary to our intuitions, material implication does not lead to arguments that we would intuitively regard as invalid being found valid. (Most introductory textbooks that treat material implication simply assert this to be so without giving a justification.) Likewise, to complete this thought, one would never try to establish $p \ \& \ \neg q$ by denying the truth of the conditional $p \rightarrow q$, since that denial would be understood as simply denying that q does indeed follow from p, i.e., as an attack on the reasoning by which someone had purported to establish the connection between p and q.

The foregoing discussion suggests the following resolution of the paradox of material implication. It is paradoxical if we assume that every use of "if...then..." in English (or its equivalent in other languages) is accurately represented by the Philonian conditional. In many, perhaps even most, uses of "if...then...," a non-truth-functional connection between antecedent and consequent may be intended. In the vast majority of cases, however, such a connection is irrelevant; all that is relevant to most inferences is the truth connection, accurately represented by the Philonian conditional. If a connection in meaning is relevant to the validity of an inference, this meaning connection can be made explicit by an added premise or premises, and then a logical analysis based on the Philonian conditional will no longer lead to paradoxical results.

Returning to the above statements, we regard (A1) as false because Socrates' being dead is incompatible with all philosophers' being immortal. We would regard it as true if his not being dead ($\neg D$, the denial of the consequent) were incompatible with I, the antecedent. Similarly with (A2): we would regard it as true if and only if breaking your leg ($\neg\neg L$, the denial of the consequent), were incompatible with jumping out of the window (F, the antecedent), which it is not. This means that when we deny the truth of a conditional like (A1) because of the meaning connection or causal connection between antecedent and consequent, we are implicitly applying the Chrysippian criterion mentioned in the box above: a conditional is true if the contradictory of its consequent is incompatible with its antecedent, and otherwise false. When a conditional is regarded as true or false by virtue of a connection between its antecedent and consequent, then it is the latter criterion we are applying in analyzing it.

Nevertheless, as argued above, this does not matter in the context of argument. We would never try to establish the truth of a conditional using one of the versions of the paradox of material implication and then proceed to use it in a modus ponens. In logical inferences and proofs a conditional has the force of the Philonian conditional. Thus (A1) is a true statement in exactly the same sense that the following statement is true:

(B1) "Either it is untrue that all philosophers are immortal, or Socrates is dead."

This disjunction is true because at least one of the disjuncts is true; in fact, both are. But it is not true by virtue of some connection in meaning between the two disjuncts. Similarly (A2) is equivalent to

(B2) "Either it is untrue that you will fall out of the window, or you will not break a leg."

If I deny (B2), $\neg F \vee \neg L$, then I am indeed asserting F & L.

SUMMARY

- On the Philonian analysis, a conditional $p \rightarrow q$ is true if its antecedent is false or if its consequent is true, and is otherwise false.
- This is also called the Material Conditional. It is logically equivalent to $\neg p \vee q$, and this equivalence underwrites the law of Material Implication (MI).
- On the Chrysippian analysis, a conditional $p \Rightarrow q$ is true if the denial of its consequent is incompatible with its antecedent, and is otherwise false.
- Probably the great majority of conditionals used in ordinary language are Chrysippian, and embody some connection or relevance between antecedent and consequent.
- Nevertheless, in any normal case where a conditional is used to make inferences, it performs its role as a Philonian (i.e., material) conditional;
- and in the rare cases where the validity of an inference depends on some relevant information connecting the antecedent and consequent, this information can be made explicit as an added premise or premises, and the argument analyzed as if the conditional stands for material implication.

A Little History: *Consequentiae*

In chapter 12 we saw how the Hypothetical Syllogism could be expressed as a valid *sequent schema*

(1) $p \rightarrow q, q \rightarrow r \vdash p \rightarrow r$

We saw too how the same information could be expressed as

(2) $\vdash [(p \rightarrow q) \mathbin{\&} (q \rightarrow r)] \rightarrow (p \rightarrow r)$

where (2) may be obtained from (1) by conditionalizing, i.e., supposing its two premises. This example has some historical significance. Aristotle, who apparently single-handedly invented what we now call Predicate Logic, did not recognize conditional statements and rules of inference based on them as the proper subject of logical inquiry. Yet he would make statements like

(3) "If every A is B, and every B is Γ, then every A is Γ."

to justify inferring "every A is Γ" from the two premises "every A is B" and "every B is Γ."[1] (3) is a *conditional statement*. Aristotle's pupil and immediate successor Theophrastus, however, expressed such rules as explicit argument schemas:

---

[1] See William and Martha Kneale, *The Development of Logic* (Oxford: Clarendon, 1972), pp. 73, 111. A more literal rendering of Aristotle's statements would be "If B is predicated of all A, and Γ is predicated of all B,...," and so forth. Note the Greek letters, A, B, Γ, etc. Aristotle used them because he was Greek; I have used them because they do not stand for statements but categories or predicates.

(4) "Every A is B; and every B is Γ; therefore every A is Γ."

Clearly this amounts to the same thing, if all one is concerned with is what follows from what. Yet Theophrastus' casting of (3) into the form (4) allowed him to formulate rules of inference for conditional statements themselves. The rule that one can find implicit in Aristotle as

(5) "If given that-P it is necessary that-Q, and given that-Q it is necessary that-R, then given that-P it is necessary that-R."

is explicitly expressed by Theophrastus as an argument schema for the Hypothetical Syllogism:

(6) "If A then B; and if B then Γ; therefore if A then Γ."

In the Middle Ages, some logicians would slip back and forth between these two ways of stating rules as if they were the same thing. They would express the same rule, which they called a *consequentia* (literally, a consequence, "what follows from what"), indifferently in conditional form as in (3) or (5), or as an argument schema as in (4) or (6). This led to some confusion between antecedents and premises, and between consequents and conclusions, and between validity (of inferences) and truth (of statements). Still, the sense in which they wished to call a conditional statement schema like (3) or (5) "valid" is captured by its expression as a *sequent schema*. Expressed as sequent schemas, (5) becomes (2) and (6) becomes (1), both of which are valid according to our definitions above.

THE *CONSEQUENTIA MIRABILIS*

One consequentia with a particularly interesting history is the so-called *consequentia mirabilis* (Marvellous Consequence). This is the sequent schema

Consequentia mirabilis: $p \rightarrow p, \neg p \rightarrow p \vdash p.$

Here strictly speaking the first premise is not necessary, since we can derive it as a theorem. Only the convention, found in both Aristotle and the Stoics, that every argument or sequent must have exactly two premises and one conclusion makes it necessary. The Stoics, in fact, had derived it from their argument schema: $p \rightarrow q, \neg p \rightarrow q \therefore q$. Here, since q stands for any statement, we can let it stand for whatever p stands for (i.e., sub p for q), yielding $p \rightarrow p, \neg p \rightarrow p \therefore p$. They had even used it to refute skepticism, arguing as follows:

If there is proof, there is proof; but if one succeeded in proving that there were no proof, then there is proof. Therefore, there is proof.[2]

But although the *consequentia mirabilis* was known in antiquity—indeed, it is exploited in an ingenious proof in Euclid's *Elements*—it was made famous in the early modern period by Gerolamo Saccheri (1667-1733).[3] In his *Logica Demonstrativa* (1697) Saccheri explicitly identified it, named it, and sought to make it the basis of proof for all tautologies in logic. What is interesting about Saccheri is not just that he gave it pride of place in his logic, but that using it he almost discovered non-Euclidean geometry (later used by Einstein in his theory of curved spacetime). For, more than 30 years after his *Logica Demonstrativa*, Saccheri published a book called *Euclides ab Omni Nævo Vindicatus* (*Euclid Freed of Every Blemish*), in which he set about trying to prove Euclid's famous Fifth Postulate (the Parallels Postulate) by this method. The postulate states

If a straight line falling on two straight lines makes the interior angles on the same side less than two right angles, the two straight lines, when produced indefinitely, meet on that side on which the angles are less than two right angles.

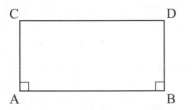

Cardan had shown that this was equivalent to constructing a quadrilateral by erecting equal perpendiculars AC and BD on a straight line AB, and then positing that the two equal angles at C and D must be right angles (call this R). Saccheri's idea was to suppose R was false, and then from this supposition together with the other postulates of Euclidean geometry to prove R's truth. There were two cases: the angles at C and D are either (i) obtuse, or (ii) acute. For case (i) Saccheri worked out lots of consequences of the first four postulates + ¬R (thus proving theorems in what would later be termed elliptic geometry), and thought he had proved that ¬R implies R; but he had unwittingly smuggled in an assumption that is true for Euclidean geometry, but untrue in elliptic geometry. For case (ii) (what is now called hyperbolic geometry) his claim that ¬R leads to contradiction (and thus to R by reductio) also contains a blemish (ironically); otherwise Saccheri might

---

2 As the Kneales observe, the same way of refuting the skepticism was taken up by Augustine, and more famously by Descartes in his *cogito ergo sum*. Descartes argued that the one truth he could not doubt was that he was doubting (*Meditation III*).

3 See Euclid, *Elements*, ix, 12; Kneale and Kneale, *Development*, pp. 173-74, 380.

have discovered non-Euclidean geometry almost a century before hyperbolic geometry was surmised by Gauss and independently worked out by Lobachevsky in the 1820s, and even longer before Riemann's discovery of elliptic geometry became known in 1867.[4]

It was mentioned above that the first premise of the *consequentia mirabilis* is a logical truth, and actually redundant. Shorn of this redundant first premise, it may be expressed as $\neg p \rightarrow p \vdash p$, or equivalently, as the theorem

$$\vdash (\neg p \rightarrow p) \rightarrow p$$

In this form, the *consequentia mirabilis* reappears as the third of Łukasiewicz's three axiom schemas for statement logic, $(\neg p \rightarrow p) \rightarrow p$: see chapter 12. Other examples of the application of the *consequentia mirabilis* may be found in the exercises to that chapter.

---

[4] Whether Saccheri's work had any influence on the discovery of non-Euclidean geometry is not clear.

Logic Diagrams

VENN DIAGRAMS

In the text we have used a version of Logic Diagrams pioneered by Lewis Carroll (i.e., Charles Dodgson), in preference to the usual Venn diagrams employed not only in many logic textbooks, but in many other fields besides. In this appendix I am going to discuss the relative merits of the two approaches.

A Venn diagram for an argument involving 3 predicates is drawn with three overlapping circles. It was Venn's invention to put an 'x' in a region we know to be occupied, so that the following diagram would represent "Some A are N":

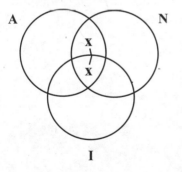

In Venn's method, any region we can see to be empty is shaded. Thus to diagram "All senators are politicians" we must shade the area representing senators who are not politicians. This is done in the figure below testing the validity of the following argument:

Some POLITICIANS are CORRUPT.
<u>All SENATORS are politicians.</u>
Hence, some senators are corrupt.

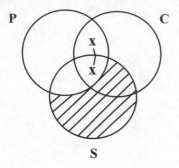

Carroll himself was not shy in boasting the advantages of his diagrams over Venn's:

> My Method of Diagrams *resembles* Mr. Venn's, in having separate compartments assigned to the various Classes, and in marking these Compartments as *occupied* or as *empty*; but it *differs* from his Method, in assigning a *closed* area to the *Universe of Discourse*, so that the Class which, under Mr. Venn's liberal sway, has been ranging at will through infinite space, is suddenly dismayed to find itself "cabin'd, cribb'd, confined," in a limited Cell like any other Class!

Actually, this disadvantage of Venn's method is easily taken care of, by simply including the three circles in a square. Then Carroll's criticism that here "we have only *seven* closed Compartments, to accommodate the *eight* Classes whose peculiar Sets of Attributes are [PCS, PCS̄, PC̄S, etc.]" will no longer apply:

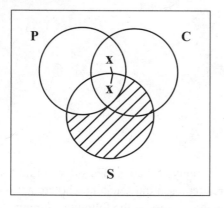

Also, Carroll continues, "I use *rectilinear*, instead of *curvilinear*, Figures; and I mark an *occupied* Cell with I (meaning that there is at least *one* Thing in it,) and an *empty* Cell with an O (meaning that there is *no* Thing in it)." It must be admitted, I think, that Carroll's figures have a more aesthetically pleasing appearance than Venn's. Ignoring for now the fact that Carroll symbolizes A-statements with existential import, the resulting figure for the above argument would be

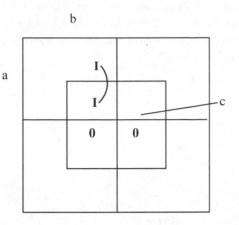

As can readily be seen, both methods give the same result: the argument is invalid. We do not know from the given premises whether the corrupt politicians are senators or not, so the negation of the conclusion, "No senators are corrupt," is consistent with the premises' being true.

Where Carroll's diagrams really seem to have the advantage over Venn's, however, is in arguments involving 4 or more predicates or classes. Carroll quotes Venn: "With four terms in request, the most simple and symmetrical diagram seems to me that produced by making four ellipses intersect one another in the desired manner," commenting that "this, however, provides only *fifteen* closed compartments."

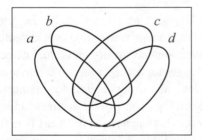

Again, a box around the whole figure will give a sixteenth compartment for individuals not in classes *a*, *b*, *c*, or *d*. But if it is difficult to draw the four ellipses with the required overlap, it is even more difficult to fill this diagram in without making mistakes.

All of this is even more the case with Venn's diagram for an argument involving 5 predicates of classes:

For *five* letters, "The simplest diagram I can suggest," Mr. Venn says, "is one like this (the small ellipse in the centre is to be regarded as a portion of the *outside* of *c*; i.e., its four component portions are inside *b* and *d* but are no part of *c*). It must be admitted that such a diagram is not quite so simple to draw as one might wish it to be; but then consider what the alternative is if one undertakes to deal with five terms and all their combinations—nothing short of the disagreeable task of writing out, or in some way putting before us, all the 32 combinations involved."

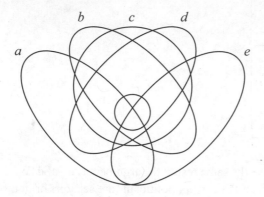

Carroll's diagram for 4 classes, on the other hand, is simplicity itself. Let me now turn to a comparison of his diagrams and my modifications of them.

CARROLL DIAGRAMS

The three main changes I have made to Carroll's diagrams are (i) to simplify the grids to make them easier to use, (ii) to adjust them to the modern convention on existential import, and (iii) to adjust them to the modern convention concerning individual names, which Carroll counted as singleton classes. Other minor changes involve replacing Carroll's 'I' by Venn's 'x' for an arbitrary individual, and using capitals for predicates instead of Carroll's lower case letters. The first change loses some of the aesthetic appeal of Carroll's diagrams, but it makes them easier to use. This can be seen most easily in the case of the diagrams for 3 classes, where Carroll's demand for bilateral symmetry, while pleasing to the eye, leaves awkward L-shaped corner regions which interfere with ease of use (this criticism can only really be appreciated if you try both methods for a while).

For example, the two statements "Some AFRICANS are BANTUS" and "No CHEROKEES are AFRICANS" would be represented on Carroll's own diagrams as follows:

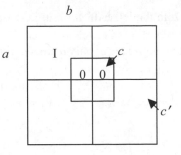

From this it is possible to read off the conclusion, that "Some Bantus are not Cherokees," but I believe this is easier to see on my modified versions of his diagrams:

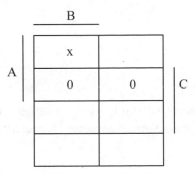

We can illustrate Carroll's diagram for 4 classes by reference to one of his own arguments:

> No TERRIERS wander among the signs of the ZODIAC. Nothing that does not wander among the signs of the zodiac is a COMET. Only terriers have cURLY tails. [U := has a curly tail]

Carroll himself uses lower case letters as variables: a := is a terrier, b := wanders among the signs of the zodiac, c := is a comet, d := has a curly tail. His basic grid for 4 letters is as follows:

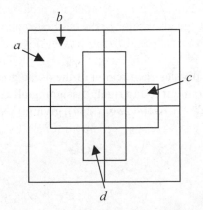

The areas for *a* are in the top half of the figure, for *b* in the left half, for *c* in horizontal rectangle, for *d* in the vertical rectangle.

The information from the premises is: No *a* are *b*; no non-*b* are *c*; only *a* are *d*. Adding it gives

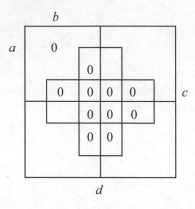

From this we can deduce that "no *c* are *d*," "No comets have curly tails"—a delightfully perverse conclusion, given the facts! Compare with the diagram for chapter 18, exercise 9

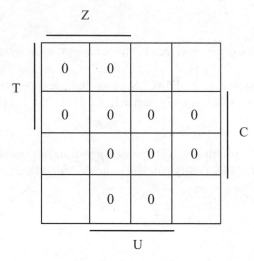

For arguments involving 5 categories, Carroll divides each region of the 4-category diagram into two with a diagonal slash from bottom left to top right, "assigning all the *upper* portions to *e*, and all the *lower* portions to *e'*" (*Symbolic Logic*, 244), giving

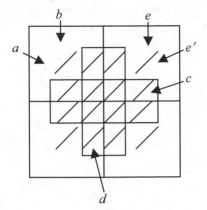

Carroll's generalization to 6 categories is by means of a diagonal slash dividing each region from top left to bottom right. I think it can be appreciated that these diagrams are not all that easy to use, and I hope my diagrams for 5-and 6-category diagrams are a little easier (see chapter 18).

Glossary

ABSTRACT ARGUMENT: what is obtained by symbolizing an argument. The premises are represented as wffs separated by commas; they are followed by the triple-dot symbol, and a wff symbolizing the conclusion; e.g., B ⊃ C, ¬Λ ∨ B ∴ C ∨ ¬Λ.

ABSTRACT STATEMENT: what is obtained by symbolizing a statement. It is simply an interpreted wff.

ANTECEDENT: the "if-clause" of a conditional statement. Thus p is the antecedent of $p \rightarrow q$, where p and q are statement variables. Despite its name, the antecedent may occur last in an English statement: "He would if he could."

ARBITRARY INDIVIDUAL: one that has not already been mentioned in the statement of the argument, and has been introduced in the proof solely in anticipation of generalizing from it later. The letters **u**, **v**, and **w** are reserved for arbitrary individual names assumed in a proof by universal generalization (UG), and **i**, **j**, and **k** for the arbitrary individual names involved in an existential instantiation (EI); they must not have occurred either in the symbolization of the argument or on any previous line of the proof.

ARGUMENT: a chain of (one or more) inferences from some initial premises to an overall conclusion.

ARGUMENT FORM: an array of logical symbols containing *statement variables* rather than statements, such that a single-inference argument is produced when statements are consistently substituted for the variables; e.g., $p \vee q, q \rightarrow r \therefore p \vee r$.

AXIOM SCHEMA: a statement form assumed without proof in the Propositional Calculus. A valid argument form is represented by a statement form derivable from these axiom schemas using certain rules of inference, understood as representing the conclusion of a valid premiseless sequent form.

413

BICONDITIONAL (STATEMENT): any statement of the form $p \leftrightarrow q =_{\text{def}} (p \to q) \ \& \ (q \to p)$.

BICONDITIONAL EQUIVALENCE (BE): the equivalence rule, from $p \leftrightarrow q$ infer $(p \to q) \ \& \ (q \to p)$, and vice versa, i.e., from a biconditional statement, infer the conjunction of the corresponding conditional and its converse, and vice versa.

BINARY OPERATOR: a statement operator that forms a compound statement from two component statements. The truth-functional binary operators are '$\to$,' '$\&$,' '$\vee$,' and '$\leftrightarrow$.'

BOUND VARIABLE: a variable x occurring within the scope of a quantifier $\forall$x or $\exists$x is said to be bound by the corresponding quantifier.

CANINE LOGIC: the kind of reasoning engaged in by dogs; usually expressed in strings of wffs; but dogs also reason silently, as when (as Chrysippus observed) they employ disjunctive argument to follow a scent in a forked path.

CARROLL DIAGRAM: a rectangular array in which statements involving categories may be represented. Any individuals of a given category **C**, or of which a given predicate **C** is true, will lie in the areas opposite the **C**. Any individuals of which the predicate is not true, i.e., those of category **not-C** or $\overline{\textbf{C}}$, will lie in the remaining area.

CLOSED PATH OF A TRUTH TREE: if on the same path there occurs both a statement and the negation of that statement, then the *path closes*, as indicated by a short line at the bottom of the path with a $\perp$ under it.

COMPLETENESS: A *system of rules of inference* is said to be *complete* if and only if any sequent or argument form that is formally valid is provably valid by these rules. A *truth tree rule* is *complete* iff the premise also has the truth value T whenever all the statements derived from it by the rule on at least one branch have the value T. A *truth tree* is *complete* if and only if either (i) every path is closed, or (ii) there is at least one open path that is either complete or effectively complete.

COMPLETE OPEN PATH: a path of a truth tree that has not closed in which all the statements on that path are either compounds that have been decomposed, or literals.

COMPLEX CONSTRUCTIVE DILEMMA: an argument with a disjunctive premise, each of whose disjuncts implies a different consequent, and whose conclusion is the disjunction of these consequents. Its form is: $p \vee q, p \to r, q \to s \ \therefore \ r \vee s$.

COMPLEX DESTRUCTIVE DILEMMA: an argument of the form: $p \to r, q \to s, \neg r \vee \neg s \ \therefore \ \neg p \vee \neg q$.

COMPONENT STATEMENT: One statement is a *component* of another if substituting it within the original by any other statement whatever still yields a meaningful statement.

COMPOUND STATEMENT: any statement that contains one or more COMPONENT statements, generated by the application of a STATEMENT OPERATOR on those components.

CONCLUSION: the statement or proposition an argument is intended to establish.

CONCLUSION INDICATOR: a word or phrase indicating that a conclusion is being given.

CONDITIONAL: a conditional statement, a statement of the form "if p then q," or $p \rightarrow q$, where p and q are statement variables.

CONDITIONAL PROOF (CP): the rule of inference: from a derivation of any statement q from the supposition of p, infer $p \rightarrow q$.

CONJUNCTION: two statements joined by the statement operator 'and,' symbolized '&.'

CONJUNCTION (CONJ): the rule of inference: from p and q, infer p & q, i.e., from the denial of a conjunction and the assertion of one of its conjuncts, infer the denial of the other conjunct.

CONJUNCTIVE SYLLOGISM (CS): the rule of inference: from $\neg(p$ & $q)$ and p, infer $\neg q$, i.e., from any two statements stated separately, infer their conjunction.

CONJUNCTS: the components p and q of any disjunction p & q.

CONSEQUENT: the "then-clause" of a conditional statement. Thus q is the consequent of $p \rightarrow q$, where p and q are statement variables. Sometimes the 'then' is merely understood, as in "If you are bitten by a tsetse fly, you should get checked for sleeping sickness symptoms."

CONSEQUENTIA: a term from medieval logic, literally, a consequence, "what follows from what." It was ambiguous between a logically true conditional statement form and an argument form. The most famous is the CONSEQUENTIA MIRABILIS (APPENDIX 2).

CONSEQUENTIA MIRABILIS: expressed as an argument form, this is $p \rightarrow p$, $\neg p \rightarrow p \therefore p$.

CONSISTENCY: A system of rules of inference is said to be consistent if and only if any sequent or argument form that is provable using the rules is itself formally valid. A truth tree rule is consistent iff whenever the premise has the truth value T, all the statements derived from it by the rule on at least one branch also have the value T.

CONTINGENT STATEMENT: a truth-functional compound statement that is neither a tautology nor a contradiction. Its truth table contains at least one F and at least one T.

CONTRADICTION or LOGICAL FALSEHOOD: a truth-functional compound statement whose form is such that its truth value is F for each possible combination of truth values of its components: its truth table consists only in F's. It is therefore any statement from which an EXPLICIT CONTRADICTION is derivable.

CONTRADICTORIES: two statements p and q are *contradictories* if and only if the truth of p is incompatible with the truth of q, and the falsity of p is incompatible with the falsity of q. A-statements and O-statements are contradictories of one another, as are I-statements and E-statements.

CONVERSE OF A CATEGORICAL STATEMENT: the statement formed by exchanging the subject and predicate terms of a categorical statement; for instance, the converse of 'All A are B' is 'All B are A.'

CONVERSE OF A CONDITIONAL: the statement formed by exchanging the antecedent and consequent of a conditional. In symbols, the converse of $p \rightarrow q$ is $q \rightarrow p$.

CONVERSION: A categorical statement is *validly convertible* iff it is logically equivalent to its converse. I-statements and E-statements are validly convertible, A-statements and O-statements are not.

DE MORGAN'S LAWS (DM): the equivalence rules: from $\neg(p \lor q)$, infer $\neg p \And \neg q$, and vice versa, i.e., from the denial of a disjunction, infer the conjunction of the denials of each of its disjuncts, and vice versa; and from $\neg(p \And q)$, infer $\neg p \lor \neg q$, and vice versa, i.e., from the denial of a conjunction, infer the disjunction of the denials of each of its conjuncts, and vice versa.

DILEMMA: an argument involving a disjunction, which shows that each of the two disjuncts leads to a certain conclusion—often an undesired or surprising one.

DILEMMA (DL): the rule of inference: from $p \lor q$, $p \rightarrow r$ and $q \rightarrow r$, stated separately, infer r, i.e., from a disjunction and two conditionals whose antecedents are the disjuncts, and which have the same consequent, infer their consequent. This is the form of a simple constructive dilemma.

DISJUNCTION: any two statements joined by the binary statement operator 'or,' symbolized '$\lor$.'

DISJUNCTION (DISJ): the rule of inference: from p or q (either one stated alone), infer $p \lor q$, i.e., from any statement, infer its disjunction with another statement.

DISJUNCTIVE SYLLOGISM (DS): the rule of inference: from $p \lor q$ and $\neg p$, infer q, *or*, from $p \lor q$ and $\neg q$, infer p, i.e., from the assertion of a disjunction and the denial of one of its disjuncts, infer the other disjunct.

DISJUNCTS: the components p and q of any disjunction $p \vee q$.

DOUBLE NEGATION (DN): the equivalence rule: from p infer $\neg\neg p$; from $\neg\neg p$ infer p, i.e., from any statement infer the negation of its negation, and vice versa.

EFFECTIVE COMPLETENESS: an OPEN PATH of a truth tree involving application of $\forall$ or $\neg\exists$ or both is *effectively complete* when these rules have been instantiated with all the names appearing in the argument—that is, any proper names occurring in the premises or conclusion, or any names **i, j, k**...resulting from any previous applications of $\exists$ and $\neg\forall$ rules on the path—the path being otherwise complete.

ENTAILMENT: zero or more statements $p, q, r,\ldots$ *entail* another statement s if the latter *follows from* the former, written $p, q, r, \ldots \vdash s$. Thus, in the case of a valid argument (where all the premises are asserted) such as $\neg C \rightarrow D, C \rightarrow E, \neg D \therefore E$, we say that the premises entail the conclusion, symbolized $\neg C \rightarrow D, C \rightarrow E, \neg D \vdash E$.

ENTHYMEME: an argument presented with at least one premise or conclusion left implicit.

EQUIVALENCE CLASS: the class of all individuals standing in an EQUIVALENCE RELATION to one another.

EQUIVALENCE RELATION: a binary relation that is *transitive, reflexive*, and *symmetric*.

EXISTENTIAL GENERALIZATION (EG): the rule of inference: infer an existential quantification from any instance of it; i.e., from Φ**n**, where **n** is any individual name, derive $\exists x \Phi x$.

EXISTENTIAL IMPORT: if there is an individual in the class denoted by the subject term, a categorical statement is said to have *existential import*. On the interpretation adopted here, only I- and O-statements have existential import, and universal quantifications such as A- and E-statements do not.

EXISTENTIAL INSTANTIATION (EI): the rule of inference: from an existential quantification infer a suitably arbitrary instance of it, i.e. from $\exists x \Phi x$ derive Φ**i**, where **i** is an arbitrary individual name, i.e., one that has not occurred either in the symbolization of the argument or on any previous line of the proof.

EXISTENTIAL QUANTIFICATION: a QUANTIFICATION (q.v.) consisting in a propositional function in x (or y or z) preceded by an existential quantifier $\exists x$ (or $\exists y$ or $\exists z$, respectively).

EXPLANATION: an account intended to show how it came to be that a fact or event is the way it is. Many philosophers claim that not all explanations are arguments. But here we are concerned with explanations only insofar as they can be construed as arguments.

EXPLICIT CONTRADICTION: a statement of the form q & $\neg q$, where q as always is a variable standing for any individual statement, such as C, or A & $\neg$B, or (A v B) $\rightarrow$ C, etc. It is denoted by the symbol $\perp$. Thus (A & $\neg$B) & $\neg$(A & $\neg$B) is an explicit contradiction, and so is $\neg$P & $\neg\neg$P; on the other hand, D $\rightarrow$ $\neg$D is not.

FALLACY OF AFFIRMING THE CONSEQUENT: this is the *invalid* reasoning $p \rightarrow q$, q $\therefore$ p.

FALLACY OF DENYING THE ANTECEDENT: this is the *invalid* reasoning $p \rightarrow q$, $\neg p$ $\therefore$ $\neg q$.

FORMAL VALIDITY: an argument is formally valid if it has a valid argument form. An argument form, on the other hand, is valid if and only if there is no argument of that form which has all true premises and a false conclusion. Also called Philonian validity.

FORMULA: a string of (one or more) logical symbols e.g., [$\neg$, A $\rightarrow$ (}v.

FREE VARIABLE: a variable x not occurring within the scope of a quantifier $\forall$x or $\exists$x.

GOVERNING OPERATOR: the last operator used in building a wff according to the rules of wff formation.

HYPOTHETICAL SYLLOGISM (HS): the rule of inference: from $p \rightarrow q$ and $q \rightarrow r$ (stated separately), infer $p \rightarrow r$, i.e., from two conditionals such that the consequent of the first is identical to the antecedent of the second, infer the conditional with the antecedent of the first and consequent of the second.

IDENTITY: the identity relation is an EQUIVALENCE RELATION: its symmetry and transitivity are derivable; its reflexivity is posited: $\forall$x x = x. If the validity of an argument depends on this reflexivity property, $\forall$x x = x is included as an additional implicit premise.

INDIVIDUAL NAME or SINGULAR TERM: an expression used to refer to an individual thing or person. Individual names are symbolized by lower case letters from a to w.

INFERENCE: an inference is the drawing of a conclusion from one or more premises.

INFERENCE INDICATOR: a premise or conclusion indicator, each of which indicates that an inference is being drawn, described, or invited.

INSTANCE OF A QUANTIFICATION: what is obtained when the initial quantifier $\forall$x is dropped and all instances of the free variable x in the resulting propositional function are replaced by the same individual name **n**.

INVALID: an *invalid* argument or inference is one that is not valid. Statements are never said to be valid or invalid in logic; the term is reserved only to characterize reasoning.

INVALIDITY OF A SEQUENT: a sequent is *invalid* when at least one open path of its TRUTH TREE is complete or effectively complete.

LITERALS: statements that cannot be further decomposed by any truth tree rules; they will be either component statements or negations of component statements.

LOGICAL EQUIVALENCE: two statements p and q are *logically equivalent* iff each entails the other, $p \dashv\vdash q$. Logically equivalent statements will have identical truth tables.

LOGICAL INCONSISTENCY: Two statements p and q are *logically inconsistent* iff together they entail both a statement and its negation, i.e. if $p \,\&\, q \vdash \bot$.

MATERIAL IMPLICATION (MI): the equivalence rule: from $p \rightarrow q$ infer $\neg p \vee q$, and vice versa.

MODUS PONENS (MP): the rule of inference: from $p \rightarrow q$ and p, infer q, i.e., from a conditional statement and its antecedent, infer the consequent.

MODUS TOLLENS (MT): the rule of inference: from $p \rightarrow q$ and $\neg q$, infer $\neg p$, i.e., from a conditional statement and the negation of its consequent, infer the negation of its antecedent.

NEGATION: the *negation* of a statement p is what we get when we precede it by the operator "It is not the case that" or its equivalent, symbolized $\neg p$. If a statement is true, its negation must be false; and conversely, if a statement is false, its negation must be true.

OPEN PATH OF A TRUTH TREE: any PATH that is not CLOSED.

PATH OF A TRUTH TREE: the collection of all the statements from the bottom of a branch up to the top of the trunk (first premise).

PENEVALID ARGUMENT: an argument whose validity depends upon one of its universal premises being taken to have an existential import that is implicit in the context.

PREMISE (PREMISS): a statement given in an argument in support of the conclusion.

PREMISE INDICATOR: a word or phrase indicating that a premise is being offered.

PROOF OF THE VALIDITY OF AN ARGUMENT FORM: a numbered sequence of lines, each of which contains either a premise of the argument, a supposition, or a statement derived from one of the preceding lines by a rule of inference; and whose last line is the conclusion of the argument, occurring after all suppositions have been discharged.

PROPOSITION: whatever may be asserted or denied; whatever is expressed by a sentence, or part of a sentence, that can be true or false.

Certain logicians reject the concept of propositions on the grounds that no one has been able to give an adequate account of when two propositions could be regarded as identical. But one could say much the same about any of our basic concepts, including 'concept' itself, so that this criticism probably amounts to a misplaced demand for formality. At any rate, it cannot be denied that a declarative sentence is used to assert something, and that something (however ill-defined) is what a 'proposition' is understood to be.

PROPOSITIONAL FUNCTION Φx : a formula containing at least one variable x that results when one or more quantifiers are deleted from the front of a quantification.

QUANTIFICATION: a formula that is a wff according to the rules of formation for wffs in predicate logic when (and only when) clause (iv) is applied last. See 19.3.1.

QUANTIFIER NEGATION: the rules of inference: (i) from the negation of a universal quantification infer the existential quantification whose propositional function is the negation of the original one, and vice versa, i.e., from $\neg \forall x \Phi x$, derive $\exists x \neg \Phi x$, and vice versa. (ii) from the negation of an existential quantification infer the universal quantification whose propositional function is the negation of the original one, and vice versa, i.e., from $\neg \exists x \Phi x$, derive $\forall x \neg \Phi x$, and vice versa.

QUANTIFIER SHIFT FALLACY: a fallacy consisting in the inversion of the order of existential and universal quantifiers in an expression, thus illicitly changing their scope. For example, "Everyone has a mother" is true if it means that for each person there is someone who is his or her mother ($\forall y \exists x$ xMy, with a UD of people); but to infer from it that there is someone who is everyone's mother ($\exists x \forall y$ xMy) is an example of this fallacy.

REDUCTIO AD ABSURDUM (RA): the rule of inference: from a derivation of $\perp$ (i.e., $q \, \& \, \neg q$) and, from the supposition of p, infer $\neg p$.

REITERATION: from a statement p, infer the same statement p (on another line in a proof).

SCOPE OF A QUANTIFIER: the shortest propositional function immediately following the quantifier that is not itself immediately followed by either a variable or a name.

SELF-CONTRADICTORY FORM: a statement form every instance of which is a contradiction.

SEQUENT: an assertion that one abstract statement or wff (the *conclusion*, written to the right of a turnstile, $\vdash$) follows from a sequence of zero or more statements or wffs (the *premises*, written to the left of the turnstile and separated by commas).

SEQUENT FORM: an array of logical symbols containing *statement variables* rather than statements, such that a sequent is produced when statements are consistently substituted for the variables; e.g., $p \lor q, q \rightarrow r \vdash p \lor r$.

SIMPLE CONSTRUCTIVE DILEMMA: an argument with a disjunctive premise, each of whose disjuncts implies the conclusion. Its form is: $p \lor q, p \rightarrow r, q \rightarrow r \therefore r$.

SIMPLE DESTRUCTIVE DILEMMA: an argument of the form: $p \rightarrow r, p \rightarrow s, \neg r \lor \neg s \therefore \neg p$.

SIMPLE STATEMENT: any statement that has no components.

SIMPLIFICATION (SIMP): the rule of inference, from $p \& q$, infer either p or q stated separately, i.e., from a conjunction, infer either one of its conjuncts.

SINGULAR STATEMENT: a statement of predicate logic containing one or more singular terms and no variables.

SOUND: An *argument* is *sound* if and only if its conclusion is *validly* inferred from *true* premises.

STATEMENT: a sentence, or part of a sentence, that expresses something true or false. Individual statements are represented symbolically by uppercase letters. (See 1.1 and 3.1.1 for a justification of this definition vis-à-vis alternative definitions.)

STATEMENT FORM: an array of logical symbols containing statement variables such that an abstract statement or wff is produced when statements or wffs are consistently substituted for the variables; e.g., $p \lor q, \neg[q \rightarrow r]$.

STATEMENT OPERATOR: a word or phrase which operates on a statement or statements to form a compound statement.

STATEMENT VARIABLE: the lowercase italicized letters p, q, etc., standing for any arbitrary individual statement. They act as placeholders in the statements of rules of inference, like the Stoics' "the first" and "the second" in "If the first then the second."

SUBSTITUTION INSTANCE of an argument form: any argument that results when the same statement or wff is substituted for each different occurrence of the same statement variable, e.g., (A & B) for each occurrence of p, $\neg$C for each occurrence of q, and so forth. Thus $\neg$E $\rightarrow$ (B $\lor$ C), $\neg$E $\therefore$ B $\lor$ C is a substitution instance of the form $p \rightarrow q, p \therefore q$.

SUBSTITUTION OF IDENTICALS: the rule of inference: If two individuals **i** and **k** are identical, then **k** can be substituted for **i** anywhere it occurs in any statement involving **i**: i.e., from **i** = **k**, Φ**i**, infer Φ**k**.; e.g. from a = b, Sa $\rightarrow$ $\neg$aLc, infer Sb $\rightarrow$ $\neg$bLc.

SUPPOSITION (SUPP): a statement p that is not actually given as a premise in an argument, but is simply assumed for the sake of argument. A supposition may be made at any point in a conditional or a reductio proof, and is justified respectively by Supp/CP or Supp/RA.

TAUTOLOGOUS FORM: a statement form every instance of which is a tautology.

TAUTOLOGY or LOGICAL TRUTH: a truth-functional compound statement whose form is such that its truth value is T for each possible combination of truth values of its components: its truth table consists only in T's.

THEOREM: a sequent form with no premises, validly derived entirely by using the rules of inference.

TRANSPOSITION (TR): the equivalence rule, from $p \rightarrow q$ infer $\neg q \rightarrow \neg p$, and vice versa, i.e., from a conditional, infer its transpositive.

TRUTH-FUNCTIONAL OPERATOR: a statement operator that forms a compound statement whose truth value depends only on the truth values of the component statements.

TRUTH VALUE: the truth value of a true statement is true (T), that of a false statement, false (F).

UNARY OPERATOR: a statement operator that forms a compound statement by operating on one component statements. The only unary truth-functional operator is '$\neg$.'

UNIVERSAL GENERALIZATION (UG): the rule of inference: infer a universal quantification from a suitably arbitrary instance of it; i.e., from Φu derive $\forall x \Phi x$, provided (i) Φu neither is nor depends upon an undischarged supposition involving u, and (ii) Φu does not contain a name i (or j or k) introduced by an application of EI to a formula involving u.

UNIVERSAL INSTANTIATION (UI): the rule of inference: from a universal quantification infer any instance of it; i.e., from $\forall x \Phi x$ derive $\Phi \mathbf{n}$, where $\mathbf{n}$ denotes any individual name.

UNIVERSAL QUANTIFICATION: a quantification (q.v.) consisting in a propositional function in x (or y or z) preceded by a universal quantifier $\forall x$ (or $\forall y$ or $\forall z$, respectively).

UNIVERSE OF DISCOURSE (UD) or DOMAIN: the set of individuals concerned in a given statement or argument. The UD or DOMAIN of a particular quantifier such as $\forall x$ is the set of individuals over which x is assumed to range.

UNSOUND: an argument or inference is *unsound* if it is not sound, i.e., if it is not valid, or if its conclusion depends on at least one untrue premise, or both.

VALIDITY: an *argument* or *inference* is *valid* if and only if denying its conclusion is incompatible with accepting all its premises. Also called Chrysippean validity.

WFF = WELL-FORMED FORMULA: a formula that is formed in such a way that it can always be interpreted as a statement. It is defined recursively in 12.1.1 (statement logic only) and in 19.3.1.

Index

From the Publisher

A name never says it all, but the word "Broadview" expresses a good
deal of the philosophy behind our company. We are open to a broad
range of academic approaches and political viewpoints. We pay
attention to the broad impact book publishing and book printing has in
the wider world; for some years now we have used 100% recycled
paper for most titles. Our publishing program is internationally oriented
and broad-ranging. Our individual titles often appeal to a broad readership too; many are of interest as much to general readers as to
academics and students.

Founded in 1985, Broadview remains a fully independent company
owned by its shareholders—not an imprint or subsidiary of a larger
multinational.

For the most accurate information on our books (including information
on pricing, editions, and formats) please visit our website at
www.broadviewpress.com. Our print books and ebooks are also
available for sale on our site.

broadview press
www.broadviewpress.com